The Mexican American Experience in Texas

The Texas Bookshelf

Other books in the series

Bill Minutaglio, *A Single Star and Bloody Knuckles:*
A History of Politics and Race in Texas

Frank Andre Guridy, *The Sports Revolution: How Texas*
Changed the Culture of American Athletics

Stephen Harrigan, *Big Wonderful Thing:*
A History of Texas

*The publication of this book was made possible
by the generous support of the following:*

Christine and Charles Aubrey

Roger W. Fullington

Jeanne and Mickey Klein

Marsha and John Kleinheinz

Lowell H. Lebermann Jr.

Joyce and Harvey Mitchell

Brad and Michele Moore

Office of UT President William Powers Jr.

Ellen and Ed Randall

Jean and Dan Rather

Tocker Foundation

Judith Willcott and Laurence Miller

Suzanne and Marc Winkelman

The Mexican American Experience in Texas

Citizenship, Segregation, and the Struggle for Equality

MARTHA MENCHACA

University of Texas Press ❖ Austin

Requests for permission to reproduce material from this work should be sent to:
Permissions
University of Texas Press
P.O. Box 7819
Austin, TX 78713–7819
utpress.utexas.edu/rp-form

♾ The paper used in this book meets the minimum requirements of ANSI/NISO
Z39.48–1992 (R1997) (Permanence of Paper).

Library of Congress Cataloging-in-Publication Data

Names: Menchaca, Martha, author.
Title: The Mexican American experience in Texas : citizenship, segregation, and the
    struggle for equality / Martha Menchaca.
Other titles: Texas bookshelf.
Description: First edition. | Austin : University of Texas Press, 2022. | Series: The
    Texas bookshelf | Includes bibliographical references and index.
Identifiers: LCCN 2021010737 (print) | LCCN 2021010738 (ebook)
ISBN 978-1-4773-2437-0 (hardcover)
ISBN 978-1-4773-2438-7 (library e-book)
ISBN 978-1-4773-2439-4 (non-library e-book)
Subjects: LCSH: 973/.046872. | Mexican Americans—Political activity—Texas—
    History. | Mexican Americans—Texas—History.
Classification: LCC F395.M5 M455 2022 (print) | LCC F395.M5 (ebook) | DDC
    976.4/0046872—dc23
LC record available at https://lccn.loc.gov/2021010737
LC ebook record available at https://lccn.loc.gov/2021010738

doi:10.7560/324370

Never doubt that a small group of thoughtful, committed citizens can change the world; indeed, it's the only thing that ever has.
MARGARET MEAD, ANTHROPOLOGIST

Every moment is an organizing opportunity, every person a potential activist, every minute a chance to change the world.
DOLORES HUERTA, UNITED FARM WORKERS ACTIVIST

Just because you're paranoid doesn't mean they aren't after you.
JOSEPH HELLER, NOVELIST

Contents

The Mexican American Experience in Texas

Introduction

This book offers a historical overview of Mexican Americans' social and economic experiences in Texas from the Spanish period to the present. My aim is to focus on the political struggles that Mexican Americans faced in their pursuit of equal rights after Texas joined the United States. As I develop this narrative, I examine major turning points in the advancement, denial, or reversal of their civil rights quest by revisiting events that had statewide impact on their lives.[1]

The narrative begins with the settlement of Texas during the Spanish and Mexican periods because it is necessary to look at who initially colonized the territory and how their ancestry influenced their incorporation into US society. Spanish and Mexican census records indicate that most settlers were a racially mixed people of Indian, Spanish, and African descent and that they were governed by a numerically small, elite white population. I argue that the mixed racial heritage of the Mexican American population affected the types of opportunities they were extended by Texas governments after independence. In 1836, Anglo-American immigrants who had settled in Texas broke away from Mexico and established the Republic of Texas. A few years later, Texas was annexed by the United States. Over the generations, and until the passage of the Civil Rights Act of 1964, Mexican Americans remained an ethnic minority population distinguished by their ancestral origin and mixed racial heritage. Treated as second-class citizens, they were not extended the political rights and social privileges enjoyed by Anglo-Americans.[2]

The two main political struggles that Mexican Americans endured were how to assert their legal rights of citizenship and how to retain possession of their Spanish and Mexican land grants. Land and citizenship were interrelated social issues: if Mexican Americans were denied citizenship, their legal rights over property could be nullified. By the turn of the twentieth century, the fact that they were US citizens was no longer being questioned. Unfortunately, they continued to be treated as second-class citizens subjected to legal and social segregation. Under US law at the time, segregation was not seen as a violation of a person's constitutional rights. The US Supreme Court, in the *Slaughter-House Cases* (1873) and in subsequent decisions, ruled that state legislatures had the authority to determine what actions could be considered a violation of a person's civil rights. In Texas, it was not illegal to segregate Mexican Americans and African Americans from white people in public accommodations. The first exclusion law affecting Mexican Americans was affirmed by the Texas Supreme Court in 1885, and in 1907 such laws were expanded by the Texas Legislature to cover all forms of public accommodation. Allegedly, the intent of Texas's exclusion laws was to protect citizens' rights to operate their establishments as they pleased. By law, business owners and members of organizations and clubs could exclude any person from the use of their facilities or confine patrons to restricted areas. The outcome of Texas's exclusion laws led many white residents to intentionally embarrass, mock, and deny services to Mexican Americans and African Americans.

From the 1920s to the mid-1950s, the Texas Legislature passed additional laws to separate Mexican Americans and African Americans from Anglo-Americans in residential districts and schools. Zoning laws, home rule authority, language policies, housing covenants, and cultural backgrounds were used to implement this separation. In the late 1920s, Mexican American parents in Del Rio, Texas, challenged the unfair treatment of their children in the town's "Mexican" schools. After a series of confrontations over school finances, the parents sued the local school board, and in 1930 their lawsuit reached the Texas Appellate Court in San Antonio. The judges ruled that separating students by ethnicity and race did not violate state law. In *Independent School District v. Salvatierra*, the court upheld the right of school boards to segregate Mexican students. Mexican Americans nonetheless repeatedly challenged segregation laws and policies by appealing to the courts or to the governor's office. Unfortunately, the court system continued to affirm that Texas's exclusion laws did not violate federal or state laws (see, for example, *Terrell Wells Swimming Pool v. Rodriguez* [1944]). By the end of World War II, LULAC and the American GI Forum had emerged as the leading Mexican American civil rights organizations challenging the legal basis for segregating Mexican Americans.

During the late 1940s, fighting the state's exclusion laws, particularly regarding education, continued to be the main political struggle of Mexican Americans. Many Mexican schools did not offer a curriculum above the fourth or sixth grade, and this prevented Mexican American students from receiving the education necessary to qualify for high school admission. Because civil rights activists identified school segregation as the most severe problem affecting the social mobility of Mexican Americans, I provide an overview of the main cases that challenged Texas laws and eventually led to school reform. Of particular significance was the milestone legal victory against school segregation in 1948, an effort headed by Gustavo "Gus" García, who worked with Dr. George I. Sánchez and other LULAC and GI Forum activists. In *Delgado v. Bastrop Independent School District*, García was able to prove that Mexican American students were being segregated on account of their ethnicity and that this policy violated the Equal Protection Clause of the Fourteenth Amendment, because no federal or state law required this separation. Judge Ben Rice instated a statewide order requiring Texas schools attended by white and Mexican American students to be desegregated within one year. But the state legislature disregarded the judge's mandate and continued to segregate and underfund Mexican schools.

The disassembling of Texas exclusion laws began in the post–World War II era when national social movements to desegregate the United States were launched by minority groups and liberal whites. President Harry S. Truman ordered the desegregation of the armed forces in 1948, a time when Congress and most state legislatures did not support such a change. Nonetheless, civil rights activists across the nation, including those in Texas, continued their quest for equality. By the mid-1960s, the civil rights movement had strengthened, gaining massive national support and influencing many Americans to work toward dismantling segregation and other prejudicial practices. Civil rights advocates placed substantial political pressure on the federal government to set up a legal framework and a system of financial penalties to stop state governments from enforcing discriminatory laws against racial minorities. In Texas, the legislature initially refused to implement the Civil Rights Act of 1964, which President Lyndon B. Johnson had signed into law. Consequently, Mexican Americans and African Americans collectively placed pressure on the legislature to begin dismantling segregation. In 1967, Mexican American youth in Texas, working together with civil rights activists across the Southwest, took the lead in challenging social inequities affecting their communities. Their collective agenda and organizational activities came to be known as the Chicano Movement. MAYO, the Mexican American Youth Organization, and La Raza Unida Party (RUP), an official third party, became the leading organizations representing the Chicano Movement in Texas.

In 1967, Governor John Connally acknowledged that many Texas laws were in violation of the Civil Rights Act, and he asked the Texas Legislature to begin desegregating the state. Within a few months of the governor's call, all state buildings except schools were desegregated. Furthermore, all policies that used race, ethnicity, national origin, or religion to deny people government services were cancelled. Neither the governor nor the legislature, however, was prepared to end Texas's exclusion laws affecting the private sector. Two years later, after a large number of Texans demanded the extension of Civil Rights Act protections to the private sector, segregation theoretically ended. Sadly, many schools remained segregated for another thirty years, and employment mobility for African Americans and Mexican Americans did not make significant progress until the early 1980s.

Nonetheless, it was a significant change when segregation in public accommodations ended in Texas. Racial discrimination was prohibited by law, and as a result of new laws, a social process began that transformed how space was inhabited. Race, ethnicity, religion, and national origin could no longer be used to determine or regulate the interaction of people of different races and cultures. Shared public places were no longer locations of inequality where one group was to acquiesce in the demands of allegedly superior others. As the rules of interaction changed in public places, modes of correct social comportment mutated and came to influence the socialization of people's behavior, which, for later generations, culminated in helping many people accept or embrace difference as a fact of life and not a marker of superiority or inferiority.

The advancements made in the sharing of public spaces, however, did not end the civil rights struggles facing Mexican Americans. School finance, election redistricting boundaries, and racial profiling are the most serious challenges that Mexican Americans have had to address in the twenty-first century. These issues became entangled with immigration politics in Texas. Economic problems in Mexico led to increased immigration to the United States during the early 1980s and mid-1990s. For many Americans, this was an unwelcome demographic change, and it triggered the formation of social movements to reduce immigration from Mexico, specifically unauthorized migration. In many cities anti-immigrant sentiments evolved into anti-Latino movements.

This book was commissioned by the University of Texas Press as part of the Texas Bookshelf Project, a work in progress that will include over a dozen books exploring Texas's history and cultures. My charge was to write about the culture and history of Mexican Americans in Texas from the settlement of the territory to the present. Because of the large scope of the book and the time period to be covered, it became necessary to concentrate on major events shaping the national and statewide experiences of Mexican Americans in Texas. I did not want to write an encyclopedia of unrelated accounts about the life of either wealthy Mexican Americans or unsung heroes. My aim, rather, was to write about political and social acts that determined or changed the course of Mexican American history. Specifically, I wanted to understand how Mexican Americans challenged segregation and how their political rights as citizens evolved over time. These two issues were interrelated.

Previous research had made me aware of the abundant archival data that were available and, so far, have not been adequately studied. My goal, therefore, was to draw on both the findings of well-known studies and the richness of archival sources to contribute new insights into Texas history. In the area of segregation, I wanted to better understand how the exclusion of Mexican Americans was justified and masked by governmental officials under the public rationale that Mexicans were discriminated against because of social class differences, not racism. Of particular significance were the Spanish *casta* (legal racial system) census records, which provide indispensable information about Mexican Americans' racial background and reveal how the *mestizaje* (racial mixture) process evolved in Texas. Likewise, I wanted to know what Representative José Antonio Navarro heard during the annexation convention of 1845, when many legislators were not in favor of extending US citizenship to Mexicans.

Equally important was to study the depositions in *Delgado v. Bastrop ISD* (1947, 1948) in order to understand why Gus García had to ask school district superintendents to explain why they decided to educate Mexican American students in shacks, while white students were placed in classrooms in modern brick buildings with indoor bathrooms and water fountains. Compared with the summary accounts found in the published case reports, these depositions contain much more information about the abuse that students underwent. In those depositions, I found the reason why García passionately dedicated his life to fight for social justice, despite the difficult life he had to lead for challenging savage inequalities. For many years, I had wondered why he took that path when, as a member of the Mexican American elite, he could have easily assimilated and used his education to generate income and fund a life of luxury. People like García, who could phenotypically "pass" for Anglo-American, chose to fight and change Texas's discriminatory laws instead of acquiescing in their imposition in exchange for personal gain.

In writing this book, I also wanted to capture part of the daily life of

Mexican Americans during the nineteenth century. To do so, I found valuable information in legal cases that established state-level precedents defending Mexican Americans' property and civil rights. For example, Antonio De La Garza's and Fernando De León's court records review Texas's land grant history, but also—and this is much more noteworthy—give insight into the terror and violence their families experienced when they stood up for their rights and refused to be run out of town.

In sum, I hope that this book will provide valuable insights into the history of Mexican Americans in Texas and illustrate how they fought for equality and to make Texas a place where diversity is appreciated and not feared. The case studies and events are offered to promote critical thinking, in the hope of dispelling stereotypes about how things came to be in Texas—my aim being to help readers overcome popular beliefs that depict Mexican Americans as foreigners who have not contributed to the betterment and progress of the state.

CHAPTER 1

The *Pobladores* and the *Casta* System

When chronicling the main events affecting Mexican Americans' political struggles for social and economic equality in Texas, it is essential to first examine their racial formation, which occurred in the aftermath of the Spanish conquest of Mexico. This early phase provides the foundation for understanding how Mexican Americans' mixed racial heritage affected their incorporation into American society after the United States acquired Mexico's northern frontier in the mid-nineteenth century. Mexican Americans are descendants of the Indigenous populations of Mexico and the Spaniards who conquered them. Some Mexican Americans are also descendants of enslaved African people brought to Mexico during the transatlantic slave trade.

To keep the conquered population under control and to give themselves economic privileges, Spaniards designed a legal system called the Sistema de Castas (*casta* system). This legal structure gave them superior economic rights and social privileges while severely constraining the livelihood of Indigenous and racially mixed people. As the Spanish Empire expanded its territorial conquest of Mexico northward, the *casta* system prompted the large-scale settlement of present-day Texas. The settlers who migrated to Texas were a racially diverse population seeking land and fortune. Most of them were people of color in search of a better life, since social conventions on the frontier allowed significant social mobility within the *casta* system. This chapter offers an overview of how Spain's racial order encouraged Indians, Spaniards, mestizos, and people of African descent to migrate north in search of social and economic opportunities. It concludes with the end of the Spanish period, when Mexicans united to obtain their independence from Spain.

The Spanish Colonization of Mexico and the Move North to Texas

Scholars estimate the size of the Native American population in what today is Mexico and the United States at around 30 to 37 million before European contact, with most of them residing in Mexico. Mexico's central region, where the Aztecs established an empire, is estimated to have had around 25 million people before contact.[1] North of the Rio Grande, population estimates for the United States range from 1 million to 18 million, with the lower estimate considered to be unreliable.[2]

In 1518, Spain came into contact with the Indians of southern Mexico, and Hernán Cortés, the captain general of the Spanish forces, through war and treaties, established alliances with many kingdoms.[3] The confederation of nation-states that constituted the Aztec Empire politically controlled central Mexico. In 1521, after three years of warfare, Cortés's forces and Indian allies defeated the Aztecs. Nearly two decades later, the Maya nations of the Yucatán, who had also chosen to fight the Spanish, were defeated.

The Indians of northern Mexico, more difficult to conquer, resisted for several decades. Six Chichimeca nation-states formed a military alliance to deter the advancement of the invading forces.[4] In 1591, the Spanish finally defeated the people of the Gran Chichimeca.[5] The fall of the Chichimeca is significant for the history of Texas because their conquest by the Spaniards opened new pathways to the North. The first Spanish colony in Mexico's farthest northern frontier was founded in 1598 by Juan de Oñate, and the province was named New Mexico. Oñate led a colony of Spaniards, Indians, mestizos, and two enslaved African males, numbering altogether 348 men plus their families. They first settled among the Pueblo peoples in an Indian village called Caypa Pueblo (Ohkay Owingeh), later renamed San Juan de Los Caballeros, and a few months later established more settlements.[6]

In 1680, the settlers were forced to leave New Mexico after Pueblo and Apache Indians united to expel them, an event known as the Pueblo Revolt. Two thousand colonists and 317 of their Pueblo allies fled southward and settled near the mission of Nuestra Senõra de Guadalupe, in a small settlement called El Paso del Norte.[7] When they arrived, they gave life to the sparsely populated village by establishing new settlements and mission communities. Among these settlements were present-day Ciudad Juárez and El Paso Valley. Following a series of disputes between Apache and Pueblo leaders, a group of Pueblo Indians negotiated a treaty with the Spanish to remove the Apache from New Mexico. In 1692, a Spanish-Pueblo military alliance reconquered New Mexico, and Spain maintained control of the province until the early nineteenth century. El Paso del Norte remained part of

New Mexico during the Spanish period and El Paso Valley was not incorporated into Texas until the United States acquired Mexico's northern frontier.

The reconquest of New Mexico was part of a large-scale initiative to colonize the northern frontier of the Viceroyalty of New Spain, the name given to modern Mexico. Two additional colonization projects had been initiated to expand the Spanish Empire into present-day Texas and into the Arizona-Sonora region. The colonization of Texas was put into action a few years after France challenged Spain's claim to New Spain's northeastern frontier.[8] Louis IV, the king of France, commissioned René-Robert Cavelier de La Salle in 1684 to explore the Gulf of Mexico and establish a French colony.[9] Spain feared that if La Salle was successful, France might establish colonies along the Texas coast.

In 1688, Don Gaspar de la Cerda Sandoval Silva y Mendoza, the viceroy of New Spain, was commissioned by Charles II, the king of Spain, to begin settling Texas. The viceroy appointed Father Damián Mazanet and four other Franciscan friars to explore the northeastern part of the territory and establish a mission among the Hasinai Indians.[10] Captain Alonso de León and a party of soldiers accompanied Father Mazanet to the northeastern border of present-day Texas and Louisiana. They left Monclova, Coahuila, on March 20, 1690, and within a few weeks arrived at a Hasinai village called Nabedache, where they set up camp and established two missions nearby.[11] If the settlement succeeded, colonists and troops would soon follow.

The first attempt to settle Texas failed, however, when Father Mazanet and the other missionaries were unable to live off the land or acquire aid from the local Indians. They left nearly three years later, after France no longer posed a threat to Spain's claim over Texas. By then, La Salle's colony had collapsed. The Karankawa Indians had attacked La Salle's fort and killed most of the French settlers. In mid-March 1689, British intelligence agents reported news of the colony's demise. Spanish explorers later confirmed it when they found the fort in ruins. The survivors were found by Spanish troops hiding in bushes and nearly starving. The French colonists were sent to Mexico City, where they recounted tales of disorder, starvation, and other problems.[12]

The First Spanish Settlements in Texas

With the French threat diminished, it was no longer necessary for the Spanish to establish a colony in northeastern Texas, and Spain reverted to its earlier settlement plan. New forts and villages were to be established within two days' travel from a populated settlement so that military assistance could be sent if they came under attack. Three missions and a fort were established between 1700 and 1703, five miles south of the Rio Grande in a region that came to be known as the San Juan Bautista complex.[13] The missionaries formed amicable relations with the local Indians, and a large number of Coahuiltecan Indians formed alliances with the missionaries.[14]

Within a few years, the French resumed their plans to colonize Texas. In 1714, French agents were sent to explore the Texas coast and establish a colony near the Red River on what today is the Louisiana-Texas border. Having gained the confidence of some Caddo Indians, the French established a village near them, called Natchitoches. When the Spanish Crown and the Catholic Church learned of the Caddo-French alliance, they immediately made plans to move the financial resources of the San Juan missions into the interior of Texas close to Natchitoches. They hoped to set up a large settlement composed of missions and villages that would stretch westward from the Arroyo Hondo near Natchitoches toward the Neches River, in the same location where the earlier northern missions had been built. Because Spanish officials were aware that establishing a settlement in a distant area was risky, they tried to ensure that it was well financed and that the colonists were equipped to survive on their own. In mid-February 1716, Captain Domingo Ramón took approximately seventy-eight colonists into the northeastern part of Texas.[15] Twenty-five soldiers accompanying the captain were encouraged to bring their families. Four months later, several missions and a presidio with a civilian settlement had been established five miles west of the Neches River and approximately thirteen miles from Natchitoches. The colony eventually came to be known as Los Adaes. Among the colonists were mestizos, Indians, Spaniards and one Black person.[16] The colonists lived in the presidio (military headquarters) and on its outskirts, and the fathers lived in the five missions that they had established nearby. Under Spanish law, missions were to be located apart from civilian settlements and used to attract local Indians. The separation was to ensure that conflicts between the civilians and Indian allies did not destabilize the colony. Spain had learned from previous experience that colonies in the northern frontier failed when settlers and mission Indians lived together. Disputes often erupted over land and water rights and culminated in Indian revolts. In Texas, the sensitivity of the colonization project meant that this mistake could not be repeated. To befriend local Indians and recruit them to live in the missions, Indians from the San Juan Bautista missions were carefully selected to act as the fathers' guides, negotiators, and assistants.

Within a year, life in the colony became unbearable, even though most of the colonists were frontier people accustomed to living in hostile regions. Local Indians were hostile, and the soldiers believed that the French in Natchitoches were inciting the Indians to attack them. To help fortify the region, Spanish officials in Mexico City decided to establish a network of settlements in Texas. Preparations to found a second colony in present-day San Antonio began. In 1718, Martín de Alarcón, the governor of Coahuila and Texas, was told to recruit settlers and establish a civilian colony. A mission was to be established by Father Antonio de San Buenaventura y Olivares, who was in charge of developing the mission system in San Antonio. Both Alarcón and Olivares planned to populate San Antonio with white Spanish settlers, but soon found that it was mainly people of color who were willing to make the journey from the interior of Mexico. The only white persons would be the missionaries and some of the Spanish soldiers. Once Alarcón had recruited seventy-two settlers, he prepared to march north. In his letters to the viceroy of New Spain, Alarcón described the settlers as mulattos (Spanish-Black), *lobos* (Black-Indian), *coyotes* (Indian-mulatto), and mestizos from Coahuila.[17] Among them were artisans and masons who had been hired to construct buildings in San Antonio. Because of the small size of the colony and the risks associated with its protection, the civilians had to be governed by a military administration.[18]

When all the recruits were assembled, Alarcón separated the settlers into two companies, with the governor leading the civilians, and Olivares the mission Indians. On their arrival in San Antonio, the Indians were to be housed apart from the colonists and placed under the governance of Olivares. Two missionaries and five Indians were appointed to help him manage the mission community and recruit local Indians.[19] In late April 1718, the settlers arrived in San Antonio, and Alarcón selected the location for the settlements a few days later. On May 1, Mission San Antonio de Valero was founded, and four days later they established the Villa de Béxar, which contained a civilian settlement and a military presidio.[20] The mission later became the present site of the Alamo, and the complex of settlements formed the foundation of San Antonio. By 1720, San Antonio had a colonial population of three hundred, along with several hundred mission Indians.[21] The population of the villa and mission grew after the fathers made alliances with several Coahuiltecan *ranchería* (village) chiefs. The alliances were beneficial to both sides.[22] The Indians helped protect the mission from hostile Indians, and Indian allies obtained food and commodities from the fathers. Some of the chiefs chose to relocate their *rancherías* near the mission, and some families chose to live inside the mission grounds.

While the residents of San Antonio managed to do well, Governor Alarcón received news that the French planned to attack the northeastern settlements.[23] Numerous letters from the settlements corroborated that information—many settlers were desperate to leave. Alarcón ordered the civilians of Los Adaes to temporarily seek refuge in San Antonio. Faced with such grave problems, the viceroy of New Spain knew that he had to find a benefactor who would be willing to fortify and expand the settlements in that region. In 1719, José de Azlor y Virto de Vera, known as the Marqués de Aguayo, was named governor and captain general of the province of Coahuila and Texas. He had the financial resources and determination to fortify the Northeast and end the French threat.

Two years later, Aguayo began the reconquest of the Northeast. In mid-July 1721, he departed Monclova, Coahuila, with the goal of ousting the French and forcing them to retreat eastward toward Natchitoches.[24] Equipped with numerous cannons and a large amount of artillery, his battalion, composed of several hundred men, easily forced the French to retreat to Natchitoches and agree to a truce.[25]

Once the French had left Los Adaes, Aguayo sent news to San Antonio for the colonists to return and join the mission fathers, who had not left the embattled region. In preparation for the refugees' return, Aguayo left one hundred soldiers and six cannons to protect the colony. Twenty-eight of the soldiers were commissioned to send for their families, in an effort to increase the number of settlers. Near the mission of San Miguel de Los Adaes, Aguayo established the Presidio de Nuestra Señora del Pilar de Los Adaes. One additional mission and presidio were also established in the old encampment zone. Altogether, six missions and two well-fortified presidios were established, and Los Adaes was named the capital of Texas.[26]

Aguayo next tried to deter any further French attempts to settle the central Texas coast. Two previous French attempts to claim the area had failed.[27] After resting for the winter in San Antonio, Aguayo erected a military outpost on Matagorda Bay. In 1722, his troops founded Presidio Nuestra Señora de Loreto and established Mission Nuestra Señora del Espíritu Santo de Zúñiga nearby.[28] Nine soldiers were left to protect the area. Four years later, the settlements were moved inland near the Guadalupe River, and a new mission was established. The presidio was renamed Presidio Nuestra Señora de la Bahía del Espíritu Santo, and the region came to be known as La Bahía. By 1763, the missions had an Indian population of 312 and a colonial population of 50 families.[29]

Aguayo's actions brought stability to Texas. The fortification of San Antonio, La Bahía, and Los Adaes proved that Texas could be settled, and this convinced formerly reluctant people to choose the region as their home. In 1749, José de Escandón led one of the largest land movements in the history of the northern frontier, and many chose present-day South Texas as their home. Escandón established Nuevo Santander along the current border between Texas and the Mexican state of Tamaulipas. Six thousand people were recruited, and over twenty-three towns were established. Laredo was founded in 1755, and hundreds of settlers established ranches in what today is South Texas. By the turn of the nineteenth century, Laredo had over 718 settlers, and the towns and ranches in Nuevo Santander grew to over 20,000 colonial inhabitants.[30]

The Evolution of the *Casta* System in New Spain

While the Spanish Empire expanded in New Spain, the Crown's administrators instituted a racial order providing them with superior social and legal rights. Spaniards, who consisted of *peninsulares* born in Europe, and criollos, who were American born, governed the overseas colonies, while Indians and racially mixed people had limited political and social privileges. This social-racial hierarchy was initially shaped by intermarriage and war. By the mid-1570s, Spain had replaced the governing Indigenous elites, who had resisted the new regime, with faithful Native rulers. For decades following the conquest, to obtain the confidence and allegiance of the Indigenous people, the Crown and the church encouraged the intermarriage of Spanish soldiers with Indigenous women. Once the insurrection movements ended, however, the Crown discouraged viceroys, governmental officials, and their families from marrying Indians. Intermarriage was to proceed, but only among the commoner colonial groups, whose children came to constitute the racially mixed *casta* groups.[31]

New Spain's Sistema de Castas (*casta* system) evolved from Spain's Limpieza de Sangre (purity of blood) legal system, which dated back to the fifteenth century.[32] In Spain, Spaniards of Jewish and Muslim descent were prohibited from obtaining high-level appointments within secular, ecclesiastical, or royal governments. It was believed that these kinds of people were "sullied" by their non-Christian ancestry, and they were considered untrustworthy subjects who might revert to their idolatrous religions. To ensure that high-level occupations and appointments were not given to heretics, an applicant had to provide proof of purity of blood, consisting of a genealogical study and witnesses who could confirm the applicant's family history. This discriminatory social practice was transported to the overseas colonies, with racial exclusions added. People of Indigenous and African descent became part of the banned populations.

The first law distinguishing Spaniards from people of color was adopted by King Philip II in 1568. It stipulated that Blacks, mulattos (Spanish-Black), and mestizos (Spanish-Indian) were prohibited from carrying arms unless given a dispensation by the royal government.[33] A few years later, the king introduced a series of laws that, according to scholars, signified the institutionalization of the Sistema de Castas, which was used to maintain people of color in a subordinate position.[34] The laws prohibited those of mixed racial heritage from becoming municipal magistrates or public notaries, or from holding any title of authority over Indians.[35] The king also ordered that people of mixed African and Indian heritage pay a special tax in order to remain part of the free population.[36] Under Spain's Siete Partidas (seven divisions) laws, the children of enslaved males married to Indian and mestiza women obtained the legal status of their mothers, that is, the children were born free. The Siete Partidas laws, however, were not extended to enslaved women, and a child of a female slave was born a slave.[37] Racial labels were used to distinguish people who were free and racially mixed, such as mulatto, *pardo* (black mixture), or *morisco* (child of a mulatto and a white person), whereas slaves were generally referred to as *negros* regardless of their ancestry.[38] To maintain a record of people's racial lineage, parish priests and municipal governments were required to register the race of those issued marriage and baptismal certificates, or of a person of African descent who settled in a community.

In 1582, Philip II extended the occupational restrictions and ordered the viceroy of New Spain to ascertain that Spaniards born in the New World seeking high-level appointments and occupations were not mestizos or mulattos. Limpieza de Sangre certificates were required, and exemptions were given only to sons born from legitimate marriages between conquerors and women of noble Indigenous ancestry.[39] Under the Sistema de Castas, people who were of mixed racial heritage were called *castas*. Because it was important to enforce the racial decrees, especially at the highest levels, royal administrators and clergy from the Holy Inquisition Office were charged with investigating complaints and enforcing the mandates.

By this time, the Catholic Church had established its own *casta* policies. Indians were prohibited from joining the Franciscan orders in 1525, and forty years later, Indians and racially mixed people were banned from the priesthood altogether.[40] Exemptions, however, were permitted for meritorious men of Indian descent if they spoke Indian languages and were born from legitimate marriages.

Following the royal decrees, secular institutions began placing Limpieza de Sangre restrictions on many occupations, prohibiting *castas* and Indians from joining guilds. If the guilds hired Indians or *castas*, they were restricted to journeyman roles.[41] Spaniards controlled the municipal governments, and it was common for hereditary or Limpieza de Sangre statutes to be adopted in order to prevent nonwhites from holding office.[42] Municipal governments in turn passed local laws reserving some occupations for Spaniards.

The municipal laws and practices blocking mestizos and people of African heritage from local government did not affect Indians, since in 1571 they were banned from participating by royal order.[43] Under the República de Indios laws, Indigenous communities were to form their own municipal governments and select their representatives and judges.[44] They were also required to pay annual tribute on the harvests and goods they produced, and if they lived in missions or *corregimientos* (land grant communities) they were told what crops to grow.[45] To prevent mestizos and people of African heritage from interfering in the political life of Indian communities, by law they were prohibited from living in Indian pueblos.[46] Indigenous people, however, were permitted to live and work in Spanish towns, where most of them were employed as servants.[47]

In the early 1600s, institutions adopted additional exclusionary laws against Indians and people of mixed descent. By 1630, universities had barred Indians, mestizos, and mulattos of illegitimate birth from attending, and occupations in many cities were closed to them in hospitals, accounting offices, and the royal lottery office.[48] The Holy Inquisition Office ten years earlier had tried to impose similar restrictions on criollos, but King Philip IV vetoed the proposal. Administrators had advised the king that criollos should not be appointed to high-level offices because most of them were racially mixed. Allegedly, they were submitting fraudulent papers to prove that they were not of Indian or African descent.[49]

Oddly, the occupational exclusions and college-admission bans occurred during the period when opportunities within the military opened for Black males.[50] Additional Black units were needed to catch runaway slaves and to help oversee the Black population, which had grown tremendously during the height of the transatlantic slave trade, especially in the coastal cities. Black men had participated in the military since the mid-sixteenth century, but their numbers were few because of the cost of enlisting.[51]

The Black population in Mexico increased after a series of epidemics in central Mexico radically reduced the number of Indigenous people during the mid-1570s. Scholars estimate that the Indigenous population of central

Mexico fell from 25 million (precontact) to around 2.8 million, and possibly as low as 1.3 million.[52] The ongoing population decline created a tremendous labor shortage for the *peninsular* elite, who had been given enormous land grants. As the Indigenous population plummeted, the Spanish Crown authorized slave traders to bring more captives to Mexico. Within sixty years after the epidemics spread, approximately 150,000–200,000 African people had been forcibly brought to Mexico.[53] But in 1630, King Philip IV canceled most commercial slave-trading licenses, since the Indigenous population had rebounded.[54]

In 1714, the Bourbons took control of Spain after Charles II died without leaving any descendants to inherit the Spanish throne.[55] For over a decade, the Spanish nobility had been divided over whether Philip V, the grandson of Louis XIV of France, should inherit the crown and place the Bourbon dynasty in power, or whether Spain should remain faithful to the Habsburg dynasty by selecting the archduke of Austria to inherit the crown. When Philip V ascended to the throne, a large portion of the nobility opposed his succession, so he decided to reduce their power and centralize the government in the Castilian region, where his allies resided. He ordered the restructuring of the judicial system, required military offices to be headed by professional men who had attended military academies, ended hereditary governmental offices, nationalized the customhouses, and appointed his supporters to the Spanish parliament and other high-level positions.

In New Spain, the reforms did not begin to take effect until the mid-1700s. The primary goal was to reduce the authority of the criollo elite, who the king believed had excessive power over markets and the collection of taxes.[56] According to his advisers, this had resulted in reducing Spain's overseas revenues. To remove influential criollos from office, the king suspended hereditary political appointments and the sale of new appointments. Positions within the government were now supposed to be awarded on merit and education, but in fact the king replaced officials with *peninsular* bureaucrats in order to centralize his power. The monarchy justified this reform by invoking Spain's Limpieza de Sangre legal codes, which required that high- and midlevel appointments be held by officials without Jewish, Arabic, Indian, or African ancestry.[57] To remove more officeholders, a new policy required the spouses of officials to prove their racial purity, too, which led to the appointment of more *peninsulares*.[58]

To end the criollos' monopoly over municipal governments, the king reduced the authority of the councils (*ayuntamientos* and *cabildos*) and transferred their duties to ministries directly responsible to him.[59] He also instituted an *intendente* system, making professional military officers responsible for tax collection, roads, and oversight of a range of treasury interests, including the suppression of smuggling.[60] The governance of New Spain was divided between the viceroy's administration and the commandancy-general system. This was done to decentralize the authority of the viceroys and create a more efficient system in the frontiers. In the northern territories a captain general was put in charge of the Internal Provinces, which consisted of California, Sonora, New Mexico, Nueva Vizcaya, Texas, and Coahuila. The captain general, who took direct orders only from the king, was authorized to appoint governors, town councils, and career military officers.[61]

Reforms were also instituted in commerce in order to end criollo dominance in that sphere. New restrictions ended criollos' trading monopoly with Peru and other New World colonies. New licensing requirements were imposed to regulate trade.[62] The Casa de Contratación (House of Trade), based in Seville, controlled commerce, and criollos saw its practices as highly discriminatory. For example, many products could not be produced in Mexico and could be imported only from Spain.[63] Furthermore, licenses for overseas commerce were confined to large-scale trading firms, which were generally owned by *peninsulares*. With the new restrictions, criollo merchants were placed at a serious disadvantage.

While restrictions were placed on criollos, opportunities opened for mestizos and Blacks in lower-level occupations. Prestigious occupations, however, remained closed to them.[64] The enforcement of occupational restrictions in the craft guilds had become lax and was not of concern to royal administrators. In 1754, a government report titled "Decrees of the Baratillo of Mexico" concluded that the Limpieza de Sangre laws were primarily enforced in high-ranking occupations and within commercial houses. This weak implementation was attributed to changing economic patterns. Many persons of color had opened their own shops, and they did not enforce the occupational restrictions.[65] Likewise, employers in many regions, out of economic necessity, competed for the most skilled workers. Toward the end of the eighteenth century, the royal government further liberalized its treatment of racially mixed people by selling Limpieza de Sangre licenses, permitting wealthy persons to seek occupations and governmental appointments that had previously been unattainable. Under the Gracias al Sacar (certificates of merit) laws of 1795, people of color could assume the political status of criollos.[66]

Criollos resented the opening of opportunities for the *castas*. They saw this as a fraudulent form of *blanqueamiento* (whitening) and a disrespectful form of social leveling. In addition, they resented Spanish authorities for refusing to treat them as fully European and expecting them to prove their racial purity.[67] Criollos, therefore, became the strongest opponents of any laws that would encourage the whitening of mestizos, Indians, and Blacks. Instead, they chose to harden the lines that separated them by retaining their social distance.[68] They were well aware that royal officials were liberalizing the *casta* practices in order both to gain political support and to undermine their local authority.

Elite criollo families turned to Spain's marriage laws to distance themselves from their social inferiors by invoking the Pragmática Sanción law of 1776. The law required that people younger than twenty-five obtain the approval of their parents before being wed.[69] Although the law did not prohibit interracial marriages, it allowed criollos to forbid their children from marrying people from racial groups that they considered socially unequal. Many criollos, therefore, used the law to affirm their social superiority and assert their distinct ancestry. Sadly for them, the royal government did not share their perspective: it had become common knowledge that nearly all criollos were racially mixed, and their fictitious heritage stopped being the basis for preferment and privileges.[70]

The *Casta* System on the Northern Frontier

When Texas was founded, Spain's racial order was strictly enforced in the interior of New Spain. On the frontier, however, people needed incentives to become settlers, including a relaxation of the distinctions between racial groups. The king's administrators preferred to recruit Spanish settlers, but because volunteers were scarce, most people who applied had to be accepted if they were free and in good health, pledged their loyalty to Spain, and had some assets. Consequently, settlers in Texas were given land grants, and occupational restrictions were not strictly enforced.[71] Distinctions in the craft guilds were also irrelevant, since they did not exist in sparsely populated Texas. The Crown's administrators recruited blacksmiths and other skilled workers who could construct buildings, make clothing and shoes, and erect irrigation systems, irrespective of their race. Thus, the economic needs of Texas and the sparse colonial population created the conditions for Spanish administrators to be flexible in how they interpreted the *casta* restrictions. To build a united community, administrators accorded people the status of their professional and productive worth, rewarding those who were industrious. For Spanish males with racially mixed families in particular, the North became a place where their children were not bound by *casta* social distinctions and would be allowed to claim the father's racial status.[72]

During the early eighteenth century, San Antonio continued to be the most stable settlement in the province. To further strengthen it, plans were made to send additional European settlers.[73] The Council of the Indies decided that ten to twelve families from the Canary Islands could be sent periodically until two hundred families were distributed across Texas. In 1731, the first colonists from the Canary Islands arrived in Texas.[74] They were given land near the Presidio de San Antonio de Béxar, where the military was housed and the earlier colonists resided. They were commissioned to establish the villa of San Fernando de Béxar and establish the first *ayuntamiento* (town council) in San Antonio.[75] With the arrival of the first fifty-nine Canary Islanders, who were called Isleños, San Antonio's military officials shared the settlement's governance with the *ayuntamiento*.

Within a few months of the Canary Islanders' arrival, serious problems erupted. The Isleños believed that they had legal rights superior to those of the locals, who were predominantly people of color, and that the latter had to abide by their rules. Juan de Acuña y Bejarano, the viceroy of New Spain and the Marqués de Casa Fuerte, received an official complaint from the friars of the San Antonio missions, informing him that the Isleños were misbehaving and threatening the stability of the settlement.[76] The complaint was supported by spokesmen representing the earlier settlers and by Captain Francisco Pérez, who, in the absence of the governor, was in charge of the presidio. The missionaries reported that the newly appointed *ayuntamiento*, which had jurisdiction over the civilians of San Antonio, had passed a water ordinance to enrich the Isleño families, but at the cost of destabilizing the colony. Only Canary Islanders were appointed to the town council at this time. The council had ruled that the local creeks and rivers belonged solely to the Isleño families. The rest of the settlers, including the mission Indians, were to pay a fee for water. Furthermore, the fathers reported that many of the men were trying to force local Indians to work without any compensation. Essentially, the Canary Islanders were attempting to reproduce a rigid *casta* system in which Indians would be obliged to work for free and the earlier settlers would be forced into debt servitude. When the viceroy ordered the provincial governor, Juan Antonio de Bustillos y Zeballos, to hold a hearing to collect the facts, the Isleños' representatives denied the charges and petitioned for the water ordinance to remain in effect. They argued that King Philip V had given the Isleños legal jurisdiction over the civilians in San Antonio when he chose them to establish a new village. They also complained that the water ordinance had been passed because Captain Pérez, who had previously held the authority to distribute water, gave the missions and the presidial families more water than they needed.[77]

After the investigation concluded, Viceroy Juan de Acuña y Bejarano supported the missionaries' claims. The viceroy ordered the Isleños to accept the authority of Captain Pérez and share the water. The following year, the Isleños appealed, but the viceroy rejected their petition.[78] He had received additional evidence of the Isleños' misbehavior. Ten colonists formed a caucus and wrote a letter complaining that the Isleños were endangering the settlement's safety by periodically organizing posses to capture and punish Indians with whom they had financial conflicts. These raids, which often ended badly, forced Captain Pérez to send troops to rescue the Isleños. The letter emphasized that the Indians were not the aggressors; the problem was the Isleños' vigilante attitude.

By the mid-1700s, Spanish officials had become convinced that the growth of Texas should proceed by recruiting frontier settlers rather than bringing more people from the Canary Islands.[79] Most Isleños were experiencing difficulties in running their farms and ranches, and they had to rely on the resources of the earlier settlers or on the provisions owned by the military. Although the Isleños initially had a series of conflicts with the earlier settlers, including monopolizing the *ayuntamiento*, within two decades of their arrival their children had married locals and formed a more inclusive community. The non-Isleños had to push for this inclusion by demanding to be part of the *ayuntamiento*. Like other people of color in New Spain, they had to petition for the right to be included in municipal governments, which were monopolized by *peninsulares* and criollos. After a series of petitions sent by non-Isleños to the viceroy in Mexico City, on September 1, 1745, they were permitted to participate in the local government.[80] A few years later, the Isleños' hereditary *ayuntamiento* appointments, which allowed fathers to pass on their appointment to their sons, were terminated, and council membership was opened to other candidates.[81]

Indian Hostilities and the Reorganization of the Settlements

In 1768, Cayetano María Pignatelli Rubí Corbera y San Climent, commonly known as the Marqués de Rubí, submitted a report to King Charles III, who had commissioned it, recommending that Los Adaes, the northernmost settlement in Texas, be abandoned because of Indian hostilities and its failure to prosper.[82] In Texas, he proposed that the Crown invest in La Bahía, San Antonio, El Paso del Norte, and Laredo. The last two, if militarily strengthened, could provide additional assistance when Texas settlements came under attack. He argued for relocating the Los Adaes colonists to San Antonio and La Bahía.

To Rubí, Los Adaes had lost its strategic military significance after the Bourbons came to power in Spain and ended many long-standing conflicts between Spain and France. During this peaceful phase, France ceded Louisiana, including Natchitoches, to Spain in order to prevent Great Britain from acquiring the territory following France's defeat in the French and Indian War.[83] To Rubí, the military expense of protecting Los Adaes could no longer be justified in the absence of a French threat. Five years later, because Los Adaes continued to experience unresolvable problems, Charles III ordered the northeastern settlements to be relocated to San Antonio and La Bahía.[84] San Antonio was then named the capital of Texas.[85]

The consolidation of the settlers in San Antonio and La Bahía improved the fortification of those settlements. The reorganization also increased the financial assistance given to the military in El Paso del Norte and Laredo. In both colonies, the resources were used to maintain and forge new alliances with Indian communities.[86] Officials were able to purchase more goods to trade with or give to their Indigenous allies. Since around 1,500 Indian allies living in the *visita* of San Agustín (Christian village) surrounded and protected Laredo, this assistance was a wise expenditure and critical to Laredo's prosperity.[87]

Racial Diversity and the Politics of Passing

Following the reorganization of Texas, the fortification of the colonies improved, but sporadic Apache and Comanche attacks continued to be a problem. These raids became an obstacle to recruiting settlers to Texas. Consequently, the growth of the Texas settlements was mainly due to internal birth rates and the acculturation of Indian people. The racial composition of the colonies, however, continued to be diverse. In the village centers, the inhabitants consisted of Spaniards, people of mixed descent, and *amestizado* (acculturated) Indians from Mexico and the local area. The missions, on the outskirts of the village centers, provided housing for new Indian converts, while most Indigenous people lived in *ranchería* villages surrounding the colonial settlements. Generally, only Indigenous people who were part of mixed Indian-settler families lived among the colonists.[88]

The provincial and regional censuses of Texas provide an overview of the racial diversity of the colonial and Indian populations, but also reveal that a whitening process was taking place in the late 1700s. That is, census tabulations over the years indicate that residents of color were decreasing in number, while the figure for the Spanish category was increasing significantly.[89] This trend did not make any sense unless the Indians, mestizos, and those of African ancestry were not having children. Likewise, the whitening process in Texas did not reflect the national demographic pattern or the region's settlement history. According to the censuses, Texas had a higher percentage of Spanish residents than the national pattern, which was unlikely. New Spain's national censuses indicate that by 1742, few Europeans lived in Mexico, accounting for only 0.4 percent of the total population. Their numbers had fallen to 0.2 percent by the late 1700s.[90] Likewise, from 1742 to 1793 the criollo population was estimated to range from 21.2 percent to 17.8 percent.[91]

One of the earliest civilian censuses of Texas, taken in 1777, indicates that the province's population numbered 3,103, and the inhabitants were racially diverse.[92] Nonetheless, according to this census, the percentage of Spaniards living in Texas was higher than in other parts of New Spain. The census of 1777 included the entire colonial population, the mission Indians, and military personnel. Not counting enslaved persons and members of the military, the civilian population numbered 957 Spaniards, 870 Indians, and the *castas* numbered 124 mestizos and 669 persons *de color quebrado* (of partial African descent). The rest of the inhabitants were soldiers and officers whose race was not noted, as well as 20 enslaved people solely classified as "slave men" and "slave women."[93] A narrative accompanying the census reveals that the racial enumeration of the settlers was most likely inaccurate. Juan María Vicencio Ripperdá, the governor of Texas, wrote a note stating that the provincial population was indeed increasing but that the additional colonists were of low social quality (*calidad*). He wrote, "The exceptional people are the fathers, *Españoles* and *Europeos*, but their numbers are few. It is a misfortune that most [of the people] are of low quality, with most being *de color quebrado* or *Zinanbanzos* [Black and Indian]."[94] Father Juan Agustín Morfi, who was in Texas that year to conduct a geographic and historical study of the northeastern settlements, offered a similarly derogatory observation. He reported that the majority of the colonists in Texas were lazy people *de color quebrado* who were unworthy of the land grants they received.[95] A year later, Viceroy Teodoro de Croix expressed similar sentiments when he wrote to José de Gálvez, the minister of the Indies, that the quality of the recruits needed to improve.

The viceroy described the settlers intending to move to Texas as mulattos and other people belonging to the impure *castas*.[96]

A comparison of the San Antonio de Béxar censuses of 1782 and 1783 indicates that people preferred to claim that they were Spaniards, regardless of their racial makeup. In 1782, excluding the missions, the family census for San Antonio reported that 60 percent of the heads of household were mulatto and 35 percent were Spanish.[97] Oddly, in the census for the following year the figure for the Spanish category had increased to 54 percent, and the mulatto category was eliminated. Instead, 15 percent of the inhabitants were reported to be *de color quebrado*, and 6 percent, mestizo. A whitening process was at work as administrators accepted the enumerators' observations of the population.[98] The historians Gerald Poyo and Jesús de la Teja found a similar pattern in their review of San Antonio's eighteenth-century family censuses.[99] The head of household was often described as Indian or Black, yet the rest of the family was identified as Spanish or mestizo. This nonsensical pattern suggested the *casta* counts were imprecise. Furthermore, Poyo found that in the San Antonio settlements, an analysis of occupations listed in the censuses indicates that some skilled artisans over the years whitened themselves by claiming different racial labels.[100]

In 1790, based on letters written by the alcaldes (municipal heads) of Nacogdoches, La Bahía, and San Antonio to Governor Rafael Martínez Pacheco, local authorities refused to use the racial category *de color quebrado* when preparing the civilian census.[101] By this time, the Los Adaes settlers had been given permission to return to the Northeast and establish a new settlement called Nacogdoches.[102] When Governor Pacheco submitted the provincial census for Texas, he was ordered to retake it because he had not enforced the use of the *casta* categories.[103] Three years later, a similar dispute took place, and the next governor, Manuel Muñoz, was reprimanded by royal administrators for supporting the alcaldes and refusing to make them redo their census reports. The governor wrote that the 1793 census reflected the use of local categories because the alcaldes preferred to count most residents as either Spanish or Indian, and they would not use the category *de color quebrado*.[104] When the national census was prepared the royal demographers chose not to use the Texas data, and instead projected a figure for the general population based on previous censuses.[105] A year later, royal administrators deferred to Governor Muñoz and allowed the alcaldes to use their own racial labels as long as a precise count of the general population was submitted annually.

In the aftermath of the new policy, Texas's census reports lacked uniformity. Some jurisdictions reported racial data, while others omitted it altogether. In 1804, the provincial census contained only the number of people in the settlements and of Indigenous people residing in the missions, a total of 3,980.[106] In sum, because of the freedom the alcaldes had when reporting the size of their settlements, the category "Spanish" was no longer associated with the *peninsular*-criollo genealogical distinctions, but rather reflected a community's cultural membership within colonial Spanish society. Unlike the interior of Mexico, where criollo elites sought recognition as full Europeans and asserted their racial purity, in Texas the term "Spanish" evolved into an ethnic category that was not contested by the government or local elites.[107]

The Texas-Louisiana Border and Runaway Slaves

At the turn of the nineteenth century, relations between the United States and Spain became strained over boundary disagreements and Spain's runaway slave laws. Spain had adopted a policy to allow runaway slaves from the United States to settle in Texas. It is uncertain how many African Americans migrated to Texas as a result, but this issue became a major source of conflict.

On October 15, 1802, Spain returned Louisiana to France, and less than a year later France sold the territory to the United States in the Louisiana Purchase.[108] The United States and Spain immediately began talks over the location of the Texas-Louisiana border. Spain claimed that it lay between Natchitoches and the Arroyo Hondo, while the United States maintained that the border was the Sabine River, twenty leagues west of the Arroyo Hondo.[109] If the US claim was correct, it would mean the loss of over 84,000 acres for Texas. Associated with the border dispute were grievances raised against Nemesio de Salcedo y Salcedo, the commander general of the Internal Provinces, who refused to allow US agents to enter Texas in search of runaway slaves. US officials charged that the commander's interpretation of international-border policy was wrong. Salcedo had informed them that upon entering Texas, slaves gained their freedom and that this policy did not violate international law or the property rights of US slave owners. US official disagreed because Spain's laws were encouraging slaves from Louisiana and the Carolinas to run away and seek refuge in Texas.

Salcedo was named commander general of the Internal Provinces in 1802.[110] He had full political authority over the territories of Texas, New Mexico, Coahuila, Sonora, Sinaloa, and Nueva Vizcaya (Durango and Chihuahua).[111] The distance of the northern frontier from the viceroy's command center in Mexico City made bureaucratic control of the region impossible. Consequently, the Crown placed a commander general in control of most of the northern frontier settlements, with his office located in northern New Spain. Thus, the commander general could act swiftly without waiting for the viceroy's orders. The commander general was responsible only to the king of Spain, and he could execute military orders or make most decisions without consulting the viceroy or any of the courts that interpreted the application of Spanish law in New Spain. Only legal matters of high importance, such as treason, fell under the jurisdiction of the Audiencia of Guadalajara (the royal court for the northern provinces), with viceregal oversight.[112] Thus, after the Louisiana Purchase, Commander Salcedo became the Crown's primary representative on the northern frontier.

In 1804, through intelligence reports obtained by Salcedo, Charles IV, the king of Spain learned that the US government planned to acquire parts of Texas.[113] Spanish spies in New Orleans reported that US agents proposed to gain permission to enter Texas under the pretense of capturing runaway slaves. Their actual plan was to convince Caddo and Comanche groups to form military alliances and attack Spanish settlements. Nacogdoches was identified as the most vulnerable settlement, and if it fell, La Bahía would be the next target. According to Spanish agents, Congress was in support of this aggression because Spain refused to cede northern Texas and most of the coast to the United States. Under the Louisiana Purchase, US officials alleged that since France had erected forts along Matagorda Bay before Spain established its colonies in Nacogdoches and La Bahía, the United States, and not Spain, should have possession of the disputed territories.[114]

Since US plans to annex parts of Texas were obtained through the interception of news crossing spy networks, Spanish bureaucrats needed to retain a diplomatic façade while they negotiated the location of the border. If those negotiations failed, Spain would have to prepare for military action. Charles IV, therefore, advised Commander Salcedo to have his agents carefully evaluate the reason for entering Texas given by any person coming from Louisiana. He was also to strengthen the military fortification of Nacogdoches and the surrounding area.[115] Complicating matters, American spies, with the aid of Canary Islanders, were expected to enter Texas and instigate revolts. Canary Islanders had the right to obtain a license to enter Texas as Spanish subjects seeking to relocate to New Spain.

Twenty years earlier, when Louisiana belonged to Spain, Canary Islanders were brought in to populate the region. Over 2,000 of them settled in Louisiana. Spanish officials now feared that these settlers' loyalties lay with the United States. When Spain took over Louisiana, it suspended France's slave laws, and many Isleños owned slaves and preferred the old system.[116] It became public knowledge that when the US government acquired Louisiana, many Canary Islanders celebrated the change of government.[117]

While Louisiana was a Spanish territory, Charles IV had issued the Real Cédula (royal decree) of May 31, 1789, revising Spain's slave codes in the New World.[118] In Louisiana, many slave owners insisted that the king's *cédula* did not apply to them because, under international law, France's Code Noir of 1724 could not be nullified. Under the reforms of 1789, the king issued several controversial edicts. He ordered that slaves were to be emancipated if unspeakable crimes had been committed against them. Also, slave owners were required to emancipate slaves if they could purchase their freedom. These policies were radical for the times, and many considered them violations of the property rights of slave owners.[119] At first Texas was not greatly affected by these changes, since slavery was uncommon in the province. After the Louisiana Purchase, however, Texas officials had to enforce the king's emancipation and border policies. Based on the king's orders, any slave who reached Spanish soil from another nation came under Spain's jurisdiction and could be emancipated. For Salcedo, this was a delicate issue that complicated the enforcement of the king's border policies to keep American spies out of Texas.

Runaway African American Slaves in Texas

After the Louisiana Purchase, Spanish and American diplomats could not agree on the location of the Texas-Louisiana border, and Commander Salcedo had to remain vigilant against attempts by American troops to enter East Texas.[120] Regardless of the standoff, William Claiborne, the governor of Louisiana, continued to complain to José de Iturrigaray, the viceroy of New Spain, that Salcedo failed to follow international policies regarding runaway slaves. He charged that news of Salcedo's policy had spread among the slave populations of Louisiana and the Carolinas, and that this had caused slave owners to demand US military intervention in Texas. They also threatened to enter Texas and take the law into their own hands. Salcedo, knowing of the public uproar over his policy, responded that he would retaliate if slave owners tried to circumvent it. Governor Claiborne knew that the commander had the final word on this matter, so he chose to undermine Salcedo by appealing to influential Spaniards with direct contact to the king of Spain.[121]

Salcedo's position was based on his interpretation of the king's order issued under the Real Cédula of 1789.[122] By law, he was required to emancipate enslaved people who entered Texas and presented themselves to Spanish authorities. This was not a request; it was an order that he legally had to follow. Slaves were to be returned only if they committed theft before leaving a US territory; otherwise, after a judge heard their story and concluded that they had lawful reasons to run away, they were given permits to remain in Mexico. They became legal immigrants and were not to be enslaved in Mexico.[123]

Governor Claiborne, rather than turning to the last Spanish governor of Louisiana, who was knowledgeable about the enforcement of Louisiana slave laws but was also Salcedo's brother, chose to contact the Marqués de Casa Calvo. The marqués, Sebastián Nicolás Calvo de la Puerta y O'Farrill, had served briefly as interim governor of Louisiana, and it was likely that he would be sympathetic to US grievances.

On receiving news of the commander's slave policies, the marqués sent a series of letters to Salcedo, demanding the return of all runaway slaves.[124] He rudely told the commander that under the Treaty of San Lorenzo (signed in 1795 to establish the border between the United States and Spanish Florida), Spain had agreed to respect US law along the borders of Spain's colonies and that Salcedo had no right to emancipate any slave.

When Salcedo ignored the marqués's insolent letters, the Marqués de Casa Calvo turned to other influential friends of the king, and when this failed, he began to harass lower-level bureaucrats in Nacogdoches. In particular, the marqués attempted to intimidate Captain José Joaquín Ugarte, the military commander of Nacogdoches, who was the official directly in charge of handling runaway slaves in the settlement. Salcedo traveled throughout the northern frontier, and since his main office was located in the city of Chihuahua, the capital of the Internal Provinces, he did not directly manage the capture or emancipation of runaway slaves. In 1804, Salcedo instructed Ugarte to not return any slave entering Texas.

Ugarte fulfilled the commander's orders, but in December 26, 1804, when he received a letter from the Marqués de Casa Calvo to disobey Salcedo, he was uncertain how to proceed.[125] Ugarte, as a lower-level bureaucrat, feared the wrath of the marqués. Caught between his superior and the marqués, he continued to follow Salcedo's orders but sought legal advice on an issue that was unclear in the Real Cédula of 1789.[126] Rather than contact Salcedo, Ugarte wrote to Don Bernardo Villamil for legal advice. Villamil, one of the king's leading authorities on international law, was stationed in Chihuahua and had direct contact with the king. Ugarte asked whether slaves violated their right to apply for asylum if they were carrying arms when they turned themselves over to Spanish authorities? If so, were they to be arrested and returned to the United States?

On January 22, 1805, Don Villamil wrote to Ugarte that in his legal opinion, Salcedo had correctly interpreted the king's orders. He had consulted other legal advisers on international law and asked them under what circumstances could slaves be returned to the United States. All authorities on this subject concluded that the final decision involving slaves, including those who were armed, was a matter left to Salcedo. Villamil told Ugarte to direct any further inquiries regarding runaway slaves to Salcedo.[127]

On January 23, 1805, Salcedo sent a report to the king about the conflict over runaway slaves.[128] Some of the commander's statements were defensive, but he reassured the king that giving refuge to runaway slaves benefited Mexico, especially on the northern frontier. In the report, Salcedo first addressed the legal questions raised by the marqués and Governor Claiborne, and then he delineated the strategic military value that emancipated slaves offered Texas. Concerning the Treaty of San Lorenzo, Salcedo wrote that after carefully studying the treaty, he had found no evidence that Spain had agreed to allow foreigners to enter Spanish territory to retrieve runaway slaves. The treaty only addressed giving US merchants permits to temporarily dock their ships in Louisiana ports and cross Spanish maritime borders to enter the Mississippi River.[129]

Salcedo then addressed the second major issue raised by the marqués and Governor Claiborne. They had argued that under international law, French and American laws could be enforced in Texas. Their argument was that since Spanish officials had not enforced the Real Cédula of 1789 in most of New Spain's territories, the de facto practice was to recognize the earlier laws as still being in force. Salcedo acknowledged that France's Code Noir had been reinstated by the US government in Louisiana, and he did not dispute the de facto claim. But he asserted that only in Louisiana and Santo Domingo were the king's orders ignored. In Texas, as in other regions of New Spain, the Real Cédula of 1789 was enforced; therefore, arguing that the de facto laws of Louisiana superseded Spain's slave laws was absurd. There was no legal precedent allowing the laws of another nation to invalidate the laws of Spain in its own territories.

Salcedo then explained why the Real Cédula of 1789 served the interests of the Internal Provinces. He concurred with the popular opinion that US slaves should not be allowed to reside in the interior of Mexico. He therefore advised the king to require emancipated people to remain in Texas or be sent to other northern colonies. Settlers were needed to populate these remote places, and former slaves could easily be trained to defend the frontier from foreign military invasions. Earlier that month, Salcedo had deployed a squadron of 200 Black soldiers to protect the Sonoran coast near Mazatlán against British intrusion. The Milicia de Caballería de Pardos Libres posed no problems and was operating efficiently and independently.[130]

The commander's report reassured Charles IV that his policy was sound. The king was pragmatic, and he did not revoke Spain's slave codes. On the contrary, he chose to go beyond Salcedo's liberalism. He recognized that New Spain's changing racial demographics necessitated some flexibility in the *casta* system. The king was not prepared to nullify the occupational and political laws privileging the nobility and other *peninsulares*, but he realized that some social mobility was needed in order to maintain the loyalty of his subjects. On October 15, 1805, he issued the Cédula de Limpieza de Sangre, which allowed the children of *peninsulares* married to women of color to acquire the status of a Spaniard.[131]

While decisions over runaway slaves were being finalized, American and Spanish diplomats reached a temporary agreement over the Texas-Louisiana border. The negotiations were timely, since tensions kept mounting; both Commander Salcedo and General James Wilkinson were increasing their troop numbers and preparing for battle. During the autumn of 1806, Wilkinson and Lieutenant Colonel Simón de Herrera agreed that while a boundary accord was being negotiated, no colonies or settlements would be placed in the disputed territory.[132] Under this Neutral Ground Agreement, the zone between the Sabine River and the Arroyo Hondo was demilitarized and each side agreed to obtain a permit before entering the other's nation. The temporary truce brought some calm to the border conflicts, which highly benefited Spain: within a few years, the royal government would be attacked by French forces and weakened by domestic divisions.

Dismantling the *Casta* System and Mexican Independence

In the last years of the eighteenth century, Spain's hold over most of its Latin American colonies, including New Spain, gradually began to collapse. Charles IV, to avert the growth of independence movements, appealed to the criollo elite's economic interests. He did not eliminate the Limpieza de Sangre occupational and military requirements passed by previous administrations, but he did expand their economic opportunities in the hope that criollos would suppress regional independence movements. In the 1790s, the Crown passed a series of commercial reforms giving Latin American merchants the authority to retain a higher percentage of their profits generated in international markets.[133] This was done by lowering commerce taxes and custom duties.[134]

In New Spain, although the reforms benefited the criollo elite, the new policies did not pacify them. Criollo merchants continued to resent the political and financial monopoly that *peninsulares* held over the administration of the ports. The Mexico City consulate office controlled the ports, and only *peninsular* officials were appointed to posts within it. Consulate administrators were in charge of issuing passports, determining port authority policies, and limiting who had access to the warehouses, a privilege primarily accorded to *peninsular* merchants.[135] The appointments in the ports reflected the overall pattern found in Latin America. *Peninsulares* continued to occupy around 95 percent of all high-level administrative offices in the colonies.[136]

The criollos' anger was further fueled by the Crown's plans to restrict their participation in the Mexico City *audiencia*. By tradition, the *audiencia* was a powerful institution whose members gave the viceroy advice in shaping colonial policies; in the absence of the viceroy, it was authorized to govern New Spain. By 1789, the king had restricted criollos' participation in the *audiencia* and stopped appointing them to it; in subsequent years, fewer than four of the sixteen members were criollos.[137] Their removal was prompted by ongoing grievances and petitions submitted to the royal government by criollo members of the *audiencia*, requesting the equalization of political rights for the inhabitants of Spain's overseas colonies.[138]

The discontent of the criollos was not the main concern of the royal administration, since a serious international conflict was about to burst. In March 1808, Charles IV was pressured to abdicate, and two months later his son who ascended to the throne, Ferdinand VII, was kidnapped by French spies and held in captivity.[139] Napoleon Bonaparte, the emperor of France, had embarked on a quest to conquer the Iberian Peninsula, and after Portugal fell, he declared war against Spain. After defeating the Spanish military, Napoleon replaced the Spanish monarch with his brother Joseph Bonaparte. This created political chaos in Spain and forced the Supreme Royal Junta (head council) to take over the governance of the Spanish Empire. A year later, the junta collapsed and the Spanish parliament, the Cortes, took over.[140]

While the Cortes attempted to stabilize the government, its representatives acknowledged that Spain would lose Mexico if reforms were not enacted. The Mexico City *audiencia* recommended reforms in manufacturing, commerce, and agriculture. A declaration of equality between the citizens of the overseas colonies and the peninsula was also suggested in order to generate support for the royal government.[141] Although not prepared to dismantle the *casta* system, the Cortes agreed that commoners should be given new political rights. In Mexico, the majority of the population consisted of people of color; the Spanish elite was very small. In 1800, Indians and mestizos constituted 72 percent of the population, Spaniards 18 percent, and people of African descent 10 percent.[142] Of the Spanish population, less than 1 percent were *peninsulares*.[143]

On September 16, 1810, Miguel Hidalgo, a priest who had lost the support of the Catholic Church for refusing to stop protesting against Spain's unfair laws, issued Mexico's proclamation for independence. He called for the Grito de Independencia in the town of Dolores and told his followers to take up arms against the state. The rebellion was squashed by the military, but the movement spread throughout Mexico, and communities began organizing against the Crown. To dissuade people from supporting independence, the colonial government, within a few days of the call for independence, gradually introduced strategic reforms that had been approved by the Royal Junta of the Cortes. These reforms nearly dismantled the *casta* system. The first changes were aimed at the Indians, the majority population. The logic was that an independence movement would fail if the Indigenous communities could be convinced to remain loyal to the Crown. On September 25, 1810, Indians were released from paying tribute to the Crown and to the local government.[144] They were to be taxed in the same manner as other subjects. On February 9, 1811, under Decree 31, the Cortes rescinded occupational restrictions in the craft guilds and allowed Indians to enter any profession and to transact business with whomever they wanted.[145] Indians were also permitted to raise any crop they chose. Within days, the occupational decree was extended to other races. Decree 31 stipulated: "The Americans, Spaniards, as well as Indians, and the children of both classes, shall have equal option as the European Spaniards for all classes of employment or destiny, as well in the Cortes as in any other place of the monarchy, whether they be of an ecclesiastical, political, or military career."[146] Essentially, most race-based economic and occupational restrictions were ended.[147]

The Spirit of Mexican Independence Reaches Texas

After Father Hidalgo's call for independence, his followers amassed a huge army and won many battles throughout Mexico, but by mid-1811 the royalist army was back in control. On April 26, 1811, Commander Salcedo's army captured Father Hidalgo after his troops were defeated by royal forces at the Wells of Bajan in northern Coahuila.[148] He was turned over to the bishop of Durango, and a date was set for his trial by a military tribunal. Father Hidalgo, if found guilty of treason and acts of war, could no longer negotiate amnesty for himself. A few months earlier, in an attempt to stop the insurrectionist movements, the Royal Junta of the Cortes had informed Father Hidalgo that if he publicly denounced Mexican independence, they would stop pursuing him. He valiantly refused to be co-opted and continued to lead the rebellion. After his capture, Salcedo appointed his nephew, Manuel María de Salcedo, the governor of Texas, to head the tribunal. On July 29, 1811, the court found Father Hidalgo guilty of treason.[149] Witnesses reported that he was tortured, shot by a firing squad, and then beheaded.[150]

After Father Hidalgo's execution, the independence movement was led by the Supreme Governing Junta of America, with José María Morelos and other generals commanding the insurgent forces. The independence movement reached Texas after two agents were sent to negotiate assistance from the US government. Ignacio Aldama and Bernardo Gutiérrez de Lara were commissioned to purchase arms from the Americans. Aldama was to take a cart of gold to purchase the arms, and Gutiérrez was to meet diplomats in Washington, DC. [151] Although Aldama was captured by Spanish forces in San Antonio, Gutiérrez reached Washington, DC, in February and met with Secretary of State James Monroe. When Gutiérrez determined that US officials were unwilling to support the insurrectionist movement, he abandoned diplomacy and acted on his own. The US government was interested in supporting the Supreme Junta only if it agreed to move the Mexico-United States border to the Rio Grande and to cede Texas to the United States. Before Gutiérrez left Washington, he met William Shaler, who historians believe was a US government agent. Shaler informed Gutiérrez that Augustus Magee, a retired army officer in New Orleans, might be willing to help him. Gutiérrez met Magee in New Orleans, and together they assembled the Republican Army of the North, composed of Anglo-Americans and Mexican rebels, with the intent of liberating Texas from royal control.

On August 18, 1812, Gutiérrez's troops returned to Texas and took over Nacogdoches and, within a few months, La Bahía.[152] The entire Bexar region fell on April 1, 1813, after citizens in San Antonio offered little resistance.[153] When San Antonio was captured, Gutiérrez declared Texas an independent republic and ordered the execution of Governor Salcedo.[154]

When William Shaler learned that Gutiérrez had no plans to cede the province to the United States, he orchestrated the replacement of Guti-érrez by José Álvarez de Toledo.[155] The Mexican historians Josefina Z. Vázquez and Lorenzo Meyer propose that the secret agreements between Gutiérrez and Magee are unknown, but it is unlikely that Gutiérrez in-tended to continue with the independence movement.[156] Most likely, he was waiting for Mexican reinforcements, but when Shaler intervened, the course of Texas history changed, since Toledo was a secret agent working for Spain and the United States. Toledo, a Cuban exile living in New Orleans, allegedly favored independence for Cuba. Replacing Gutiérrez was not dif-ficult. When Magee died in the battle over La Bahía, the Anglo-American volunteers disliked Gutiérrez, so when Toledo arrived, they voted to replace him. Although the American and Mexican factions of the Republican Army squabbled over the future of Texas, they maintained a united coalition pre-pared to fight the Spanish forces that had set up camp in Nuevo Santander. By then, independence movements were breaking out throughout Mexico.

The Constitution of Cádiz Dismantles the *Casta* System

In January 1810, the Royal Junta of the Cortes called for an assembly to be held in the city of Cádiz to begin drafting laws and a constitution that would unify the nation against Napoleonic forces, address the concerns of the overseas colonies, and bring closure to the independence movements that were being organized throughout Latin America. A year later, after a series of liberal laws were issued for the overseas colonies, a committee composed of twelve men, two of them from the Americas, completed a draft of the constitution. It was now ready to be debated and voted on by the elected representatives. Out of 179 representatives, 52 came from the Americas, 15 of them from Mexico.[157] The main disagreement at the con-vention was the question of whether Indians and racially mixed groups in the Americas should be extended citizenship. Some delegates, including the representatives of Peru, proposed that Indians should be given citizenship because they had proved to be faithful to the Crown, but it was unlikely that mestizos and the descendants of Africans would remain loyal. Deny-ing them citizenship would prevent them from being eligible to run for office and to vote. In many districts, *casta* groups composed the majority of the population, and if they could run for office, they would not vote for *peninsular* officials.

The Mexican and the Central American delegations, led by Miguel Ramos Arizpe, the representative from Coahuila, Mexico, challenged the unfairness of the plan, accusing the representatives of politically disenfranchising one-third of the Spanish Empire's American population. After an eight-day debate, a compromise was reached. On March 19, 1812, article 1 of the constitution stipulated that "the Spanish nation is the sum of all Spaniards of both hemispheres," and articles 8 and 18 declared that Indians and all free people of Spanish heritage were citizens with equal rights.[158] Because some of the delegates had argued against making people of African descent citizens, regardless of whether they were also of Indigenous or Spanish descent, a compromise was reached by giving automatic citizenship to members of the military but requiring others to qualify. Article 22, the compromise resolution, required nonmilitary people of African descent to come before a governmental official and prove that they were of legitimate birth and that they deserved the rights of citizenship based on merit.[159]

The plans and reforms passed by the Cortes did not last long. In 1813, France released Ferdinand VII and ended the takeover of Spain. Upon resuming office, the king immediately put an end to the Cortes's liberal legislation.[160] He reinstated the tax system, abolished the reforms in the craft guilds, ended the secularization of the mission system, and declared the Constitution of Cádiz null and void. This reversal was a monumental mistake, because the king needed to convince people to be loyal rather than to anger them by restricting their political rights.

Texas residents experienced additional political problems, including loss of the right to form a civilian government. Before the king returned to power, the Cortes ordered the reconquest of Texas. In the summer of 1813, Joaquín de Arredondo, the new commander general of the Eastern Provinces who replaced Nemesio de Salcedo, led three thousand royalist soldiers to suppress the Republican Army of the North. By August 18, all the Texas settlements had been recaptured.[161] General Arredondo immediately placed Texas under military rule and suspended the regional government. He then undertook an exhaustive investigation to determine which locals had aided the Republican Army, and he ordered their execution. In San Antonio, where the rebels' command center was housed, several hundred civilians were sentenced to death for supporting Mexico's independence. Several hundred other people were arrested and placed in prison. Around thirty civilians in Nacogdoches were executed; those who could escape fled to Louisiana.[162] After Texas was placed under military rule, few Texas residents sympathized with the royal government. Although the historians Josefina Z. Vázquez and Lorenzo Meyer assert that the reconquest of Texas was not a significant event in the drive for Mexican independence, it influenced the course of Texas history.[163] Thanks to the Gutiérrez-Magee alliance, many foreigners became familiar with the territory and learned that Texas was sparsely populated but had many natural resources.

Border Politics and African American Immigrants on the Eve of Mexican Independence

Most residents of Texas favored independence from Spain. The people of Nuevo Santander, however, supported the royal government, and civilians there were prepared to aid the royal forces if insurrectionist movements erupted in Texas. As the struggle for independence grew, and in an attempt to prevent the US government from intervening, Spain ended the dispute over the Louisiana border. In 1819, Luis de Onís, the Spanish minister to the United States, finalized an agreement to delineate the territorial boundary between the United States and New Spain, including the question of the Neutral Zone. In addition, Spain agreed to cede Florida to the United States under the Adams-Onís Treaty (also called the Transcontinental Treaty of 1819).[164] In the Neutral Zone, Spain relinquished all claims east of the Sabine River, giving the United States ownership over the disputed territory. The treaty also laid out the western border of the United States and Mexico, with Spain ceding all claims to the Pacific Northwest and to most of the Rocky Mountains north of New Mexico.[165] In return, the United States relinquished all claims to the Texas coast.

The treaty, however, did not contain an article dealing directly with runaway slaves reaching Texas.[166] Most likely, this was because agreements concerning slavery were such a sensitive issue that they could derail critical territorial negotiations. Capturing people and returning them to their nation of origin were minor problems that could be handled by local officials.

Spain, despite its weakened state, continued to enforce the Real Cédula of 1789 on the northern frontier. The number of slaves entering Texas from Louisiana and the United States during the Spanish period is uncertain; what is public knowledge, though, is that Spain continued to enforce the *cédula* during the war for Mexican independence. At this time, slavery in Texas was uncommon. Spanish censuses indicate that from 1782 to 1821, the number of slaves in Texas year to year never exceeded thirty-seven.[167]

A court hearing held in the city of Monterey in 1820 illustrates what was required of escaped slaves hoping to stay in Mexico. To be emancipated and allowed to become immigrants, they had to demonstrate good character and convince a judge or *audiencia* that they had suffered intolerable cruelty at the hands of their masters.

The Monterey hearing dealt with five emancipated African Americans who were given asylum in Texas but were later charged with being part of a band of thieves and stealing a horse. If found guilty, they were to be extradited to the United States.[168] The investigation centered on the evidence presented against Martín, one of the runaway slaves. In his testimony, Martín unwittingly implicated Juan Pexos, Ricardo Moran, Samuel, and Tivi. (The last names of Martín, Samuel, and Tivi were not recorded in the hearing's transcripts.) For their profession, Juan Pexos and Ricardo Moran reported that they were shoe cobblers, Tivi was a domestic worker, and Martín was a blacksmith. Juan and Martín had fled from South Carolina, and the rest from Louisiana. They all spoke Spanish except Ricardo, who needed an interpreter. After they were given emancipation papers, Martín moved to San Antonio, and the others lived in San Antonio and Nacogdoches.

The extradition proceedings began in 1820 after the arrest of Martín, who was age twenty-seven. A San Antonio judge, whose name was not recorded in the depositions, reported that a witness testified that when Martín arrived in Nacogdoches, he was associated with Spanish thieves hiding in the Neutral Zone. When Martín heard about the accusation, he turned himself in and pledged his innocence. He, however, confessed to authorities that before leaving South Carolina, he stole a horse from his master's estate, but denied that he knew the thieves.

Martín's confession placed him in danger of being extradited. Under Spanish law, enslaved persons could be returned if they had committed theft against their masters. To remain in Texas, Martín had to prove that he was not part of the band of thieves, and he needed to find a legal argument to obtain amnesty for stealing a horse. To invoke the Real Cédula of 1789 in self-defense, Martín had to convince the court that his master had tortured him.

After Martín's confession, he was arrested, and a date was set for a hearing to be held in San Antonio on April 4, 1820. His companions, who had met Martín on their way to Nacogdoches, were also arrested. Juan Pexos was arrested in San Antonio, and Ricardo Moran and Tivi in Nacogdoches. By that time, Ricardo had become a successful businessman. Tivi was his house companion, but it is unclear whether she was his wife. The three were charged with conspiracy for stealing a horse and being associated with a band of Spanish thieves.

Because the group's criminal charges were serious, the hearing was moved to Monterey to be heard by higher-level judicial authorities in the Audiencia of the Reino de Nuevo León. Juan Pexos, the first to testify, informed the *audiencia* that he met Martín on the road to Nacogdoches. They had both escaped from South Carolina, but he was originally from Louisiana and he did not know his age. When Juan first met Martín, he was surprised to see a Black man riding a horse and assumed that it was stolen. Juan assured the court that he did not conspire to steal the horse.

Martín corroborated the testimony and cleared Juan of any criminal association. Martín testified that he escaped from his master's home with the help of three local slaves.[169] He met Juan on the road, and when they were near Nacogdoches, they met Ricardo (age forty-eight), Tivi (age twenty-seven), and Samuel. Martín did not know Samuel's age. He recalled that Samuel was ill and could barely walk. And he knew that they had fled from Louisiana.[170] When they finally reached the outskirts of Nacogdoches, soldiers arrested them. A few days later, Samuel died in the hospital at Nacogdoches, and the local judge decided to release them and handed them emancipation certificates. Martín and the others were allowed to move to any of the Texas settlements. Tivi and Ricardo remained in Nacogdoches, while Juan and Martín settled in San Antonio. Juan lived in La Bahía for a short time but did not like it there, so he returned to San Antonio.

During the hearing, the defendants were asked a series of questions to determine their innocence or guilt. They were also asked to share their experiences of enslavement. Each of them recounted sad and cruel memories about their despotic masters. Tivi recognized that her master had lost at least $1,000 when she escaped, but in her view, running away was the only way of ending the years of torture she had endured. She accused Santiago Cochran, her master, of committing unspeakable crimes against her.[171]

At the conclusion of the hearing, the members of the *audiencia* found Martín guilty of stealing a horse, but did not recommend his extradition, because of the inhumane acts committed against him.[172] The *audiencia* concluded that stealing the horse was his only way to escape. The *audiencia* ruled in addition that none of the accused had conspired with the band of Spanish thieves, nor had they helped Martín steal the horse. All the defendants had satisfactorily proved that they were industrious and self-sufficient people who deserved to be emancipated. The *audiencia* records end with their acquittal and do not provide further information on their lives in Texas. What we do know is that a year later, the war for independence officially ended, and all free people, including Black civilians, became Mexican citizens.

The war for Mexican independence ended after Vicente Guerrero, part of the landed elite from Veracruz and a descendant of Indian and Black slaves, consolidated the insurgent movements throughout Mexico during the winter of 1820.[173] He convinced part of the royal army to support independence. Earlier that year, King Ferdinand's last attempt to regain the loyalty of the masses had failed, even though he had reinstated the citizenship articles of the Constitution of Cádiz recognizing the equality of citizens of Spain and the Spanish subjects in the overseas colonies.[174] Guerrero's forces, in alliance with one of the most important royalist officers who turned against Spain, Colonel Agustín de Iturbide, defeated the Crown's army in Mexico City and forced it to lay down its arms. On February 24, 1821, the Plan de Iguala was adopted by the insurgent forces. It proclaimed their independence from Spain and declared that all inhabitants of Mexico were citizens without distinctions, other than their differences in merit and virtue, and were free to choose any form of employment.[175] Seven months later, on September 27, 1821, the Crown's military forces ceded power and the rebels obtained their independence. Within three years, Mexico was transformed into a republic, and the citizenship articles of the Constitution of Cádiz inspired the debates over equality and the rights and obligations of the government towards its people.[176]

At the end of the war, the settlements in present-day Texas grew substantially. From North Texas to South Texas, the inhabitants numbered 7,801, including the mission Indians. Laredo alone had a population of 2,041, with hundreds of other people scattered in South Texas ranches.[177] Many of these ranches evolved into municipalities, becoming the towns of Zapata, Cuevitas, San Diego, San Juan, Palito Blanco, Agua Dulce, El Sauz, Los Alamos, San Luis Peñascale, San Ygnacio, Dolores, and Los Saenz.[178] El Paso del Norte, which remained part of New Mexico during the Mexican period, grew to around 8,000 people.[179] The largest settlements in the El Paso Valley were the mission communities of Ysleta and Socorro and the presidial village of San Elizario. Many residents were scattered in ranches across present-day downtown El Paso and in the Canutillo district. Although the majority of the settlers in Texas welcomed Mexican independence, they knew that the survival of their settlements would be difficult. For Texas to prosper as part of an independent Mexico, the settlers had to become financially self-sufficient and find ways to defend their settlements against the Apache and Comanche Indians, who continued to control large regions of Texas. For generations, nearly all attempts to establish Spanish colonies in western and northwest Texas had failed from a lack of military forces to protect those areas.

CHAPTER 2

New Racial Structures:
Citizenship and Land Conflicts

Less than thirty years after Mexican independence, the people of Texas experienced a series of epic political changes. Mexico's territorial claim over Texas ended after Anglo-American immigrants, and later the US government, took possession of this borderland territory. This chapter chronicles the experiences of Mexican Tejanos from Texas independence to the end of the US Civil War. After Texas independence, Mexicans became a minority ethnic population that had to navigate new social systems in which they were viewed as aliens and undesirables. Racial and ethnic stereotypes became commonplace, and were often used by governmental officials to deny Mexican-origin people citizenship and land rights. The *casta* system in Texas was replaced by a political system that discriminated against people based on national origin and racial ancestry.

From Mexican Independence to Texas Independence

In the aftermath of Mexican independence, the Plan de Iguala became Mexico's provisional constitution, ending all legal distinctions between people born in Europe and Mexico. Decisions about the territorial divisions of the nation, the abolition of slavery, and Mexico's governmental structure would not be finalized until a formal constitution was drafted and the political rights of the states were determined. Before a constitution could be adopted, however, the political discord that had erupted against General Iturbide, who had become the head of state, had to be resolved. Mexicans also had to address the disastrous conditions of their nation in the aftermath of the war. The Mexican economy was in ruins. Farms and ranches had been destroyed, and the nation's agricultural production had fallen drastically. The mines, formerly one of Mexico's most lucrative industries and sources of employment, had closed down.[1] Spain had left Mexico with an international debt of 76 million pesos, which the Crown had incurred during its attempt to stop independence.[2] On the northern frontier, the physical destruction of the countryside was not as severe as it was in the interior. In Texas the main challenge was how to protect settlements from Apache and Comanche attacks. The federal government continued to help finance the military and the regional government, but for the most part, the settlers had to depend on themselves. To assist them, the Iturbide administration allowed a few families from the United States to settle in Texas under a contract previously issued by the Spanish government to Moses Austin.[3] The contract had been provisionally approved, but had to be confirmed by an immigration commission before it could be fully executed.

By January 1822, a few Anglo-American families had settled in Texas under the Austin contract. They settled near the Brazos River approximately sixty miles west of present-day Houston and then dispersed into North and Central Texas.[4] Because Moses Austin had died in 1821, his son Stephen Austin inherited the contract, giving him the responsibility of obtaining approval to bring the rest of the 300 families originally agreed upon. For the Iturbide administration, allowing Anglo-Americans to settle in Texas was essential for the economic prosperity of the northern frontier, but also controversial. It was expected that Anglo-American settlers would bring slaves into Mexico. This posed a moral dilemma, since slavery was uncommon in Mexico and the country was in the process of abolishing the practice. In March 1822, the urgency to approve the Austin contract and the need to recruit more American settlers to come to the northern frontier, specifically to Texas, prompted Iturbide to establish the Colonization Commission to finalize an immigration plan. Bernardo Gutiérrez de Lara, one of the commissioners, knew Texas well and proposed that immigration be encouraged, but specified that Indians and local residents be given priority in setting land claims. Another commissioner, Valentín Gomés Farías, recommended that immigrants be prohibited from bringing slaves. Iturbide decided to postpone the commission's recommendations and instead allow these policies to be debated during the first constitutional convention.[5]

Many Mexicans detested slavery, and when Mexico's constitutional convention convened in November 1822, the political battle to officially eradicate slavery commenced.[6] The delegates at the convention were divided, and the majority resented Iturbide, who, with the support of the Junta Nacional Instituyente, had proclaimed himself emperor of Mexico six months earlier. The junta was composed of officials appointed by Iturbide. During the first constitutional convention, the debates over Mexico's colonization laws became contentious when some delegates refused to separate the topic of slavery from immigration. The majority view was that Mexico needed immigrants to populate Texas, but most delegates did not support allowing foreigners to bring slaves.[7] Those who favored slavery argued that Americans depended on slave labor, and if this practice was abolished in Mexico, Anglo-Americans would not immigrate there. The opposition argued against such claims and proposed that slavery went against the spirit of Mexican independence. They supported abolishing slavery altogether. The debate ended on January 4, 1823, and Iturbide approved the final plan. Overall, Mexico's General Colonization Law was generous in the amount of land it made available to new settlers, yet it contained abolitionist policies. Immigrants were prohibited from bringing slaves, and enslaved children living in Mexico were to be emancipated upon reaching age fourteen.[8]

All these plans fell apart when a military junta overthrew Iturbide, forced him to abdicate, and annulled the convention's proceedings.[9] After new delegates were elected, the second constitutional convention assembled on November 20, 1823, and closed on October 4, 1824.[10] The delegates were authorized to draft a new colonization law, revise Mexican laws and decrees, adopt a constitution framing the structure of the government, and determine the rights and obligations of the Mexican people. In article 1 of the Actas Constitutivas, the delegates declared all inhabitants residing in the territories previously called New Spain to be part of the Mexican nation. Mexican historians propose that the concept of citizenship was left abstract in article 1, but it was clarified in the articles determining a person's citizenship rights.[11] Under article 2, the rights of male citizens were protected by law. Articles 5 and 9 stipulated that upon reaching age twenty-five, people born or residing in Mexico, regardless of race, had the right to vote and run for office.

When the question of slavery was introduced for debate in January 1824, it was forwarded to a committee, to prevent differences of opinion from disrupting the convention. To keep the delegates united, committee members compromised and decided to pass a law rather than a constitutional amendment.[12] On July 13, the delegates issued a decree that the sale and trafficking of slaves within Mexico was prohibited.[13] Any slave illegally introduced into Mexico was to be set free. Although Congress did not pass an article ending slavery, the decree and two additional laws prevented the growth of slavery. Article 162 of the Constitution prohibited the states from importing or exporting cargo that was not permitted by federal law; thus, under the Decree of July 13, slaves could not be introduced into Mexico.[14] Likewise, under the Colonization Law of 1824, immigrants were required to obey all federal laws, including the Decree of July 13.[15]

For the Texas delegation, headed by Erasmo Seguín, the new colonization law and slavery agreements posed a serious threat to the recruitment of American settlers. These laws, however, were considered improvements over those drafted by Iturbide's congress.[16] The Texas deputation also believed that the Decree of July 13 was vague and would not be enforced because slaves were personal property, which the Constitution protected. But they were concerned that slavery might be banned in Texas if their province was not allowed to become its own state.[17] Over May 5–7, 1824, when the states and territories of the republic were constituted, the delegates voted to merge Texas and Coahuila into one state.[18] The Texas delegation, including Stephen Austin, vigorously opposed the union because Coahuila was an older, extensively populated region and would be apportioned more representatives than Texas.[19] At that time Texas had 3,334 inhabitants, and Coahuila, 42,937.[20] It was likely that slavery would be abolished in Texas because Congress authorized each state to draft its constitution and establish state laws, including those regarding slavery.

Following the convention, Texas became one of twelve departments of the state of Coahuila-Texas. Each department was assigned a number of state representatives based on population. Saltillo, Coahuila, became the capital and the seat of government. Texas lost its governor position and instead was assigned a departmental political chief, who was in charge of maintaining law and order and commanding the departmental militia. His office was located in San Antonio, which remained the capital of Texas and the location of the Bexar Departmental Ayuntamiento (regional council). The *ayuntamiento* was authorized to develop departmental policies, advise the political chief, and appoint one legislative representative to the state government.[21] The number of state representatives apportioned to Texas could be increased based on its population growth.

In the aftermath of the convention, federal officials promoted the colonization of the northern provinces by establishing an empresario system. Mexican citizens and foreigners were commissioned to recruit settlers and establish colonies in the frontier zones. In return, the recruiters were awarded thousands of acres and named the political heads, or empresarios, of their colonies. In Texas, Stephen Austin became the most active empresario, and within a few years he had brought in 900 families. For his effort, he was granted 239,628 acres in Texas and recognized by the Mexican government as the main political spokesman for the Anglo-American colonists.[22] Twenty-three other empresarios obtained colonization contracts, but only Martín De León brought Mexican citizens to Texas. The rest of the settlers came from the United States or Europe. De León established his colony in Victoria, along the Texas central coast.

In 1825, the legislators of Coahuila-Texas began writing the state constitution, and in article 13 they supported abolishing slavery.[23] When Stephen Austin learned of this, he contacted other Anglo-American leaders, and they sought the support of influential Mexican Tejanos.[24] Austin warned his allies that if slavery were abolished in Texas, most colonists would leave. Austin projected that this exodus would ruin the nascent, flourishing cotton economy and endanger the commercial ties that US companies were forming in Texas. According to the historians Raúl Ramos and Andrés Tijerina, Mexican merchant elites in San Antonio considered this a threat to their livelihood, and since they controlled the state's political machinery, they chose to assist Austin.[25] The Navarro, Veramendi, Ruiz, Arciniega, Flores, Padilla, Seguín, and Músquiz families composed an inner circle, united by marriage bonds. When Austin asked the Bexar Ayuntamiento for support, they headed his warning.

The *ayuntamiento* had elected Felipe Enrique Neri, the Baron de Bastrop, an immigrant from the Austin colony, to be their state representative. When the baron arrived in Saltillo to report on the *ayuntamiento*'s opposition to article 13, among his allies was José María Viesca, a wealthy landowner and future governor of the state. Viesca and his brother Agustín were in the process of converting their landholdings into large cotton farms, and any threat to Texas's link with US commercial networks would be detrimental to their wealth.

The constitutional debates dragged on for nearly two additional years. Dionisio Elizondo, a Coahuila representative, led the charge to abolish slavery. On March 11, 1827, a compromise was finalized. The Coahuila representatives did not adopt all of Texas's demands. Stephen Austin, who led the Anglo-Tejano alliance, had lobbied for people in bondage to remain enslaved, for children to not be emancipated until age fifteen, and, most importantly, for immigrants to be indefinitely allowed to bring slaves. Once finalized, article 13 did not abolish slavery, but laid the groundwork for dismantling slavery within a generation. Article 13 stipulated: "In the state no one is born a slave and six months after the publication of this constitution in the centers of each part of the state neither will the introduction of slaves be permitted under any pretext."[26]

Article 13 angered many immigrants in Texas, and slave owners refused to comply with its provisions.[27] To resolve this dispute, Austin proposed that his compatriots pursue political separation from Coahuila. Under the Constitution of 1824, if Texas became a separate state, its residents would be allowed to retain slavery and govern themselves.[28] In the meantime, it was necessary to find a way around the federal and state laws prohibiting the importation of slaves into Texas. Austin introduced a plan designed by Peter Ellis Bean, and obtained the support of the Bexar Ayuntamiento. Bean had found a loophole that allowed immigrants to continue introducing slaves into Texas. Enslaved people would be brought to Texas as indentured servants. First, while slave owners were residing in US territory, they would take their slaves to a notary public, emancipate them, and afterward require them to sign a contract indenturing themselves and their children for life. Once transported to Texas, the enslaved would never be paid wages high enough to allow them to purchase their contract.[29] José Antonio Navarro and José Miguel de Arciniega, both residents of Bexar and Texas's new legislative representatives, introduced the proposal. (Because of the growth of the immigrant population in Texas, the state legislature had apportioned Texas an additional representative.) On May 5, 1828, Navarro and Arciniega's proposal passed, and was adopted as Decree 56. They had convinced the legislature that it was urgent to allow settlers to bring indentured servants. Allegedly, many families from Ohio, a free state, were waiting to settle in Texas if they could bring indentured servants. Navarro and Arciniega had deceitfully hidden the fact that the indentured contracts were for life and not for a few years.[30]

A little more than a year later, a harsh blow temporarily shocked proslavery advocates when, on September 15, 1829, President Vicente Guerrero issued Mexico's Emancipation Proclamation.[31] Guerrero was of African descent. José María Viesca, who had become the governor of Coahuila-Texas, immediately contacted Guerrero to obtain a temporary exemption for Texas.[32] He argued that his state did not have sufficient funds to enforce the proclamation, because slave owners would have to be immediately indemnified.[33] He also warned the president that if the proclamation was enforced, violence would erupt. Texas was given a temporary exemption, but officials were ordered to stop the entry of additional slaves.

In late December 1829, Guerrero was removed from office and the new Anastasio Bustamante administration decided to address international border issues affecting Texas. The most urgent one concerned unregulated immigration from the United States. Two years earlier, General Manuel de Mier y Terán had been appointed to head the Comisión de Límites, which was to investigate the botanical and mineralogical resources of Texas and define the limits of Mexico's northern border.[34] While in Texas, he observed that Americans were settling in regions outside the empresario districts. On his return to Mexico, he was promoted to inspector general of the Eastern Provinces and land commissioner of Texas.[35] In 1829, the general wrote a report on Texas affairs and recommended a series of reforms affecting immigration, slavery, and commerce. The Bustamante administration implemented his reforms and drafted the Law of April 6, 1830.[36] The general recommended that immigration from the United States to Texas be prohibited because Anglo-Americans outnumbered the Mexican population, and this imbalance posed a serious political threat to Mexico's hold over Texas. He reported that thousands of settlers were coming in on their own and settling wherever they saw open land. He requested that only two empresario contracts approved before April 6 be authorized to move forward.[37] Mier y Terán also proposed that to discourage immigration, Americans should be prohibited from bringing slaves and be warned that manumission would be enforced.[38]

To better integrate Texas's economy into Mexican markets, the general recommended that new commerce laws restrict and tax trade with US companies. If this were not done, Mier y Terán cautioned, US merchants would soon control the Texas economy.[39] To address the general's recommendations, three customhouses were established along the northern coast and the Texas-US border; Mexican soldiers were instructed to stop unapproved commerce.

After the reforms, US immigration to Texas did not stop, and by 1835 the Anglo-American population had grown to over 30,000.[40] The enslaved population increased from 2,000 when General Mier y Terán issued his report to 5,000 in 1836.[41]

As Anglo-Americans became increasingly dissatisfied with the reforms, and as Stephen Austin's attempt to gain separate statehood failed, more residents of Texas supported seceding from Mexico. Mexican elites with commercial ties to American settlers likewise supported independence. In 1834, when General Antonio López de Santa Anna ascended to the presidency, his administration attempted to stop Texas secession by nullifying parts of the reforms of April 6, 1830. The ban on North American immigration was lifted, Americans who had entered unauthorized were to be given land, and more political representation was extended to the immigrant population. The Mexican Congress, however, issued a no-tolerance order for slavery in Texas.[42] The concessions came too late. The rebels distrusted the Mexican government and demanded independence.[43]

On November 7, 1835, Anglo-American settlers declared war against Mexico.[44] The Mexican population was divided, including some of the elite families. José Antonio Navarro supported independence, while his brother Angel sought a leadership role within General Martín Perfecto de Cos's Mexican Army. Likewise, Gregorio Esparza died in support of the rebels at the Battle of the Alamo, but his brother Francisco fought on the side of Mexico. In San Antonio and Victoria, several militias supporting Mexico were formed by hundreds of locals, whereas the Seguín family organized several militias for the rebel cause.[45] Most Mexican families, however, were shocked that a statehood matter had somehow led to secession, and they preferred to be left alone. During the revolt and afterward, hundreds of Mexican families sought refuge in New Orleans, Saltillo, or Monclova. After a series of battles, the Anglo-Americans defeated the Mexican Army. The war ended on April 21, 1836, at the Battle of San Jacinto, and Texas became an independent republic.[46]

Citizenship, Slavery, and Land in the Republic of Texas

The exact size of the territory lost by Mexico became a contentious issue between representatives of Mexico and those from the Republic of Texas. They differed on where the border of Mexico and Texas lay. Mexican officials claimed that only Central and North Texas had been lost, including part of the coastline. They alleged that the land from the Nueces River to the Rio Grande belonged to the state of Tamaulipas and to other northern Mexican states.[47] To support their claim, they referred to the territorial history of Texas, including the state boundaries decided on by the Mexican Congress during the Constitutional Convention of 1824. In the case of El Paso del Norte, which was also under dispute, Mexican officials claimed that it had never been part of Texas. For most of its existence, that region had belonged to New Mexico, and after Mexican independence it was appended to the state of Chihuahua.

Officials for the Republic of Texas, on the other hand, claimed that present-day Texas plus most of northern New Mexico belonged to them. This argument was based on their assertion that because Texas and New Mexico had been part of the Internal Provinces, they retained possession of sections of New Mexico.[48]

The territorial claims made by opposing governments were debated for nearly a decade. Irrespective of this conflict, the most radical change in the daily lives of Mexican Tejanos was the new racial order that was codified into law. Race came to determine who was a citizen, who could own land, and who was a free person. Most of the liberal racial policies enacted by the Mexican government were rescinded and declared null and void. Texas officials encouraged slavery and the importation of slaves. To be eligible for citizenship in Texas, a person could not be Black or Indian.

The Constitution of the Republic of Texas (1836) extended citizenship to all persons residing in Texas on the day of the declaration of independence as long as they were not Black or Indian.[49] Mexicans who were white and mestizo became citizens of Texas. With respect to land, officials adopted some of Mexico's property laws, but placed racial restrictions on those who would be able to recertify their grants. Under Mexican law, occupational land rights were recognized, and a person did not have to hold a deed to the land he lived on. Under the laws of the new republic, however, Indians and Blacks were prohibited from validating their Spanish and Mexican land grants, regardless of whether they held a deed. They also became ineligible to apply for new land grants.

The adoption of Mexican land policies was necessary because many Anglo-Americans did not hold deeds to their land, and those who did had obtained their land grants under the laws of Mexico. Texas officials had to uphold Mexican property laws lest possession by force become the new way to establish ownership and the Anglo-American land grants issued by the empresarios become null and void. The General Provisions adopted by the constitutional convention in 1836 decreed that all persons who were residing in Texas on the day of the declaration of independence and were eligible to become citizens were entitled to the land they occupied. If they did not possess land, they would be granted property. Section 10 stipulated: "All persons (Africans, the descendants of Africans, and Indians excepted) who were residing in Texas on the day of declaration of Independence, shall be considered citizens of the republic, and entitled to all privileges of such. All citizens now living in Texas, who have not received their portion of land, in like manner as colonists, shall be entitled to their land."[50]

After the decree was issued, the "Act to Establish a General Land Office for the Republic of Texas" was passed.[51] Its purpose was to establish in the upcoming months an office to confirm land claims issued under Spanish and Mexican rule and to certify new claims. Land officials were commissioned to inform Mexicans whether their claims needed to be validated by a court. The less property owned by Mexicans that officials deemed eligible for certification, the more of it they would make available for Anglo-American claims.

Pushing *Afromexicanos* and Tribal Populations out of Texas

In 1840, the Republic of Texas began to address the liberal racial policies it had inherited from Mexico. The political status of *afromexicanos* and emancipated slaves was the most critical issue at hand. For most Anglo-Americans, *afromexicanos* were a nuisance, since they had the freedom to move freely among them and act as equals.[52] Plus, free persons of African descent posed a political threat to Texas's new racial order because they were symbols of the social status that enslaved people could aspire to. The Texas Congress, therefore, chose to remove *afromexicanos* from Texas and then nullify all emancipation certificates. Under the new plan, immigrants such as Martín, Juan Pexos, Tivi, and Ricardo Moran, would be reenslaved, and *afromexicanos* asked to leave Texas.

The act of February 5, 1840, entitled "Concerning Free Persons of Color," forced all free Black people to leave Texas. If they refused, they would become slaves. Under the act, persons of African descent already in residence in Texas had two years to leave, and potential immigrants of African descent were prohibited from entering. The law did not make exceptions for *afromexicanos*, whose ancestors were part of the founding families of Texas. Black people who refused to obey the law were to be incarcerated, sentenced to a life of servitude, and sold at auction.[53] The act encouraged Texans to turn in any person whom they suspected of violating this law. Texans were to contact a judge and identify the alleged criminals. Judges were authorized to arrest the accused, determine their race, and give them the option of leaving or being sold at auction. If a person decided to leave, they were to pay a $1,000 fine before being released; otherwise, they would remain in jail.[54]

After the act was passed, many influential Texans protested that it was vague, far reaching, and in need of revision.[55] They argued that more reasonable legislation would merely ensure the return of runaway slaves to their owners. On December 12, 1840, Congress revised its policy toward free Black people. Under the "Act for the Relief of Certain Free Persons of Color," commonly referred to as the "Ashworth Act," people who could prove that during Spanish and Mexican rule they had never been slaves did not need to fear deportation or enslavement.[56] This revision, however, did not end the denunciation investigations. The accused still had to prove that they were not runaway slaves.

Indigenous people who lived outside the Mexican municipalities also became targets for expulsion. At first, their removal was concentrated in western and northern Texas, where the Apache and Comanche dominated the territory. Plans were made to push them into Mexican territory, and if they resisted, they were to be killed. The Texas Rangers, founded in 1835, were commissioned to move out tribal peoples in order to make room for incoming settlers.[57] Indian removal expanded into other territories after the United States annexed Texas in 1845. A few years later, the Apache and Karankawa survivors were pushed into Mexico, and the Comanche, Caddo, and Wichita were placed in Oklahoma (Indian Territory) reservations.[58]

Few Indigenous people were allowed to remain in Texas after the republic was formed. Among them were the secularized mission Indians, who, despite not being given citizenship and having their land grants voided, were permitted to remain in the Mexican towns. Likewise, the only recognized tribal Indian group not expelled from Texas was the Alabama-Coushatta. The Alabama-Coushatta was a reorganized tribe composed of Indian peoples who entered Texas in 1804 and established several communities.[59] Under the Republic of Texas, they were acknowledged to be a peaceful and industrious people who posed no danger. After the Alabama-Coushatta Indians were removed from their homes, they were given a small land grant and allowed to remain in Texas.

The US Annexation of Texas and the Citizenship of Tejanos

A few years after Texas obtained its independence from Mexico, influential Anglo-Americans argued that Mexicans were a culturally and racially inferior people who should be denied US citizenship. This issue came up for debate when the US government finalized its plans to annex Texas. In March 1845, the US Congress submitted its request for annexation and gave the government of Texas the opportunity to determine which of its residents would become citizens of the United States. At the time, Congress had not passed a uniform law prescribing the procedures and requirements for acquiring US citizenship. States had the authority to delineate the racial prerequisites of citizenship eligibility.[60] Congress did not clarify these issues until the adoption of the Fourteenth Amendment to the US Constitution.

On July 4, 1845, fifty-seven delegates met to approve the annexation of Texas and write the Texas Constitution. The most important issue was to decide who in Texas would be given American citizenship.[61] Whether to allow people of Mexican ancestry to become US citizens became a heated topic of debate at the convention. By this time, Mexican Americans' ethnic heritage had become a marker of cultural inferiority and racial impurity. Some delegates feared that even in the bloodlines of Mexicans who appeared to be solely descended from Caucasians remained traces of their ancestors' Black and Indian heritage. Such racial mixtures were alleged to taint the mind and reason; therefore, it was not prudent to allow them to become citizens with voting rights. Furthermore, because migration from Mexico to Texas was expected to rise considerably after annexation, some delegates claimed that Mexican immigrants should not be allowed to become citizens. Many delegates, therefore, considered it imperative to adopt policies stipulating which Mexicans, if any, would be extended citizenship.

During the constitutional convention of 1845, the delegates debated several key issues. First, would only "free whites" be considered citizens of Texas and the United States and be allowed to vote? Second, since most Mexicans were racially mixed, did they come under the definition of "free white" person? And third, should immigrants be allowed to vote if they were not citizens, and how would a decision on this issue apply to Mexican immigrants?

The rationales for limiting citizenship and voting to free whites included racist beliefs that the Anglo-Saxon race was superior, as well as convoluted arguments claiming that only some Mexicans were white. On the far right were representatives such as Mr. Moore, who argued that Mexicans should be denied citizenship because they were "not Caucasian." Moore stated:

> I fear not the Castilian race, but I fear those who though they speak the Spanish language, are but the descendants of that degraded and despicable race which Cortez conquered. . . .
>
> Talk not to me of a democracy which brings, the mean groveling yellow race of Mexico, I say the Indian race of Mexicans, upon an equality of rights and privileges with the free born race of Europe. The God of nature has made them inferior, he has made the African and the red man inferior to the white. Let them if they wish like the Choctaws and Cherokees form a separate government; but not come here to poison the institutions of the Caucasian race.[62]

Mr. Hogg agreed, but presented a less exclusionary plan. Unlike Moore, he was not opposed to most Mexicans voting or being considered citizens. He merely wanted to make sure that Mexicans who were tainted with African blood would not be allowed to vote.[63] He argued that if the phrase "free white" was inserted in the citizenship clause of the Texas Constitution, county officials would have the authority to prevent undesirable Mexicans from voting.

Mr. Kinney, who disagreed with Hogg and Moore, argued that the term "free white" was ambiguous and was being considered only to ensure that Mexicans did not vote. By using the term "free white," the delegates knew that they were giving county officials the power to manipulate elections. To support his argument, Kinney pointed to the well-known fact that

José Antonio Navarro

throughout Texas, county officials during close elections used race to allow or disqualify Mexicans voters by ignoring a person's bloodline for political convenience.[64]

The delegate from Bexar, José Antonio Navarro, the only Mexican American at the convention, became angry at the callous remarks. He opposed the free-white proposal and affirmed that Mexicans were not an ignorant and inferior race.[65] Including this phrase, he argued, would have broad implications beyond voting. Navarro, a distinguished Texan, was respected for having fought against Mexico during the Texas Revolution.[66] He knew that if his opponents' views triumphed, most Mexican Americans would lose their citizenship and voting rights.

Navarro's experience at the convention revealed a sad reality and exposed the social atmosphere of the times. In Texas, Mexican Americans' ethnic and racial heritage, regardless of their social standing, was being used as a cultural marker to deny them equal rights.

After the closing arguments, the delegates voted to strike out the phrase "free white." The citizenship clause from the Republic of Texas Constitution was adopted. Every free male person who was at least twenty-one years old and a citizen of the Republic of Texas would become a citizen of the United States. (US citizens residing in Texas would of course retain their US citizenship.) This compromise allowed Mexicans who were citizens of the Republic of Texas to gain US citizenship, but it disqualified Indians and people of African descent.[67]

A clever attempt to resuscitate the free-white argument and politically disenfranchise Mexican mestizos was introduced when the delegates debated giving the right to vote to immigrants who were not citizens of the United States or Texas. The issue was raised because in several counties, German immigrants composed two-thirds of the population, and many of them were not citizens of the United States or Texas. If they were not allowed to vote, some delegates feared that counties with large European populations would be governed by a small minority of voters who would not necessarily share the economic interests of the immigrant populations.[68] Delegates who supported giving European immigrants the right to vote proposed inserting the free-white requirement in order to prevent nonwhite Mexican immigrants from voting, since it was generally expected that in the near future, immigration from Mexico would increase substantially. After a long debate, the delegates reached a consensus not to use the term "free white," but instead to clearly stipulate that Black or Indian immigrants could not vote.[69] The immigrant-voting-rights clause was a liberal policy that gave many noncitizens the right to vote, including Mexican immigrants.

In the aftermath of the convention and annexation, Mexicans were made US citizens with the right to vote. The main problem they faced was the political machinery at the county level, where officials had the power to determine their bloodlines and decide whether they belonged in one of the prohibited classes ineligible to vote.

Property Rights from Marriage and Inheritance

After Texas joined the United States, the republic's marriage and inheritance laws remained in effect. This policy served to protect the inheritance property rights of all people whose parents had acquired land grants under Spanish and Mexican law, including the rights of Mexican heirs.

One of the main legislative tasks of the Republic of Texas had been to determine whether Spanish and Mexican marriage laws were valid under the new political regime. The resulting legislation would affect the inheritance rights and economic livelihoods of most families in Texas. The Texas Congress had adopted English common law regarding marriage practices. If Congress nullified the former governments' marriage laws, all marriages that took place before Texas independence would be declared null and void, including those of Anglo-Americans. Families formed under the previous governments' laws and conventions would be deemed illegitimate, and under English common law, any children from such families would be unable to inherit property from a deceased parent, including land grants issued by empresarios under Mexican law. The legitimate inheritors would be the extended family of the deceased rather than the nuclear family.

In 1837, to quickly resolve this problem, Texas congressmen validated all marriages occurring before independence, in an effort to legalize the inheritance rights of Anglo land grant heirs.[70] To do so, the Texas Congress decreed on June 5, 1837, that all marriages certified before that date were valid and that the children of these marriages were legitimate and able to inherit.[71] Interracial marriages between white and Black partners that occurred before that date were also validated under section 2 of the act, since Congress declared that marriages contracted under the customs and practices of Spain and Mexico were valid.[72] Under section 2, the Texas Congress also upheld section 4 of Spain's Las Siete Partidas cohabitation marriage laws, which declared that couples who cohabited and were publicly recognized as husband and wife were legally married, regardless of whether a certified state clerk or priest had solemnized their unions.[73] This validation was necessary because many Anglo-Americans had not been married by a priest or certified clerk. For Mexican Americans, the act of 1837 created the legal basis for validating the inheritance rights of Mexican heirs whose parents were Mexican and Anglo-American. It also served to protect the property rights of children who had one African-descent parent, since Texas property laws did not nullify the land grants of whites married to afromexicanos.

The inheritance rights of Mexican Americans were further clarified in 1845 after the Texas Supreme Court ruled on an interethnic-marriage case involving a Mexican woman. Less than a year after Texas was annexed to the United States, María de Jesusa Smith's right to inherit property from her Anglo-American spouse came into question when a US citizen asserted that he held legal rights superior to hers. It was a complicated case that involved Spanish, Mexican, Texas, and US law.

María de Jesusa Smith was a native Tejana, a member of the aristocratic Mexican families that claimed descent from Canary Islanders. Her family, the Curbelo-Delgados, was among the wealthiest property owners in San Antonio. During Mexican rule, María de Jesusa Curbelo-Delgado married

John Smith, an American investor who actively participated in the Texas Revolution. Smith fought in the defense of the Alamo, and he became San Antonio's first mayor after independence.[74] The Smiths had three daughters, who were well received in Anglo-Texan social circles and were married to prominent Anglo-Americans. Upon John Smith's death, his wife inherited his estate, including property valued at over $400,000, $10,000 in cash, a monthly stipend based on the collection of tenant rents, and the earnings of three seamstress slave girls whom the Smiths hired out.[75]

In 1845, Samuel Smith arrived in San Antonio to challenge María de Jesusa Smith's right to inherit her husband's estate, on the grounds that he was the deceased's only legitimate heir. In court, he claimed to be John Smith's son from an earlier, common-law marriage. Samuel Smith lost after being unable to prove his paternity. He appealed the case to the Texas Supreme Court. In the second trial, *Smith v. Smith* (1846), Samuel Smith's attorneys had to prove that his father was John Smith and convince the judge that Mexican and Spanish laws were invalid when they came in conflict with US state and territorial laws. The political rights of people like Samuel Smith, a citizen of the United States, had to be defended against the laws of foreign nations. Samuel Smith's attorneys argued that Mrs. Smith was a foreigner and had been wrongly protected by the laws of a foreign government. His appeal rested on the assertion that marriages consecrated under Mexican law were outside the customs and traditions of US society and were therefore invalid. Samuel Smith's attorneys also argued that María de Jesusa Smith could not inherit the Smith estate because John had committed bigamy. She had married John Smith when his first wife, Harriet Stone, was alive. Consequently, under English common law, María de Jesusa Smith and her daughters did not form a legitimate family, and therefore could not inherit property from John Smith. Under Missouri law, only Samuel Smith could inherit his father's estate, because a marriage certificate was unnecessary when a common-law son or daughter claimed a parent's inheritance.

To support Samuel Smith's inheritance claim, his mother's brother, Samuel Stone, testified on his nephew's behalf. The witness was convincing, yet María de Jesusa Smith's lawyers were able to find inconsistencies in Stone's stories, and nearly impeached his testimony. He was unable to prove that Harriet Stone had been John Smith's common-law wife, nor did he offer corroborating accounts in order to meet Missouri's evidentiary common-law requirements: Stone had neither met John Smith nor attended his wedding. He also did not know when his alleged brother-in-law had left his sister and moved to Texas.

After Stone's disastrous cross-examination, Samuel Smith's attorneys informed the judge that their client was willing to settle for a lesser amount. Samuel Smith agreed to give María de Jesusa Smith a monthly stipend and allow her to keep her house if she agreed to settle all property claims, including turning over ownership of the three enslaved seamstresses. María de Jesusa Smith did not accept the terms. She was the widow of John Smith, whose marriage ceremony had been a public affair, and for years everyone had acknowledged her as Mrs. Smith. She would not settle for anything less than a public acknowledgment that under the law, she and her daughters were John Smith's only family.

Although the arguments against María de Jesusa Smith's case were compelling, the Texas Supreme Court upheld the lower court's decision. It ruled that when John Smith was alive, he did not acknowledge Samuel Smith or Harriet Stone to be his family. On the issue of Mexican law, the judges ruled that Mexico's Las Siete Partidas marriage laws were legally binding under US law because the Republic of Texas had upheld them. The judges added that marriages executed during Spanish and Mexican rule were not void merely because they had been performed in Catholic ceremonies or followed traditions not practiced in the United States.

The legal and cultural arguments used in defense of the Smiths' interethnic marriage set precedents for the defense of Mexican Americans' political rights. *Smith v. Smith* became the precedent in Texas for upholding Mexico's marriage and inheritance laws. The legal and cultural arguments used in defense of the Smiths' interethnic marriage were later found to be equally applicable to interracial marriages. That is, although immediately after independence the Texas Legislature passed a series of "antimiscegenation" laws prohibiting the marriage of whites and Blacks, this type of interracial marriage was deemed legal if it had been conducted during Spanish and Mexican rule, and the children born from these marriages were eligible to inherit.[76] In addition, María de Jesusa Smith's case provided the legal standard for rejecting foreignness as a principle to justify placing Mexicans under different legal standards from Anglos. When the Texas Supreme Court ruled that cultural difference was an invalid reason for stripping people of their inheritance, it set a precedent that protected Mexican Americans' property rights.

The Mexican-American War, 1846–1848

After the annexation of Texas by the United States, determining the location of the Texas-Mexico border became a critical issue that had to be immediately resolved. Acting unilaterally, the US Congress set the border at the Rio Grande, claiming that South Texas and the El Paso Valley were part of the annexed region. Mexico disputed the boundary, holding that the border lay farther north on the Nueces River. Congress disagreed, and the dispute became so contentious that the United States declared war against Mexico on May 11, 1846.[77] Fourteen months later, the US military defeated Mexico and began treaty negotiations.

US congressmen debated which parts of Mexico the United States should acquire. Some proposed that the entire country be occupied, while others favored taking only Mexico's northern territories, which today include the US Southwest and the Mexican states of Tamaulipas, Nuevo León, Chihuahua, Coahuila, Sonora, and Baja California.[78] The less expansionist plan was chosen, largely because most congressmen conceded that it was best to acquire the least populated territories. Congress expected problems in determining the legal rights of the conquered population because it was common knowledge that Mexicans were a racially diverse people. Incorporating whites as US citizens would not pose a problem, but determining the legal status of racially mixed peoples presented legal ambiguities, and it was best to limit their numbers. In the end, the United States acquired California, New Mexico, and northern Arizona, along with the land below the Nueces River, including South Texas, the El Paso Valley, and other parts of southwestern Texas. Congress appended the El Paso Valley and South Texas to Texas, rather than creating a new state. Mexico also lost the parts of its northern frontier that today constitute Nevada, Utah, parts of Colorado, and small sections of Oklahoma, Kansas, and Wyoming.[79]

To bring closure to the Mexican-American War, the Treaty of Guadalupe Hidalgo was executed on February 2, 1848, and ratified on May 30, 1848.[80] The treaty stipulated the political rights of the inhabitants of the ceded territories, set the US-Mexico border, delineated the political responsibilities of each country in stopping Indian insurrections along the border, and finalized several agreements on economic relations. The most important agreements were articles 8 and 9, which gave US citizenship to the annexed population and recognized the validity of their Spanish and Mexican land grants as well as their legal possession of the land they occupied.

Within a year of ratification, the US government violated the treaty's citizenship stipulation and began a process called racialization, which gave Mexicans different legal rights, based on their race. The Mexican government's definition of who was a citizen of Mexico was not upheld. After Mexican independence, people living in Mexican territory had been declared Mexican citizens, and in 1829, after the Emancipation Proclamation issued by Mexican President Vicente Guerrero, enslaved people were also extended citizenship.

Instead, Congress decided to not make people of African descent or Native Americans US citizens, and thereby created the legal infrastructure to prevent the legislative governments of the acquired territories from extending them such a privilege. Congress decided that the territorial populations, when writing their new constitutions, might try to incorporate Blacks or Indians as citizens. Of particular concern were the Mexican American delegates in New Mexico, who were expected to outnumber the Anglo-American delegates because of the numerical superiority of the Mexican population. To prevent the extension of citizenship to Blacks or Indians there, New Mexico was organized as a territory. Under the Constitution, Congress has the authority to govern a territory and rescind or approve any of the laws passed by its legislature.[81] Thus, if the delegates in New Mexico tried to extend citizenship to Blacks or Indians, Congress could revoke those policies. The other territories and states were not of concern, because Anglo-Americans outnumbered Mexicans in California and Texas. Likewise, since northern Arizona did not have colonial settlers at the time, this issue was not then relevant.

Native Americans were divided into two legal categories: peaceful and warlike Indians. Indians who had not been conquered by previous governments were classified as warlike and placed under the management of the US War Department.[82] Mexico's Indigenous allies and mission Indian communities were deemed peaceful, and Congress commissioned agents to visit them and prepare a report on what to do with them.[83] They were to advise Congress whether it was necessary to relocate them onto reservations or treat them as Mexicans.[84]

Congress gave the legislative bodies of the ceded territories the authority to determine which Mexican people would be given US citizenship. At this time, the states and territories had the legal right to determine citizenship eligibility requirements, a power given to them by the US Constitution.[85]

In Texas, most decisions over which Mexicans qualified for US citizenship had already been decided. After the Mexican-American War, the Texas Legislature once again decided to extend citizenship to Mexicans who were white or mestizo. California was not as liberal as Texas and chose to extend citizenship only to whites.[86] Legislators in New Mexico were the only ones who did not place racial restrictions on its citizenship statutes. In 1850, New Mexico extended US citizenship to everyone in the territory, irrespective of race.[87] Congress immediately nullified New Mexico's citizenship policy pertaining to Blacks, and in 1853 did the same for Indians.[88]

In Arizona, since only the northern region was acquired after the

Mexican-American War, and since it was populated only by Native Americans, the laws of New Mexico were extended to the territory. A few years later, the US government realized that not having negotiated the annexation of southern Arizona was a mistake. US officials learned that they needed the Mexican settlements there in order to establish safe routes for travelers moving back and forth from California to Texas. The Mexican villages and mission settlements could serve as resting places and refuge zones. In 1854, the US government purchased southern Arizona, and New Mexico's citizenship laws were extended to it.[89]

Certifying Spanish and Mexican Land Grants in Texas

After the Mexican-American War, Texas acquired a vast territory where property boundaries and deeds had to be certified. The US government handed the Texas Legislature this undertaking as long as the land under review did not contain Indigenous communities. In what was considered "Indian Country," the federal government retained jurisdiction.

Most Spanish and Mexican land grants in North and Central Texas had been processed by the time the US government annexed Texas. Around 72.5 percent of the claims had been validated by the Texas General Land Office; only in Nacogdoches were a large percentage of the claims rejected.[90] The certification rates, however, did not include the property lost by people of African descent or Indians, because they were ineligible to keep their grants.

Land grants in South Texas and the El Paso Valley were reviewed after the Mexican-American War. They were the only two acquired regions that contained large concentrations of Mexican citizens. The residents of South Texas did well in comparison with those of the El Paso Valley. In South Texas, 364 claims were submitted and 325 were confirmed (89.2 percent).[91] In the El Paso Valley, very few claims were confirmed: 8 out of 14 petitions were rejected.[92] Although the number of rejected grants was few, the amount of acreage lost was large because these were communal grants owned by many villagers.

In both regions, many controversies over the certification process emerged within a few years. In South Texas, land grant heirs claimed that their acreage had been reduced when new deeds were issued by the Texas General Land Office. A shadow of doubt about the land office's trustworthiness was raised when one-third of the grants submitted for review were lost. In February 1850, the legislature commissioned William H. Bourland and James B. Miller to locate and register the South Texas grants. Over 150 land grantees gave the commissioners their documents, which were placed on board the steamer *Anson*.[93] Unfortunately, in November the *Anson* sank in the Gulf of Mexico, near Matagorda Bay, and the records were never recovered.

The loss of these documents caused many South Texas residents to believe that this was not a tragedy, but rather a scheme to steal their property. Over the years, most reasonable people, even without believing in conspiracy theories, acknowledged that the loss of the documents was suspicious, since the commissioners were not on board with the deeds. Andrés Tijerina, in his classic text *Tejano Empire: Life on the South Texas Ranchos* (1998), addresses this mystery. He argues that although the land office recovered copies of the original titles lost at sea, from Mexican and Spanish archives, the copies do not necessarily identify the correct owners of the ranches or their exact boundaries. He advances an important theory. The Spanish and Mexican archives do not contain all the transactions that followed the initial granting of property. Over the years, many people sold their land or partitioned their grants among relatives. These changes were not documented in the original titles. Likewise, Tijerina proposes that because the titles were copies, judges had to certify their authenticity, and in the process they had the opportunity to reduce the acreage contained in the surveys. Judges could invalidate titles that looked suspicious and reduce acreages when overlapping claims were submitted.

Tijerina challenges the Texas General Land Office's position that all South Texas applications were processed. His analysis is supported by formal complaints submitted by the Mexican government. In 1852, the Mexican government's General Commission for U.S-Mexico Relations (Agencia Mexicana ante la Comisión General de Reclamaciones entre México y los Estados Unidos—Reclamaciones Mexicanas) concluded that 440 Mexicans had not been allowed to submit claims or had been asked to withdraw their applications.[94] Most of the rejected applications came from South Texas, along with some from Liberty, Nacogdoches, Goliad (La Bahía), and Travis counties. Furthermore, Alan Minter, a former Texas assistant attorney general, assessed the confirmation rates of the Mexican land grants and concluded that the grantees in general did quite well.[95] He asserted, however, that a different scenario emerged when the analysis looked at the amount of acreage confirmed. In total, 17 million acres (10 million in Spanish land grants and 7 million in Mexican land grants) were claimed by Mexicans and Anglo-Americans.[96] All Spanish land grants were held by Mexicans and Christian Indians, and most of these grants were rejected. Thus, the confirmation rate primarily reflects the grants processed during the Mexican period, and the largest percentage of the grants belonged to Anglo-Americans. The confiscated Spanish land grants were converted to public land and made available for distribution. Settlers were given the authority to identify vacant lots and file petitions to obtain ownership.

Regardless of the controversy over the sinking of the *Anson*, these were not the worst land grant machinations that took place after the Mexican-American War. The El Paso Valley's Spanish and Mexican land grant rejection rate reached 57 percent, and it cannot be denied that the loss of property was caused by greed and racism.[97] San Elizario, Socorro, Ysleta, present-day downtown El Paso, and Canutillo comprised the El Paso Valley.[98] The controversy over the disputed land grants is complicated. The Texas Legislature rejected all grants issued from 1836 to 1847 because, it decreed, Mexico did not have the authority to issue title. This position was based on the allegation that following Texas independence, the El Paso Valley belonged to the Republic of Texas, and therefore only the Texas General Land Office had the right to issue land titles. Some land grants were also dismissed on the basis that they were communal. Communal land grants were invalidated because they did not exist in US law. As a consequence, all communal lands reverted to the government and became public lands. The majority of the land loss in the El Paso Valley, however, was related to federal Indian land policy. The mission Indians of Ysleta gradually lost their land because the US government and the State of Texas refused to validate their Spanish land grants.

After the Mexican-American War, the mission communities of Ysleta came under federal jurisdiction. The mission lands were treated as "Indian Country," which could not be settled by homesteaders without congressional authority. Unfortunately, in 1850, when the US government finally established the boundary between New Mexico and Texas, Ysleta became part of Texas and was put under the jurisdiction of the state legislature.[99] As soon as Ysleta became part of Texas, the land was gradually sold or given to Anglo-Americans. Under Texas land laws, originally drafted during the republic period, the Texas Legislature had the authority to nullify Spanish land titles issued to Indians. The people of Ysleta attempted to prevent the dissolution of their mission communities by invoking federal law protecting Indian lands.[100] This strategy failed when the federal government reclassified the people of Ysleta as Mexican, which denied them all federal Indian protections. Overall, the people of Ysleta lost more than 11,000 acres.[101] The Ysleta Indians were allowed to keep only their homes. The land improvements made in Ysleta over the previous 150 years, including the construction of irrigation systems and roads, made this land very valuable. A few years after the annexation of Ysleta to Texas, the legislature granted a large percentage of the confiscated acreage to the Pacific Railway Company, and in turn the company sold it to Americans migrating from the interior of the United States.

Alien Enemy Property Laws and Mexicans

Mexican land grant owners, whether or not they held deeds, faced many obstacles in retaining possession of their property. In court, Anglo-Americans often tried to dispossess Mexican Americans of their property by charging that people who had fought on the side of Mexico during the Texas Revolution were traitors and did not deserve to own land in Texas. The sad saga of the De León family from Victoria exemplifies this chapter in Texas history. Victoria was settled by Martín De León in 1824, becoming the last colony founded by Mexicans in Texas. A large percentage of the land in Victoria was passed on to his heirs. In 1837, his son Sylvester De León was killed. Upon his death, his Anglo-American neighbors attempted to steal his estate, under the rationale that the De León heirs were alien enemies. The De León family fought back in court, and their plight ended when the Texas Supreme Court issued its final ruling in *Hardy v. De Leon* (1849). The court ruled that conquered people after a war do not become aliens by law, nor do they lose their property rights.

The De León family's ordeal began on June 22, 1844, when Fernando De León filed a lawsuit in the Victoria District Court on behalf of his nephews.[102] Fernando De León charged that in 1841, Milton H. Hardy, without the authorization of the De León family, appeared in front of a judge in the Victoria County Probate Court and applied to be the executor of Sylvester De León's estate. Sylvester (Fernando De León's brother) and his wife had died several years earlier. They left three boys named Martín, Francisco, and Francisco Santiago.

During the probate hearing, Hardy claimed that he was eligible to become the executor of the De León estate because Sylvester De León owed him money. To prove his charges, Hardy brought William Gamble and Thomas Newcomb as witnesses. Under Texas law, a person who was owed a large sum of money could become the executor of a deceased person's estate. To repay what was owed, Hardy planned to sell the De Leóns' land grant, which was assessed at 4,000 acres.[103]

In 1843, Hardy held an estate auction, without notifying the De León family.[104] At the auction, Gamble, Newcomb, Mr. Van Horn, Mr. Cunningham, and Mr. Ingram purchased half of the property, and Hardy purchased the rest. After the auction, Gamble and Ingram sold their shares to Hardy, amounting to 1,700 acres.

A few months later, Fernando De León learned of the estate sale and filed a petition in the Victoria District Court to dissolve the sale and to investigate why Hardy had been appointed executor of the estate. It was strange that a person not related to his family had been appointed by the probate court to manage the estate. The trial was delayed for five years, most likely because after annexation, the Texas courts needed to be restructured. Afterward, the outbreak of the Mexican-American War must have delayed the proceedings further. The court records do not provide any information about the delay.

The court trial began on October 8, 1848. At trial, Fernando De León accused Hardy of leading, organizing, and conspiring with others to steal his brother's estate. He testified that Hardy paid people to falsely claim in probate court that Sylvester De León owed them money, since this would have allowed Hardy to become executor of the estate. De León also charged that the officers in the probate court knowingly conspired to defraud his family by falsely claiming that back taxes were owed.

In response to the charges, Hardy tried to derail the proceedings by introducing a legal theory that would lead the court to dismiss the suit. Hardy charged that it was a moot point whether the probate court erred on his behalf because Sylvester De León had already lost the grant. He had evidence that Sylvester and the rest of the De León family were alien enemies, and under state law they could not own land in Texas.

Despite Hardy's accusations, the district judge did not dismiss the suit. Fernando De León's attorneys had submitted sufficient evidence to prove that Hardy had committed crimes against the state. Besides colluding with probate court officials and other citizens to sell the De León estate, Hardy had withheld evidence possibly proving that Sylvester De León was an alien enemy. If that were true, Hardy had no right to auction the estate, since the land grant would have reverted to the State of Texas. Furthermore, the possibility that the De León family might be alien enemies was not a cause to dismiss the case. Under Texas law, alien enemies could not be plaintiffs in a case, but they were allowed to present their grievances as defendants.

Once it became public knowledge that Hardy was being tried for failing to disclose that the De León grant might belong to the State of Texas, his conspirators changed their testimony and confessed that they had lied. Van Horn and Cunningham were apologetic and pleaded guilty to perjury. They admitted that De León did not owe them money, and disclosed that Hardy had paid them to purchase the property at the auction. Gamble, another conspirator, confessed that he had worked with Hardy to develop the tax scheme. But unlike the other two witnesses, Gamble was not ashamed of his actions. He testified in court that Mexicans were alien enemies and did not deserve to own land in Texas.

At trial, Hardy's attorneys, Mr. Paschal and Mr. Neil, tried to dismiss the damaging testimony that had been presented against their client. They argued that the important issue was that the De León family had lost their property after Texas independence for supporting Mexico. It was their legal opinion that after a war, conquered people are incorporated as aliens and not citizens. Some are legally classified as alien enemies, like Sylvester De León, while others are considered friendly aliens. Paschal and Neil asserted that the property of alien enemies became public land. Therefore, although Hardy had acted badly, he was the rightful owner of the De León estate because he had followed the proper procedure for acquiring public land. He surveyed it, registered it, and obtained legal title. In their opinion, once the Texas General Land Office issued a new deed, that title was legitimate and irrevocable.

Mr. Phillips, the attorney for the De León family, argued that Sylvester De León, as well as most Texas residents, was given citizenship at the end of the Texas Revolution. No precedent in Texas law substantiated the claim that Mexicans were incorporated as aliens. Phillips also charged that it was untrue that the boys' father was an alien enemy.

The facts were more complicated, Phillips charged. After Texas independence, Sylvester De León briefly moved to New Orleans. His wife was ill at that time, and about to give birth to Francisco Santiago; he took his family to New Orleans to protect them from their angry neighbors. Once his family was safely relocated, he immediately returned to Texas and lived there until his death. While in Victoria, Sylvester De León learned that his wife had died during childbirth. He returned to New Orleans to pick up his children, and then took them to temporarily live with his mother-in-law in Matamoros, Mexico. After he settled his affairs in Victoria, he returned to Matamoros to retrieve his sons, but on his way, he was ambushed and killed south of the Nueces River. After Sylvester De León's death, his sons were dispersed among relatives. Francisco Santiago, the boy born in New Orleans, moved to Texas, and his two older brothers remained in Mexico. In 1844, Fernando De León was appointed guardian of Francisco Santiago.[105]

When Fernando De León learned that his brother's property had been sold for unpaid taxes, he knew that the alleged reason was untrue. Phillips declared that it was impossible for Sylvester De León to owe back taxes, because under Mexican and Texas law, he did not need to begin paying taxes until 1844, and by that time Hardy had sold the estate. Furthermore, Phillips added that the De León heirs could not have accrued any back taxes, because child heirs do not owe taxes until an estate is settled. Phillips concluded that because these issues were standard knowledge, the officials in probate court knowingly colluded with Hardy to steal the estate.

At the end of the trial, the jury rendered a mixed opinion. It concluded that Sylvester De León was never a citizen of Texas, because he was presumed to be an alien enemy. Further, the jury decided that there was sufficient evidence to indict Hardy on all charges. The judge concurred with the jury, but interjected that the land grant would not become public property, because Francisco Santiago was the legal heir. When the boy's father took his family to New Orleans, his son Francisco Santiago was born in US territory after Texas Independence. His date and place of birth, therefore, prevented him from being considered an alien enemy. And since Francisco Santiago was a US citizen, he had the legal right to inherit his grandfather Martín De León's land grant. His brothers, Martín and Francisco, however, could not inherit any part of the grant, because they were born in Texas before independence, and thus they inherited their father's alien enemy status.

After the trial, Hardy appealed. The case was sent to the Texas Supreme Court. The justices accepted the appeal, since many issues remained unresolved and needed to be clarified. The jury had rendered a favorable decision for Francisco Santiago, yet a dangerous precedent on the political status of Mexican Americans in Texas had also been established. If the Texas Supreme Court did not overturn the district court's opinion on how a person became an alien enemy, many Mexican Americans could potentially be converted into alien enemies and dispossessed of their land and voting rights. Furthermore, because the district court had ruled that the classification "alien enemy" was inheritable over the generations, a potential precedent was established for retaining Mexican Americans in a perpetual caste-like political position.

In the December term of 1849, the Texas Supreme Court ruled on Hardy's appeal. The justices upheld the lower court's ruling on Francisco Santiago's inheritance. But it reversed the district's ruling on his father's legal status. The justices concluded that there was insufficient evidence to prove that Sylvester De León was a traitor. His actions after Texas independence were the normal reactions of a man who needed to defend his family against the hostile acts of neighbors who were trying to steal his possessions.

The justices also overturned the district's court ruling on alienage. Justice Wheeler, who wrote the opinion of the court, stated that it was an international principle for conquered people to obtain the political status of their new nation.[106] Wheeler also concluded that people who were declared by law to be alien enemies did not retain that status for life, nor did their children inherit their political status. On property law, he added that it was an accepted international tenet for the land titles of the conquered to be validated unless new policies were enacted by the conquerors.[107]

Wheeler also admonished the lower courts for their actions in handling the De León case. The officers of the probate court and the sheriff of Victoria acted improperly. Hardy was allowed to pursue a claim that was obviously fraudulent.[108] Although the justices chose not to fine the officers, they established a precedent that had to be followed by public officials when handling land grant and other property cases. District, county, and probate judges, as well as other governmental officials who participated in legal proceedings to confiscate property, were prohibited from selling or purchasing the same property. Likewise, the court ruled that lower-level administrators, juries, and district judges did not have jurisdiction over determining whether a Mexican was an alien enemy.

Following the ruling, Fernando De León and other Mexican Americans were able to use the precedent to litigate similar claims in their self-defense. In Victoria County, many land grant heirs won their district court rulings; others appealed to the Texas Supreme Court and had district court rulings overturned.[109] Judge Robinson, the district court judge of Victoria County, was notorious for making rulings against land grant heirs. After the Texas Supreme Court ruled in favor of the De León family, Robinson was forced to return a large portion of the acreage that he had purchased from litigants whom he ruled in favor of, against Mexican land grant heirs.

The Use of Violence against Mexican Land Grant Heirs

The *Hardy v. De Leon* ruling was a monumental triumph for the advancement of Mexican Americans' civil rights. But Anglo-American settlers did not stop using violence, or conspiring with local officials, to fraudulently obtain the land owned by Mexicans.

After the Mexican-American War, migration to the US Southwest from

Europe and the interior of the United States increased. Most immigrants settled in Texas and California. Many newcomers found the best plots of land were occupied by Mexicans or by Anglo-American settlers who had arrived during the Mexican period. Most recent migrants accepted this land-tenure pattern and moved on to find vacant or public lands. Some entrepreneurs, however, used violence or colluded with local officials to illegally obtain the land they coveted.

In an analysis of the history of land grants in Texas, Ana Carolina Castillo Crimm argues that the most contentious legal conflicts over property took place in the Stephen Austin, Green DeWitt, and Martín De León colonies, where fighting often broke out between old and new settlers.[110] The old settlers were the original Mexican inhabitants and the Anglo-Americans who had joined the empresario colonies before 1830 and owned registered land grants. Problems arose after the Mexican-American War when district judges often colluded with investors and friends to make it difficult for old settlers to keep their property. The main scheme used by the judges was to transfer title to investors by pressuring old-timers to relinquish possession of their land for back taxes, as in the fraudulent scheme discussed in *Hardy v. De Leon*. It was common knowledge that settlers who obtained land grants during Mexican rule owned parcels larger than 4,000 acres. Entrepreneurs, therefore, searched for ranches where land taxes might be owed, surveyed the targeted land, and then approached the courts to transfer title. Violence often accompanied the appropriation process. The case of Antonio De La Garza illustrates how entrepreneurs used fraudulent surveys and violence to appropriate the property of land grant heirs.

Antonio De La Garza's problems began a year after the Mexican-American War. In 1849, William Cook filed legal papers against Antonio De La Garza, and a trial of possession was held in the Victoria District Court.[111] Cook charged that he owned Antonio De La Garza's ranch because when he purchased several parcels from locals, his surveyor included the ranch as part of the property sold to him. In court, Antonio De La Garza submitted evidence that he held legal title to the ranch and he did not owe back taxes. The judge ruled in De La Garza's favor, since Cook's survey was insufficient to prove ownership. After the ruling, many witnesses heard Cook threaten De La Garza and swear that he would take the ranch by any means.

Two years passed, but Cook refused to give up. He hired two local thugs to beat up De La Garza whenever they saw him. On occasion, the Harper brothers and other vigilantes hired by Cook would go to the De La Garza ranch and harass his family and workers. Although De La Garza reported the assaults to local authorities, the sheriff said he could not intervene.[112]

When violence against Antonio failed, Cook decided to harm his family. He hired eight vigilantes to visit Mrs. De La Garza. They waited for a time when Mrs. De La Garza and her children were alone.

On a morning when De La Garza left the ranch to sell his cattle, Cook's men attacked. Three of the Harper brothers let the animals out of the barn and then moved on to destroy the pens, fences, and barn walls. After the ranch was left in shambles, Cook walked into the house and told Mrs. De La Garza that he was taking possession of the ranch, including the furnishings. When she protested and tried to protect her family, Cook ordered the Harper brothers to restrain her, and then he violently struck her.[113] Once the Harpers had finished destroying the house, they stole the furniture and forcefully picked up Mrs. De La Garza by the arms and threw her out of the house while she was carrying her infant child. They warned her never to return.

After the ordeal was over, Cook's hit men took possession of the ranch. Upon his return, De La Garza had no other recourse than to seek justice in the courts. In 1851, De La Garza filed suit in the Victoria District Court to recover his property.[114] Once again, he won the lawsuit. Judge R. B. Moore ordered Cook and his conspirators to pay damages and return all confiscated property. Cook and the other vigilantes were found guilty and ordered to pay De La Garza nearly $4,000 in cash. Because Cook was found to be the principal aggressor, he was required to pay $600 and to guarantee payment of his accomplices' fines and debts. Although the court records do not specify the crimes that Cook's accomplices were convicted of, they must have been heinous, since their fines were substantial. Mr. Moore and Mr. Baldwin were together assessed $600.[115] William Vannell and Casino Villanueva were fined the heavy sum of $1,800.[116] Mr. Ashworth and Mr. Lampkin, who must have had a less aggressive role in the altercations, were to pay together $764.72.[117] Sheriff James W. Cunningham was ordered to see that the damages were paid either in cash or by having the assailants transfer title of property owned by them.

Cook appealed to the Texas Supreme Court on the grounds that he had not received a fair trial. On January 10, 1853, Antonio De La Garza once again received a favorable ruling.[118] The justices admonished Cook and his companions for their cowardly behavior toward Mrs. De La Garza and ordered Cook to leave the family alone.

Dissatisfied with the Texas Supreme Court ruling, Cook applied for an injunction to temporarily stop payment of the fines. Rather than submitting this request to the Texas Supreme Court, he filed a petition in the Victoria District Court, where a new district judge had been recently appointed. On August 2, 1853, Judge R. E. Baylor accepted the petition and set in motion preparations for a hearing to reduce the fines. Further, he temporarily suspended payment of all fines and ordered Sheriff Cunningham to help Cook find new witnesses who could challenge Antonio De La Garza's account. In the meantime, Cook's attorneys appealed the Texas Supreme Court for a reconsideration of the case, claiming that errors had been committed by court officials.

On September 9, 1853, Cook received bad news from the district court. Judge Baylor had been removed, and the new judge dissolved the injunction. The judge also increased the fines because Cook had submitted fraudulent deeds for property that he expected to give De La Garza in lieu of payment. The problem was that the deeds were for ranchland owned by the De León family.[119]

In November 1855, the Texas Supreme Court ruled on Cook's appeal.[120] In an opinion written by Justice Wheeler, the justices concluded that a retrial was unnecessary and that the earlier ruling was affirmed. Cook's attorney, W. Paschal, had not submitted sufficient evidence to prove that the witnesses who testified against Cook had lied, or that technical errors had been committed by the Texas Supreme Court. Paschal had tried to impeach De La Garza's witnesses by charging that the testimonies of Mexicans could not be trusted.

Wheeler then moved on to discuss why Cook had no standing to request a rehearing at the district level. Wheeler explained that Judge Baylor had been removed from the case because he did not have the authority either to issue an injunction or to hold a new trial to reconsider the fines. In fact, Baylor's actions amounted to a legal scheme to retry the case. But under US law, a case cannot be retried merely because a different judgment is expected from a new judge.

After the appeal was rejected, Cook did not file new lawsuits against De La Garza.[121] But the Texas Supreme Court had not resolved all issues affecting land grant heirs. The legal theory that Texas courts did not have the authority to invalidate deeds recorded by the Texas General Land Office remained a conclusion that entrepreneurs were unwilling to abide by, and the issue had to be settled by the US Supreme Court. In 1860, Joseph Sheirburn, a wealthy investor from Guadalupe County, took his land dispute to the US Supreme Court.

After purchasing part of the Antonio María Esnaurrizar Mexican land grant in Guadalupe County, Sheirburn had the property surveyed, and as required by law, he submitted the survey and the sale records to the Texas General Land Office. He was then issued a deed. Jacob De Cordova and several Mexican and Anglo-American residents challenged his claim and filed a class-action lawsuit in the federal court for the Western District of Texas. Their main complaint was that Sheirburn's surveyors had knowingly included land that did not belong to him. The court ruled against Sheirburn and dissolved his deed.

Sheirburn appealed to the US Supreme Court, using an argument similar to Hardy's when he tried to dispossess the De León family of its grant. In *Sheirburn v. De Cordova et al.* (1860), Sheirburn's attorneys claimed that although their client's survey contained parcels of property owned by his neighbors, his claim had been approved by a US institution and therefore his title became the only legitimate deed, superseding those issued by a foreign government. The Supreme Court justices dismissed Sheirburn's arguments and affirmed the lower court's decision. The Court ruled that an original deed is not dissolved when another claimant surveys that property and registers it as his own. The ruling created a precedent preventing claimants from obtaining titles to land under fraudulent premises. Deeds issued by US offices were invalid when the officials processing the documents colluded with petitioners or mistakenly certified false documents.[122]

The rulings rendered by the courts, from the De León family's fight against Hardy to the class-action suit filed against Sheirburn in Guadalupe County, were progressive, indicating that US law was evolving in an equitable direction. On the other hand, the cases illustrated that Mexican Americans had to struggle to retain their property. A common element among the cases was that the litigants who won favorable rulings had the financial means to pursue a lawsuit. It was uncertain how less wealthy Mexican Americans fared when faced with the need to litigate their complaints.

Land, Slave Labor, and the US Civil War

Following Texas independence, Anglo-American landowners became increasingly dependent on slave labor. The enslaved population of Texas increased from 5,000 in 1836 to 58,161 in 1850, an increase of more than 1,000 percent.[123] In 1860, when tensions leading to the US Civil War were intensifying, the enslaved population of Texas had grown to 182,566, 30 percent of the total population of 604,215.[124]

By the time the US Civil War broke out, the ethnic makeup of Texas had changed radically. Most Native Americans had been pushed out of the state, and Anglo-Americans and African Americans outnumbered the Mexican population. Mexican Americans were spread throughout Texas, but were primarily concentrated in El Paso and Bexar Counties and in South Texas. The Mexican-origin population in Goliad (La Bahía) and Victoria had dwindled to a small minority. Although Texas prospered economically after US annexation, it became highly dependent on slave labor. Anglo-Americans acquired an immense territory after the Mexican-American War, and slave labor became the key to making this land profitable. By 1860, Anglo-Americans were distributed across Texas in 151 counties, 17 of which had a population larger than 6,000 inhabitants. Except in the counties in South Texas, El Paso County, and a few of the smallest counties in Texas, such as Brown, Clay, and Eastland, slavery grew immensely across the state. In over 33 counties, slaves either outnumbered the free residents or accounted for half the population. The largest slave populations were concentrated in Central Texas in the counties of Washington, Fayette, and Walker, and along the Brazoria coast. By this time, Bexar County was no longer the most populous county in Texas; Washington County had outstripped it when its enslaved population grew to nearly 8,000, accounting for over half of the county's residents.[125]

In the former Mexican settlements, slavery was nearly nonexistent. Only in the De León colony, which had become Victoria County, and in Goliad had slavery increased radically, to nearly one-third of the inhabitants. In both these former Mexican settlements, the fertile land near the coast drew hundreds of settlers, who quickly made claims on the land and eclipsed the Mexican population in size. In most South Texas counties, enslaved residents were few in number, and the region became the home of half of Texas's free Black population, numbering in total 397. But in the northern counties of South Texas, slavery began to spread after European immigrants and people from Alabama, Tennessee, Mississippi, Georgia, and Louisiana settled there.[126] Karnes, San Patricio, and Atascosa Counties had non-Mexican populations of 28 to 46 percent, and these were also the South Texas counties with the largest number of slaves, ranging from 97 to 327.[127]

In 1860, following the election of President Abraham Lincoln, the southern states threatened to secede.[128] The North and South were divided on many economic issues, but the immediate and primary one was the South's dependence on slavery and the North's increasing opposition to it. Because of its reliance on slave labor, Texas likewise threatened to secede from the Union. One month after Lincoln's election, South Carolina took the lead and made good on its promise to secede; within months, Mississippi, Florida, Alabama, Louisiana, Georgia, and Texas had followed suit. As the rebellion intensified, Virginia, Arkansas, North Carolina, and Tennessee joined the other southern states. On April 12, 1861, Confederate forces attacked federal troops at Fort Sumter in Charleston Harbor, South Carolina, and the Civil War began.[129]

The war lasted almost exactly four years, and by late April 1865, the Confederacy had surrendered. The nation faced a difficult and tumultuous process of unifying the country and moving forward. Unfortunately, after the war ended, President Lincoln was assassinated and Vice President Andrew Johnson assumed the presidency. He had been selected as Lincoln's running mate during the president's reelection campaign because Johnson was the only sitting southern Democratic senator who had not joined the rebellion.

Johnson's plans for the nation differed radically from the majority opinion of Republican representatives and senators, who controlled Congress. He favored quickly restoring the political rights of the rebellious states and did not support making African Americans citizens. Congress disagreed, fearing that the immediate restoration of southern governments, and the seating of southern legislators in Congress, would impede or completely obstruct the passing of federal legislation to improve the political rights of African Americans.[130] In 1865, President Johnson moved forward with his plans and appointed provisional governors in the southern states. They were to assemble the state legislatures, rescind the Confederate-era constitutions, and prepare the states to be readmitted to the Union.

Texas complied. On April 2, 1866, the state representatives completed the revisions to a new constitution that abolished slavery but gave few rights to the newly freed population. Black codes were passed to keep African Americans on the estates of their former masters, and no plans were developed to make them citizens with voting rights.[131] Congress was disturbed at President Johnson's policies and his support of the southern states' new constitutions.

After the congressional election of April 1866, Republican representatives were able to slow the restoration of the southern states' political authority when they gained a two-thirds majority in Congress. This gave them the power to pass Reconstruction legislation and override presidential vetoes.[132] Within days, Republicans passed the Civil Rights Act of 1866, which was meant to protect African Americans from the Black codes and force southern states to rewrite their constitutions. On April 9, 1866, Congress decreed under the Civil Rights Act of 1866 that all people born on US soil and not subject to any foreign power, excluding Indians, and irrespective of race and color, were citizens of the United States, regardless of any previous condition of slavery or involuntary servitude.[133] Two months later, Congress went further and used the core principle of the Civil Rights Act of 1866 to draft the Fourteenth Amendment.[134] The amendment would, among other fundamental changes, make African Americans citizens. On June 13, Congress passed the Fourteenth Amendment, which declared that all people born on US soil were citizens of the United States, as were the foreign born who obtained naturalization. The only American-born people exempted from US citizenship were Native Americans.[135] In the near future, this exemption would have negative consequences for Mexican Americans, and would be used in Texas to promote a social movement to deny them citizenship.

Congress acknowledged that it would be very difficult to convince the former Confederate states to adopt the Fourteenth Amendment. In the meantime, Congress passed a series of Reconstruction laws as the Military Reconstruction Acts. The acts required the rebel states to pass the amendment before they would be readmitted to the Union. Until then, the states would remain under military control and not be allowed to govern themselves. On July 9, 1868, the Fourteenth Amendment was ratified. The former Confederate states of Tennessee, Alabama, South Carolina, North Carolina, Georgia, West Virginia, Arkansas, Florida, and Louisiana had passed the amendment.[136] Texas, which had refused, remained under military control.

Within months of the ratification of the Fourteenth Amendment, it became apparent to most Texans that it was useless to continue resisting the nation's new political agenda. All political avenues for restoring their state government without ratifying the Fourteenth Amendment had been exhausted. When state leaders informed Congress that they were prepared to pass the amendment, it authorized General W. S. Hancock, a military commander, to organize a constitutional convention. On March 30, 1870, Congress readmitted Texas to the Union, restored the state's political representation in Congress, and authorized the Texas Legislature to govern the state.[137]

Although the state had complied with federal law, the majority of white Texans resented the intrusion of Congress into their political affairs. Two years later, they converted Texas into a one-party state run by Democrats, the former Confederates. Democrats took over the legislature, and the following year a new governor was elected, Richard Coke, who opposed the civil rights that African Americans had gained in Texas, especially Black suffrage.[138] (The Fifteenth Amendment, which guaranteed Black men the right to vote, had been ratified in February 1870.)

For Mexican Americans in Texas, the new government did not display the intense political animosity it showed to African Americans. The Texas Legislature for decades had acknowledged that US and Texas laws made Mexican Americans citizens and thus eligible to vote. Nonetheless, Mexican Americans experienced many forms of racial discrimination during Reconstruction. The freedom of movement that African Americans had obtained under federal law intensified the animosity many whites held against all people of color.

CHAPTER 3

Violence and Segregation, 1877–1927

This chapter examines social injustices that Mexican Americans underwent from 1877 to 1927. The period just after the Civil War was a particularly troublesome time. Mexican Americans experienced increased violence along the US-Mexico border, and their status as US citizens was questioned. Segregation laws were passed to keep persons of color apart from whites. In 1873, the US Supreme Court ruling in the *Slaughter-House Cases* gave the courts and state legislatures the authority to segregate people of color, including Mexican Americans. In Texas, de jure segregation of Mexican Americans began in 1885 after the Texas Supreme Court gave the boards of organizations and business owners the authority to exclude any person, for any reason, from using public accommodations. The chapter closes by examining how the segregation of Mexican Americans intensified during the early twentieth century after the Texas Legislature authorized municipal and county officials to institute residential and school segregation. In the later chapters, case studies examine how school segregation unfolded and how the segregation of Mexican Americans in public accommodations was enforced by the state and by local governments.

The Texas Rangers and the US-Mexico Border

In 1875, during Reconstruction, Governor Richard Coke commissioned several companies of Texas Rangers to patrol the US-Mexico border, and an era of abusive policing began.[1] Their main mandate was to protect the border from Mexican bandits who entered Texas to steal cattle, but their policing practices became seriously corrupt. Wealthy Anglo-American settlers who had purchased Spanish and Mexican land grants along the border used the state's police force to advance their economic interests against the Mexican population.[2] Major John B. Jones commanded the Frontier Battalion, consisting of six companies of seventy-five men each. They were responsible for patrolling El Paso County. Captain L. H. McNelly was placed in command of the Special Force of Texas Rangers, a smaller unit of forty men responsible for maintaining law and order in South Texas between the Nueces River and the Rio Grande. The Rangers indiscriminately attacked people, instilling terror in Mexican communities. Mexicans were shot or arrested merely because they were suspected of being bandidos or because they were accused of protecting cattle rustlers.

In South Texas, many Rangers were on the payrolls of Anglo-American cattle barons and helped them steal cattle from Mexican ranchers. Richard King, an American entrepreneur, had become the wealthiest rancher in the region. It was rumored that King exerted significant influence on the Rangers, paying them to arrest Mexicans who questioned his authority. The Rangers had a camp on the King Ranch. Mexicans were often arrested for allegedly stealing cattle from the ranch. Several incidents were so grave that the attacks on Mexican communities came to the attention of Congress and investigations were made. On June 12, 1875, the Rangers captured thirteen Mexican cowboys near Brownsville and accused them of cattle rustling.[3] Rather than giving them the opportunity to defend themselves in court, the Rangers shot them and then hung their corpses in the public square in Brownsville. The Rangers were later accused by Mexican Americans and news reporters of using public hangings to instill fear in Mexican American communities. Newspapers across the United States reported that after the federal government investigated the affair, the Mexican cowboys were found not to be rustlers, but cowboys returning from a stock-buying trip in North Texas. When the cattle were inspected for stolen brands, most were found to be unbranded, proving that the cowboys were not thieves.

McNelly's Special Forces were also known for committing brutalities across the border, and in Mexico they were considered outlaws with licenses to kill. In 1875, McNelly and his Rangers crossed the border without federal authorization and attacked the Mexican village of Cachuttas.[4] On their return to the United States, they alleged that Juan Flores Salinas, the mayor of Camargo was at fault for not allowing them to pursue the bandits that had stolen cattle from the King Ranch. The conflict began after the Rangers set up camp at Cachuttas and Flores ordered them to leave. When they refused, he returned with one hundred men, and the conflict exploded. McNelly's Rangers reported that they fought back, and after overpowering the villagers, eighty Mexicans were dead, including Flores. The Rangers then retrieved the stolen cattle and pursued the alleged thieves hiding in nearby villages. The Rangers collected four hundred cattle and returned to the King Ranch. The Mexican government complained, and the US Department of War investigated the incident, finding that of the cattle taken from Mexico, 250 were unbranded and that only a few had a King Ranch brand.

McNelly was admonished for his actions by the Secretary of War, but the governor of Texas did not suspend his commission. The incident caused bad feelings between the Mexican government and the State of Texas. It also alerted the US government to maintain oversight of the Texas Rangers when it came to international affairs, and the War Department was put in charge of investigating all matters dealing with Texas Rangers crossing the border. After the Cachuttas affair, the US government could not ignore major international incidents. Therefore, when Major John B. Jones, commander of the Frontier Battalion in El Paso County, became embroiled in the most explosive crime committed against a Mexican American community in Texas, the federal government was forced to intervene and to maintain federal surveillance over unjust state policing. President Rutherford B. Hayes began an investigation of what became known as the Salt War Riots, after federal troops reported that Texas Rangers were committing atrocities against the civilians of El Paso County and the Mexican communities across the border.

Violence, Political Corruption, and the Salt War Riots

One of the most violent incidents committed against Mexican Americans during Reconstruction took place in El Paso County during the winter of 1877.[5] The largest municipalities in the county were El Paso, Ysleta, Socorro, San Elizario, and the village of Canutillo, northwest of El Paso. The violence that broke out in El Paso County was the outcome of political disputes between influential Anglo-Americans seeking to obtain ownership of public land in El Paso County that had recently been opened for sale or claim by the Texas Legislature. Anglo-Americans had begun settling in El Paso County in 1850 after Congress appended the American side of El Paso del Norte to Texas rather than New Mexico. A decade later, during the Civil War, the number of Anglo-Americans increased when the Confederate government opened up mission lands for settlement. Afterward, during the first years of Reconstruction, Republicans assumed political control of the Texas Legislature and took advantage of their authority. In El Paso County, Republicans who controlled the local government chal-

El Paso Street, El Paso, circa 1859–1879

lenged the land claims that the former Confederate government had issued. During the Civil War, a significant percentage of the land in the county had been transferred from the Mexican and Indigenous populations to Anglo-American newcomers, and it was these claims that Republican politicians were contesting.[6]

Albert J. Fountain, a Republican Unionist, was appointed land surveyor of El Paso County after the war, and he had the authority to approve all survey petitions for land claims before they were submitted to the legislature. When competing land claims arose, he generally favored his Unionist friends. Fountain became more politically powerful when he was elected state senator for El Paso County and chairman of the Texas Indian Commission. Although Fountain was well liked by the local Mexicans, they were unaware that he was secretly working with a ring of entrepreneurs to acquire large tracts of public land in El Paso County. He was also working with the legislature to convert the last parcels of mission land into public property without compensating the occupants.[7]

In 1871, the Texas Legislature made available for redistribution additional Spanish and Mexican land grants in El Paso County when it decreed that any Spanish and Mexican land grant claims that remained unresolved became public property.[8] If Mexicans and Native Americans had not already received deeds to their land grants, they lost the property to whoever could retitle it. The legislature also allowed people to apply for land that had been previously used for community civic buildings. Ysleta and Socorro were the most severely affected settlements, since the mission titles had been invalidated, having originally been issued to mission Indians.[9] This land grant reorganization brought many Anglo-Americans to El Paso County, including powerful men who could purchase large tracts of land from the state government. Throughout the county, roads and streets were treated as public lands and sold to influential Anglo-Americans.[10]

Fountain's political influence diminished in 1872 when the former Confederates took control of both houses of the Texas Legislature. With the transition of power from Republican to Democratic rule, former Confederate politicians once again helped their friends acquire property in El Paso County. Among them were Charles Howard and his father-in-law, George Zimpleman, who came to El Paso County in search of land that the legislature had deemed public property. At that time, the legislature confirmed all claims to public lands, including those containing rivers, lakes, and salt. Obtaining the support of legislators was not difficult for Howard and Zimpleman, since they had many political connections. Both men were highly respected Civil War heroes and former Texas Rangers.[11] Zimpleman was also a wealthy entrepreneur who had the financial means to pursue any land claim.[12]

Mexicans did not have the political power to stop the Texas Legislature from selling El Paso County's public lands to private entrepreneurs. In 1876, however, the Mexican community could no longer tolerate this land-grabbing scheme after learning that the Texas Legislature had sold the county's salt lakes to Zimpleman. They became aware of this when Howard began charging locals a fee to harvest salt. For the Mexican community this was intolerable. Adding to the indignity of having their public lands privatized, they lost their main source of salt.

To resolve this problem, a few people from San Elizario and Ysleta approached Louis Cardis to speak to Howard on their behalf. Cardis was the district's state representative. (By this time, Fountain had left El Paso.) Cardis met Howard in San Elizario and attempted to convince him to relinquish his family's title to the salt lakes and give it to the people of El Paso County. Howard ignored Cardis and instead hired gunmen to protect the salt lakes.[13]

As the Mexican community grew angrier, Cardis decided to take legal action against Howard. He organized a committee of six prominent Anglo-Americans to represent the district and begin proceedings.[14] It was

Ysleta Mission, late 1800s

necessary to do this because Howard had begun working with local authorities to have people arrested for failing to pay his fee. To locals, Howard was a thief who had bribed local authorities and put them on his payroll. It was widely believed that local law officers were Howard's allies, including Charles Kerber, the county sheriff, and the García brothers, who were the judge and sheriff of San Elizario.[15] Their only ally was Cardis.

The Salt War Riots Begin

In early September 1877, José María Juárez and Macedonio Gandera organized local residents to stop paying the salt fee. They were prominent local citizens and *salinero* merchants who harvested salt and sold it across the border in Ciudad Juárez.[16] When Howard learned of their actions, he asked Gregorio N. García, the county judge, to arrest the organizers. García held a hearing on September 20. He found the men guilty and placed them in the San Elizario jail.[17] San Elizario, the county seat, contained the only courthouse and jail, and the principal Catholic parish. More than two-thirds of the residents of El Paso County resided in San Elizario, Ysleta, and Socorro.[18]

Nine days later, sixty residents went to Judge García and demanded the men's release. This came to be considered the first riot. To calm matters, the county sheriff, Charles Kerber, assured locals that he would personally get Juárez and Gandera released from jail. Two weeks later, after no progress had been made in getting the men out of prison, a second riot erupted on October 1. A much larger crowd demanded the men's release and the arrest of Howard. Locals wanted Judge García to ask Howard to sign papers forfeiting his father-in-law's claim to the salt lake. When García refused to help them, the leaders of the crowd took Howard prisoner.[19] Sheriff Kerber negotiated his release, but became alarmed at the size of the crowd, which he estimated to be more than two hundred.[20] After people went home, Kerber immediately contacted Governor Richard Hubbard and asked for a troop of Rangers to be dispatched to El Paso. He did not tell him about the conflict involving Howard and the salt fees. Instead, he lied, reporting that Mexicans from across the border were causing trouble in El Paso and were planning to loot American stores.[21]

On October 10, Howard killed Representative Cardis in San Elizario. While Cardis sat behind a desk in the Shultz County Store, writing a letter, Howard entered the store carrying a rifle.[22] Without warning, Howard shot him dead. After the slaying, Howard fled to Mesilla, New Mexico, but

San Elizario's first courthouse, circa 1888–1900

left his gunmen to continue collecting the fees. Rumors spread that Howard had murdered Cardis for organizing the land committee to challenge
his father in-law's claim. He also blamed Cardis for the embarrassment he
endured when locals took him prisoner.[23] When the Mexican community
heard of Cardis's death, they escalated their plans to challenge Howard's
claim. Father Borrajo, the parish priest of Guadalupe, a church across the
border, was identified as the lead organizer.

Father Borrajo's contempt for Howard was deeply rooted. Several
years earlier, Howard had asked the bishop of El Paso to remove Father
Borrajo from the parish in San Elizario and transfer him somewhere
else. Borrajo was transferred across the border to Ciudad Juárez, where he
could continue stirring up trouble.[24] Howard blamed Borrajo for organizing locals to challenge his family's land claims in El Paso County.

On November 6, 1877, another protest broke out in San Elizario, this
one involving around 500 participants. Father Borrajo was once again rumored to be the leader. Although the crowd dispersed peacefully, Governor
Hubbard was informed about the event, and he summoned Ranger Major
John B. Jones, the commander of the Frontier Battalion, to investigate
the troubles in El Paso.[25] On November 16, Jones held a town meeting in
San Elizario and warned the residents that they would be arrested if they

refused to pay the salt fees. They would also be arrested if they continued with their disorderly conduct. The crowd became incensed when Jones failed to assure them that Howard would be arrested for Cardis's death.

A few days later, Jones left San Elizario and put Sheriff Kerber and John Tays, one of his Rangers in charge, giving them the authority to recruit and deputize volunteers. Tays was disliked by Mexicans, and also rumored to be one of Howard's men.[26] Jones informed the governor that Borrajo and Cardis were to blame for the troubles in El Paso.[27] Anticipating that a larger riot would soon break out, he asked the governor to send more Rangers and to solicit the US War Department for aid. Jones knew that Sheriff Kerber had found recruits in Silver City, New Mexico, and among them were desperadoes.[28]

Within a couple of days, Rangers arrived in San Elizario. Tays instructed them to arrest any person who attempted to steal salt from the lakes. On December 12, another riot broke out. It began at the salt lakes and continued into San Elizario. By then, Howard had returned to El Paso. On the fifth day of the riot, locals overpowered the Texas Rangers and Howard's gunmen. The prisoners were temporarily held in the San Elizario jail, and Howard and two of his men were executed by the rebels. After the siege, Tays's men were released without their guns. The residents were not naïve and expected retaliation. News spread that federal troops had arrived in El Paso and were preparing to enter San Elizario. The spokesmen for the Mexican residents were prepared to give federal investigators their side of the account and to report the atrocities that Howard's men had committed against them. During the last riot, around fifteen Mexicans were killed and over forty-five wounded.[29]

Federal Troops Arrive to End the Salt War Riots

On December 22, sixty federal troops from New Mexico's Fifteenth Army Infantry, under the command of Captain Thomas Blair, arrived in San Elizario, and they observed the community under attack.[30] A rampage against the locals had broken out. People's homes were pillaged for wine and tobacco, those accused of imprisoning the Rangers were shot, and women were ravaged and raped.[31] It is uncertain whether the federal troops were unable or unwilling to stop the attack on the civilians. San Elizario was the first town attacked, and then the violence spread to communities along both sides of the border.

Although Anglo-American civilians in El Paso were not the target of the

Rangers or Sheriff Kerber's men, the violence spread to their district. J. P. Miller reported to Captain Blair that his family was attacked by men pretending to be Rangers. He was physically assaulted after he refused to tell them where his womenfolk were hiding. Before they left El Paso, the Rangers destroyed his house and stole everything they could carry.[32]

Unable to stop the chaos, Blair asked for a large battalion to be sent from Fort Davis. He reported that the well-armed Silver City desperadoes refused to follow his orders. Sheriff Kerber had given them the authority to do as they wanted. Blair personally witnessed a Ranger robbing an Anglo-American merchant in Kerber's presence. When Blair demanded that Kerber arrest the Ranger, the sheriff responded that he did not take orders from lower-level officers.[33] In the meantime, news about the riot spread throughout the United States, with reports blaming the disorder on the Rangers. News reports also stated that Juan D. Ochoa, the vice-consul of Mexico, had informed the offices of President Hayes and the US secretary of war that Rangers were attacking Mexican villages across the border. This was no longer just a Texas incident.

When Hayes received news from the War Department about the Rangers' brutal misconduct, he contacted Governor Hubbard. The governor denied all the allegations and blamed the disorder on Captain Blair. He told the president that this was a Texas matter that he would handle. In response to the governor's defiant stance, Hayes summoned federal troops to intervene and take control of El Paso County. He informed the governor that a federal military investigation was underway. In retaliation, Hubbard sent more Texas Rangers to the area and stated that he would be investigating why Mexicans from across the border were plundering and robbing Texas residents.

The Federal Investigation Begins

In late December after federal troops had contained the Rangers' disorder, President Hayes ordered an immediate investigation into the affair. American citizens had been killed by state authorities and forced to flee their homes. George W. McCrary, the secretary of war, headed a commission to investigate the Salt War riots. The commission was composed of two military officers and one Texas representative. When Governor Hubbard chose Major Jones as the Texas commissioner, McCrary opposed the appointment. He charged that Jones could not participate in the commission because he was implicated in crimes committed against the residents of El Paso. Also, Jones was accused of escalating the conflict after ordering Captain Tays to imprison any person who failed to pay the salt fee. Under Texas law, failure to pay was punishable by a small fine, not imprisonment. Finally, Jones was accused of breaking state law when he refused to detain Charles Howard for the murder of Representative Cardis. After Governor Hubbard dismissed the conflict-of-interest charges and refused to appoint another commissioner, the president's legal advisers recommended that Jones's role be limited.[34] Under federal law, his report did not have to be included in the commission's findings, and he could be prevented from interviewing witnesses.

When news spread that Major Jones was being accused of crimes and that he would not play a meaningful role in the investigation, many Texas Rangers fled the state to avoid prosecution. The field investigation began on January 3, 1878, and witness statements concluded on March 4.[35] Colonel Edward Hatch and Judge Advocate General John Dunn were in charge of the investigation. Colonel Hatch had arrived in the El Paso Valley on December 23 and observed some of the atrocities that the civilians experienced. Therefore, besides being responsible for assembling the eyewitness accounts, his testimony became a critical part of the investigation.[36]

The federal commissioners compiled the investigators' reports and submitted their findings to the secretary of war on April 2, 1878, and a month later to President Hayes and Congress. Major Jones also submitted a minority report, which interpreted the events differently. The commission's report concluded that the Texas Rangers and Sheriff Kerber's deputies had knowingly broken many laws and committed atrocities on both sides of the US-Mexico border. The Silver City desperadoes had pretended to be Texas Rangers when they entered people's homes, and many eyewitness accounts identified actual Rangers as the persons who had shot at unarmed civilians. Victims also charged that several Texas Rangers had raped women.[37] Jones's minority report disputed the main commission's findings, reporting that the Rangers killed civilians only in self-defense. Hatch's testimony, however, questioned the truthfulness of Jones's report. When Hatch examined the bodies of the murder victims, Jones's explanation did not hold up. It was false that Mexicans were shot because they were resisting arrest, since the victims' bodies indicated that they had been shot at close range in the head, face, or back.

In the report, Hatch's testimony became one of the most damaging eyewitness accounts against several Rangers. Hatch reported that he arrived on December 23, 1877, at around nine or ten in the morning and observed scenes of violence and terror:

On approaching Socorro on the morning of the 23d of December, 1877, about 9 or 10 O'clock I heard sharp desultory firing, rode rapidly into the town with an orderly, found armed men (citizens) rallying rapidly, women and children fleeing to the opposite bank of the river. Finding also the justice of the peace, learned from him that the Texas Rangers were killing residents of the village . . . I then met the sheriff of the county, Charles Kerber, who informed me that the men killed about the town were killed resisting arrest, and learned that two men were killed, two wounded, and one woman shot through the lungs.

On approaching Ysleta found two dead men . . . This led me to examine the men carefully. One had some five or six-bullet holes in his head, shot through the hat-band; the other was shot in the forehead and in the side. So near was the shot in the side it was evident the gun had been near his clothing.

I was then assured in my own mind that these prisoners were killed without necessity. . . . I then denounced this inhumanity in no measured terms, and informed the sheriff it was his duty to arrest the murderers immediately; that the troops were sent there to assist the civil authorities in enforcing order and making arrest; that atrocities of this nature would not be for a moment tolerated. The sheriff did not arrest the parties who committed the murders or take any further notice of the matter.[38]

In the final report, the commissioners added that the Rangers had tried to intimidate witnesses during the investigation. Military officers reported that most Mexican civilians refused to testify because the Rangers had threatened to harm them if they did. The same complaint was raised by two Americans. Boyle Leachy, the tax assessor, testified that a Ranger called McDonald or McDaniel told him that he would kill him if he did not stop talking to Colonel Hatch.[39] George Zwitzers, a clerk in Socorro, was threatened, and he testified that he saw Leachy being threatened by a Ranger.

Major Jones's report countered the commission's findings and instead accused the troops from Fort Davis of corruption and incompetence. Based on his investigation, it was the soldiers under Captain Blair who had pillaged the villages and stolen the wine and tobacco. Because of Captain Blair's failure to control his men, Sheriff Kerber was left to deal with the disorder. The sheriff had done his best to protect the civilians against the looting, but he did not have enough men to arrest them.[40] Jones concluded by asking that Congress dismiss the commissioners' final report because the investigation violated the political autonomy of the State of

US military post, El Paso, 1880-1890, originally the Juan María Ponce de León Ranch, built 1849

Texas. President Hayes had abused his power and violated the jurisdictional division between the federal government and the state.[41]

In the aftermath of the commission's final report, Congress reopened Fort Bliss and kept the El Paso District under federal oversight. Fort Bliss was founded in 1854, but had been closed during Reconstruction. Several warrants were issued for the arrest of men who had committed the worst atrocities against civilians, but no one was arrested. Warrants were also issued for the six Mexicans who were concluded to have led the civilian attacks, but they fled to Mexico and, like the rest, did not stand trial.

Unfortunately, federal oversight of El Paso was ineffective, since Governor Hubbard increased the number of Rangers assigned to police the area. Hubbard commissioned Captain Tays and Sheriff Kerber to find the Mexicans who had led the Salt War riots. The pursuit of the alleged Mexican bandits continued until 1881. In the end, the salt lake fees were reinstituted, but lawsuits over who owned the land lasted for years. The Pacific Railway Company challenged Zimpleman's claim over the salt lakes, charging that the land was part of a grant given to the company by the State of Texas. Eventually, Texas declared the salt lakes to be public land open for redistribution.[42]

In retrospect, the federal government's inadequate oversight of the El Paso affair reflects the changing political atmosphere of the nation. At the time, most states favored less federal intervention and supported state control. Reconstruction had ended with the election of President Hayes

San Antonio Street, El Paso, late 1882

Texas Rangers, El Paso, 1896

Old Fort Bliss, at Hart's Mill, late 1800s

in the hotly disputed presidential race in 1876, and southern states were therefore generally left free from federal intervention.

As a result, matters worsened for Mexican Americans in Texas. News reports confirmed an escalation of attacks against Mexicans along the US-Mexico border.[43] In 1877, a series of articles in the *New York Times* reported that the Texas Rangers often did not defend Mexicans against vigilantes who took matters into their own hands. Over one hundred Mexicans were attacked and lynched by thugs hired by Anglo-American ranchers in the latter half of that year.[44] South Texas became particularly vulnerable to the authority that land barons exerted over the economy and the political life of the region. They had the money to hire men to pursue their enemies, and the political clout to convince Texas Rangers to detain and, if necessary, kill Mexicans suspected of stealing cattle. These victims were not given trials or any other form of due process.

Railroads, Land Barons, and Mexican Migration

During Reconstruction, the Texas Legislature began a statewide project to improve the state's transportation infrastructure. Cities and towns throughout Texas were to be connected by rail. The construction of railways in the United States had stopped during the Civil War and through the first years of Reconstruction. State legislatures and the federal government offered companies enormously generous land grants to build rail lines. In Texas, the legislature purchased or obtained through eminent domain the land that railroad companies identified as preferred sites for development. By 1890, investors had financed 8,709 miles of track throughout Texas—an enormous achievement, since before Reconstruction the state had only 711 miles.[45] Abuses accompanied this building spree. When laying track, railroad companies had the authority to appropriate private property, and once in possession, they sometimes turned around and sold the acreage instead of building on it. The construction of railways across the country turned railroad executives into land barons.

The main railroad investors in South Texas were Uriah Lott, Richard King, and Mifflin Kenedy. From 1876 to 1879, they built 162 miles of track connecting interior counties to the coast and to the Mexican border. A few years later, their company laid track connecting South Texas to San Antonio, Galveston, and Houston, and those cities became the main hubs connecting Texas to other parts of the United States.[46] The companies received grants so large that they sold off unneeded land.[47] Soon other Anglo-American entrepreneurs replicated the economic projects the railway investors had started. The King family had proved that great wealth could be made in cattle ranching. Richard King gradually obtained, through purchase, intimidation, and government concessions, 614,000 acres of land in South Texas, and Mifflin Kenedy acquired nearly 400,000 acres in Cameron and Hidalgo Counties.[48]

Wealthy Anglo-American cattle ranchers were accustomed to fencing their property, while Mexicans preferred the open range. When Anglo entrepreneurs acquired vast tracts of land, they fenced their property, making it very difficult for small- and mid-scale ranchers to take their herds to the local watering holes, since they could no longer cut across their neighbors' property.[49] For many farmers, this ended the open range and devastated their source of income. Mexicans retaliated by cutting fences, but were met with a harsh response.

Throughout Texas, small-scale farmers lost their property to railway corporations or land investors in the same way. In 1884, wealthy land barons, including King and Kenedy, successfully lobbied the state legislature to pass a law making fence cutting a felony.[50] Within a few years of the passage of the law, many farmers and ranchers were forced out of business because of the difficulty of feeding and watering their animals. In South Texas, approximately 50 percent of the Mexican stock herders switched to full-time farming or entered other occupations.[51]

The railway system contributed to the enormous population growth of South Texas and El Paso County. As corporations and land barons sold their surplus land, Anglo-Americans moved in to buy cheap land. In El Paso County and many South Texas counties, the population more than doubled from 1870 to 1890. As the railway system expanded and a great deal of land became available for purchase, Texas's population grew from 819,899 to 2,235,523 (an increase of 173 percent), South Texas counties increased from 40,136 to 107,457 (168 percent growth), and El Paso County grew from 3,671 to 15,676 (327 percent growth; see appendix 3.1).[52]

In 1883, El Paso County's population boomed after it was connected by railway to South Texas and to Mexican border cities. Within a couple of years, track was laid connecting El Paso to New Mexico and California, and the region continued to increase in population.[53] This boom had devastating effects on Ysleta after the Texas and Pacific Railway Company sold its land to newcomers. By 1890, the people of Ysleta had lost most of their land, retaining only sixty-six acres.[54]

In South Texas, a great deal of land became available for sale when many Mexican Americans were unable to pay their land taxes during the last decade of the nineteenth century. The region's economic troubles were caused by environmental catastrophes. In the period of 1885–1887, a cycle of drought and blizzards hit South Texas, driving many Mexicans out of ranching and destroying their crops.[55] Economically devastated, many families that could not afford to pay their land taxes or support themselves sold their property to land barons at very low prices. The new owners sold the land to families from the Northeast who had heard cheap land was available in South Texas.

The railway system benefited Anglo-American land barons in other ways. In 1881, King, Kenedy, and Lott became the first US entrepreneurs to obtain a contract to construct railroad stations connecting Mexico and the United States. From 1881 to 1884, their corporations and others laid track connecting central and northern Mexico to Texas.[56] The first branches entering US soil were constructed near the homes of Texas land barons, which served them well. They had an outlet to move their commodities from farm to market quickly, and a way to move people from Mexico to the United States just as easily. The railroads allowed landowners to acquire a cheap labor force: workers escaping Mexico's political instability.

Toward the end of the nineteenth century, Mexicans began entering the United States in large numbers. They were migrating in search of work because of the economic and political crisis caused by the Porfirio Díaz administration. Díaz became president of Mexico in 1876 and changed the nation from a democratic republic into a political dictatorship that gave the masses few political rights. He initiated a modernization program that reorganized Mexico's land system. Millions of acres were transferred from private owners to railroad corporations and Mexican elites. The rationale was that only the wealthy could make land productive. US railroad corporations, including ones in Texas, received millions of acres for surveying and laying track in Mexico. This was done in partial payment for constructing the railway system. Mexico's Land Act of 1883 led to the appropriation of ranchland owned by thousands of small-scale farmers. Under the law, corporations were hired to survey Mexico's public land, and in lieu of payment, they received one-eighth of the land surveyed; for a few cents an acre, they were given the option of purchasing more land. Within a few years of the law's passage, one-fifth of Mexico's land, 68 million acres, was transferred to foreign corporations and Mexico's ruling class.[57]

For Mexican landowners whose land was subject to a claim by a railroad company, their only recourse was to seek justice in the courts. But the Díaz administration had appointed most of the judges in Mexico, and they were there to help fulfill the president's modernization program. Unsurprisingly, many Mexicans lost their land when they appealed to the courts. Their deeds were nullified, and the corporations' claims upheld. When Mexicans found themselves without land or a source of income, many chose to move north. Mexican migration to the United States increased radically during the development of the American and Mexican railway systems. In 1870, 42,435 Mexican immigrants resided in the United States, and by 1890 their numbers had nearly doubled, to 77,853.[58] Over 66 percent of Mexican immigrants resided in Texas, mostly in El Paso and South Texas counties. The exodus of poor Mexicans served Texas land barons well, since it coincided with the expansion of their estates.

Declining Political Representation

As the Anglo-American population increased in settlements founded by Mexican Americans' ancestors, the governance of the counties and cities came into the hands of the newcomers. In San Antonio, La Bahía, and Victoria, Mexicans lost political control immediately after Texas independence, and in El Paso after the Mexican-American War. In South Texas, Mexican Americans were able to elect city council representatives until the late 1890s, but lost political control of the judicial system and most positions in county government. Only in Webb, Zapata, and Starr Counties did this not occur.[59] At the state level, only one Mexican American,

Thomas A. Rodriguez, representing District 90 in South Texas, remained in office during this time. Nonetheless, Mexican Americans remained an important sector of the electorate. Anglo-Americans running for office needed voters, and Mexican Americans were an important constituency when elections were close. This was particularly important in congressional elections, particularly in District 11, which covered all of South Texas and a few coastal counties. Whoever ran for that seat needed the Mexican vote. The significance of the Mexican American vote increased when Mexican immigration more than doubled during the late nineteenth century and many immigrants and their adult sons became eligible to vote.

In 1896, however, a social movement began in Texas to politically disenfranchise Mexican voters. A third party, the People's Party, formed an alliance with the Republican Party to challenge Democratic rule.[60] The Republican Party by this time had reorganized in Texas, and most liberal Republicans had left the state or joined the Democratic Party if they wanted to pursue a political career. The Republican Party had become highly conservative; most chapters did not accept Black members and supported policies that adversely impacted Mexican communities.[61]

The People's Party decided that reducing the number of Mexican-origin voters would allow it to gain the congressional seat that represented South Texas, as well as many county offices in areas where Mexicans were the swing vote.[62] Thus, the alliance between the People's Party and the Republican Party thrust Mexican-origin people into the center of a deeply disturbing social movement for the sake of taking power away from the Democratic Party. The plan was to argue that all people of Mexican-origin were in fact Indians, who could not, under the Fourteenth Amendment and federal naturalization laws, be US citizens or vote. The second disenfranchisement argument rested on the logic that treaty provisions, when in conflict with US laws, became null and void. The Treaty of Guadalupe Hidalgo had extended citizenship to the annexed population, and the Naturalization Treaty of 1868 allowed Mexican immigrants, irrespective of race, the privilege of acquiring US citizenship via naturalization. But if Mexicans were legally Indians, as members of the People's Party and the Republican Party claimed, then these parts of the treaties were without effect.[63]

The movement to politically disenfranchise people of Mexican descent began on May 11, 1896, when members of the Republican Party and the People's Party filed in the Western District Court of San Antonio a petition to stop Mexican-origin people from voting.[64] The petition culminated in a court trial held a few days later to determine whether Mexicans like Ricardo Rodríguez, the defendant, were Indians. Because of the complexity of the case, and the research required to address its questions, Judge T. S. Maxey did not render his final decision until nearly a year later.

On May 3, 1897, in *In re Rodriguez*, Judge Maxey offered his ruling. He concluded that although Mexicans were not white in the ethnological sense, Mexican-origin people did not come under the laws applied to Native Americans, because they were a detribalized people.[65] Maxey stated that in regard to Rodríguez and Mexicans like him: "If the strict scientific classification of the Anthropologists should be adopted, he would probably not be classed as white. . . . After a careful and patient investigation of the question discussed, the Court is of opinion that, whatever may be the status of the applicant viewed solely from the standpoint of the Ethnologists, he is embraced within the spirit and intent of our laws."[66] Maxey added that a review of treaty law indicated that the US government had never intended to deny US citizenship to the populations acquired from Spanish and Mexican territories. For more than a century, he stated, the United States had enacted treaties with the governments of Mexico and Spain, and since gaining Louisiana and Florida, the US government had not denied the annexed populations US citizenship. The Treaty of Guadalupe Hidalgo and the Naturalization Treaty of 1868 demonstrated the intention of Congress to extend US citizenship to Mexican people brought into the United States via territorial acquisition and immigration. According to Maxey, the naturalization laws of the United States, which allowed only whites to apply for US citizenship, had been waived for Mexican immigrants under the Treaty of 1868.

Without a doubt, the *Rodríguez* case was a monumental advance for Mexican Americans' political rights. They would continue to vote and remain an important part of the Texas electoral process. Judge Maxey not only upheld the US citizenship of people of Mexican descent born in this country, but also concluded that even if Mexican immigrants were not white, they should be allowed to apply for US citizenship. This was a privilege that at that time was denied to Asians and Native Americans, but had been extended to Black immigrants in 1870, a few years after the Civil War.[67] US citizenship, however, did not protect Mexican Americans from other forms of discrimination.

State-Ordered Segregation, the *Slaughter-House Cases*, and the *Civil Rights Cases*

Since Texas independence, Mexican Americans had experienced different forms of social discrimination on account of their ethnicity and mixed racial heritage. A new era, however, began toward the end of Reconstruction when the US Supreme Court's ruling in the *Slaughter-House Cases* (1873) gave state legislatures the authority to determine what actions constituted violations of a person's civil rights. The ruling was intended to unite the country and reduce federal and state tensions over the civil rights policies that could be adopted by the states. Congressional representatives were bitterly divided over what political rights the Fourteenth Amendment had given African Americans, and in turn they disagreed whether these rights violated the civil rights of white people. For Mexican Americans, the Court's decision ushered in a period when states had the authority to pass segregation legislation affecting them. In the aftermath of the *Slaughter-House Cases* ruling, the Texas Legislature and state courts passed laws giving clubs, organizations, and businesses the authority to refuse entry or services to any person, for any reason. Mexican Americans could be denied the use of public spaces if those in charge of the accommodations wished it.

In February 1873, the US Supreme Court heard the appeal of a group of cases from Louisiana consolidated as the *Slaughter-House Cases* (1873). The Court's ruling reversed the liberal direction that the nation was moving in, that is, toward equalizing the political rights of all citizens. The justices ruled that state legislatures had the power to determine what social practices in everyday life constituted discriminatory actions and violated a person's constitutional rights. This opinion therefore allowed the state legislatures to pass laws segregating racial minorities from whites.

The *Slaughter-House Cases* involved a dispute between a group of white butchers in New Orleans and the legislature of Louisiana. When the Louisiana Supreme Court ruled against the butchers, they appealed to the US Supreme Court. The butchers' arguments rested in part on the Privileges or Immunities Clause of the Fourteenth Amendment, ratified just five years earlier.[68] Throughout the United States, courts disagreed on the meaning of the Fourteenth Amendment, with some ruling that it applied only to political rights associated with citizenship, while others argued that the spirit of the amendment was more extensive.

The lawsuit centered on whether the Thirteenth and Fourteenth Amendments protected the political rights of citizens to practice their professions without interference from state governments. Butchers in New Orleans sued when the Louisiana Legislature passed a law forcing butchers to move south of the city and putting all slaughterhouses under the control of a single corporation. Previously, butchers had been allowed to slaughter within the city limits. The stench made life miserable for the residents of

New Orleans, blood and entrails polluted streets and waterways, and discarded animal parts were suspected of contributing to cholera outbreaks. When the Louisiana Supreme Court ruled in favor of the legislative action, the butchers appealed.

On April 14, 1873, in a 5–4 decision, the justices offered their interpretation of the Thirteenth and Fourteenth Amendments and destroyed the legal basis for federal intervention in most civil rights disputes involving racial minorities. The Court ruled that the amendments were not designed to protect a person's profession. The Thirteenth Amendment had been specifically designed to prohibit the enslavement of African Americans and prevent the indentured servitude of Mexicans and Asians. The justices wrote: "While the thirteenth article of amendment was intended primarily to abolish African slavery, it equally forbids Mexican peonage or the Chinese coolie trade, when they amount to slavery or involuntary servitude; and the use of the word 'servitude' is intended to prohibit all forms of involuntary slavery of whatever class or name."[69] The Court ruled that the Fourteenth Amendment likewise did not apply to the professions, since it had been designed to solely protect a person's political rights as a US citizen.[70]

Although the opinion of the justices was morally meritorious because it upheld the authority of a progressive biracial state legislature that had nullified the Black codes passed by the recently disbanded Confederate government, the Court set a dangerous precedent.[71] By limiting federal intervention in the affairs of the states, the ruling gave state legislatures the authority to regulate most aspects of a person's daily activities and empowered governmental officials to mobilize the police and marshals to enforce state laws. The justices concluded that the federal government could not intervene in state affairs unless a person's liberty was being endangered, or a person was being denied the right to peaceably assemble or to possess property of any kind.[72]

Perhaps most importantly, the justices ruled that state legislatures were the governing bodies empowered by the US Constitution to determine what represented a violation of a person's civil rights.[73] The ability of the states to do this placed racial minorities in a precarious position; at the time, most states did not consider racial segregation to be discriminatory or violative of a person's civil rights. Segregation was considered a normal practice necessary to maintain social order and prevent race wars at the local level. The federal government could intervene in civil rights disputes only when a state violated political rights associated with citizenship. After the *Slaughter-House Cases* ruling, state assemblies went far beyond passing segregation legislation aimed at keeping African Americans apart from whites.[74] They passed exclusionary laws discriminating against Jews, Mexican Americans, Native Americans, and Asian Americans.

In an attempt to protect racial minorities from the impact of the *Slaughter-House Cases* ruling, on March 1, 1875, the Republican-controlled Congress passed a civil rights act to nullify the authority the Court had given the states to pass laws segregating public accommodations. In 1883, the US Supreme Court heard a challenge to the act, and the justices affirmed the right of states to pass segregation legislation. In an 8–1 decision, the justices ruled in the *Civil Rights Cases* (1883) that denying persons of color access to or privileges in hotels, inns, theaters, and other public accommodations was not a violation of federal law, because neither the Bill of Rights nor the Fourteenth Amendment protected such rights of access. The justices did, however, stipulate that when it came to public transportation, people of color could not be denied service if they had purchased a ticket. Conveyance companies were to provide services according to states' racial policies. According to the Court, segregation was legal because not all types of discrimination could be considered unconstitutional. The justices argued that since the inception of the United States, discrimination had taken place between people of different social classes, and such actions had not been considered violations of the US Constitution. American law, therefore, could not be used to force private citizens to provide accommodations to persons of color. In sum, the Court refused to force whites to interact with people of color, because doing so amounted to reverse discrimination. (Although the opinion did not use that phrase, this was the spirit of the ruling.) The enforcement of segregation laws, however, was not a violation of the civil rights of people of color, because freedom from segregation was not a fundamental right.

After the *Civil Rights Cases* ruling, Congress chose not to pass legislation negating the Court's ruling. By then, southern Democrats controlled at least one chamber of Congress, as they did for the rest of the century.

Texas and the Passage of Exclusion Laws

Across the nation, segregation laws were adopted by state legislatures. In the South, they replaced the Black codes that had previously been used to deny Black citizens entry into public spaces reserved for whites.[75] The provision of separate accommodations to Blacks was touted as a progressive improvement, since they were now being given services. In Texas, the legislature began passing segregation laws targeting African Americans in 1876. African Americans were to be schooled apart from white students, and the segregation of public transportation, including separate waiting areas in stations, was required by law.[76] A few years later, the courts and the state legislature began passing segregation laws that applied also to Mexican Americans. These new exclusionary laws focused on the rights of business owners and the representatives of organizations. By wording the laws in that way, Texas legislators avoided legal challenges based on possible constitutional violations. Separating whites from Blacks was not against the law, but separating some members of the white race from other whites could be considered discrimination and a violation of a person's constitutional rights. Mexican Americans, therefore, could not be named as a targeted group because many of them were phenotypically white. Likewise, they could not be segregated as a group based on their national origin, because no such federal statute or US Supreme Court ruling allowed it. Segregation laws aimed at Mexican Americans, therefore, needed to be written to allow for their exclusion without mentioning racial or ethnic criteria.

In 1884, the Texas Supreme Court handed down the first ruling that empowered organizations to exclude any person from membership. Mexicans were not named in the case, but the privilege given by the court to clubs and organizations established a practice that would evolve in Texas and have detrimental effects on Mexicans. The court ruled in *Manning v. San Antonio Club* that "clubs or societies, whether religious, literary or social, have the right to make their own rules regarding the admission and exclusion of their members."[77] According to the judges, a denial of admission (or as in this case, the expulsion of a member) was not a violation of federal or state law because governments should not interfere in the social intercourse of people in places of pleasure or amusement. Although the judges did not mention business owners as members of a protected class, the spirit of the ruling was later interpreted to include them.[78]

When the court issued its ruling on behalf of the San Antonio Club, banning Mexicans from public accommodations had already begun in San Antonio.[79] A year earlier, Mexicans had been banned from the dance platforms of the San Pedro Springs Municipal Park after its developer, Frederick Kerble, obtained a lease from the San Antonio City Council. Under the lease agreement, he was required to build amusement facilities and pathways in the park. Kerble chose to limit the space where Mexicans were allowed. By this time, a more general ethnic-separate recreational activity pattern had emerged in San Antonio. Anglo-Americans no longer attended Mexican religious festivities nor the annual Mexican Independence fiesta, a practice that had been common before 1860.[80] Mexicans were also required to obtain a permit to organize public events using public space, a practice that had started five years earlier after the city council passed an ordinance to prohibit Mexicans from organizing *fandangos* (a fiesta centered on Spanish dance moves using castanets and tambourines). This type of festivity was considered a public nuisance and morally unacceptable.

In 1907, the Texas Legislature expanded its support of de jure segregation when it passed a statewide law stipulating that public amusement services could be segregated. The intention of the law was to clarify the political rights of individuals to require segregation in public accommodations. Under a 1907 law titled "Theaters, Etc.—Prohibiting Discrimination Between Persons Desiring to Lease Same," the legislature stipulated that business owners, managers, and lessees who offered public amusement services in theaters, playhouses, opera houses, and similar types of buildings had the right to refuse service to "objectionable characters" and to provide separate accommodations ("assign seats to patrons").[81] The act did not define "objectionable character." For Mexican Americans, *Manning* and the 1907 law became the legal bases to segregate them without naming their ethnicity directly.

The Spatial Logic of Racism: Home Rule and Residential Zoning Laws

In 1913, legislative representatives revised the Texas Constitution and authorized cities and towns of 5,000 residents or more to adopt home rule charters.[82] The charters allowed municipalities to pass city ordinances to govern the behavior of residents and to zone neighborhoods into districts restricted for manufacturing, commercial businesses, and residential use.[83] This authority was used to intensify the racial segregation of African Americans and Mexican Americans, since the charters gave city leaders the power to establish boundaries separating white neighborhoods from those of racial minorities. This boundary-making policy became the intellectual foundation for zoning plans that sequestered manufacturing and hazardous commercial businesses in racial minority neighborhoods.[84] Although different policies were enacted for African American and Mexican American neighborhoods, the intent and outcome of the ordinances were the same. For African Americans, their residential districting necessitated a relocation plan because their homes were scattered throughout the cities and often located near vacant public lots. For Mexican Americans, home rule charters primarily formalized a de facto segregation practice established following the Texas Revolution and the Mexican-American War. District-ing became a way of officially designating the Mexican side of a city. Mexican Americans were already concentrated in the old sections of most cities as a result of social conventions.[85] As cities grew in the twentieth century, districting led to consolidating minorities in their own ethnic districts or in biracial or biethnic African American and Mexican American districts.

Before home rule charters, the segregation of Mexican American neighborhoods began with de facto housing patterns.[86] De facto residential segregation is defined as the separation of people based on the use of social norms rather than legal ordinances.[87] The de facto segregation of Mexican American neighborhoods began after Texas independence when Anglo-American settlers moved out of their colonies and obtained land claims in Mexican pueblos. As the number of Anglo-Americans increased in San Antonio, El Paso, Nacogdoches, and Victoria, they constructed new neighborhoods for themselves. The older sections of the cities where Mexican Americans lived came to be known as the Mexican wards or the Mexican towns. For example, in 1845, when Texas was annexed by the United States, 64 percent of the acreage in San Antonio was owned by Spanish-surnamed people; by 1860, that figure had fallen to 7.8 percent.[88] Many new neighborhoods were constructed throughout San Antonio, and the Anglo-American population spread outside the Mexican quarters.

A similar pattern took place in El Paso County. Around 1900, an influx of Anglo-American newcomers moved in. By 1915, Mexican Americans constituted only 52 percent of the city's population, and they became concentrated in the older settlements.[89] Socorro and San Elizario, located south of downtown El Paso, became exclusively Mexican American, and Ysleta became known at the "Barrio de los Indios."[90] The area that today is downtown El Paso became ethnically mixed, with Anglo-Americans establishing residential niches for themselves in the northern sector. Many Mexican American families continued to live in the downtown area, but were pushed toward the southeast of downtown and along the Texas-Mexico border.[91] Anglo-American elites lived in the northeastern neighborhoods, and lower-income whites in the northwest part of the city.

The second de facto segregation pattern also began after Texas independence. Anglo-Americans established new cities in Texas, and as the economy prospered, elites needed workers and employment became available. Mexican-descent people migrated to such cities as Houston and Dallas.[92] Mexican Americans formed new neighborhoods near their places of employment, and were hired to work on farms or ranches, or in sawmills and stockyards.

Mexican immigrants crossing the Rio Grande by car, 1910

The de facto residential concentration of people of Mexican descent intensified during the Mexican Revolution (1910–1920).[93] Immigration from Mexico to Texas had accelerated during the late 1870s when President Díaz's modernization program led to the transfer of property from small-scale farmers to railroad corporations. Immigration increased when Díaz lowered the minimum daily wage from 35 centavos in 1876 to 15 centavos in 1910.[94] Díaz's policies eventually became intolerable, and the Mexican Revolution broke out on November 20, 1910. A steady stream of Mexican refugees flowed into Texas, leading to the massive growth of Mexican American neighborhoods. In Houston, for example, Mexican migration started in the late 1800s, and Mexicans settled near the sugarcane fields they worked. In 1900, 500 Mexican-origin people lived in Houston. As the city's economy prospered, many jobs became available and thousands of Mexicans entered new occupations. They moved onto the outskirts of Anglo-American and African American neighborhoods located near the shipyards, gas fields, and oil fields where they worked.[95] By 1930, the number of Mexican immigrants and their native-born children in Houston had reached 15,000.[96] This demographic growth paralleled migration patterns across Texas. In 1900, Mexican immigrants in Texas numbered 71,062, and by 1920 they had increased to 251,827 (see appendix 3.2).[97]

The consolidation and residential segregation of African Americans were part of a national process intended to increase the property values

Mexican Immigrants crossing the Rio Grande by canoe, 1910

of white neighborhoods—and of public property adjacent to former Black residential clusters—and to regulate urban growth. In 1910, state legislatures authorized cities to segregate African Americans in designated wards. Baltimore became the first city to enact ordinances for race-specific residential-districting zones.[98] Within a few years, Norfolk, Richmond, Atlanta, Birmingham, and Winston-Salem had replicated Baltimore's zoning ordinance. Municipal governments in Texas began relocating Blacks to separate districts in 1916. Dallas was the first city in Texas to prohibit African Americans and whites from living in the same neighborhoods.[99] Before the adoption of the Dallas ordinance, Blacks had been allowed to purchase property near white neighborhoods or in white working-class neighborhoods, where they formed small residential clusters.[100]

Once Dallas instituted a residential zoning law segregating African Americans, the League of Texas Municipalities gave city governments advice on how to pass similar laws. In 1917, T. C. Russell, the chairman of the league, supported the passage of residential segregation ordinances similar to the one in Dallas. He saw such measures as necessary for regulating urban growth. But because each city's racial composition was different, municipal officers needed advice on how to implement lawful ordinances. Russell therefore asked league members to lobby the state legislature to pass statewide segregation laws in order to protect cities from retaliatory lawsuits.[101]

Indeed, state laws allowing cities to pass segregation ordinances took care of any city's potential legal liability. In 1927, the Texas Legislature began to pass laws to support cities' segregation plans. Texas had received guidance from the US Department of Commerce on how to develop segregation ordinances without violating the US Constitution, namely, by clarifying the powers of home-rule charters. Different strategies were implemented to keep African Americans and Mexican Americans apart from whites. The Dallas racial-districting plan became the model applied to African Americans. For Mexican Americans, the use of housing covenants prohibiting them from living in certain districts became the most effective way to maintain them in their ethnic neighborhoods; in addition, city officials allowed Mexican Americans to live in African American neighborhoods.

Herbert Hoover, who was the US secretary of commerce, finalized the revisions of the Standard State Zoning Enabling Act in 1926, which was designed to give state legislatures guidance on how to write laws requiring cities to enact zoning regulations, including residential segregation. Cities were to zone land into residential, commercial, and industrial use to plan for future urban growth. Hoover acknowledged that adopting statewide residential segregation laws would be complicated, but nonetheless, he advised doing it.[102] Following the secretary's directive, agents from the Commerce Department advised state legislatures to pass statewide zoning-enabling acts and avoid using terms such as "segregation" or "exclusion." It was best to employ phrases such as "regulate and restrict" when referring to policies intended to separate groups into racial residential districts. The model statute made this explicit: "'*regulate and restrict*': This phrase is considered sufficiently all-embracing. Nothing will be gained by adding such terms as 'exclude,' 'segregate,' 'limit,' 'determine.'"[103] Such language could not be construed to be discriminatory and could not be legally challenged. The Commerce Department also advised state officials that it was necessary for state legislatures to enforce zoning ordinances by authorizing municipalities to impose fines or imprisonment penalties for violations of the law.

In 1927, the Texas Legislature adopted the recommendations of the US Department of Commerce and passed a series of laws affirming the authority of municipal officers to pass city ordinances under home rule authority. This authority was extended to cities and towns with fewer than five thousand residents. During the regular session of the Fortieth Texas Legislature, representatives passed a series of statewide zoning laws. Some of the laws were designed to regulate and restrict the platting of land, the construction of buildings, and street development (SB 270, SB 277), while other laws were instituted to formalize segregation (HB 87, SB 275).

On March 16, 1927, the legislature passed Senate Bill 275, requiring local governments in Texas to segregate Blacks and whites in separate residential districts.[104] It included provisions designed to forestall litigation, such as might arise from the US Supreme Court ruling in *Buchanan v. Warley* (1917).[105] This ruling prohibited city governments from passing ordinances to forbid the sale of property to Blacks, in violation of freedom of contract. The Texas Legislature mandated that local officials follow federal law, but still used Senate Bill 275 to keep whites and Blacks separated. *Buchanan v. Warley* did not stipulate that a customer had to be allowed to live in the house purchased, or that private citizens were prohibited from refusing to sell their homes to potential buyers based on race, religion, or national origin.[106] To ensure that Texans complied with Senate Bill 275, local officials were instructed to withhold building permits to whites and Blacks who planned to reside in neighborhoods that did not correspond to their race, and to assist private citizens who did not want to sell property to members of racial minority groups.[107]

Although Senate Bill 275 did not name Mexican Americans as a group to be segregated in separate districts, sections 3 and 4 of the law allowed city officers to segregate them by other means. Section 4 required officials to enforce housing-covenant restrictions instituted by corporations or individuals. Private citizens were allowed to use race, national origin, or religion to prohibit Blacks and Mexican Americans from living in certain neighborhoods.[108] A year earlier, the US Supreme Court had ruled in *Corrigan v. Buckley* (1926) that it was not unconstitutional to use housing covenants to prohibit different races from living in a residential tract as long as the restrictions were made by private citizens.[109] Such exclusionary policies could also be based on national origin or religion.[110]

Section 3 of the law allowed local officials to include Mexican Americans as a group that could reside in Black districts. Officials were authorized to define what characteristics constituted the "negro and the white races," and to determine which communities could be considered white. Section 3 thus allowed municipal authorities to create districts composed of Black and Mexican American residents based on local norms. Municipal officials could decide whether Mexican American communities were to be treated as white or nonwhite, and thereby determine where they could live.

To give local governments further authority to segregate whites from African Americans and Mexican Americans, the legislature enacted House Bill 87, "City Zoning Law—Authorizing Cities and Incorporated Villages to Pass Zoning Regulations." Cities were empowered to divide existing neighborhoods into districts and determine the future planning of those districts.[111] This zoning law was particularly useful in cities that had large African American and Mexican American communities. Even if Mexican Americans and African Americans lived in different neighborhoods, city officials could place these neighborhoods in one district and force residents' children to attend segregated schools. In cities where African Americans and Mexican Americans constituted a significant percentage of the population, such Black-Mexican districts emerged. Dallas, Houston, Austin, Fort Worth, Baytown, and Nacogdoches contained Black–Mexican American districts or triracial districts where whites lived apart.[112] This act permitted the zoning of commercial and manufacturing industries within these residential districts.

In Austin, Using Different Strategies to Segregate African Americans and Mexican Americans

By the turn of the twentieth century, African Americans were Austin's largest racial minority, constituting 20 percent of the population, while Mexican Americans were numerically small—approximately 335 residents.[113] Both populations were scattered throughout the city and the rest of Travis County. In 1927, after Senate Bill 275 and House Bill 87 became law, Austin officials began to relocate African American neighborhoods to the eastern area of the city. Mexican Americans were gradually restricted to the same side of town by the use of housing covenants. It was not illegal to confine Mexican Americans to the East Side, since city officials chose not to treat them as white.

In 1927, city officials hired the Koch and Fowler Consulting Engineering Firm to create a master plan for the future growth of Austin. The firm had developed such plans for many of the largest cities in Texas. The plan was to include zoning recommendations for the locations of segregated neighborhoods and to identify suitable areas for future industrial and hazardous waste plants.[114] The consultants Oscar Koch and James Fowler completed a comprehensive analysis and advised city officials that the property values in predominantly white parts of Austin would increase considerably if African American neighborhoods were relocated to the East Side. The engineers claimed that Black neighborhoods were lowering value of both private and public land throughout Austin.[115] Koch and Fowler added that concentrating African Americans on the East Side would reduce the cost of building duplicate schools and parks for whites and Blacks throughout the city. As long as the relocation was done intelligently, addressing the city's

State of Texas }
County of Travis }

a. No lot shall be sold or leased to any Mexican or person of Negro blood, or to any corporation or firm composed of Negroes or Mexicans.

Travis Heights restrictive housing covenant, Austin, 1913

"race segregation problem" would not be found unconstitutional, since Black residents would be provided all of the necessary facilities and conveniences in their district. Koch and Fowler made reference to the spirit of the "separate but equal" doctrine, adding that as long as superficially equal facilities were provided, the proposed segregation would not be declared unconstitutional.[116] They wrote:

> At the last session of the Texas Legislature an enabling act was passed, permitting cities to control the nature of their growth through zoning. . . . Experience has shown that where a zoning ordinance is based upon the safety and health of the community and is broad and comprehensive in its requirements, there is very little chance of it being declared unconstitutional. . . . There has been considerable talk in Austin, as well as other cities, in regard to the race segregation problem.
>
> This problem cannot be solved legally under any zoning law known to us at present. Practically all attempts of such have been proven unconstitutional . . . It is our recommendation that the nearest approach to the solution of the race segregation problem will be the recommendation of this district as a negro district; and that all of the facilities and conveniences be provided the negroes in this district . . . We further recommend that the negro schools in this area be provided with ample and adequate playground space and facilities similar to the white schools of the city.[117]

Koch and Fowler also recommended that the city place its main industrial zone in the East Side, since doing so would enhance the property values in the rest of the city by clearing industrial waste and improving the beauty of the landscape. They projected that more warehouses and industry would be needed as the city grew, and to avoid creating visual blight, unpleasant buildings should be concentrated on the East Side. In 1928, the city adopted Koch and Fowler's plan and zoned half of the East Side as a mixed residential, industrial, and commercial area. It left the other half of the land, which was undeveloped, as a nonrestricted zone, allowing for future industrial projects to be built there as the city grew.[118]

By 1930, the size of the Mexican American population in Austin had grown tremendously. People of Mexican descent numbered 5,014, and African Americans 9,868.[119] Austin contained nearly half (10,225) the Mexican-origin residents of Travis County, and 62 percent (15,832) of the African Americans. The demographic growth of the Mexican American community was a result of the general influx of Mexicans entering Texas in the aftermath of the Mexican Revolution. After the revolution, political and economic problems continued to plague Mexico, causing Mexicans to search for employment in the United States.

By 1932, the segregation of African Americans was complete.[120] Their churches, schools, and stores had been relocated to the East Side, and new parks had been built for them. Within ten years, the Mexican American population had doubled in size, and they were also concentrated on the East Side, next to the African American neighborhoods.[121] East Avenue bound the East Side neighborhoods on the west, First Street on the south, Springdale Avenue on the east, and Seventh Street on the north. This demographic pattern did not occur by accident. Throughout Austin, restrictive housing covenants were used to prohibit Mexican Americans from living outside the East Side.[122] In 1934, the City of Austin conducted a study of home loan practices and found that mortgage companies did not approve loans for houses on the East Side if the applicants were white.[123] The East Side of Austin had been redlined as a district for Mexican and Black residents and zoned as a site for hazardous and industrial enterprises.[124]

Once Mexican Americans were confined to the East Side, the wide-scale segregation of minority students followed. In upcoming decades, the East Side became the home of hazardous-chemical storage tanks and the Holly Street Power Plant; Interstate 35 was built atop the former East Avenue.[125] In sum, Mexican Americans in Austin, as in most Texas cities, were not treated as part of the white population. Over the years, governmental officials rationalized the segregation of Mexican-origin people by a variety of excuses, not least by claiming that social class differences between Mexicans and Anglo-Americans were a natural cause of the separation. They shrugged off discriminatory business practices by claiming that business owners had the legal right to not serve Mexicans.

Texas's Triracial Schooling History

The passage in 1927 of state laws in Texas requiring segregated residential zoning happened during a period when states were expanding their public education systems. By the 1920s, the availability of public education was increasing throughout the country. Not wanting to lag behind the nation in this area, the Texas Legislature made adjustments to the state budget to improve the public schools. The resulting plan, however, required racial minorities to be schooled apart if they were to receive an education.

Texas's triracial school segregation system dates back to 1884, when a statewide funding system was established.[126] State officials were not concerned with educating most African American or Mexican American students, as special exemption policies allowed local officials to decide which students would receive an education. Under the Texas Constitution, the distribution of state funds was left to the governor and his educational commission.[127] State law did not require equitable school financing. Texas's public education system, like those in the rest of the United States, focused only on schooling from kindergarten through the eighth grade. Schooling past the eighth grade was uncommon, and it was left to parents to send their children to private academies.[128]

In the late nineteenth century, the legislature did not intend to offer schooling to all children and exempted many counties from the educational mandate.[129] Only large metropolitan areas were required to establish city or county school districts. But local officials did not have to establish schools in all residential areas.[130] County commissioners were given the option of sending local students to schools in other counties if they chose to share the cost of educating students rather than build new schools. Together, these provisions were designed to allow municipalities to opt out of establishing schools near minority neighborhoods.

The lack of schools in the fifty-five counties exempted from the statewide public school mandate overwhelmingly affected minority students. If parents in the exempted counties wanted to establish schools, they were required to file a petition with the state; otherwise, they would not receive any state funds.[131] Before their petition could be accepted, they had to obtain the approval of a county judge. Although the exempted counties were located across the state, they included nearly all the counties along the coast and most South Texas counties. These counties were heavily populated by residents of African and Mexican descent. The rest of the exempted counties were newly formed and sparsely populated; they were located in western and northern Texas. Thus, the legislature's school-by-petition policy placed onerous hurdles in front of minority parents and left the decision of educating Black and Mexican American students in the hands of Anglo-American county judges. In 1884, with the exception of Webb and Zapata Counties, all the exempted counties were controlled by Anglo-American judges, and they had the power to certify or reject the school petitions.[132] The legislature also made sure that parents in these counties would not run the schools. Schools formed by petition were not authorized to elect a school board. The county judge was in charge of managing the schools, distributing funds, drawing school

Judge Roy Bean, Langtry, Texas, in Val Verde County. Bean is emblematic of the powerful county judges who ruled the region with unquestioned authority.

neighborhood boundaries, and selecting parents to advise him on school policy.[133]

In 1909, when the demand for public schooling exploded in Texas, the state attorney general offered the opinion that it was unconstitutional for the state to allow some counties and cities not to establish schools.[134] The exemptions had created an unequal educational-access framework that denied some students schooling while concomitantly enforcing an unfair tax structure to fund the schools. The state required all men ages twenty-one to sixty to pay a school poll tax and imposed a twenty-cent tax on each $100 of property valuation, yet not all children had access to an education. Essentially, the attorney general stated that if residents were to be taxed, then all cities and counties had to provide access to schools.

To address this problem, the legislature approved a statewide multi-school districting system in which all children, regardless of the number of inhabitants in a county, would have access to a nearby school. Following the reforms of 1909, many new school districts were formed, and racial-minority children had more access to schools.[135] Many school districts expanded their curriculums past the eighth grade and constructed high schools.[136] The numerical growth of high schools in Texas followed a pattern seen across the United States. For example, in 1890 there were

2,526 public high schools nationwide; by 1910 the number had increased to 10,213.[137]

Regardless of the educational improvements, Annie Blanton Webb, the state superintendent of education, reported to the legislature in 1920 that additional reforms were needed. The legislature should require all counties to establish schools. She found that 50 percent of students in rural areas did not attend school because local city or county governments refused to build schools.[138] Webb also reported that more high schools were needed in communities where the majority of students were Mexican American. In El Paso, for example, one public high school served the entire county. In South Texas, the counties of Starr, Zapata, Jim Hogg, Kenedy, and McMullen did not have any high schools. Hidalgo, Cameron, and Nueces Counties each had three or more public high schools, which they shared with other counties. All other South Texas counties had one public high school that served the entire county. Of the eleven high schools in the city of San Antonio, only six were public, and the number of seats was insufficient.[139]

On November 2, 1926, the Texas Legislature completed the financial restructuring of Texas schools and significantly expanded the educational budget after voters approved the schooling plan. New high schools were to be built across Texas, and counties and cities needing more elementary schools were identified.[140] The state government increased its financial contribution to education, providing one-fourth of the revenue for the public school system. The legislature also chose to turn over to school boards the authority to draw school district boundaries and to locate and construct schools.

This local-control mandate reflected a legislative consensus to separate whites from racial minorities in schools as well as neighborhoods, since its adoption all but coincided with the passage of the 1927 residential zoning laws. Within a few months of passing the schooling district reforms, state legislators turned over to cities and counties the residential zoning of their districts.[141] Municipal and county governments could place African American and Mexican American neighborhoods in the same district, or create triracial districts that separated whites, Mexican Americans, and African Americans.[142] School boards could then use these residential district plans to draw school boundaries and assign students to specific neighborhood schools. The lack of state oversight over school district boundaries allowed for the educational separation of racial minorities from whites. State districting and zoning laws on the surface appeared to be racially neutral, but in the end negatively affected persons of color. Local officials, whether in municipal or county governments or on school boards, did not have to dis-close their reasoning for drawing district boundaries. As the urbanization of Texas increased in the following decades, the state legislature did not have to be concerned with being legally challenged for orchestrating the segregation of Mexican Americans, since it was local officials who were drawing the residential and school boundaries.

CHAPTER 4

Challenging Segregation, 1927–1948

This chapter examines why the State of Texas considered the social segregation of Mexican Americans an ordinary part of life. It begins by examining two landmark cases in which Texas courts ruled that it was not unconstitutional to segregate Mexican Americans. *Independent School District v. Salvatierra* (1930) illustrates how district zoning laws were used to segregate Mexican American students. *Terrell Wells Swimming Pool v. Rodriguez* (1944) explores exclusion laws applied to public accommodations and the state's application of these laws to Mexican Americans. In addition, the analysis examines a series of desegregation battles engaged in by Mexican American political activists. Their requests to the state government and the courts for equal treatment were denied, and Mexican Americans were told that the social distance between Anglo-Americans and themselves was the result of class differences, not racism.

The chapter closes with an overview of the national debate over segregation and the changing politics around the practice that began after the World War II. In Texas, Mexican American civil rights activists won their first school desegregation ruling in *Delgado v. Bastrop Independent School District* (1948) when they convinced a federal court that segregating Mexican Americans was unconstitutional.

Statewide School Segregation Adopted by Texas Courts

In 1930, Mexican Americans from Del Rio, Texas, solicited legal advice from an attorney named John Dodson when their children were removed from integrated elementary schools and placed in a separate school for Mexican students. Jesús Salvatierra led the parents' campaign against this unfair practice, and with Dodson's aid, they filed for an injunction to stop the segregation of their children. Judge Joseph Jones, Del Rio's district judge, heard the case and granted an injunction to temporarily stop the transfer of additional students to the Mexican school. The Fourth Court of Civil Appeals, in San Antonio, took the case after the Del Rio Independent School District appealed the injunction. While the court studied the case, Salvatierra sought the legal and financial support of a newly formed civil rights organization called the League of United Latin American Citizens (LULAC).

Three of LULAC's members were attorneys, and they joined Dodson to litigate the case. At that time, José T. Canales, Alonso S. Perales, and Manuel C. Gonzales were the only Mexican American attorneys practicing law in Texas.[1] Gonzales was the vice president of LULAC, and Canales and Perales were among the founders of the organization. The parents in Del Rio knew that this would be a difficult struggle but were not intimidated by the institutional bureaucracy they were up against. What ensued was a legal battle between white school board members, who asserted their authority to assign students to specific schools, and the Mexican American parents who demanded equal treatment. To explore the conflict that culminated in *Independent School District v. Salvatierra* (1930), it is necessary to first examine how the segregated school system began in Del Rio and expanded over the years. In Texas history, the *Salvatierra* case is of monumental significance because it set a legal precedent upholding the authority of city, county, and school officials to determine when Mexican American students could be segregated.

The city of Del Rio was originally part of the Spanish settlement of San Felipe, located on the US-Mexico border near the Mexican city of Acuña.[2] The name of San Felipe was changed to Del Rio after the village grew during the American period. In 1885, Del Rio became the principal municipality of the newly organized county of Val Verde in West Texas.[3] A few years later, several Anglo-American investors purchased property in Del Rio, established an irrigation system, and sold plots of land. Del Rio had grown to nearly 1,980 residents by 1890, approximately 70 percent of Val Verde County's population of 2,874.[4] As Del Rio grew, the community remained biethnic, with Anglo-Americans dominating the political life of the village. By the turn of the twentieth century, the Anglo-American population lived in the downtown neighborhoods, while Mexican Americans were spread throughout the village. The majority of Mexican Americans were concentrated on the East Side, known as the Mexican ward or the San Felipe Barrio.

In 1890, county officials established the Del Rio Independent School

District and opened the first public elementary school in Val Verde County.[5] The school was located in Del Rio, and students from the East Side were not admitted. At that time, schooling did not have to be offered to all students. In 1908, the county commissioners established a separate school for Mexican students in the San Felipe Barrio. A one-room wooden shack was built for Mexican students.[6] To maintain separate funding for the schools, the county commissioners established the San Felipe Common School District No. 2 for the East Side students.

In 1909, the county commissioners established a second school in the East Side. It is uncertain whether this was done because of overcrowding or because of the state mandate that all students have access to schools. The much larger second school housed students in a two-story building. But the East Side schools offered a curriculum only up to the seventh grade. If San Felipe Barrio students planned to attend high school, they had to enroll in the downtown elementary school in order to finish the eighth grade. By this time, the Del Rio ISD had one elementary school and a high school. The high school accepted students from across the county.

During the Mexican Revolution, Val Verde County's population expanded tremendously from Mexican immigration. By the late 1920s, over three-quarters of the county's residents lived in Del Rio, and 64 percent (9,542 out of 14,924) were of Mexican descent.[7] Among the Mexican immigrants were wealthy merchants from Ciudad Acuña who had left the political chaos in Mexico and started a new life on the East Side of Del Rio. Ciudad Acuña, located six miles from Del Rio, was one of the largest Mexican cities along the border.[8] When Mexican entrepreneurs moved to the East Side, they gave the Mexican ward a new life by opening shops, establishing artistic centers, and constructing new houses. The Southern Pacific Railroad Company contributed to the financial prosperity of the East Side shops when a train stop was established in the San Felipe Barrio. It became routine for passengers to rest and eat there while they waited to resume their journey to Louisiana, California, or the Mexican cities of Acuña and Piedras Negras. As San Felipe prospered and the village grew in population, property values went up, and the San Felipe Common School District acquired funds to improve the schools.

In 1928, the Del Rio ISD found itself in financial trouble. The county commissioners decided to annex part of the San Felipe neighborhoods to the Del Rio ISD in order to increase the tax base for the Del Rio schools.[9] The commissioners, who were all Anglo-Americans, were interested in annexing only the higher-income neighborhoods on the East Side.[10] Based on the zoning laws of 1927, the county commissioners believed that they had the authority to redraw residential and school district boundaries without obtaining the consent of the East Side residents. On June 18, 1928, the county commissioners approved the annexation plan.

East Side Mexican parents were outraged when the commissioners reorganized their school district. Parents believed that this was merely a scheme to steal their tax revenue and use it to improve the schools attended by Anglo-American students. Santos Garza, a local merchant and benefactor of the arts community, organized the East Side parents to appeal the annexation. After failing to convince the county commissioners to reverse their decision, Mexican American parents won a temporary injunction in the district court. The Del Rio ISD appealed to the Texas Fourth Court of Civil Appeals and lost. On November 7, 1928, the court dissolved the annexation and ruled that the procedure used to annex part of the neighborhoods in District 2 violated the Texas Constitution.[11] Under Texas law, county commissioners could not redraw school boundaries without consulting the county judge of Val Verde, which the commissioners had not done. More grievous were the violations of election laws. The zoning laws of 1927 did give city and county officials the power to redraw school district boundaries. But in school annexation cases, an election approving the measure was mandatory, and such an election had not taken place. The justices also opined that the county commissioners had not given any consideration to how the annexation would affect the East Side schools. It was obvious that the plan would have deprived the San Felipe school district of enough revenue to pay for its schools. The justices concluded that the county commissioners could not take San Felipe's tax base, and they had to find additional funds elsewhere to stabilize the Del Rio schools.

The Del Rio school board did find an alternate solution, which in a few years had statewide consequences. In a mean-spirited response, surely motivated by its defeat in court, the school board in Del Rio raised its district's revenue by cutting what it spent on educating its Mexican students. It planned to reassign all Mexican students attending the two downtown elementary schools to a third, newly constructed school designed for Mexican students. The board's official rationale was that this move would reduce the costs of educating "students with cognitive language problems" by putting them all in one school and thereby eliminating the need to duplicate services across the schools.[12] Under the zoning laws of 1927, the Del Rio School Board and the county commissioners could place all Mexican-origin students in the Mexican school by assigning their neighborhoods to that school. To execute this plan, a bond election was placed before the voters.

On January 7, 1930, the voters approved the financing of a $185,000 bond for school improvements. Parents were informed that the schools were overcrowded and that it was necessary to transfer some students to a new building with five classrooms. The bond would also finance improvements in the other two schools. What voters were not told was that the "new building" was in fact an old building that would be converted into the school for Mexican students.

After the new school was ready and only Mexican-origin students were transferred there, Mexican Americans parents protested. Jesús Salvatierra organized the families and hired John Dodson to file for an injunction. After the injunction was granted by the district judge, the Del Rio ISD filed an appeal with the Fourth Court of Appeals in San Antonio. Dodson, now joined by the LULAC attorneys, received a devastating blow. The appellate court blocked the injunction, ruling that it was legal to segregate Mexican students because Texas laws allowed school boards and county officials to assign students to specific schools.[13] The court found no violation of state law in the actions of the Del Rio school district. The judges stated that the court would stop the transfer program only if the defendants could prove that it was based on racial bias. If such evidence was presented, the district would be in violation of state law because no state or federal statute stipulated what race Mexicans belonged to. Because the transferred students were of both "Spanish and Mexican" extraction, the district could claim that race was not the determining factor—meaning that some students were white and others were not. In the absence of evidence of racial bias, the court had to uphold as truthful the rationale presented by school officials.[14]

The judges also commented that the school board had the statutory power, under the acts of 1927, to manage the schools, establish school assignment boundaries, and group students according to their abilities.[15] In their opinion, Texas law gave school boards the statutory power to select the location of schools and make all decisions on the construction of school buildings. Salvatierra's attorneys had objected to the inferior facilities of the new school, but the judges dismissed their concerns: "As has been held in this opinion, the matter of locating and constructing school buildings is an administrative function of the board, and may not be questioned except in the manner and by the processes prescribed by the statutes. . . . Where the board has exercised its discretion in such matters, its action thereon is final and conclusive, at least as against an attack by the process here invoked."[16] After the ruling, the Mexican American parents appealed for a rehearing to the US Supreme Court, but the request was denied.[17]

In the aftermath of the *Salvatierra* decision, it became common for very specifically worded language to be used as a smoke screen to justify segregating students in Texas and California. School boards were careful not to invoke race or national origin as reasons for segregation. In many cases, even if Mexican-descent students were monolingual English speakers, school officials continued to segregate them on the basis that they were not English proficient.[18]

After the San Antonio appeals court upheld the school segregation of Mexican students, East Side parents were on alert, prepared to challenge the county commissioners for their fair share of the state funds given to Val Verde County schools. In 1934, the San Felipe School Board fired its superintendent, who they believed was colluding with the county commissioners to ensure that the East Side Schools did not receive adequate funding. The community had recently opened its own high school and needed a strong advocate to lobby on its behalf for adequate funds.

The San Felipe School Board hired Carlos Castañeda as the new superintendent. He had recently obtained his doctorate in history from the University of Texas at Austin, and he was an experienced archivist knowledgeable in locating and interpreting records. He was in fact the first Mexican American in Texas to obtain a doctorate. When Castañeda began studying the county records, he found that all county schools were segregated.[19] In Del Rio, Mexican students attended the East Side schools or the Mexican school. He also concluded that the commissioners were underfunding the East Side schools. In 1934, the East Side student enrollment was 1,988, accounting for over half the students in both districts, yet the San Felipe schools received less than half the state funds.[20] Castañeda found that the county commissioners were intentionally manipulating the county's enrollment data to undercount East Side students and thereby justify hiring more teachers and purchasing more supplies for the downtown schools. The commissioners did not report the year-round attendance record of the schools when they submitted their annual figures to the state. Instead, they submitted attendance data from the beginning of the school year, which lowered the enrollment count for the East Side schools, because migrant students did not return to Del Rio until a few days after the school year began. This accounting practice gave a false picture of the actual number of Mexican American students attending the schools year-round. When Castañeda presented his findings to the commissioners, they ignored him. When he later contacted several state legislators, they were unwilling to intervene. The unequal distribution of state funds across Texas schools was a common problem.

After nearly two years in Del Rio, Castañeda realized that he would be unable to make any changes, and he returned to the University of Texas, where he worked as a librarian and a history professor. On October 24, 1934, before he left his post in San Felipe, Castañeda collaborated with Eleuterio Escobar, a businessman and influential member of LULAC, to organize an educational meeting in San Antonio. At the meeting attended by 13,000 people, Castañeda and many educators gave papers on the problems faced by Mexican-descent students.[21] The LULAC board assembled the papers into a report that they submitted to the state superintendent of instruction, L. A. Woods. Woods did not respond to their grievances, but the LULAC activists did not give up.

Catholic School Segregation

Mexican American students were also being segregated in Catholic schools by the late 1920s. Their segregation, however, was not a result of the zoning laws of 1927, since private schools were exempt from public school policies. The school segregation practices in Catholic schools also differed. The high schools were integrated, and the schools reserved for white students accepted some Mexican American students. Because the Catholic schools offered education from elementary school through high school, many Mexican American students were able to attend the higher grades. Thus, Catholic schools equipped Mexican American students to qualify for college admission. Most public schools designed for Mexican American students, on the other hand, generally offered education only through the seventh grade, and it was common for schools to offer a curriculum only up through the fourth grade.[22]

When the Catholic school system was established in Texas, following the Mexican-American War, the schools and the parishes were not segregated. The Catholic Church's involvement in education in Texas became part of its effort to regain the trust of the Anglo-American population after the war. Most Anglos were Protestants who distrusted the Catholic clergy, seeing them as allies of their defeated enemy.[23] To address the concerns of the Anglo-American population, Catholic administrators in Rome removed all Mexican priests and replaced them with ones from European religious orders. The Society of Mary, the Oblate Brothers, the Sisters of the Incarnate Word, the Order of the Blessed Sacrament, and the Ursulines became the principal Catholic orders that invested financially in Texas.[24] These organizations came to accept that Anglo-American Catholics preferred to attend church services apart from Mexican Americans and not to have their children attend the same parochial schools.

To regain the trust of governmental officials, the Catholic orders established schools and hospitals, which were scarce in Texas. In 1850, the Ursulines established the first Catholic schools in Galveston. The next year, the sisters opened a school in San Antonio, taking over one that had operated since the Mexican period. They made major building improvements and increased the school's attendance.[25] At this time the schools were integrated.

The number of schools established by the Catholic orders had increased by the late nineteenth century.[26] Many of the schools evolved into academies providing a curriculum beyond the seventh grade. The expanded curriculum attracted non-Catholics as well as students from communities that did not have schools. To accommodate the demand for the education they offered, many Catholic schools established dormitories, providing room and board. A gender pattern of education was formed: priests taught boys, and nuns focused their attention on educating girls, orphans, and poor children. By the early 1900s, Catholic schools had been established in the largest cities in Texas, including Galveston, Dallas, Brownsville, San Antonio, Corpus Christi, Laredo, Austin, El Paso, Houston, Victoria, Robstown, Fort Stockton, Rockport, Nacogdoches, and Fort Worth. New schools had also been constructed in smaller towns and cities where Catholics constituted a significant percentage of the population.[27]

At this time, the administrators of Catholic schools shifted their position toward Mexican American students and decided to school them apart from white students.[28] Income differences between whites and Mexican Americans may have affected the placement of students, but that did not explain why only Mexican-descent students, and not poor whites, were required to attend separate schools. Language differences also do not explain why Mexican Americans were segregated, since white non-English speakers were not placed in the Mexican schools.[29]

Gilberto Hinojosa, in a critical analysis of the Catholic Church, recognizes the significant contributions of the Catholic orders in restoring parishes in Texas and establishing new schools following the Mexican-American War.[30] His groundbreaking, coedited book *Mexican Americans and the Catholic Church, 1900–1965*, however, also delineates how the orders supported the segregation of Mexican Americans in separate schools and parishes. Hinojosa found that school segregation was strategically instituted during the late 1800s in the four archdioceses of Texas. A common pattern emerged in the dioceses of San Antonio, Galveston, Dallas, and Browns-ville. Each diocese constructed schools only in cities predominantly pop-ulated by Anglo-Americans and neglected to establish schools in counties where the majority of the population was Mexican American. In ethni-cally balanced cities, schools were located on the Anglo-American side of town. According to Hinojosa, these school-siting patterns prevented Mex-ican American children from attending parochial schools in their neigh-borhoods, since none were available.[31] In San Antonio, where the majority of the residents were of Mexican-origin, the situation was worse. By the late 1800s, the Catholic orders had shifted to primarily educating white students. Only one school focused on the education of Mexican-descent students. If parents wanted their children to receive a Catholic education, they had to send them to the San Fernando Cathedral School for Mexicans.

Hinojosa adds that the church intentionally underfunded the Cath-olic schools serving Mexican American students. For example, by 1930, the Brownsville Diocese, serving South Texas counties, had 100,000 more Catholics than the predominantly Anglo-American diocese in Galveston, yet many more Catholic schools were opened in the Galveston Diocese. The Galveston Diocese enrolled 37,000 students, while the few parochial schools in the Brownsville Diocese could serve only 5,000 students.[32]

Father Robert Wright and Father James Talmadge Moore offer differ-ent explanations of the process by which Mexican Americans came to be segregated. Neither denies that in most communities, Mexican Americans were segregated in separate parishes and churches. On the contrary, both state frankly that the Catholic schools were segregated. Wright, however, contends that Hinojosa's critique is unfair and distorted.[33] He argues that the Catholic orders did not initiate the segregation of Mexican Americans in separate schools or parishes. Rather, the practice reflected changing demographic patterns. In 1880, when Anglo-American Catholics began to move to Texas in large numbers, they chose to live in residential areas apart from Mexican Americans. As white Catholic communities increased in number and size, the church established parishes and schools near their residential areas. Segregation resulted from these residential patterns and not from any policy designed by the church.

Wright adds that Hinojosa ignores how the Mexican Revolution affected the growth of segregation in Catholic communities. From 1910 to 1920, the Mexican-origin population of Texas more than doubled because of the influx of refugees. Consequently, the Catholic Church became the main institution providing medical, financial, and social service aid to the refu-gees, which left it without sufficient funds to erect new parishes in Mexi-

can American communities. The building of new schools and parishes required local residents to contribute financially, and Mexican-origin people
did not have the means to help finance such projects at that time. Robert
Treviño, in a historical study of the Catholic Schools in Houston, admits
that the Mexican Revolution created great financial stress on the Catholic
Church.[34] But he argues that most financial assistance given to Mexican
immigrants was raised by Mexican American civil rights organizations in
Houston, and not by the church. Other scholars support Treviño's analysis:
in most cities, Mexican American charitable organizations and the Mexican
consulate raised funds to help Mexican immigrants. Among these organizations were the Cruz Azul Mexicana, the Sociedad Honorífica Mexicana, the
League of Mexican Women (in Laredo), and other local mutualist associations.[35] Treviño demonstrates as well that a pattern of neglect continued
after the Mexican Revolution. From 1925 to 1951, the Catholic Church allocated the Mexican parishes in Houston $39,000 and the Anglo-American
parishes nearly $1 million dollars, even though two out of three Catholics
were of Mexican descent.[36]

Father Talmadge Moore acknowledges that it was common for Mexican
Americans to be segregated in separate parishes and churches.[37] Language
differences among Mexican and white Catholics was the official justification
for the separation, but in reality, it was a choice made by administrators
and parishioners. Talmadge Moore admits that by 1903 the church had
chosen to primarily invest in the welfare of the white districts, but agrees
with Wright that this pattern emerged because white communities had
the assets to sponsor building projects. For example, by 1900, thirty-nine
schools had been established in the dioceses of San Antonio, twenty-eight
in Galveston, twenty-four in Dallas, and eight in Brownsville (Vicariate).[38]
Because the State of Texas prohibited governmental funds from being used
to construct or financially support parochial schools, most of them had to
rely on enrollment fees for financing. So when the church built new schools,
it did so in white districts where residents could pay for tuition and donate
money to the schools. Nonetheless, Talmadage Moore acknowledges that
school boards often voiced public opposition to admitting Mexican American students.[39]

Carlos Castañeda, who was commissioned by a Catholic organization,
the Knights of Columbus, to write the history of Catholics in Texas, likewise concluded that Mexican American students were segregated in parochial schools. He found that the Catholic orders practiced a tripartite
school-segregation system in communities that were multiracial. Separate
schools for African Americans were established in San Antonio, Galveston,

Houston, Corpus Christi, Ames, Marshall, Beaumont, and Port Arthur.[40] Once students graduated from eighth grade, only Mexican Americans were admitted to the Anglo-American Catholic high schools; African Americans were not.

In 1937, Pope Pius XI issued a statement condemning school segregation in the United States. He did not, however, revise the church's stance on this issue.[41] The policy of the Catholic hierarchy in Rome was to allow US archdioceses to determine their own racial policies regarding the admission of students to parochial schools.[42] The archdioceses in turn allowed the Catholic orders to determine local policy, because the societies provided the academic labor and a large percentage of the schools' finances. The choice to integrate or segregate students based on race or ethnicity was left to high-ranking school officials. In making their decisions, school administrators would assess the opinions of parishioners and the clergy who taught the students, and obtain advice from their archdiocese. To provide insight into how parochial-school segregation developed in Texas, a brief detour into the history of San Antonio's Catholic schools illustrates this process. It also shows that like the public schools, the Catholic orders provided inferior school facilities when children were segregated.

The Ursulines in San Antonio had begun to remove poor Mexican American students from integrated Catholic schools by 1860, but left them in the classroom if they paid tuition. The formal segregation of Mexican American students in San Antonio began in 1875 when Father Simler recommended that Mexican students be put in separate schools in order to improve the finances of the American Catholic schools.[43] In many schools across the country, Mexican Americans were charged lower tuition fees, based on their family income, and this policy, according to Father Simler, had to end. He was the Catholic Church's inspector of American schools. The Society of Mary, which had established St. Mary's Institute for boys, the premier school in San Antonio, rejected the plan. The Marianist priests who were the teachers and administrators did not want to exclude Mexican American students. It is uncertain why the fathers resisted the plan—perhaps it was related to the nostalgic belief that Mexican Americans were part of the old mission system that needed to be preserved. The institute's founding and success were largely due to the income it received from Mission Concepción. Bishop Odin transferred the title of Mission Concepción to the Marianist order during the Civil War, and this gave the priests the financial means to establish a high-quality school. They used the mission's property to raise revenue. Perhaps the knowledge that the financial stability of the institute was related to a mission that had once served Native

Americans and Mexican-origin people influenced the fathers to not stigmatize their Mexican American pupils.

Nonetheless, a few years after Father Simler visited St. Mary's Institute, the Mexican American students were removed from the integrated classes and confined to two classrooms. When their teachers protested that the classrooms were overcrowded and asked that some of the Mexican American students be returned to the integrated classrooms, the administration denied their request.

In 1888, a school for Mexican students was established next to the San Fernando Cathedral, and Mexican American students from St. Mary's Institute were transferred there. Soon after, Mexican American students from other Catholic schools were transferred to the Mexican school, too. Fathers teaching in the new school complained that their facilities, compared to St. Mary's Institute, were extremely inferior and should be immediately upgraded. Unlike the modern, spacious, four-floor building at St. Mary's, which had an assembly room, labs, dormitories, a library, a cafeteria, and study rooms, the San Fernando school consisted of a modest two-story wooden building with a heating system that did not function most of the year. The Mexican school was housed in an old shabby building, while St. Mary's Institute was considered to be San Antonio's most beautiful and modern school. The Mexican school did have lower tuition. Three years later, because of distressful building conditions at the San Fernando school, the students were transferred to the Ursuline orphanage for Mexican children.

When the orphanage became overcrowded, the Archdiocese of San Antonio renovated the San Fernando Cathedral School and transferred the students back there. Though modest, the new building could accommodate at least three hundred students. There was also enough space to allow some of the Mexican orphans to attend the new school.

In 1927, the archdiocese closed the San Fernando school and transferred the boys to a Mexican American girls' school located at 216 North Laredo Street, run by the Sisters of the Incarnate Word.[44] Parents were told that the merger was necessary to reduce costs, but it is unclear why the school system was restructured. Most likely, it was related to the expansion of Texas's public school system. In the mid-1920s, the Texas Legislature increased its public school funding and allocated more money for the construction of schools across the state. These actions may have decreased the demand for Catholic schools in San Antonio.

Although segregated parochial schools in San Antonio became the norm, Mexican Americans were allowed to attend the city's Catholic high schools.

Four gender-segregated schools offered instruction past the eighth grade. Girls attended Our Lady of the Lake and Incarnate Word, and boys, Central Catholic High School and the St. Louis Academy.

The St. Louis Academy was a boarding school established in 1894 for upper-class male students and those awarded scholarships. Mexican Americans were allowed to attend. The school, a branch of St. Mary's Institute, offered education from middle school to college. Nearly all students were boarders, and those who commuted were not allowed to socialize with the residents. In 1901, the academy began to offer bachelor degrees, and a few years later it was renamed St. Louis College. Fredrick Guerra from Roma, Texas, was the first Mexican American to receive a bachelor of science degree from the college, in 1906. Throughout the history of the academy, the percentage of Spanish-surnamed students each year ranged from 29 to 32 percent.[45] They attended all grade levels, but their numbers dwindled in the high school and college ranks. The registration records for the college and the St. Louis Academy indicate that of the Spanish-surnamed students, the majority were US residents from communities in San Antonio or South Texas. A few students were from Mexico. During the mid-1920s, the curriculum at St. Louis College was restructured twice, and eventually it became St. Mary's University. Six Spanish-surnamed students graduated with bachelor degrees before St. Louis College became a university.

The Catholic orders in Texas were complicit in promoting school segregation by not challenging local norms. Writings by Catholic clergy do not deny this. Nonetheless, the admission of Mexican American students to Catholic schools allowed many of them to acquire schooling past the fourth or seventh grade, which was not possible in many segregated public schools.

The US Census and the Mexican Race

In the mid-1930s, Mexican American civil rights activists protested against government agencies using nonwhite racial terms to classify Mexican Americans. The US Census Bureau and the Department of Vital Statistics, with congressional approval, had stopped classifying Mexican-origin people as white. Other federal departments were replicating this practice. Many Mexican Americans became alarmed, since this type of classification could place Mexican Americans under the same segregation laws affecting African Americans.[46] Mexican Americans were segregated in most public facilities, but were not required to sit apart from whites on public transportation or to wait in separate depot stations. They were also admitted to the white colleges. From 1850 to 1930, the US Census Bureau counted Mexican-origin people as white unless census takers identified them as Black or Native American.[47] Vital Statistics Department regional offices, however, did not classify all Mexican-origin people as white, often using the label "Mexican" to distinguish them from Anglo-Americans. The opinion that Mexican-origin people should be officially distinguished from whites in governmental records began with these two agencies after federal and state public health experts lobbied Congress to adopt a "Mexican" racial category. The influx of refugees during the Mexican Revolution had more than doubled the size of the Mexican-origin population. Public health officials therefore proposed that for the welfare of the nation, it was essential to know their exact number, because most Mexicans were poor, experienced health problems, and died younger.[48]

In 1927, Congress authorized Herbert Hoover, the secretary of commerce, who was in charge of the US Census and the Vital Statistics Department, to consult with experts. Within the Census Bureau, officials were divided on how to proceed. Joseph Hill, the assistant director, supported the use of a "Mexican" racial category because scientific data indicated that they were nonwhite. His opinion largely rested on Manuel Gamio's study of Mexico, *Forjando Patria: Pro-Nacionalismo* (1916), which claimed that Mexicans constituted a separate mestizo race. Gamio, an anthropologist, had served as Mexico's secretary of education and was currently the secretary of Mexico's Department of Demography. Hill also relied on the advice of the American Economic Association and the American Statistical Association, which had determined that the new immigrants arriving from Mexico were more racially mixed than most Mexican Americans. A report prepared by Daniel Folkmar for the congressional Dillingham Commission was also consulted; his study offered the opinion that Mexicans were largely an Indian or mixed-origin race.[49] Congress approved the terminology change, but acknowledged that the count for the "Mexican race" category might be inaccurate because it would include some persons who were white. Consequently, Congress requested that a study be conducted to estimate the number of Mexican families that were white.

In 1930, the US Census counted 1,422,533 people belonging to the "Mexican race." This category included persons born in the United States and Mexico.[50] To estimate the percentage of whites within the "Mexican race" category, a special report on families was prepared for Congress.

In *Fifteenth Census of the United States: 1930, Population Special Report on Foreign-Born White Families by Country of Birth of Head, with an Appendix Giving Statistics for Mexican, Indian, Chinese and Japanese Families*, Mexican-descent families, irrespective of place of birth, numbered 277,700 nationwide.[51] Of these families, 73 percent (203,086) were of foreign stock, and only 6,631 were classified as white.[52] For a family to be counted as white, the head of household had to be of the white race. Based on this data, the census estimated that most Mexican-descent families in the United States were not white. Similar results were found when the Census sampled selected cities (see appendix 4.1). In San Antonio, 67 percent of the 16,860 Mexican-descent families were classified as foreign born, and within these families, only 765 persons were identified as white.[53]

On the release of census data adopting the "Mexican race" category, Mexican Americans in New Mexico immediately protested. New Mexico Spanish-language newspapers strongly criticized the use of this racial category, and reporters argued that Mexicans were of Spanish descent. In Texas, LULAC members at first were divided. Alonso S. Perales, an influential attorney, did not find the term problematic and emphasized that this change allowed for a more accurate enumeration.[54] Other LULAC members were concerned that this category classified Mexicans as people of color and could mean a loss of rights. All LULAC chapters changed their position against the use of the "Mexican race" category in the mid-1930s when the Department of Vital Statistics issued a directive that its offices across the nation classify Mexicans as "colored people" and identify them as an "other race." In October 1936, Alex K. Powell, the El Paso city registrar, announced that his office would join four other Texas cities in classifying Spanish-speaking residents as "colored."[55] This ignited a firestorm, since in Texas, "colored" was associated only with African Americans. Immediately, state senators and mayors in New Mexico and Texas protested that the new classification was inappropriate. Mexicans were a mixed-Caucasian race, more similar to Italians than Blacks. The Department of Vital Statistics responded that "colored" did not mean "Black." It applied to the nonwhite races.

Officials representing the Census Bureau and the Vital Statistics Department disagreed with LULAC. To gather support for their position, they contacted scientists and Mexican demographers. The director of Mexico's census bureau, Emilio Alanis Patiño, and Manuel Gamio concurred that for scientific purposes and the control of disease, it was important to have an accurate count of the Mexican population. Patiño opined that Mexicans were predominantly an Indian people, while Gamio suggested using an "Indo-European" category. American scientists offered similar opinions, adding that using a separate race category was supported by the Public Health Service, the Department of Labor, the Social Security Board, the Department of Agriculture, and the War Department.[56]

Although Patiño and Gamio had supported a separate enumeration category, consular officials working for Mexico's Foreign Office disagreed, and lobbied the State Department to order all US agencies to stop the practice. The Foreign Office supported the position taken by LULAC chapters, namely, that the actual purpose of this type of enumeration was to limit Mexican Americans' political rights. Mexican officials were particularly concerned that this move was the first step in changing US naturalization laws, which at that time allowed Mexican immigrants to apply for US citizenship irrespective of race. Across the United States, scientists and some congressional members opined that Mexican immigrants should not be allowed to become naturalized citizens because they were not white. This position was based on the perspective that the federal Western District Court in Texas had erred in *In re Rodriguez* (1897) by wrongly exempting Mexicans from the "white only" citizenship-eligibility clause of the Naturalization Act of 1790. With the use of the new classification gaining support in congressional circles, the Mexican government understandably took the position that all governmental enumerations of Mexican people as nonwhite had to stop.

On November 20, 1939, the US Census Bureau informed Castillo Najera, Mexico's ambassador, that the bureau had been instructed by Congress not to use a separate racial classification for Mexican-origin people.[57] In 1940, the US Census returned to its traditional enumeration system, which offered detailed information about Mexican foreign-born families and their US-born children (e.g., race, occupation, housing) and counted nonimmigrant Mexican American families in the "white" category. In 1950, the Census continued to count most Mexican-origin people born in the United States in the "white" category, yet it prepared a special report on the nonwhite population of the United States that included all people with Spanish surnames.[58]

The battle to not count Mexican-origin people as nonwhite was a triumph for Mexican American activists and the Mexican government. But it did not protect them from being socially excluded from public accommodations, nor did it have any impact on school-segregation practices. In Texas, Mexican Americans continued to struggle for equality and better treatment.

No Dogs, Negroes, Mexicans: Lonestar Restaurant Association, Dallas

Social Segregation in Texas Public Accommodations

The social exclusion of people of color from public accommodations had been legal in the United States since the *Slaughter-House Cases* ruling of 1873. The Texas Legislature upheld this practice in 1907 when segregation laws allowed businesses and organizations to exclude any person for any reason.[59] But it was not until 1913, when the Texas Legislature empowered cities to write home rule charters, that municipal officials began to write specific laws to segregate racial minorities in public places and use fines and imprisonment to frighten them into compliance.[60]

Under section 4 of chapter 147 of the Home Rule Act of 1913, city and town officials had the power to determine what public behavior was considered a nuisance or immoral. Municipal officials could enforce the separation of the races without needing to mention race or ethnicity as the real cause. Officials had the power to regulate all public behavior in restaurants, hotels, parks, theaters, athletic grounds, speedways, and boulevards. For example, if a city wanted to protect a business owner's right to offer segregated services, a person who resisted being seated in the "Mexican or Black" section of a restaurant or theater could be arrested by police and fined for being a public nuisance.

Mexican Americans complied with Texas home rule laws and accepted the school segregation of their children, too. During World War II, however, Mexican Americans began to challenge the legality of segregation in public places. They had lost the battle against school segregation, but they questioned the legal theories behind their exclusion from restaurants, amusement places, and theaters. They got indirect assistance from an earlier court ruling that did not go their way. In the *Salvatierra* school-segregation lawsuit, the Fourth Court of Appeals upheld the segregation of Mexican-descent students under the districting laws of 1927, but also ruled that race could not be the only basis of their segregation.

In 1942, LULAC civil rights activists, along with representatives of the Mexican consulate, submitted official complaints to Governor Coke R. Stevenson about what they saw as the misapplication of home rule segregation policies. They charged that Mexican-origin people were being segregated in public accommodations on account of their national origin. The complainants also stated that Mexican Americans were part of the Caucasian race, and business proprietors did not have the authority to treat them differently from Anglo-Americans. The letters acknowledged that Texas segregation laws allowed organizations and businesses to exclude people, but noted that it was against federal law to not apply these laws uniformly. If business owners did not exclude Anglo-Americans from their premises, then they could not legally exclude Mexican Americans either.[61]

Stevenson responded by supporting the right of business owners and government officials to segregate Mexican Americans. On October 2, 1942, he replied to official grievances submitted by Federico P. Jiménez, the consul-general of Mexico: "Such incidents are indeed unfortunate. I am sure that you understand that in a democracy each businessman is free to establish standards and regulations concerning the operation of his business."[62] Stevenson added that after investigating the consular office's complaints, he had concluded that city officials had the authority to enforce local ordinances and that private citizens had the right to exclude anyone from their premises. Jiménez had complained that in Atascosa, Mexican Americans were not given permits to celebrate September 16th, a Mexican holiday, because permits were not issued to organizations solely composed of Mexicans. In a case from Harlingen, signs illegally prohibited Mexicans from entering the roller rink, according to the consul. And in Alvin, Texas, the city attorney had informed the consul that business owners did not have to serve Mexicans.

Jiménez continued to submit complaints. In letters to the governor, he insisted that he had not received citations to the US laws that allowed Mexicans to be treated differently from other Caucasian ethnic groups. Furthermore, he complained that the governor's office had not specified which federal law gave city officials and business owners the right to expel consulate staff from places reserved for whites. Jiménez cited a case from New Braunfels. In 1942, Narcisso Ortiz, a consulate staffer, was forced to sit in the section of the Rialto Theatre reserved for African Americans and Mexicans.[63] Ortiz's experience was so humiliating that he sought legal representation from Manuel C. Gonzales, who at that time worked for the Mexican consulate and was the secretary of the San Antonio LULAC chapter.[64] Nothing resulted from the complaint.

Jiménez raised other serious issues. He charged that in Willacy County, city attorneys refused to investigate assault complaints filed by Mexican Americans against highway patrolmen. In one instance, an elderly man was brutally beaten in front of many witnesses, yet the city attorney refused to arrest the officer. After consulate staff filed a formal grievance against the city for failing to take action and contacted Willacy County officials for support, the county attorney's office replied that it would not intervene in "a case against fellow officers when they have to work with them in the preparation of criminal cases." Jiménez also complained that when Mexican Americans submitted formal charges against law enforcement personnel in Willacy County, officials threatened to deport them if they proceeded with the complaint.[65]

Jiménez submitted documents alleging that incidents similar to the one in Willacy County had occurred in Bee, Cameron, and Nueces Counties, but the governor refused to intervene.[66] On one occasion, however, several incidents of racial discrimination were investigated because they involved military servicemen. In January 1942, Manuel C. Gonzales and Consul Jiménez wrote a series of letters to Governor Stevenson, informing him that throughout Uvalde County were signs reading, "ONLY WHITES, NO MEXICANS." They asked for the signs to be removed. Gonzáles and Jiménez added that Mexican American soldiers were being refused service in many Uvalde County restaurants. They believed that during a time of war, this was unpatriotic and objectionable behavior. They asked for an immediate investigation and suggested that it begin with the Club Café. Several incidents had been reported of servicemen and their guests being forcibly ejected from the restaurant. The most recent complaint involved Juan Reyes, who was arrested by police when he refused to leave. At the time, the Reyes family was celebrating his last days as a civilian before being deployed abroad.

Stevenson handed over the case to Tom Wheat, his assistant secretary, since the charge was serious. The US government had recently declared war against the Axis powers, and this was not the time to treat soldiers disrespectfully. On January 30, 1942, W. F. Hare, the mayor of Uvalde, responded to the governor's investigation. After surveying the county's restaurants, Hare had concluded that the charges of racial discrimination were false. The problem, in his assessment, was that "some troublemakers," meaning Mexicans, did not want to respect the status quo. In Uvalde, it was well known that the races did not marry or mix. In his view, only trouble-makers and repulsive persons refused to respect the city's social order.[67]

After receiving Hare's letter, the governor's office closed the investigation. They were satisfied that no civil rights violations had taken place.[68] Nonetheless, Jiménez continued asking Uvalde officials to remove the offensive signs. To stop Jiménez from bothering them, city officials contacted state representative C. P. Spangler and asked him to intervene. Spangler asked Stevenson to find a way of getting rid of Jiménez. The best way, he suggested, was to deport Jiménez and everyone helping him.[69]

The Mexican Government Places Pressure on Texas

In late November 1942, Governor Stevenson became unable to continue dismissing the Mexican American civil rights complaints. The US secretary of agriculture had announced that the Mexican government's assistance was needed to meet war-related demands. The US government needed to accelerate food production. Crop production needed to more than double, since the Allies and American soldiers stationed in Europe and the Pacific depended on food exports. The problem for American farmers was that they were being required to increase food production while the military draft was shrinking their labor force.[70] In Texas, in anticipation of a projected farm labor shortage, and to avoid having to ask the Mexican government for assistance, Stevenson petitioned the Selective Service to exempt Texan agricultural workers from the draft. He requested that men employed in farm labor not be allowed to enlist. His petition was denied. Mexican Americans, who constituted the majority of the farm labor force in Texas, would be drafted.[71]

Stevenson had no option except to solicit aid from Mexico if Texas was to have enough farmworkers to replace the men drafted to war. Texas needed to participate in the Bracero Program, a binational farm labor program designed to bring workers from Mexico to US farms. President Franklin D. Roosevelt had signed the Mexican Farm Labor Agreement on August 4, 1942, to address the farmworker shortage in the United States.[72] Mexican men called braceros ("hired arms") were contracted to work in agriculture or on the railroads for six months at a time. Their contracts could be renewed as needed. During the war, approximately 167,925 braceros were employed in agricultural occupations, and a few thousand more in the railroad industry.[73]

Braceros were imported throughout the United States, but Mexico's secretary of foreign affairs, Ezequiel Padilla, refused to send workers to Texas. Mexicans would not be shipped to a state where consular staff had reported that the Mexican people's civil rights were severely violated.[74] Padilla's decision relied upon the research that Consul Jiménez had compiled on the state of affairs in Texas. The secretary informed Governor Stevenson that the program would not begin in Texas until his office provided evidence that the government was actively investigating and prosecuting cases of discrimination against Mexicans. He stressed that even the daughters of consular staff members had been humiliated by restaurant owners merely because they were Mexican and speaking Spanish.[75]

During the summer of 1943, Stevenson responded to the secretary's concerns by establishing the Good Neighbor Commission. Its first mandate was to prepare two reports on the status of Mexican-origin people in Texas. One report would provide an overview of farm labor conditions, and the second would identify which counties formally segregated Mexican Americans. The governor's office anticipated that the reports would confirm the state's official position that segregation in the case of Mexican Americans was the result of social-class differences, not racial discrimination.[76] In the meantime, the governor needed to resolve two embarrassing problems that Consul Jiménez was unwilling to drop and hindered the removal of the bracero ban. One was a minor problem that could be settled with an apology; the second was a possible civil rights violation that would take time to resolve.

The minor incident involved the owner of the Blue Moon Café in the city of New Gulf (in Wharton County). Adolfo G. Domínguez, the Mexican consul in Houston, who was accompanied by John Herrera, a Mexican American attorney, and J. V. Villareal, an employee of the Texas Gulf Sulphur Company, were humiliated by the café's owner when she told them, "NOT EVEN THE CONSUL OF MEXICO WILL BE SERVED, UNLESS HE WANTS TO BE SERVED IN THE KITCHEN."[77] Secretary Padilla asked Governor Stevenson to investigate the incident and assure him that this type of offensive behavior would not be repeated.

The more serious incident involved a clear-cut violation of federal civil rights law in Pecos County. This violation was compounded by the fact that Pecos officials were not supporting the Caucasian Resolution. On May 6, 1942, the governor worked with the Texas Legislature to enact the Caucasian Resolution (HCR 105), which on the surface addressed the Mexican government's concerns, but fundamentally did not nullify any exclusionary laws, nor did it include an enforcement policy. The resolution merely proclaimed that members of the Caucasian race could not be segregated in public accommodations.[78] After the resolution was adopted, attorneys working for the Mexican consul-general's office tried to argue that Mexican-origin people in Texas were white and that therefore it was against the law to segregate them. Not being naïve, the consulate attorneys knew that their interpretation of the resolution was broad and idealistic.

In Pecos County, the county commissioners banned people of Latin American descent from using community swimming pools reserved for whites. Attorneys for the consul-general of Mexico informed Governor Stevenson that the Pecos ordinance was unlawful because under federal law, a segregation ordinance could not be enforced in a government-owned facility. Segregation ordinances were legal only if they involved private property. Because the swimming pools in question were owned by the county and the ordinance had been passed by county officials, the commissioners were clearly violating federal law. Furthermore, the attorneys for the consul-general argued that the ordinance was illegal because Latin Americans were being taxed to pay for public facilities that they could not enjoy—also a violation of federal law. Governor Stevenson investigated the complaint and contacted state senator H. L. Winfield, who represented Pecos County.[79] The senator confirmed that the Board of Directors of the Pecos County Water Improvement District had indeed passed an ordinance banning Latin Americans from using Comanche Creek, the springs of Pecos County, and the public pools.[80] Winfield personally investigated whether provisions had been made to ensure that members of the Latin American race had a place to swim in the county. He found that the county had designated one pool for their exclusive use and had prohibited other citizens from swimming there.[81] Although the pool was "not very nice," he was working with the water improvement district to improve it.[82] The senator's actions made it clear that he would not support overturning the swimming pool ordinance.

Regardless of the setback, the Mexican consulate and the governor's office continued to discuss how both sides could reach their goals. Stevenson believed that the segregation of Mexicans was uncommon, and in most cases due to class differences. The Mexican government wanted Texas laws to be revised to stipulate that Mexicans could not be segregated. Both sides wanted to find a compromise that would allow Texas to participate in the Bracero Program. The parties agreed to wait for the Good Neighbor Commission reports to be completed. Data was needed to determine whether action was required, and if so, what type.

During winter of 1944, Pauline Kibbe, the executive secretary of the Good Neighbor Commission, who had been entrusted to prepare the studies, submitted her first report, titled "Report of Findings on Cases of Discrimination Reported to Good Neighbor Commission for Years 1942–1943."[83] Kibbe concluded that sixty-three municipalities in Texas practiced some type of segregation. Among the worst offenders were Pecos County officials. Although her findings clearly illustrated that segregation was widespread in Texas, her analysis was vague and apologetic. Kibbe reported that Mexican Americans often caused their own oppression because they were uneducated and were reluctant to report abuses: "The Latin Americans are, generally speaking, of the humblest class, and having long been denied the opportunity for educational or economic advancement, and completely lacking in leadership, have never dared to raise their voices in protest against the conditions under which they live."[84] She concluded that segregation was not a problem in all counties. And although many cities practiced school segregation, only Wharton, Matagorda, Brazoria, and Fort Bend Counties institutionalized countywide school segregation and did not allow Mexican Americans to vote in the Democratic primaries.

After Kibbe submitted her report, LULAC challenged part of the findings, and Dr. George I. Sánchez put forward a supplementary report.[85] Sánchez was a professor in the College of Education at the University of Texas at Austin. At this time, Sánchez and Carlos Castañeda were the only professors of Mexican descent employed by the university.

The LULAC-Sánchez report duplicated part of Kibbe's findings, but challenged the conclusion that countywide segregation was limited to a few counties. In LULAC's report ("Some Places Where Mexicans Are Discriminated Against in Texas either by Denying Them Service or by Segregating Them from Anglo Americans"), school segregation, residential segregation, and the exclusion of Mexican Americans from public accommodations were found in nearly every town and city in Texas.[86] The report claimed that Mexican Americans were segregated or denied services in restaurants, barbershops, swimming pools, and theaters throughout the state. And in the cities of Brady, New Braunfels, Balmorrhea, McQueeny, Corpus Christi, and Seguin, the parks were for the exclusive use of Anglo-Americans. Many cities had begun to ask Mexican Americans to sit in waiting areas otherwise reserved for African Americans.[87] Some cities required Mexicans to wait outside before receiving services. In most cities, Mexican Americans were allowed to shop in the same stores as Anglo-Americans, but it was a common store policy not to allow them to try on clothes. Austin, the capital of Texas, was found to be the worst offender when it came to all forms of social segregation. Unlike Kibbe's report, which blamed Mexican Americans for their segregation, LULAC's assessment focused on city officials.

According to Sánchez, segregation was a tool manipulated by city leaders to justify the mistreatment of Mexican American people.

On December 29, 1944, Pauline Kibbe submitted her second report ("To the Members of the Good Neighbor Commission"), on the status of Texas farmworkers.[88] Displeased with the report, the governor's office disputed her findings.[89] If the study's findings had been accepted by the governor's office, it would have given the Mexican consulate further evidence to retain the bracero ban. Kibbe found that employers provided farmworkers unsanitary housing and overcharged them when deducting rent from their earnings. Wages were so low that farmworker families lacked enough income to pay for basic necessities. Furthermore, because farmworkers did not have access to health care services, many suffered from tuberculosis and dysentery. The worst problem faced by farmworker families was the lack of schools: over 54 percent of migrant children did not attend school.

After the reports were submitted, Governor Stevenson failed to take action to address segregation in Texas or to improve the working and living conditions of farmworkers. Because of the reports' mixed findings and the criticisms made by both sides, the commission was deemed ineffective. LULAC and the Mexican government considered the commission to be a biased tool manipulated by the state government to justify segregation. The governor, displeased with the reports, decreased the commission's operating expenses in an effort to quietly dismantle it.[90]

Upholding the Segregation of Mexican Americans

In 1944, the Fourth Court of Civil Appeals, in San Antonio, ruled in *Terrell Wells Swimming Pool v. Rodriguez* that people of Mexican descent could be legally segregated in Texas. Mexican Americans were dealt a harsh political blow when they were told that racially exclusionary laws applied to all Mexicans. The incident leading to the court's opinion began July 10, 1943, when Manuel C. Gonzales, the attorney who had worked with Consul Jiménez to document abuses against Mexican Americans, purchased three tickets to the Terrell Wells Swimming Pool in San Antonio. He was accompanied by Jacob I. Rodríguez, a tax collector, and Alberto Treviño, an attorney. When the attendant asked Gonzáles whether Rodríguez was with him, she informed him that they could not enter. Company policy prohibited people of the Spanish and Mexican race from swimming at the pool. She told Gonzáles that she had sold him the tickets because she thought he was white.

As Jacob Rodríguez's legal counsel, Gonzáles filed a case of racial discrimination against H. E. Stumberg, the president of the Terrell Wells Swimming Pool Corporation.[91] On August 11, 1943, Judge Robert W. B. Terrell, of the 37th District Court in Bexar County, ruled in favor of Rodríguez, on the grounds that since he was part of the Caucasian race, he could not be discriminated against. The judge cited the Caucasian Resolution as his legal basis. Terrell also referred to the governor's public interpretation of the resolution. On June 25, 1943, the governor had endorsed the Caucasian Resolution and proclaimed that it applied to people of Mexican descent.[92]

Stumberg and his partners appealed the district court's ruling to the Fourth Court of Civil Appeals. On February 2, 1944, the lower court's ruling was reversed. The judges concluded that Texas laws allowed proprietors to deny services to anyone: "Appellee was refused admittance to the Terrell Wells Swimming Pool because he was of Hispanic or Mexican descent and his contention here is that this conduct on the part of the proprietor of the swimming pool violates the Good Neighbor Policy of this state as found in H.C. R. 105, and the Governor's Proclamation, and that therefore he is entitled to a mandatory injunction requiring such proprietor to admit him to the swimming pool. We overrule this contention."[93] The judges concluded that the Caucasian Resolution did not nullify the right of proprietors or managers to eject patrons from public amusement places. Only a legislative bill revising Texas's exclusion laws could prohibit such action. The judges added that it was a well-known fact that resolutions did not change state law.

Gonzáles submitted a petition to the Texas Supreme Court in an attempt to reverse the ruling of the civil appeals court, but was refused a rehearing. Following the ruling, Governor Stevenson was informed by Ezequiel Padilla, Mexico's secretary of foreign relations, that Mexico would not lift the bracero ban.[94] To prevent the bracero negotiations from ending and to show good faith on behalf of the state government, in spite of the *Terrell Wells* ruling, Stevenson supported passage of a pending bill, Senate Bill 1, which would end the exclusion of Mexicans and other Latin Americans from public accommodations. After a difficult debate in the legislature, Senate Bill 1 passed on May 7, 1945.[95] Although the bill superficially benefited Mexican Americans, it could not be enforced because the legislature did not pass companion legislation to nullify Texas's exclusion laws. The right of business owners and managers to expel people from their places of business remained unchanged.

World War II ended a few months after the bill passed, and the governor's office lost interest in challenging local segregation ordinances. Furthermore, the Mexican consulate lost its power to negotiate, since the farm labor shortages ended when the war did.[96] One year after the war, congressional representatives informed Mexico's Office of Foreign Affairs that the Bracero Program would not be renewed unless Mexico accepted certain changes.[97] Because of the high cost of managing the program and the absence of a national emergency, Congress would be turning over the program to employers interested in importing workers. The US Department of Agriculture and the US Department of Labor would stop managing the program. Instead, employers were authorized to administer it and set workers' minimum wage according to local demands.

Transferring the management of the program to American farmers created an abusive situation. The Department of Labor was not allowed to monitor wage scales, and only a few inspectors were permitted to investigate labor grievances. If the Mexican government chose to reject the revisions, its only alternative was to withdraw from the program and prohibit braceros from working in the United States. Instead, Mexican officials decided to continue the program and monitor abuses by having consular staff document and litigate grievances. Consequently, with the restructuring of the Bracero Program, Mexican consular offices shifted their attention from civil rights to monitoring workplace abuses. In Texas, this resulted in consular staff leaving civil rights issues to be litigated by Mexican American attorneys.

Desegregation Movements across the Country

US service members in World War II, including African Americans and Mexican Americans, fought against enemies (the Japanese Empire, Nazi Germany) driven by virulently racist views of the world. But when American soldiers of color returned home, state governments continued to deny them equal rights, based on their race, and their political representatives supported the ongoing social segregation of their families.[98] In response, American civil rights organizations began to steadily challenge segregation in a number of areas. Organizations established by racial minorities, such as the National Association for the Advancement of Colored People (NAACP), LULAC, and the GI Forum, concentrated on school segregation and employment discrimination, whereas challenges to "antimiscegenation" laws were spearheaded by religious organizations and the American Civil Liberties Union (ACLU).[99]

President Harry S. Truman's attempt to dismantle segregation in the United States was monumental in igniting political shifts in the federal bureaucracy. It was soon followed by national changes in marriage laws and school segregation policies. In 1948, Truman issued Executive Order 9981 mandating the desegregation of the US Armed Forces.[100] His executive action came in response to criticism from the Soviet Union that the US government enforced racial policies like those of the defeated Nazi regime. The Soviet Union was attempting to convince nations to adopt its way of government and not follow the racist democratic system practiced in the United States. (It should be noted that the Soviet Union under Joseph Stalin, though technically antiracist, was deeply anti-Semitic.) In an attempt to defuse this criticism, President Truman asked Congress to begin desegregating America. Although Congress did not comply, Truman's desegregation of the US military meant that the liberalization of America had begun.

President Truman encountered steep obstacles to the implementation of his desegregation order. The secretaries of the navy, army, air force, and coast guard balked. They were prepared to increase the percentage of African American recruits and include them in the officer ranks. But they opposed merging Black and white companies or integrating dormitories, recreational centers, hospitals, cafeterias, schools, and base housing. In the case of Mexican Americans, the order to integrate and diversify the military affected their recruitment but not their living spaces. For generations, Mexican Americans had been allowed to live among Anglo-American soldiers and were not segregated in separate units or housing.[101]

The secretaries of the military divisions stated that before they could implement the president's executive order, his administration would have to change federal and state laws. They could not order commanding officers in charge of military bases to break state laws if integration was against a state's constitution. In response, the following year President Truman appointed the President's Committee on Civil Rights to develop a plan to integrate the armed forces. In addition, he decided to appoint a US secretary of defense who favored integration. And he needed to place in high-ranking offices integrationists, especially those who advised the secretary of defense on military finances.

Although by the end of Truman's presidency he had replaced many high-level officers with ones who supported integration, the desegregation of the armed forces moved slowly. Nonetheless, his support for integration had prompted civilians to take similar actions and challenge segregation in the courts. In the case of Mexican Americans, one of the first major national desegregation victories took place in California when the ACLU, together with Catholic associations, challenged the state's "antimiscegenation" laws.

In 1948 in the case of *Perez v. Sharp*, the California Supreme Court removed Catholics from the state's antimiscegenation laws. Andrea Pérez, a Mexican American, and Sylvester Davis, an African American, had been prohibited from marrying due to California's antimiscegenation laws.[102] Under California law, a mixed-Caucasian could marry anyone, but a person who was white could not marry an African American. Because the Los Angeles County Clerk's Office considered Andrea to be a non-mixed Caucasian of Mexican heritage, she was prohibited from marrying Sylvester.[103] Andrea and Sylvester sought legal counsel from the Southern California chapter of the ACLU, which at that time was working with the Catholic Interracial Council of Los Angeles to challenge California's antimiscegenation laws.

Daniel Marshall, Andrea and Sylvester's attorney, who was also the chair of the Los Angeles chapter of the Catholic Interracial Council, won the suit. The California Supreme Court ruled that because Andrea and Sylvester were both Catholics, and since Catholic doctrine did not prohibit different races from marrying freely, California's marriage codes violated their religious freedom. After the ruling, Catholics, regardless of their race, were permitted to marry freely in California, and the *Perez* case created a precedent that was followed by other states. By the late 1940s, thirty-one of the thirty-eight states that had passed antimiscegenation legislation had revoked their statutes.[104] Texas was among the states that failed to follow this liberal path. Texas's antimiscegenation laws had not been altered for generations. In Texas, Caucasians were allowed to marry anyone not of African descent. If clerks issuing marriage licenses deemed Mexican Americans to be solely of the Caucasian race, Texas antimiscegenation laws also applied to them, even if both persons applying for a marriage license were of Mexican origin. Only Mexican Americans who were phenotypically mixed-Caucasian were allowed to marry Black people.[105]

Although the *Perez* case was monumental in moving forward civil rights law in the United States, the most important desegregation achievements affecting Mexican Americans were the legal challenges against school segregation. The first successful lawsuit again took place in California, which was soon followed by a Texas case. *Mendez v. Westminster* (1947) led to a dismantling of the legal arguments used by school boards to rationalize the segregation of Mexican American students in California. It became the legal foundation for overturning the school segregation of Mexican-descent students throughout the Southwest.[106] In 1946, federal judge Paul J. McCormick ruled that the Westminster School District of Orange County had segregated Mexican-descent students on the basis of their "Latinized" appearance and had gerrymandered the school districts to ensure that Mexican students did not attend school with white students. McCormick concluded that the school board's invocation of California's educational code of 1935 to justify the segregation was unconstitutional. Under California law, Mexican-descent students were identified as Indian and subject to de jure school segregation policies. McCormick disagreed, and ruled that California's educational-segregation code violated Mexican American students' civil rights, since no federal statute stipulated that they were Indian.

David C. Marcus, the lead attorney in the *Mendez* case, applied legal arguments that he had previously used in an earlier desegregation suit involving public accommodations. Three years earlier, Marcus had prevailed in a class-action suit challenging the segregation of Mexican Americans and Puerto Ricans in California's public parks. In *Lopez v. Seccombe* (1944), he argued that no statutes permitted the segregation of either group because of its national origin, and thus the segregation violated their civil rights under the Equal Protection Clauses of the Fifth and Fourteenth Amendments.[107] Using similar arguments in the *Mendez* case, Marcus won the appeal that the Westminster School Board took to the US Ninth Circuit Court of Appeals in San Francisco. On April 14, 1947, Judge McCormick's ruling was upheld. The appellate court agreed that in the absence of state statutes authorizing segregation, it was impermissible.[108]

In Texas, while the *Mendez* case was being litigated, George I. Sánchez, Dr. Hector P. García, and the attorney Gustavo García maintained close contact with the *Mendez* attorneys and waited for the results of the case. Within months after *Mendez* was settled, the three activists challenged school segregation in Texas and filed suit in federal court in Austin.

Delgado v. Bastrop Independent School District

The most successful challenges to segregation in Texas occurred in 1948, when Mexican Americans won legal victories against school segregation and restrictive housing covenants. This transformative period began with the actions of LULAC and a newly founded organization called the GI Forum. In 1947, Dr. Héctor P. García became the president of LULAC, and the next year he founded the GI Forum.[109] García had recently returned to civilian life after serving in the US Army Medical Corps during World War II. When he returned, he inspired Mexican Americans to launch a full attack on segregation and other forms of discrimination. His modus operandi was to demand immediate change through the courts and no longer wait for state representatives to pass legislation to remove Mexican Americans from Texas exclusion laws. He and other trailblazers, such as LULAC members Gustavo García (also known as Gus García) and Carlos Cadena, both attorneys, and George I. Sánchez, considered passage of the Caucasian Resolution and Senate Bill 1 to be insincere political gestures designed to publicly show concern for Mexican Americans in order to get their votes. To these activists, it was obvious that effective legislation could be introduced, but legislators chose not to do it.

On February 1, 1947, Gus García contacted Abraham L. Wirin, attorney for the Southern California chapter of the ACLU, for legal support to file suit against school districts in Bastrop, Caldwell, and Travis Counties.[110] He and Sánchez had studied the *Mendez* case and believed that they could win in Central Texas on similar grounds. But they had to be cautious because the ruling in *Independent School District v. Salvatierra* (1930) allowed Mexican American students to be segregated in Texas. In addition, García and Sánchez planned to charge that school boards intentionally denied students schooling past the fourth grade. In many Texas counties, there were no means for Mexican American students to reach middle school, which meant they would not be eligible to enroll in high school. Wirin agreed to assist García and Sánchez. García would act as lead counsel. Wirin, Robert Eckhardt, and Carlos Cadena would assist him, and Sánchez would provide advice on curriculum, language, and intelligence testing.[111]

The legal team decided to challenge school segregation after hearing Sánchez discuss his research at LULAC meetings. After collecting data on Central Texas schools, Sánchez found that most Mexican American and African American students were systematically segregated in outrageously inferior accommodations. The worst conditions were in the schools along the border of Travis, Bastrop, and Caldwell Counties. The school boards in these counties were unconcerned with offering minority students any semblance of a good education and blatantly mistreated them. When Gus García learned that Sánchez had collected data on these practices, he prompted LULAC to take legal action.

Working with LULAC and the GI Forum, Héctor García raised over ten thousand dollars to finance the legal team's research and court expenses.[112] People were asked to donate money and attend fund-raising parties and events. In the meantime, Gus García's legal team was assisted by students from his alma mater. The Alba Club, a Mexican American student organization at the University of Texas at Austin, helped Sánchez, the club's faculty sponsor, gather data and raise funds for the lawsuit.[113] At the time,

Alba Club, University of Texas at Austin, 1947

approximately 129 Mexican American students attended UT-Austin, out of a total enrollment of 17,406 (0.7 percent).[114]

On November 17, 1947, Gus García filed an official complaint in the US District Court for the Western District of Texas on behalf of Minerva Delgado and nineteen other plaintiffs against four school districts in the counties of Travis, Bastrop, and Caldwell, which bordered one another. Under Texas zoning laws, counties were authorized to share the cost of schooling students who resided in rural areas near county lines.[115] The Martindale Independent School District was located in Caldwell County, the Colorado Common School District in Travis, and the Bastrop and Elgin ISDs in Bastrop County. The Elgin schools served rural students from both Bastrop County and Travis County. In the petition, García stipulated that Mexican-descent students were excluded, barred, or prohibited from attending the regular schools near their homes, which were reserved for white students.[116] And in Travis County, white students who lived near the Mexican schools were bused to the white schools. García charged that Mexican-descent students were placed in overcrowded, dilapidated segregated schools where instruction was unavailable past the fourth or sixth

Mexican school, Bastrop, mid-1940s.

grade. He claimed that this type of segregation was capricious and arbitrary, and violated the plaintiffs' constitutional rights. García asked for the immediate termination of this schooling structure and for the plaintiffs to be paid damages amounting to $10,000.

García informed the court that he had been forced to file this suit when his letters informing L. A. Woods, the state superintendent of education, of the horrendous conditions of the schools were repeatedly ignored. (Texas educational procedures required complainants to first contact the state superintendent of education before filing a lawsuit.) García also stated that Superintendent Woods knew that the schools were segregated and that county administrators were intentionally underfinancing the schools.[117] At the time, many governmental officials nationwide considered school segregation a natural, commonsense practice, but under the law, intentionally providing unequal facilities was a violation of federal and state statutes, including those of Texas.

In response to the charges, Ireland Grace, the attorney for the school boards of the four districts, and Joe R. Greenhill, the assistant state attorney general who represented Woods, denied the charges.[118] Both attorneys asserted that García's claims were false and that the school facilities attended by the white and Mexican students were of comparable quality. They alleged that the only reason Mexican students were not allowed to

Drinking fountain at the Mexican school, Bastrop, mid-1940s

Regular school, Bastrop, mid-1940s

Regular school, Elgin, mid-1940s

Mexican school, Elgin, mid-1940s

Privy at the Mexican school in Elgin, mid-1940s

attend the regular schools was their language deficiencies. Grace and Greenhill also invoked the *Salvatierra* ruling in defense of the school assignments. They argued that under Texas law, *Salvatierra* had affirmed Woods's authority to approve school assignments developed by school districts.

From December 1947 to May 1948, depositions were taken in preparation for the trial, which was scheduled to be held in June 1948, with Judge Ben H. Rice Jr. presiding. When García and Wirin deposed Woods, his answers were defiant. He denied that students in the Mexican schools were provided an inferior curriculum or instructed in substandard facilities.[119]

When the district superintendents were deposed, they echoed Woods's defense and arguments. They each asked why their schools had been singled out, since the separation of Mexican students was common across the state; they considered this to be unfair. They denied that segregation was wrong, but admitted that the Mexican students were not given an education of the same quality as that provided to students in the regular schools. Each identified the same inequities: none of the teachers in the Mexican schools had teaching degrees or had even attended college, while all teachers in the white schools had attended college, and most held teaching degrees; the Mexican schools were overcrowded; most of the Mexican schools did not have indoor bathrooms, drinking fountains, or cafeterias; and the Mexican schools were poorly constructed. Even after disclosing these facts, the superintendents stood their ground and asserted that they had done nothing wrong because the Mexican schools met state standards.[120]

When García asked the superintendents how they expected Mexican students to qualify for high school if the fifth to eighth grades were unavailable in their districts, they did not have a response. They merely said that they were only following their school boards' policies. Mr. Brown, superintendent of the Elgin school district, did elaborate why the upper grades had been eliminated in its Mexican schools. Four years earlier, the school board had voted to close the upper grade levels in the Mexican schools in preparation for building renovations. Mexican students in grades six to eight were to temporarily attend other schools near their homes, but for some unknown reason, the transfers did not take place. Afterward, because the Mexican parents did not complain, the board decided not to reopen the higher grades. Brown distanced himself from the board's decision and commented that in Elgin, Latin Americans accepted this type of treatment.[121]

I. W. Popham, the county superintendent of Travis's rural schools, was not as apologetic. He insisted that the treatment of Mexican students in all the county's districts had improved. Gus García had charged that the Colorado Common Schools, which Popham supervised, served white, Mexican, and Black students on Austin's East Side, yet only the white school had adequate facilities. Two of the schools served Black students, two served Mexican students, and one served white students. The schools were spread out in the Montopolis area to the border of Bastrop County.[122] Popham disagreed with García's assessment, arguing that the minority schools could not be described as shacks because brick rooms had been added the previous year. Furthermore, in the case of the Mexican students in Montopolis, when the La Luz Church school became overcrowded, the county built a second school for Mexican students. Grade levels were added to the new school for Mexican students who wanted to attend classes beyond the second grade.

When García asked Popham why the white school in Montopolis did not admit Mexican students, the superintendent appeared to be appalled at the impudence of the question. The white and Mexican schools in Montopolis were located across the street from each other, yet only the white school offered a curriculum up to the ninth grade.[123] García had raised this question because Mexican students in Montopolis did not have a local school that offered classes beyond the sixth grade. Popham responded that if Mexican students really wanted to attend high school, nothing was stopping them from attending seventh to eighth grade, since several schools in Austin admitted Mexican students from outside their district. He accused the students' parents of lacking the initiative to find schools willing to admit their children in the higher grades. He did not consider it a contradiction to expect Mexican American parents to find schools for their children, whereas the white students in his district were automatically provided schooling up to the ninth grade. Popham repeatedly emphasized that things were getting better. For example, some Mexican students were sometimes given bus service if they lived near white neighborhoods. He had recently instructed the bus driver in Montopolis to return to the Mexican neighborhoods if he finished driving the white students early.

The last subject that García and Wirin raised in their inquiries concerned the evaluation methods used by the schools to assess English-language proficiency. When the superintendents were asked what type of language tests their schools administered, they admitted that students were not tested and that all school assignments were based on a student's ethnicity. The superintendents confirmed that Polish and Czechoslovakian non-English speakers, as well as white students who failed their English tests, were not placed in separate schools or classrooms.[124] These responses indicated that the schools were violating state law, since the *Salvatierra* ruling required that Mexican American students be tested for English proficiency before being segregated in separate classrooms. The schools were also not following a uniform policy for white students.

The trial was held on June 15, 1948, and after closing arguments, Judge Rice ruled for the plaintiffs.[125] He concluded that the plaintiffs' attorneys had proved that the segregation of Mexican students was arbitrary and in violation of their constitutional rights under the Equal Protection Clause of the Fourteenth Amendment. The representatives of the school districts had been unable to prove that language handicaps were the basis of their schools' segregation policies, since none of the schools administered language tests to determine English proficiency. Rice also ordered Superintendent Woods to stop approving the districts' school-placement policies if they were based solely on ancestry. Only students in the first grade, or students who did not speak English, could be instructed in separate classrooms, and only for one year. Rice added that when separate language instruction was necessary, the classrooms had to be located within the same campus attended by white and Mexican students. Finally, he ordered that the Mexican schools across the state be integrated or closed by September 1949.

In sum, Rice's ruling theoretically ended the school segregation of Mexican students in Texas. In practice, however, the struggle for equal education continued. The Texas Legislature and the governor's office disagreed with the court and continued to erect barriers to school desegregation.

CHAPTER 5

The Path to Desegregation, 1948–1962

This chapter explores the achievements and struggles of Mexican American civil rights activists in their pursuit of desegregating their communities in Texas from 1948 to 1962. At the time, Mexican Americans made great advances in dismantling the legal barriers used to exclude them from serving on juries, attending schools with white students, and residing in neighborhoods restricted to white residents. Though the courts ruled in favor of Mexican American litigants, the Texas Legislature and the governor's office found alternate methods to maintain segregation. Governmental officials and the Texas Legislature were particularly concerned with keeping schools segregated, and when ordered to desegregate, they passed laws to prevent civil rights activists from filing lawsuits.

The political successes and failures of Mexican American civil rights activists in Texas occurred when political shifts were taking place across the United States. Many Americans supported ending segregation and began to pressure Congress to end de jure segregation. Likewise, the US Supreme Court began to offer rulings in school desegregation cases that went against past segregationist agendas. In 1954, under the Court's ruling in *Brown v. Board of Education of Topeka*, all public schools, including universities, were ordered to desegregate. As part of the analysis on how desegregation unfolded in Texas, this chapter examines the first phase of the desegregation of the University of Texas at Austin, the state's flagship university. The aim of this case study is to illustrate the different kinds of segregation experiences that Mexican Americans and African Americans underwent, and it addresses how the *Brown* ruling benefited Mexican American students. The chapter concludes with the integrationist agenda put forward by President John F. Kennedy's administration and the political response of Mexican American civil rights organizations.

Farmworker Housing and Housing Covenants

In the aftermath of *Delgado v. Bastrop Independent School District* (1948), LULAC members moved forward to challenge other forms of segregation. The schools named in the lawsuit were ordered to begin immediate desegregation procedures, and Gus García was authorized to monitor the schools' desegregation plans. Winning the case was one matter—having the court's order enforced remained a challenge. Across Texas, school districts were not prepared to desegregate, and they sought support from the governor's office and the legislature. Consequently, George Sánchez, Gus García, and Héctor P. García, a doctor who was also president of the GI Forum, remained vigilant, and prepared to once again take legal action. Héctor García's next challenge was to improve the housing conditions of farmworkers, who lived in deplorable conditions throughout Texas. Unfortunately, the governor's office had no intention of supporting any reforms in this area.

In 1948, Héctor García, representing the GI Forum, conducted a survey of farmworkers' housing conditions in South Texas. He found that most employers providing camp housing rented workers dilapidated shacks without running water or trash pickup. In many towns in South Texas, Mexican Americans were segregated in areas without gas or sewage utilities. These housing conditions contributed to the spread of tuberculosis, dysentery, and other illnesses.[1] When García's report was submitted to Governor Beauford Jester, he requested that the housing violations be investigated and that something be done to improve living conditions. The governor acknowledged receipt of the report, but said that he could not get involved in municipal issues. Under Texas's home rule laws, municipal officials were empowered to make decisions about such things as the construction of buildings, the paving of streets, and the location of sewer systems. To his knowledge, the uneven infrastructural development of a city was not a violation of any state or federal law. According to the governor, the living conditions that García witnessed were certainly a tragedy, but most likely were the outcome of social class differences, not municipal neglect. On this matter, the GI Forum was unable to change state policy, since home rule laws allowed city officials to neglect sectors of a municipality. It was legal for city officials to allow agricultural corporations to rent housing that was overcrowded and lacked sanitation. This was a common pattern across the United States because state legislatures refused to pass minimum-standard sanitation and safety laws, and the federal government refused to intervene in farm labor issues.[2]

Although the GI Forum failed to convince the state government to improve farmworkers' housing, in 1948 LULAC civil rights activists won a ruling benefiting Mexican Americans opposed to restrictive housing covenants. After purchasing a house in the Mayfield Park Division of San Antonio, Abdon Salazar Puente was not allowed to move in after his neighbor sued him for violating a restrictive covenant prohibiting the sale of houses in the subdivision to people of Mexican descent.[3] The attorneys Carlos Cadena and Alonso S. Perales agreed to represent Puente. If they won the case, it would establish a precedent against using housing covenants to prohibit Mexicans from living in neighborhoods reserved for white residents. After considerable litigation, *Clifton v. Puente* (1948) was turned over to the Fourth Court of Appeals of Texas.

The prospect of Puente winning the suit was good, since on May 3, 1948, the US Supreme Court ruled in a case from Missouri, *Shelley v. Kraemer*, that the courts could not enforce housing covenants to prevent African Americans from moving into white neighborhoods. Cadena and Perales acknowledged that the Court had continued to allow the use of housing covenants when contracts were negotiated between private citizens, but the courts could no longer deploy police or sheriffs to enforce such covenants.[4] Once the police and the courts were removed from the process, enforcing a restrictive covenant became difficult.

The challenge for Cadena and Perales was to convince the court of appeals that *Shelley v. Kraemer* applied to groups besides African Americans. The Shelleys, an African American family in St. Louis, had unknowingly bought a house bound by a restrictive covenant prohibiting African American ownership, and they had been prevented from moving in by one of their neighbors. Puente's case was similar. He unknowingly purchased a house with a similar restriction. In addition, Cadena and Perales had to overcome the subjective bias that the Fourth Court of Appeals had shown against Mexican Americans. Four years earlier in *Terrell Wells Swimming Pool v. Rodriguez*, the judges had ruled that the segregation policies of private businesses did not violate Mexican Americans' civil rights.

The covenant at issue in Puente's case was put in place by the Southwestern Acreage Company in 1937. It prohibited the sale or lease of the property "to persons of Mexican descent."[5] Over the years, the Mayfield Park house had been sold to three buyers. On December 4, 1947, Puente purchased the property from P. J. Humphreys, who four months earlier had purchased it from I. N. Clifton. After Clifton learned that Humphreys had quickly resold his house to Mexicans, he believed that some type of fraud had taken place. Clifton claimed that Humphreys and Puente knowingly ignored the restrictive covenant, thereby committing fraud in the sale of his property. He immediately contacted the Southwestern Acreage Company, and was reconveyed the title to the property on the basis that Puente's title was invalid.

On December 8, 1947, Clifton received a temporary injunction preventing Puente from taking possession of or moving into the property. The dispute over the sale of the house reached the Fourth Court of Appeals several months after the US Supreme Court's decision in *Shelley*. Clifton's attorneys tried to convince the court that restrictive housing covenants were still enforceable in Texas against Mexicans, since *Shelley* involved African Americans. The justices, however, ruled in favor of Puente. The ruling became the first case in Texas to rescind the use of racial covenants in the sale or lease of houses to Mexican Americans.

Although the *Puente* case was a victory for Mexican Americans and an important legal precedent, ending the use of restrictive covenants would be difficult. People contesting the covenants had to take their complaints to the courts, and for most Mexican Americans, the cost of such legal action was out of their reach. The use of housing covenants continued in Texas for several decades, and many builders and property owners refused to sell or lease to Mexican-origin people.[6]

Exclusion Practices in Funeral Homes

In 1949, Mexican American civil rights activists sought to challenge the exclusion of Mexican Americans from funeral homes reserved for white citizens. This time they met with mixed results. The governor's office refused to assist them, yet they obtained the political support of Senator Lyndon B. Johnson, and their struggle received national attention. In late December 1948, Beatrice Longoria contacted Héctor García and asked for the support of the GI Forum. Her husband, Felix Longoria, died during World War II, and his body was being sent to Three Rivers, his hometown in South Texas, for burial. The funeral home in Three Rivers refused to prepare his body for interment. She believed that her husband, a war hero, was being discriminated against because he was a Mexican American.

Private Felix Longoria died in 1945 while fighting in Luzon, in the Philippines. Three years later, his body was recovered and scheduled to be shipped to Three Rivers for reburial. Late in December 1948, Mrs. Longoria asked Tom Kennedy, the undertaker and owner of the Rice Funeral Home in Three Rivers, to receive Felix Longoria's body and allow a funeral service to be held in the chapel. He denied her request. The reason: "The whites won't like it."[7] When García contacted Kennedy on Beatrice Longoria's behalf, the request was again denied, and Kennedy added, "The last time we let them [Mexican Americans] use the chapel, they all got drunk and we just can't control them."

Kennedy's funeral policy was common across Texas and not against state law, since it was legal for business owners to deny services to anyone. When Mexican Americans died in Texas, it was necessary to inter them quickly because in many towns and cities, mortuary services were unavailable. In most Texas cities, it was also common for cemeteries to be segregated based on ethnicity and race, and sometimes religion. Regulations governing cemeteries and funeral houses were part of the authority given to cities under home rule legislation.[8] Cities and towns could regulate cemetery and funeral home business practices as they saw fit as long as state sanitation and health policies were followed. According to state law: "The cemetery association may make, adopt and enforce rules and regulations for the use care, control, management, restriction and protection of its cemetery, and of all parts and subdivisions thereof."[9] Thus, the law was on Kennedy's side. He had not violated any civil rights laws.

On January 12, 1949, García contacted governmental officials to intervene on behalf of Mrs. Longoria. He sent telegrams to President Truman, Governor Jester, Senator Lyndon B. Johnson, Price Daniel (the state attorney general), and several other state officials.[10] He asked that an exception to Texas's funerary admission policy be made for this national hero. García also contacted news reporters in Texas and other national media outlets to publicize this social injustice. On January 13, Senator Lyndon B. Johnson responded. The rest never acknowledged García's request. Johnson told García that if Kennedy continued to refuse to cooperate, his office would arrange for Longoria to be buried at Arlington National Cemetery with full military honors.

Johnson, who had recently won his senatorial race by a razor-thin margin over former governor Coke Stevenson, was aware of the crucial support he had received from Mexican Americans. By intervening, he demonstrated his respect for the Longoria family and Mexican Americans in general.

When media outlets received news of Johnson's involvement, a scandal broke out. J. F. Gray, the state house representative for Three Rivers, and the local chamber of commerce accused García and Johnson of colluding to defame the good people of their city. Gray denied García's charges that Mexican Americans were refused funeral services or were discriminated against in Three Rivers. He asked the governor's office to establish a commission to investigate the false, outrageous charges made by García and the GI Forum. Under fire, Héctor García urgently summoned Gus García to represent him, the GI Forum, and Beatrice Longoria.

Gray was appointed chairman of the commission, despite having shown bias against the complainants. The commission first interviewed Kennedy and compared his testimony with García's and Mrs. Longoria's accounts. Kennedy placed the entire blame on Mrs. Longoria and accused her of misunderstanding him. According to Kennedy, the confusion resulted from a disagreement between Mrs. Longoria and Felix Longoria's parents. They disagreed over where the wake should take place, and not wanting to become involved in a family dispute, he denied Mrs. Longoria's request. Kennedy said that he did not recall telling her that Mexicans were not welcome in his funeral home. When Mrs. Longoria and García testified, they affirmed their previous accounts, and both agreed that Kennedy lied. They asked the interviewers to verify or dispute their charges of discrimination by soliciting local viewpoints.

When news spread that García and Mrs. Longoria had been pressured to retract their statements, the scandal worsened. Gray was put in an embarrassing position. To publicly shame García and demonstrate that he was an incompetent radical, Gray needed to prove that Mrs. Longoria had made a mistake. To impeach Mrs. Longoria's testimony, Gray ordered investigators to pressure Felix Longoria's father to verify Kennedy's account. After a long interview, the investigators were unable to convince Guadalupe Longoria that he too had misunderstood Kennedy. Instead, Mr. Longoria repeatedly asserted that Kennedy lied, and he refused to sign any document stating otherwise. When Longoria refused to cooperate, the investigators gave up. After the investigation closed, Gray filed the commission's majority report, concluding that the entire affair had been a misunderstanding.[11]

At the conclusion of the investigation, two reports were submitted to the Texas Legislature. Gray wrote the majority report, basing his analysis on the funeral director's account, which also concluded that Mexican-origin people were not segregated or discriminated against in Three Rivers. The minority report, written by Frank Oltorf, supported Mrs. Longoria's account and exposed the fact that Guadalupe Longoria had not signed the affidavit. A commission member who had initially signed the majority report later joined Oltorf's minority report when reporters learned that Guadalupe Longoria had been harassed by the investigators.

On February 16, 1949, Felix Longoria was interred in Arlington National Cemetery.[12] Gray had tried to convince Mrs. Longoria to hold the services in Three Rivers, but García advised against it. Accepting the local invitation would whitewash the whole affair and be seen as an admission that Kennedy and other Anglos in Three Rivers were not at fault. After the funeral, Senator Johnson's popularity within Mexican American communities in South Texas surged, as did the esteem felt by Mexican Americans for the GI Forum. The event also opened a direct line of communication between Johnson and García.

Hernandez v. Texas

In 1954, Gus García and Carlos Cadena headed a team of lawyers to argue before the US Supreme Court that in Texas, Mexican Americans were excluded from serving on juries. Their client, Peter (Pete) Hernández, had been indicted for murder by an all-white grand jury and convicted of the crime by another all-white jury, and they believed the case represented a clear violation of Hernández's civil rights.[13] *Hernandez v. State of Texas* became a critical juncture in Mexican American civil rights history, because García and Cadena's legal team were able to prove that Mexican Americans were excluded from juries and that this prevented Mexican American defendants from receiving fair trials. Jury exclusion was part of a widespread practice in Texas to dehumanize Mexican Americans and impose segregated rules of social comportment on them.

In 1951, Pete Hernández killed Joe Espinoza. Both men lived in Edna, Texas, the county seat of Jackson County, in East Texas, a section of the state where Mexican Americans and African Americans constituted a large percentage of the population. Jackson County was adjacent to Victoria County. In 1930, African Americans and Mexican Americans constituted 35 percent of Jackson County's residents, and Mexican Americans alone accounted for 18 percent.[14] By 1950, the county had 12,916 residents, of which 14 percent were Spanish-surnamed.[15] Edna's main economic base was agriculture, and whites enforced a system of social segregation, which was common throughout Jackson County. White students were schooled apart from Mexican Americans and African Americans, and it was common to see signs in restaurants reading, "No Mexicans Served."[16]

Hernández worked as a harvest picker, and Espinoza was a tenant farmer. After work, while Hernández and Espinoza were relaxing in the Chico Sánchez Tavern, Hernández became agitated and started talking loudly, bringing attention to himself. Based on eyewitness reports, Hernández left the cantina, returned with a shotgun, and killed Espinoza. There was no question about Hernández's guilt. What differed was Hernández's version of what happened in the tavern and why he returned with a shotgun. Hernández testified that Espinoza and another man called him a cripple and would not stop harassing him. Espinoza then forcibly shoved him out the door of the tavern. According to Hernández, once they were outside, Espinoza roughed him up and tried to rob him. To protect himself, he went home, got a shotgun, and returned to shoot Espinoza.

Hernández was charged with murder. To obtain legal representation, his family traveled to Houston and met with John Herrera and James DeAnda, who shared a law practice. Herrera referred Hernández's family to Gus García, who later agreed to act as lead counsel. Herrera and García were members of LULAC, and they had worked together on the *Delgado v. Bastrop* school desegregation case. On September 20, 1951, Hernández was indicted by the Jackson County grand jury in Edna, and three weeks later he was found guilty in the Jackson County district court.[17] In both instances, an-all white jury heard the evidence against Hernández. A year later, the conviction was affirmed by the Texas Court of Criminal Appeals, in Austin. García and Herrera then filed an appeal with the US Supreme Court. They knew that the case went beyond a small-town murder. The fundamental issue was racially based jury exclusion in Texas. Jackson County was the perfect test case because a large percentage of the residents were Mexican American, yet they were never called for jury duty.

On October 12, 1953, the US Supreme Court accepted the *Hernández* petition.[18] To prepare for trial, Gus García asked Carlos Cadena to be lead cocounsel. They were assisted by Maury Maverick Sr. and John Herrera. Maverick was a college friend of García and a respected and trusted Anglo-American ally. In the past, LULAC had helped elect Maverick mayor of San Antonio and later to the US House of Representatives for Texas's Twentieth Congressional District, which included Bexar County and parts of South Texas.[19] Cadena was a professor of law at St. Mary's University in San Antonio. He was the first Mexican American to hold such a distinguished position in Texas.

To finance the expenses for the appeal, George I. Sánchez provided $5,000 from his research funds and Héctor García organized dinner and dance fund-raisers with the assistance of LULAC and GI Forum chapters.[20] García raised additional funds by publicizing the trial on his radio program, and received many donations of $25 to $50.

During oral arguments, Howard Wimberley, assistant attorney general for Texas, presented the state's two-class theory, which had been used in previous trials to explain why Mexican Americans were not called for jury duty. Wimberley argued that in Texas there were only two races, Blacks and whites, and only Blacks on occasion needed the government's protection from hostile whites.[21] Mexicans were treated as white, and their absence on juries was not the result of racism, but rather because of their lack of education and failure to speak English proficiently.

Wimberley argued that Hernández's conviction should not be over-turned, because his rights under the Equal Protection Clause of the Four-teenth Amendment were not violated. As a member of the white race, Hernández had received a fair trial, since the jurors that convicted him were white and his peers. Wimberley claimed that Mexicans in Texas were treated as part of the white race and that discrimination against them did not exist. Thus, petitioners could not prove that jury exclusion existed in Texas, because Mexicans were members of the white race. As evidence that Mexican Americans were treated as white in Texas, he referred to Sen-ate Resolution 1, passed in 1945, which declared that Mexicans and Latin Americans could not be excluded from public accommodations. Wimberly failed to mention that the Texas Legislature, at the time of the passage of the resolution, did not nullify any of the state's exclusion laws. The rights of proprietors and managers to expel anyone from their places of business remained unchanged. For the resolution to be effective, the laws giving private citizens the right to segregate Mexican Americans or refuse them service needed to be voided. The Fourth Court of Appeals in San Antonio had made this clear when it upheld the right of proprietors to segregate Mexican Americans in the *Terrell Wells Swimming Pool* case.

Gus García presented the oral arguments for the Hernández team. His defense centered on a legal argument designed by James DeAnda and re-fined by García and Carlos Cadena, which came to be called the "class apart theory." García contended that Mexican Americans were a "class of their own" and that for generations they had been discriminated against on the basis of their national origin. Thus, he claimed, Texas courts had misin-terpreted the Equal Protection Clause of the Fourteenth Amendment by claiming that it applied to only two classes: whites and Blacks. As a result, Texas courts had concluded that Mexican Americans were not allowed to claim discrimination, because they were white.[22] In challenging this asser-tion, García had no trouble presenting substantial evidence that in Texas, Mexican Americans were not treated as white. In many counties across Texas, including Jackson County, there were three classes of people: whites, Blacks, and Mexican Americans. Mexican Americans constituted a distinct class that was segregated, denied public services, excluded from restrooms reserved for whites, and not allowed in jury boxes. García further argued that it was a contradiction for the state to claim that Mexican Americans were treated as white when governmental officials knowingly permitted their exclusion from public accommodations. Using research gathered by Carlos Cadena, he argued that plenty of evidence showed that Mexican Americans in general were not considered white. García cited the US Census of 1930 and stated that in later censuses, the bureau continued collecting data distinguishing Mexican Americans from the general white population. He also referred to anthropological studies and governmental reports offering the opinion that Mexican Americans were a people primarily of Indian descent.[23]

In concluding his arguments, García reiterated that the Equal Protection Clause of the Fourteenth Amendment was not designed to protect only African Americans, and nothing in the constitutional text makes that claim.

On May 3, 1954, the Supreme Court ruled that Hernández had been denied a fair trial because his due process and equal protection rights had been violated when his peers were not allowed to serve as jurors.[24] Texas courts were found to have erred in relying on the two-class theory and had failed to recognize that people can be discriminated on the basis of ancestry and national origin:

> When the existence of a distinct class is demonstrated, and it is further shown that the laws, as written or as applied, single out that class for different treatment not based on some reasonable classification, the guarantees of the Constitution have been violated. The Fourteenth Amendment is not directed solely against discrimination due to a "two-class theory"—that is, based upon differences between "white" and Negro. . . .
>
> The petitioner's initial burden in substantiating his charge of group discrimination was to prove that persons of Mexican descent constitute a separate class in Jackson County, distinct from "whites." . . . No substantial evidence was offered to rebut the logical inference to be drawn from these facts, and it must be concluded that petitioner succeeded in his proof.[25]

The justices were convinced that sufficient evidence had been presented to prove that Mexican Americans were discriminated against in Texas on account of their national origin. It was also absurd to accept as truth the state's claim that Mexican Americans in Jackson County had not been appointed to jury duty merely by chance. According to the justices, it was obvious that Mexican Americans had intentionally and systematically not been called to serve on juries—a clear act of discrimination.[26] The justices then ordered Hernández to be retried in another city.

Seven months later, Hernández was retried in Refugio, a town near the eastern coast of Texas. He was found guilty and given twenty years in

Gustavo García,
GI Forum legal adviser,
visiting Washington,
DC, 1952

prison. García eventually got his sentence reduced, and Hernández was released in 1960. The death of Joe Espinoza was a tragedy, but his misfortune helped expose how Mexican Americans were systematically discriminated against. Mexican Americans were treated as second-class citizens because of their national origin, language, customs, and skin color.

After *Hernandez*, Texas officials could no longer claim that Mexican Americans had unintentionally been barred from serving on juries. County clerks were put on notice that jury exclusion was against the law. But in the following decades, the state government did not monitor the situation or commission studies to determine which counties in Texas were ignoring the *Hernandez* ruling. It was not until 1970 that a study was commissioned to survey jury participation in Texas. As discussed in chapter 7, the US Commission on Civil Rights found that in some counties, few or no Mexican Americans participated in juries. Nonetheless, the historians Ignacio

García and Carlos Kevin Blanton propose that the *Hernandez* case marked a turning point in the Mexican Americans' civil rights history.[27] Many Mexican American activists began to push for a status that neither disclaimed nor asserted their Spanish ancestry, but rather emphasized their identifiable ethnic differences. Gus García had promoted this idea in 1951 when he gave a speech in Corpus Christi at the State Convention of Latin American Leaders. García maintained that Anglo-Americans historically did not consider Mexican Americans' European heritage a social marker of equality or civility. Mexican American leaders, therefore, to lessen their segregation, had to move away from invoking their Spanish ancestry when claiming why they should not be segregated.[28]

Choice Plans Designed to Prevent Desegregation

Four months after the *Hernandez* decision, the US Supreme Court, in *Brown v. Board of Education of Topeka* (1954), ruled unanimously that the school segregation of African American students under the "separate but equal" doctrine was unconstitutional. *Brown* marked the beginning of a national political shift that challenged the states' customary practices and legal right to segregate students of color. Thurgood Marshall, representing the NAACP, charged that de jure segregation was a violation of the Fourteenth Amendment. On May 17, 1954, the justices agreed: "Separate educational facilities are inherently unequal."[29] The ruling applied to state colleges as well as to public schools at all levels.[30] A new era had begun. Marshall and his legal team had convinced the Court that the purpose of segregation was to maintain Black students in separate, inferior schools, based on a doctrine that promoted the superiority of whites and the inferiority of Blacks. The ruling in *Brown* threatened other forms of de jure racial segregation, since the justices ruled that racial segregation violated the Equal Protection Clause of the Fourteenth Amendment.

After *Brown*, many members of Congress, particularly from the South, wanted to challenge the court's ruling. When news of the ruling was publicized, Texas legislators prepared for a constitutional fight. Governor Allan Shivers and Attorney General John Ben Shepperd immediately began to strategize how to prevent the enforcement of *Brown* in Texas. To do so, the governor's office turned to the political strategies that had been used to slow the desegregation of the Mexican schools after the *Delgado v. Bastrop* ruling. The governor's office had effectively used "choice plans" to obstruct the desegregation of most Mexican schools, and now the same strategy would be used to prevent the desegregation of African American students.

In the *Delgado* ruling, Judge Rice had given the State of Texas nearly one year to stop segregating Mexican American students. That meant Governor Shivers had until September 1949 to prove the state's compliance. Because the governor was against the integration of the Mexican schools, he established an administrative plan to deceive the court and designed a legal strategy to remove Mexican American civil rights activists from seeking recourse in the courts.[31]

In the wake of the *Delgado* ruling, Bastrop and Caldwell County school districts transferred Mexican American students to the regular schools. The superintendents of both counties also ordered the rest of the schools in their districts to integrate. Most school boards complied, except for those in Lockhart and San Marcos.[32] In Travis County, rather than integrate the white and Mexican schools in the Colorado Common School District, the superintendents transferred the students to schools within the Austin city limits.[33] The conditions of the Mexican schools were so deplorable that white students would not be transferred there.

To obstruct wider application of the court's order, Shivers established a commission composed of members who opposed integration. The Texas Education Commission gave school districts advice on how to delay the desegregation of their schools.[34] Because the commissioners knew that Gus García and members of LULAC and the GI Forum were monitoring the desegregation orders and would contact the court if the schools were not making plans to desegregate, the commissioners decided to stop García and these organizations from bothering the school districts. Working with the governor, the commissioners established a state policy prohibiting civil rights organizations like LULAC and the GI Forum from intervening when schools refused to desegregate. They were prohibited by law from filing complaints against schools that failed to develop desegregation plans. The only people eligible to initiate a complaint against a noncompliant school were school board members. This outrageously hypocritical strategy amounted to a mockery of the court's order, since the school boards unwilling to desegregate were the only institutional bodies eligible to complain against their own decisions. Gus García, LULAC, and the GI Forum had no legal authority to interfere unless a school board member sought legal representation from them. Even then, litigation could not take place until the Texas Education Agency, which was controlled by the commissioners, reported that negotiations between the schools and the complainants had stalled. When García informed Superintendent Woods that the commission's policies violated the court's order, he was told to take his grievance to the US Supreme Court.[35] He was also told that he was allowed to monitor only the progress of the schools involved in the *Delgado* lawsuit.

The commission then empowered school boards to stand their ground if they chose not to comply with the court's desegregation order. School boards were advised to develop choice plans. A choice plan gave parents the option to decide to send their children to the Mexican schools or the white schools. As long as the school boards informed the court that they had instituted a choice plan, the schools were technically complying, without actually making any changes. The logic behind a choice plan was that if white parents refused to send their children to a Mexican school or an integrated one, it was not the responsibility of the school boards to interfere.

The commissioners were aware that giving Mexican American parents the choice to transfer their children to the regular schools might lead to integration, so this option was strategically undermined. To obstruct the transfer of Mexican students, the commissioners told school administrators that they did not have to accept Mexican American students if classroom space was limited.[36] For schools to comply under *Delgado*, they only had to show that they had established long-term plans to make space available. In this way, schools could decide if and when some Mexican American students would be transferred to the regular schools. In addition, the commission gave schools the authority to decide when building improvements would be made.[37] After these policies were instituted, Governor Shivers reported to the court that the September 1949 desegregation deadline had been met.

Five years later, following *Brown*, the same strategy was implemented against African American students. Shivers expected African Americans to seek recourse through the courts, so he sought the advice of the Associated Citizens' Councils of Texas.[38] Council members suggested that the Texas Legislature pass strong segregationist bills, demand states' rights, boycott businesses that supported integration, and protect the legal foundation of choice plans. In the meantime, Shivers developed the "theory of interposition" to defy *Brown*. He declared that states did not have to comply with federal law when it was in conflict with state laws. Senator Price Daniel, who also opposed integration, advised the governor that if he planned to delay or prevent integration, it would be necessary to develop policies that did not defy federal law outright.[39] Shivers's theory was unconstitutional and would not be upheld by any court.

By May 1955, choice plans had been formalized across Texas and adopted throughout the South.[40] They became a legitimate bureaucratic process to demonstrate compliance with *Brown*. The US Supreme Court allowed this to happen because Congress pressured the justices to delay school integration by not requiring schools to immediately comply.[41] In *Brown v. Board of Education of Topeka* (1955), known as *Brown II*, when the justices established procedures for desegregating the schools, they set up a framework for school districts that wanted to integrate quickly, yet still allowed southern legislatures to delay mixing students in classrooms. The justices gave federal district judges the authority to determine the pace of integration and to accept, revise, or reject desegregation plans.[42] Desegregation was to proceed "with all deliberate speed." Throughout the South, judges accepted choice plans and approved plans that did not have specific deadlines for integration. In Texas, *Brown II* stalled the school desegregation of African American students and gave schools that refused to admit Mexican American students further authority to slow down the pace of building new classrooms in the regular schools.[43]

Schools That Desegregated

The desegregation of Mexican American students and African American students in Texas followed different patterns. Mexican Americans ran for school boards and pressured local schools to desegregate, while African Americans sought to enforce *Brown* by returning to the courts. Regardless of Governor Shivers's opposition to school integration, some schools desegregated within a few months of the *Brown* decision. Most Catholic schools in Texas desegregated, with the San Antonio schools being the first to do so.[44] This was a significant act of support for *Brown* because private schools were not included in its mandate to desegregate. Furthermore, by August 1955, several school districts had either desegregated voluntarily or designed short-term plans to desegregate. The cities of San Antonio, Austin, El Paso, San Angelo, Kerrville, Harlingen, Weslaco, and Mission complied with *Brown*.[45]

Schools on military bases and public schools accepting the children of service members also desegregated. Many of these schools had no choice in the matter, since they were ordered by the Department of Defense to integrate or close down. The secretary of defense, Charles E. Wilson, ordered that all military base schools and all public schools attended by military dependents be integrated by September 1, 1955, or prepare to be sanctioned.[46] These schools were not allowed to submit choice plans.

Brown gave Wilson the power to enforce the desegregation of all military-affiliated schools, even if states objected. State governments could accept the Department of Defense plans or have their schools closed. Public schools and base schools that had been erected on federal land and were receiving federal assistance were forced to meet the secretary's deadline. Schools that only received federal funds had the option of retaining segregated policies, but at the cost of losing federal funds. But schools built on federal lands had no choice, since the land belonged to the federal government.

In Texas, schools located on military bases and public schools leasing federal lands met the September deadline. Only one elementary school, associated with Reese Air Force Base, near Lubbock, refused to comply, and the school was closed.[47] Base commanders were informed that they had to follow Secretary Wilson's directive, regardless of their personal preferences regarding school integration. Wilson issued orders requiring base commanders to put pressure on civilian communities to desegregate public accommodations used by military families. If merchants refused to desegregate their place of business, base commanders were not to conduct business with the establishments. Likewise, clubs that retained exclusionary membership clauses were not allowed to use base facilities (e.g., stadiums, dance halls, meeting rooms, etc.).

In the case of Mexican Americans, many schools were desegregated through community efforts.[48] LULAC and the GI Forum ran Mexican Americans for school board positions as a way to get around the Texas Education Commission's ban prohibiting civil right organizations from intervening in school affairs. LULAC and GI Forum members elected to school boards could not be prevented from filing lawsuits against school districts. Across Texas, Mexican Americans won school board elections and pressured their school districts to close down the Mexican schools.[49] In San Antonio, Gus García was elected to the San Antonio Independent School District Board from 1949 to 1952.[50] During his tenure, he worked to increase the financial resources provided to Mexican American and African American schools and to improve school facilities.

LULAC and GI Forum members acknowledged that school integration was moving slowly. And they knew that repeatedly filing lawsuits would exhaust their organizations' resources. Gus García and George Sánchez advised school board members that the most expedient tactic was to pressure school administrators and board members to comply with *Delgado*. If diplomatic action was ineffective, they were to warn administrators that they were prepared to file suit. The intent was to convince school administrators that constructing new classrooms in the regular schools made more financial sense than spending a school district's funds on a lawsuit. By the late

1950s, this type of pressure tactic was working, and many school boards, to avoid litigation, closed down the Mexican schools, implemented transfer programs, or expanded the upper grades in the Mexican schools.[51]

After the *Brown* ruling, García and Sánchez wanted to work with African Americans to desegregate schools. But they met stiff opposition from conservative LULAC and GI Forum members, who instead favored working with the state government to desegregate only the Mexican schools. At the time, Mexican American and African American coalitions were rare, organized mainly during elections to support candidates who opposed segregation. For example, in San Antonio in 1955, African Americans and Mexican Americans worked together to elect Henry B. González to the city council and Albert Peña Jr. to the Bexar County Commission. Both were outspoken integrationists opposed to school and public accommodation segregation.[52] A decade later, collaborative events were organized by both groups, but they primarily addressed employment issues.[53]

Unlike Mexican Americans, who were sometimes successful in working with school boards, African American civil rights organization instead appealed to the courts. They experienced mixed results. In Dallas, the NAACP filed a federal lawsuit to begin desegregating the schools. In *Bell v. Rippy* (1955), Judge Atwell, who was personally opposed to integration, dismissed the lawsuit on the basis that it was premature because most schools were overcrowded and transferring Black students was impractical.[54] Judge Atwell's ruling was reversed by the US Fifth Circuit Court of Appeals, yet the school boards refused to desegregate and ignored the order. Two years later, the NAACP petitioned the appellate court to enforce its earlier ruling. Because of local resistance, the Fifth Circuit judges reconsidered their desegregation order and accepted a long-term plan that might lead to the desegregation of some schools.[55]

The NAACP was more successful against the Mansfield Independent School District. The organization obtained a favorable ruling in *Jackson v. Rawdon* (1955) against the district, southeast of Fort Worth.[56] The problems experienced by the Mansfield African American community were so shocking that the NAACP was confident that the courts would demand that African American high school students be immediately accepted in the regular high school. The city of Mansfield practiced school segregation at all levels and did not offer African Americans admission to the only high school in the district. Instead, African American students were bused to downtown Fort Worth, more than twenty miles away. When the Mansfield case was heard by the federal court in Fort Worth, Judge Joe Estes ruled against the NAACP on the grounds that the school district had the choice of setting the pace of integration of Mansfield High School. Nearly a year later, the NAACP received a favorable ruling when the Fifth Circuit Court of Appeals overturned his decision and ordered the immediate desegregation of Mansfield High. It was the first time in Texas that the immediate desegregation of a school was ordered.

On August 30, 1956, the first African American students were scheduled to enter Mansfield High School, but were prevented from registering by a mob of over three hundred angry white people.[57] Rioters attacked the students and threatened to harm them. The police held back the rioters, but failed to help the students enter the school. The mayor and chief of police had refused to ask for state assistance to help with the desegregation. Governor Shivers sent two Texas Rangers anyway—not to protect the Black students, but to prevent them from entering the high school. Needless to say, the school did not desegregate.[58]

The Texas Legislature Resists Desegregation

The legal challenges launched by the NAACP alarmed the governor's office, and procedures were set in motion to prevent the filing of further lawsuits. To make matters worse for the governor, Mexican Americans were turning to the courts to enforce the *Delgado* ruling. This action was as unwelcome as it was unexpected.

On March 15, 1957, in *Hernandez v. Driscoll Consolidated ISD,* the US District Court for the Southern District of Texas, Corpus Christi Division, ordered schools to stop arbitrarily assigning students to schools and classrooms based on their Mexican origin. James DeAnda, with the assistance of Gus García, Richard Casillas, and Albert Peña Jr., received a favorable ruling against the Driscoll Consolidated Independent School District of Nueces County. Under the *Delgado* ruling, school districts were allowed to separate students in first grade if they did not speak English proficiently. But this could be done only following the administration of a language proficiency test. DeAnda and his legal team proved that school districts across Texas were not administering language tests and were assigning Mexican-descent students to separate facilities based on their ethnicity. They also proved that the state was aware of this problem and had failed to intervene. The data for the plaintiffs had been collected by George I. Sánchez.[59] DeAnda's legal team also proved that officials of the Driscoll CISD were purposely retaining Mexican American students in the first grade for three years in order to appear to be in compliance with the language policies delineated in *Delgado*. DeAnda argued that this policy was designed to make Mexican American students feel inferior for being held back in the first grade; as a consequence, administrators expected students to eventually drop out.

Judge James Allred ordered the Driscoll CISD to immediately terminate its assignment and retention policies and ordered the Texas Education Commission to investigate other school districts that might be violating the same policies. This turned out to be a hollow victory. The Texas Legislature, supported by the new governor, Price Daniel, designed policies to stop the desegregation of minority students in Texas. In 1957, the Fifty-Fifth Texas Legislature introduced a series of bills to stop integration and, in some schools, to mix together students of African and Mexican descent.[60] Most bills targeted African American students, and two were designed for both groups. House Bill 231 cited home environments and cultural backgrounds as reasons to assign students to specific schools or classrooms. School administrators could assign Mexican Americans and African Americans to the same schools or classroom if they judged them to be from similar familial environments. House Bill 65 made it difficult for communities to integrate schools.

From May through the end of December, twelve bills were introduced in the House and Senate to strengthen Texas segregation policies and give school boards extraordinary control. Bills required cities to hold elections if some voters wanted to integrate the schools and to award tuition grants to students who chose to attend segregated academies if their schools integrated. During three of the House debates, Henry B. González, a newly elected state senator from San Antonio, and Senator Abraham Kazen, representing part of South Texas, conducted a series of filibusters lasting from ten to thirty-six hours and killed some of the bills. In May, however, House Bill 231 passed, and in December so did House Bill 65. Section 1 of HB 231 required students to take aptitude tests for placement, and section 2 mandated that students be placed in specific schools or classrooms based on their test scores.[61] Both sections appeared to be racially and ethnically unbiased, yet other sections of the bill revealed the segregationists' intent. Because legislators anticipated that many minority students might score well on the tests, section 4 was designed to keep them with their ethnic and racial peers. It stipulated that home environment would ultimately determine school placement, regardless of test scores. Minority students with above-average scores were to remain in schools with children who came from similar home environments. If minority students outperformed their peers, they would be transferred only at the request of school administrators. With no mention of race or language, the phrase "home environment" gave administrators and teachers the authority to group pupils into ethnic-racial clusters. African Americans and Mexican Americans could be mixed in the same schools and classrooms because of cultural and social class similarities, and the same argument could be used to separate white pupils.

Section 8 of HB 231 clearly defied federal law. It decreed: "No child should be compelled to attend any school in which the races are commingled, when a written objection of the parent or guardian has been filed with the board."[62] The Texas Legislature adopted HB 231 on May 6, 1957, and Governor Daniel signed the act on May 23.

HB 65 required municipalities to hold elections before school boards abolished dual school systems.[63] It also allowed parents to remove their children from schools that were integrated and place them somewhere else. The bill went beyond giving parents a choice to reject integration.

Segregationists had found legal ways to appear to be in compliance with *Delgado, Brown,* and *Driscoll.* Students were to be assigned to schools based on similar cultural and home environments, regardless of test scores. In cities where African Americans and Mexican Americans constituted a large percentage of the student population—such as Houston, Dallas, and Corpus Christi—minority students could be transferred to the same schools. Indeed, this took place, and in less than twenty years Black-Brown minority schools emerged.[64] LULAC and the GI Forum censured the new school policies during their conventions but failed to finance litigation. Conservatives took control of LULAC, and they preferred to work with Governor Daniel to improve the schools; the GI Forum sought other legal battles they could win.[65] Gus García and George Sánchez disagreed and gradually became less involved in LULAC.

College Admissions at the University of Texas at Austin after *Brown*

In the aftermath of *Brown,* public colleges were pressured to desegregate. Neither the governor's office nor the Texas Legislature could block the admission of African American students to public colleges because *Brown* was the second Supreme Court ruling mandating integration of universities and professional schools. Four years earlier, in *Sweatt v. Painter* (1950), the Court ordered Texas to admit African Americans to the graduate and professional departments of public colleges.[66] The mandate did not apply to undergraduate education. After *Brown,* undergraduate admissions were affected. If the boards of directors of public colleges resisted the admission of African American undergraduates, another lawsuit, which was destined to prevail, would be unavoidable.[67]

Only Pan American University, in Edinburg, offered admission to Blacks within a few months after *Brown*. In 1955, the University of Texas System became the next public institution to open its universities to African American undergraduates. Overall, out of the nineteen senior public colleges in Texas, seven had desegregated by 1959, and twelve refused to do so. Desegregation at the junior college level was more successful, with seventeen out of thirty desegregating. The Texas A&M Board of Regents, like those of the University of Texas System, desegregated voluntarily, while other public universities were desegregated by court order.[68] With the exception of the Catholic colleges, which had desegregated before *Brown*, most private universities in Texas remained segregated until 1963.[69]

The *Brown* ruling also significantly benefited Mexican American students, even though white colleges for years had admitted Latin American– and Asian-descent students. Mexican Americans directly benefited from *Brown* because public colleges in Texas were expected to expand in order to admit African American students. Consequently, educational space was made available for Mexican American students too. And in fact, once African American undergraduates were admitted to the University of Texas at Austin in 1955, Mexican American admissions doubled, and kept increasing over the years. Likewise, when colleges opened their academic gates to African Americans, housing policies had to change, and this benefited Mexican Americans.

A short detour into college admissions after *Brown* at the University of Texas at Austin illustrates the different kinds of segregation experiences that Mexican Americans and African Americans underwent. The focus is on UT-Austin because after *Brown*, other public universities waited to follow the lead of the UT Board of Regents. Officials may not have been able to block the admission of African Americans, but they could resist the integration of social life on campus. By making African Americans miserable at UT colleges, they hoped to discourage them from attending UT. If that strategy was successful, it could be replicated at other colleges.

The analysis begins with the experience of Mexican American students, since they attended the university before African Americans did. Their experiences of exclusion were subtler than the treatment of African Americans. Furthermore, as shown in the next chapter, when the federal government questioned the social exclusion of African Americans from student social life, Mexican American students benefited from the resulting anti-discrimination policies.

The University of Texas at Austin opened on September 15, 1883, and eight years later the first and only Spanish-surnamed student who was a Texas resident enrolled. At the time, the university had an enrollment of 1,000 students.[70] Throughout the late nineteenth century, fewer than five Spanish-surnamed students registered at the university. The number of those students increased to thirteen in 1923, nearly all of them men. In 1929, as the Great Depression was beginning, the number of Spanish-surnamed students who were US residents rose to forty-three, and half were female.[71] At the time, in general, 154 students of Mexican descent were enrolled in Texas colleges, and nearly 50 percent of them attended UT-Austin and St. Mary's University.[72] The Spanish-surnamed students at UT-Austin reported San Antonio or places in South Texas as their hometowns. Twelve other Spanish-surnamed students at UT-Austin reported Mexico or Latin America as their place of residency.

In the early twentieth century, UT social clubs did not ban Spanish-surnamed students from participating in campus activities. Annual volumes of the *Cactus* yearbook indicate that they joined campus clubs. But outside the academic, Latin, and Catholic clubs, Spanish-surnamed students do not appear as members. The main clubs that Spanish-surnamed students participated in were the Latin American Club and the Newman Club, which was sponsored by the Catholic Church and provided housing for Catholics. It was located off campus across the street from the university. In 1917, Carlos Castañeda became the first Mexican American student to live in the Newman Center dormitories. He had to work part-time as one of the center's janitors to pay for his room and board. His housing arrangement was negotiated by his hometown parish in Brownsville after he was admitted to UT-Austin.[73] Castañeda and his brothers and sisters had been orphaned at a young age, and they did not have the funds to pay for his college education. When he was an undergraduate, the Newman Center allowed Castañeda to share his room with another Spanish-surnamed student who did not have the funds to pay for his housing. In 1927, when Castañeda was completing his doctorate, he was hired by UT-Austin as the librarian for the Benson Latin Collection and as a part-time adjunct professor of Latin American and US history. That year, he became the faculty sponsor of the newly established Club Mexicano. Twenty-two Spanish-surnamed students founded the club, and two years later they renamed it the Latin American Club.[74] Throughout the years, nearly all of the members were Spanish surnamed. The club's intent was to promote good relations between students of different ethnicities. Its charter proposed: "The club serves a purpose in creating a better understanding between the Anglo-American and the Latin-American students."[75]

Spanish-surnamed students do not appear to have been banned from athletic activities. But before the late 1940s, it was rare for Spanish-surnamed athletes to participate in sports. In fact, only five Spanish-surnamed students were listed as student athletes during that time. In the early 1950s, their numbers increased but fluctuated from three to ten athletes each year. Most of them participated in boxing, baseball, cross country, and track. Their participation in basketball and football was rare until the late 1960s. According to the historian Alexander Mendoza, before the 1960s, most Mexican American athletes were recruited on athletic scholarships, and only UT-Austin recruited Mexican American baseball players.[76]

Gus García was one of the most notable Mexican American students to attend UT-Austin during the 1930s. His family dates back to the first Spanish land grant heirs in South Texas. By the turn of the twentieth century, the García family had lost most of their Los Ojuelas land grant, but remained relatively prosperous, since they owned a profitable ranch in Webb County.[77] In 1935, García received his undergraduate degree and was admitted to the UT Law School. He was the president of the Newman Club and very active in campus affairs, serving as an officer of several clubs, including the Latin American Club.[78] During his second year of law school, he was captain of the Texas Debate Squad and a member of the *Texas Law Review*, the *Daily Texan* Editorial Council, the Forensic Council, and the Hildebrand Law Society; he continued to be a member of the Newman Club and the Latin American Club. During García's undergraduate years, he met Carlos Castañeda, who was faculty sponsor of the Latin American Club. Castañeda had recently returned to university employment after having served as superintendent of the San Felipe ISD in Del Rio, Texas (see chapter 4).

Another notable graduate of UT-Austin was Dr. Héctor P. García. He attended the university at the same time as Gus García, and after graduating he enrolled in the UT medical school in Galveston.[79] Dr. García completed his medical residency requirements in Omaha, Nebraska, because Texas hospitals would not sponsor his training. Like Gus García, Dr. García came from an economically well-off family. His father was a successful merchant in South Texas. During World War II, Dr. García was called to duty after receiving his medical degree, and he joined the US Army Medical Corps. Gus García also joined the military at that time, taking a leave of absence from his law practice.

Carlos Cadena was another prominent UT-Austin graduate. He was the son of prosperous Mexican immigrants who paid for his college education. Like Gus García, he was a member of the Latin American Club and graduated from the law school.[80] As an undergraduate, Cadena had the opportunity to take classes from George I. Sánchez, who in 1942 was hired by the College of Education.[81] Cadena was drafted during World War II and served as a radio operator. Several years later, during LULAC and GI Forum meetings, Gus García, Carlos Cadena, Dr. García, and George Sánchez joined forces and became close allies working to push the Mexican American civil rights agenda.

A year after World War II ended, the number of Spanish-surnamed students more than doubled, from 56 in 1945 to 129 in 1946.[82] Nearly half of them were women. On October 10, 1946, the Alba Club was established by Mexican American students.[83] George Sánchez was the faculty sponsor. Teresa Lozano Long, who in the near future would receive a doctorate in education and later become one of the wealthiest women in Texas, was an undergraduate and a member of the Alba Club. She participated in many fund-raising activities to earn money for the *Delgado v. Bastrop* trial.[84] Lozano Long recalled that before the war, most of the Mexican American students attending UT-Austin were the sons and daughters of merchants or large-scale ranchers. After the war, many of the male students were veterans from diverse backgrounds. She also recalled that most of the female students were part of the Mexican American upper class, and they were socially accepted on campus. The main occasion when they felt left out was when the Bluebonnet Sweetheart was selected for campus queen. Mexican Americans were seldom nominated and never chosen as finalists.

On-campus housing was a slight problem for Lozano Long and her Mexican American friends. Dormitory housing shortages meant that most Mexican American female students lived off campus. The *Cactus* yearbooks verify this observation; not until 1950 did on-campus dormitories contain the names of Spanish-surnamed female residents.[85] In Lozano Long's recollection, campus social life for Mexican American women was much better than it was for young men. Most Mexican American male students were socially shunned and seldom invited to parties or other private events. They had to live in the African American and Mexican American neighborhoods on the East Side of Austin, since campus housing or lodging near the university was unavailable. Lozano Long also remembered that the sororities and fraternities were very exclusive and did not welcome Mexican Americans. The *Cactus* from 1945 indicates that one sorority accepted the first Spanish-surnamed resident, and over the years at least one Spanish-surnamed resident was admitted into the sororities annually. Fraternities did not accept Spanish-surnamed males until 1958.

A few years after the *Brown* decision, off-campus housing near the university improved for Spanish-surnamed students. The fourteen university-owned housing cooperatives made some space available for them.[86] Based on *Cactus* photographs, at least two or three Spanish-surnamed students lived in the housing cooperatives each year. Students also lived in boardinghouses near campus. It is uncertain whether Mexican Americans were allowed to live in the boardinghouses, since they were managed and owned by private citizens, and records regarding their policies are unavailable. But Texas exclusion laws of the time allowed any business, including boardinghouses, to exclude any person. In Austin, it was not until 1968 that the city council passed the Fair Housing Ordinance, which prohibited owners or managers of rental housing from discriminating against a person on account of race, national origin, color, or religion.[87] The off-campus Scottish Rite Dormitory, an exclusive residence for female students, did not accept minorities or Catholics even though it was affiliated with the university. The Scottish Rite Organization, which owned the dormitory, did not allow Catholics to live there until 1969.[88]

African Americans had many fewer housing options available to them than Mexican Americans did. In 1953, the first African Americans were allowed to live on campus after the *Sweatt v. Painter* ruling. Administrators opened Dormitory D for African American male graduate students.[89] They converted a run-down building into what was called a dormitory, although it did not have any cooking facilities. Students called it the Shack. In 1955, in preparation for the admission of 111 African American undergraduate students, the Shack was partially renovated to house male students. At this time, the number of Mexican American students nearly doubled to 230.[90] African American female students were not allowed to live on campus. White parents had complained to the university administration that their daughters should not be allowed to live or socialize with African Americans. To address this problem, Governor Shivers and the Board of Regents announced that campus clubs, the women's dormitories, and the campus dinning commons would be off-limits to African Americans. According to university attorneys, the *Brown* mandate was limited to admissions and did not apply to other areas of student life.[91]

Besides the few beds in Dormitory D, nearly all African American students had to live in neighborhoods near the East Side, where the majority of Mexican American males resided.[92] In the late 1950s, however, the university became concerned that the daughters of financially well-off African

Americans needed to be provided secure, comfortable, and wholesome ac-commodations.[93] Consequently, in 1958 the university converted two of its off-campus properties into housing cooperatives and hired housemothers to supervise the young ladies' social lives.[94] The Almetris Co-op, a property owned by the university, and a second dormitory on Whitis Street, were opened to African American female students. Both housing units were lo-cated near the university, but were strategically located far from the white female cooperatives and dormitories. This was done to appease the con-cerns of the white parents opposed to interracial socializing. A year later, Dormitory D was expanded to meet demand, and it was classified as an in-tegrated dorm. It housed Black male students, six Latinos, and one Asian.[95] The dormitory contained the largest concentration of Spanish-surnamed students housed on campus. Almetris Duren, a housing manager employed by the university, in her book titled *Overcoming: A History of Black Integra-tion at the University of Texas at Austin*, recounts that the first integrated dorms at the university housed only African American and Mexican Amer-ican males.[96] Although this may be correct, *Cactus* photographs indicate that Mexican Americans were not exclusively required to live with African Americans. As part of the housing improvements for African American students, two run-down dormitories began admitting African American males. In each dorm, one wing did not have entry to the white students' common areas. Furthermore, because the number of African American students living on campus increased, some of the dining commons opened restricted sections exclusively for them. This was a major improvement in student life, since restaurants near campus did not serve Blacks.[97]

When housing improvements were made available to African Americans, the UT Board of Regents began to reconsider the university's athletic poli-cies. Several universities accused the University of Texas System of cheat-ing in intercollegiate sports by banning African American players, from any school, from appearing on campus athletic facilities.[98] This meant that UT teams faced only other all-white teams at home, and many such teams were weak. Universities with integrated teams charged that UT System colleges used this racial ban to create unfair advantages for themselves, since Afri-can Americans were among the best athletes on visiting teams, but could not play in Austin. The regents were pressured to change their policies in this area. In 1958, teams with African American athletes were allowed to play on UT's fields and in its gyms, and this policy change led to the open-ing up of sports to African Americans at the UT System colleges as long as they participated in noncontact sports.

By the early 1960s, most Mexican American and African American athletes at UT-Austin continued to be concentrated in boxing or noncontact sports. Mexican Americans, however, made significant gains in football, and in 1960 four Mexican American athletes made the varsity and freshman football teams. African Americans would continue to be banned for another eight years.[99] UT–El Paso, formerly called Texas Western College, broke with this discrimination and in 1961 admitted five African American football players (see chapter 7).[100]

The complete desegregation of UT System colleges, however, did not take place until after passage of the Civil Rights Act of 1964. By then, many US congressional representatives were in favor of ending segregation and pressured Texas college administrators to desegregate. The desegregation of Texas colleges became part of a larger social movement to desegregate the nation.

Civil Rights Legislation and the Kennedy Viva Clubs

Because of the power that the southern bloc wielded in Congress, civil rights legislation had not been debated in the Senate or House since 1875. Powerful Democratic and Republican congressmen who formed the southern bloc prevented integration from being debated. The mood in Congress, however, began to change when John F. Kennedy, an integrationist, became president in 1961. Kennedy's efforts to move his civil rights agenda were on firm ground, since his vice president, Lyndon B. Johnson, wielded considerable power within the conservative faction of the Democratic Party, even though he was politically moderate. Johnson traditionally had been part of the southern bloc when it came to stalling integration, but in the area of voting rights, he shared many of Kennedy's ideals. Together, Kennedy and Johnson transformed the political climate in Congress and responded to the civil rights movements, which had begun to grow across the United States.

Johnson had been the Senate majority leader from 1955 to the beginning of 1961. He pushed two voting rights bills, negotiating conflicts between the progressive and conservative factions. To obtain the support of conservatives, he promised them that integration legislation would not be voted on during his tenure in the Senate, but in turn they needed to appease the liberal Democrats by passing voting legislation.[101] In 1957, Johnson brought up for debate a civil rights bill drafted by President Eisenhower's attorney general, Herbert Brownell. Southern Democrats were opposed to it because it contained desegregation legislation and gave the US attorney general the power to indict and punish people found guilty of civil rights crimes.[102] It also proposed to end states' authority to levy poll taxes for voter registration. After southern Democrats refused to support any aspect of the bill, Johnson convinced liberals to accept a revised version. The revised bill would not address segregation, but it would give the attorney general some oversight over voter registration. The bill authorized the US attorney general to investigate voter intimidation by sending federal agents, but left the prosecution and punishment of violations to local courts. Many liberals in Congress considered the bill useless and did not trust Johnson, since it was well known that judges in the South assembled all-white juries when a defendant was white and accused of committing violence against Blacks.

Although the bill had been watered down and most protective civil rights policies had been removed, powerful senators such as John F. Kennedy supported Johnson's compromise. He and others agreed that this legislation could be steadily altered. The critical thing at that point was to pass a legal framework that would allow for future constitutional protections to be inserted into an existing civil rights law. And so the Civil Rights Act of 1957 passed, the first national civil rights legislation enacted since 1875. Kennedy's prediction became a reality when in 1960 the law was amended to give the US Department of Justice the power to impose penalties on people who obstructed someone from registering to vote or casting a ballot. Federal inspectors were required to monitor polling places and registration centers that had a history of not allowing racial minorities to vote. Senator Johnson was instrumental in passing the amended legislation.

These early compromises on voting rights convinced many liberal Democrats in Congress to support a presidential ticket that contained a liberal and a moderate conservative. In 1960, John F. Kennedy won the Democratic nomination for president and chose Lyndon B. Johnson as his running mate. Johnson was expected to appeal to conservative voters.[103] Kennedy and Johnson's campaign managers knew that they would lose most white conservative voters across the country to Republicans, but were convinced that if Johnson ran, the ticket could win Texas and give Democrats enough electoral votes to win the presidential election. At that time, most progressive politicians supporting integration were part of the liberal branch of the Democratic Party.

For Texans, the prospect of electing a native son as vice president—and eventually president—appealed to many voters, who considered Johnson an effective representative. Johnson, regardless of his moderate stance on civil rights, had served Texans well throughout his congressional career in the House and Senate. Texas prospered under Johnson, since the projects he lobbied for benefited both the wealthy and the common people. He obtained congressional support for infrastructure projects such as rural electrification and hydraulic dams. This brought electricity to many parts of the state that had been without it while at the same time benefiting Texas elites, who received lucrative construction contracts.[104] Johnson's influence brought many employment, farm relief, and public housing programs to Texas, too. Many white Texans disliked Kennedy's liberalism, but were willing to support Johnson.

On Election Day, November 8, 1960, the Kennedy-Johnson ticket narrowly edged out the Republican ticket of Richard Nixon and Henry Cabot Lodge Jr., 49.72 percent to 49.55 percent.[105] Texans were stunned that the Mexican American vote in San Antonio and South Texas had swung the state in favor of the Democrats.

Immediately, the Republican Party challenged the election results in Texas and Illinois, claiming that political bosses had manipulated the ethnic vote. Texas had given Kennedy 24 electoral votes, and Illinois 27. If the votes in both states were proved to have been cast illegally, the election results could be challenged in court. In Texas, Republican operatives charged that the votes in San Antonio and throughout South Texas were fraudulent. They alleged that paper ballots had been manipulated. This claim could not be substantiated, however, because San Antonio and many South Texas counties used election machines. Challengers also voiced traditional critiques to devalue and attempt to disenfranchise Mexican American voters. For over a century, Mexican Americans had been accused of selling their votes or being forced to vote according to their employer's wishes.[106] When analysts across the country completed their election analyses, those who opposed the Kennedy-Johnson ticket had to come to grips with reality. Nixon's urban support in Dallas, Tarrant, and Harris Counties was shown to be insufficient to overcome Johnson's popularity in majority–Mexican American counties. Because the voter turnout was large in Bexar, El Paso, Duval, Hidalgo, Nueces, and Webb Counties, and the votes were overwhelmingly for Kennedy and Johnson, the liberal-moderate ticket won enough votes to swing the state's electoral votes in their direction.

In Texas, Héctor García and George Sánchez were two of Kennedy's and Johnson's main advocates. Throughout the United States, Mexican American leaders endorsed Kennedy and Johnson's civil rights vision and established Viva Kennedy Clubs to mobilize civil rights organizations to get out the vote.[107] After the election, García maintained the momentum and worked with the GI Forum and LULAC to place pressure on Democratic Party leaders to nominate Mexican Americans to high-level federal appointments (e.g., judgeships, economic commissions, etc.) and to help finance the elections of Mexican Americans running for office.[108] Of particular importance was getting Henry B. González elected to the senatorial seat vacated by Vice President Johnson.

Unfortunately, the Kennedy administration did not support filling Johnson's seat with a Mexican American candidate. Nor did it give LULAC and the GI Forum its full support. These organizations had to move on their own to advance Mexican American civil rights. LULAC and GI Forum members, however, kept pressure on Vice President Johnson to help elect Mexican American candidates to office. In 1961, when the US House seat for the Twentieth District in Texas came open, they lobbied the Democratic Party to support Henry B. González. When hardly any influential white Texan politician agreed to help, González, who at that time was the only state senator of Mexican descent in the Texas Legislature, announced that even if he did not receive support from his Democratic colleagues, he would run for the seat.

Mexican American civil rights activists diligently campaigned for González. The African American community also came out for González in large numbers, since he had the reputation of publicly denouncing segregation and supporting the school integration of African American students.[109] Four years earlier, the NAACP had bestowed an award on him commemorating González's long-term efforts to dismantle segregation in Texas. To help get González elected, Héctor García asked Vice President Johnson for support. He complained that if President Kennedy was unwilling to appoint Mexican Americans to high-level positions, the least the vice president could do was to support a Mexican American candidate running for office in a district where the majority of voters were Mexican American. The congressional seat that González was running for represented the western half of San Antonio and Bexar County. In an unprecedented break with tradition, the leadership of the Texas Democratic Party reversed course and took a risk by supporting González rather than the other white candidates. In the end, the Kennedy administration also endorsed González, and Vice President Johnson came to campaign for him.

González won the seat by more than ten thousand votes, and he became the second Mexican American at that time to join the US House of Representatives.[110] Joseph Montoya, from New Mexico, had been elected to Congress two years earlier.[111] In Texas, the González and Kennedy-Johnson victories proved that Mexican Americans could organize politically and act as a voting bloc.

A New Generation of Political Activists

By the early 1960s, the leadership of the GI Forum and LULAC disagreed on many civil rights issues. Both organizations continued to endorse the political and social mobility of Mexican Americans, yet Héctor García, who was an active member of LULAC and the president of the GI Forum, became disillusioned with the conciliatory path that LULAC's leadership was taking. Some LULAC chapters had not backed the Kennedy-Johnson ticket, and now the national board of directors was prepared to endorse any candidate who promised to appoint Mexican Americans to government boards and commissions, regardless of that person's stance on civil rights.[112] Furthermore, most LULAC chapters no longer supported financing litigation against school segregation. To García, abandoning litigation meant conceding. His longtime friend Gus García, who for many years had headed civil rights fights in court, was ill and no longer involved.

LULAC's new political position alienated the progressive branch of the organization, including García. Part of the progressive branch had left LULAC and joined a newly founded organization called PASSO (Political Association of Spanish-Speaking Organizations), which attracted young political activists who demanded immediate change. PASSO was the Texas version of a California civil rights organization called MAPA (Mexican American Political Association), which was founded during the Kennedy-Johnson campaign. PASSO's main goal was to elect Mexican American candidates to office and make politicians accountable to Mexican Americans. If necessary, it also advocated working with African Americans and other organizations that shared their goals. This was a departure from earlier civil rights organizations, since Mexican Americans had seldom worked with African Americans on political issues other than on some local elections or employment discrimination issues.

PASSO members continued to work with the GI Forum and LULAC, but did not follow those organizations' directives. For example, in 1961, when the Kennedy administration asked Mexican American organizations to support John Connally for governor, PASSO joined the GI Forum and LULAC to voice their opposition to his candidacy. Mexican Americans felt disrespected by the request, including the conservative members of LULAC, since it was public knowledge that Connally had not done anything to improve the life of Mexican Americans in Texas. Furthermore, Connally had insulted the organizations when he refused to meet with them. It was also well known that Connally was against improving the labor conditions of farmworkers, which in Texas was an important issue that many activists wanted addressed. During Connally's campaign, few Mexican Americans supported him and merely observed the full support he received from white voters. Connally handily won the governor's race in 1962.[113]

After Connally's election, Mexican American political activists decided to put more pressure on the Kennedy administration but chose different strategies to advance their causes. In general, all Mexican American organizations criticized Kennedy for his lack of support, believing that he was concerned only with the problems affecting African Americans. The GI Forum and LULAC, however, decided to pressure the Kennedy administration by working within the Democratic Party and endorsing Henry B. González's plans. Their strategy was to get the administration to fund social welfare programs in Mexican American neighborhoods and appoint Mexican Americans to federal commissions. PASSO members also supported acquiring funds from the federal government to invest in community development, but decided to set their own agenda by working with local communities rather than following the Democratic Party's priorities, which they believed did not match their own. Employment discrimination, poverty, segregation, and occupational abuses suffered by farmworkers went beyond needing federal funding. PASSO members believed that structural change was needed to eradicate these problems, and they were prepared to publicly air their grievances against the Kennedy administration. They were also ready to expose the federal government's complicity in supporting a Democratic Party agenda in Texas that was unconcerned with the needs of the Mexican American population. PASSO's stance signified a shift in Mexican American civil rights approaches. This new generation of activists took a line of attack that was prepared to use community action to challenge the status quo, and most importantly, they were prepared to work with African Americans to enact reforms in Texas.

CHAPTER 6

Institutional Desegregation, Social Movement Pressures, and the Chicano Movement

This chapter explores the social pressures that Mexican American communities in Texas placed on the Texas Legislature to enforce the Civil Rights Act of 1964. When Lyndon Johnson ascended to the presidency, the Texas Legislature was forced to confront its legacy of segregation and gradually begin dismantling the state's de jure segregation laws. The governor's office and the Texas Legislature tried to proceed gradually, and municipalities preferred to institute voluntary desegregation plans. Mexican Americans and African Americans wanted to immediately end segregation and employment discrimination. During this period, Mexican American youth and PASSO (the Political Association of Spanish-Speaking Organizations), headed by Albert Peña Jr., led the political charge for direct action. The youth were part of a national civil rights movement called the Chicano Movement. This chapter argues that the dismantling of Texas's discriminatory laws was prompted by social movement pressures and federal government reforms. Desegregation, election reforms, farmworker wages, and youth activism are the focuses of this chapter.

Social Movements to Desegregate Texas

It is uncertain which counties in Texas continued to exclude Mexican Americans from public accommodations in 1960, since the last statewide governmental study was conducted fifteen years earlier. Mexican American civil rights activists had not conducted a statewide study since the 1944 report prepared by George Sánchez (see chapter 4). What is certain is that Texas exclusion laws had not been nullified, most schools remained segregated, and desegregation in Texas was proceeding slowly and only voluntarily.

In the early 1960s, Albert Peña Jr., founder and chair of PASSO, convinced most of the group's chapters to work with African Americans, labor activists, and liberal whites to accelerate the desegregation of Texas and challenge employment discrimination.[1] In his view, Mexican Americans continued to be treated as second class-citizens with few opportunities for social mobility. Unlike PASSO, LULAC and the GI Forum preferred to work alone, since they disagreed with the political tactics used by multiracial coalitions. They disapproved of using strikes, sit-ins, and protest assemblies to put pressure on private businesses and governmental officials. Disagreeing with LULAC and the GI Forum's conservative stance, Peña demonstrated his solidarity with the goals espoused by the NAACP by joining the organization and becoming a board member of the San Antonio chapter.

In the early 1960s, the NAACP led members of multiracial coalitions to organize a series of sit-ins, pickets, and boycotts against restaurants, theaters, and stores in San Antonio, Houston, and Dallas that practiced segregation. The custom in these cities was to require African Americans to sit in a separate section of a restaurant or theater, and in department stores to shop on floors apart from the general public. In the case of Mexican Americans, business owners could treat them as part of the general public or selectively exclude patrons. In Dallas, to stop the multiracial coalitions from staging further demonstrations, many businesses chose to desegregate. In addition, the Dallas City Council agreed to develop a voluntary desegregation plan to partially desegregate the airport, hotels, restaurants, and the state fair; it encouraged school boards to desegregate schools. In Houston, most establishments resisted such efforts, and the sit-ins and pickets continued for several years.[2]

In San Antonio on March 16, 1960, a multiracial coalition headed by African Americans convinced six restaurant chains to desegregate their lunch counters. Earlier that year, the NAACP had assembled a mass meeting of 1,500 participants to protest against segregation.[3] The NAACP, with the assistance of PASSO and a multiracial coalition composed of students from St. Mary's University, Trinity University, Our Lady of the Lake, and St. Phillips Junior College was instrumental in changing local segregation policies. After countless days of picketing and a massive letter-writing campaign, the targeted businesses conceded.

The problem that persisted in San Antonio and in other cities was the reluctance of city councils to nullify their exclusion ordinances. City governments were prepared to encourage private businesses to desegregate, as well as to gradually desegregate governmental facilities, but officials refused to revoke their segregation ordinances. In San Antonio, Mayor Walter

McAllister refused to discuss any plan that would end the city's exclusion laws affecting the private sector. He firmly believed that it was not the role of government to become engaged in the affairs of private businesses. The mayor was satisfied with the progress the city had accomplished by 1960. Four years earlier, the San Antonio City Council had ordered the desegregation of city-owned public facilities, passing Ordinance 22,555 on March 22, 1956. Henry B. González, then a council member, led the desegregation debate. The new ordinance was designed to end discrimination in city-owned facilities for all persons, not just African Americans. Section 2 of the ordinance reads: "All municipally-owned facilities shall be open to all persons on an equal basis, regardless of race, color, or creed."[4] The ordinance applied also to any institution that leased or rented property from the city, including private citizens, social groups, associations, organizations, or corporations. Likewise, any public function held on city property had to follow a nondiscriminatory policy. The desegregation mandate was limited to city-owned property because most council members did not want to desegregate private facilities.[5]

Compared with other Texas cities, San Antonio was progressive. Most city councils in the state were not prepared to enact any type of desegregation municipal order. By 1962, the only city in Texas that had nullified its public accommodation ordinances affecting government and private businesses was El Paso. The desegregation of El Paso was driven by institutional and community initiatives that involved PASSO. Rescinding the segregation ordinances took place when a Mexican American became mayor.

In 1957, Raymond L. Telles Jr., a veteran of World War II, ran for mayor of El Paso and surprised everyone when he won the election.[6] He became the first Mexican American to hold that office since the end of the Mexican-American War. As mayor, Telles appointed the attorneys Alfonso Kennard and Albert Armendáriz to chair the Civil Services Committee and asked them to investigate city hiring practices within the police and fire departments. It seemed odd that in a city where over 50 percent of the population was Mexican American, seldom were people of Mexican ancestry hired as police officers or firefighters. The committee was also commissioned to investigate why African Americans had never been hired by either department.[7] When Kennard and Armendáriz interviewed the fire chief and asked him to explain his hiring practices, the chief said that Mexican Americans were not hired because white boys could not be expected to sleep in the same quarters with Mexicans.[8] After the investigation concluded, Kennard and Armendáriz reported that the exclusion of minorities from these two departments was the outcome of unwritten policies. Following their investigation, Mayor Telles put pressure on the city council to reform the city's hiring procedures and begin the desegregation of the police and fire departments.

Telles, with the assistance of Armendáriz, moved on to address the segregation of African Americans in the city's theaters. By this time, Mexican Americans and African Americans were no longer being excluded from most public places in El Paso, and students of color were dispersed throughout the schools.[9] The desegregation of the schools took place following Secretary of Defense Wilson's 1955 directive to desegregate all schools attended by students from military families, and his accompanying request to city councils that policies be instituted to encourage private businesses to desegregate.[10] Once this process was set in motion, most public facilities opened their doors to Mexican Americans and African Americans, and the city council put pressure on local school boards to desegregate the rest of the public schools. Theater owners nonetheless continued to discriminate against African Americans, requiring them to sit in the back rows. In 1960, African Americans constituted 2.1 percent of El Paso's population, and asking that they receive the same accommodations as other patrons was not an unreasonable request.

Telles and Armendáriz decided to start with the Plaza Theater, the most luxurious and popular one in El Paso. The plan was to use the Plaza as an example for other businesses to follow. Telles and Armendáriz asked the theater's owners to voluntarily end their segregation policy. If they were unwilling to comply, city attorneys were prepared to take legal action. The Plaza Theater immediately desegregated.[11]

Two years later, on June 14, 1962, an alderman named Bert Williams introduced an antidiscrimination ordinance during a city council meeting. He was certain that the city had the power to institute a nondiscrimination policy for all publicly and privately owned facilities and was not obliged to seek voluntary compliance. The city council voted in favor of Williams's proposal, passing Ordinance 2698, or what was called the El Paso Public Accommodations Act. A few days later, Ralph E. Seitsinger, who had succeeded Telles as mayor, vetoed the ordinance.[12] The mayor's actions angered many people, and on June 19, when the city council assembled, Alfonso Kennard, the regional chair of PASSO, brought two hundred Mexican Americans and fifty African Americans to the meeting and demanded that the council reconsider the ordinance. The city council responded by overwhelmingly supporting the audience and voting to override the veto. Thus, El Paso became the first city in Texas to pass a nondiscrimination ordinance affecting publicly and privately owned businesses.[13]

The Kennedy-Johnson Civil Rights Agenda

In a televised address on June 11, 1963, President Kennedy asked the public, including members of Congress, to begin the desegregation of all public accommodations in the United States and to remove employment barriers based on race, religion, and national origin.[14] The US Senate immediately began scheduling meetings to discuss the president's civil rights agenda. His call for civil rights reforms followed a series of political mobilization events led by African Americans during the mid-1950s, which continued into the early 1960s. In Montgomery, Alabama, Dr. Martin Luther King Jr., president of the Southern Christian Leadership Conference, led a bus boycott in 1955 to protest segregated public transportation systems. The US Supreme Court, five years later in *Boynton v. Virginia*, declared the segregation of public buses to be unconstitutional, yet all municipalities in the South ignored the ruling. Soon other organizations stepped up to demand the desegregation of America. The Congress of Racial Equality (CORE) and the Student Nonviolent Coordinating Committee (SNCC) were among the main ones challenging transportation segregation laws. During the Freedom Rides, beginning in 1961, civil rights activists rode interstate buses throughout the South in mixed-race groupings to challenge local laws prohibiting whites and Blacks from sitting together on public conveyances.[15] Many people were arrested by local police and assaulted by angry mobs. What galvanized the nation's attention, however, and prompted Kennedy to address the nation, were two monumental events in 1963. In March, King helped organize the March on Washington, where he delivered his famous "I Have a Dream" speech, and a month later he led a nonviolent demonstration in Birmingham, Alabama, at which Police Chief Bull Connor let loose attack dogs on peaceful protesters.[16] Televised images of these head-to-head clashes brought the civil rights movement into the homes of Americans. Sit-ins and protest marches soon followed throughout the United States.

In Texas, Governor John Connally disagreed with the president's call and responded a month later in a speech over the radio. On July 19, 1963, Governor Connally condemned the executive branch for what he perceived to be an attempt to force Americans to desegregate. He concurred that desegregation across the nation should eventually take place, but he believed that it should be a voluntary process instituted by the state legislatures and not mandated by the federal government. He did not support any law that attempted to improve the civil rights of one group by violating the civil rights of another group.[17] In Connally's assessment, the civil rights legislation that President Kennedy had asked Congress to adopt violated the rights of many Americans. The governor did not support any law that would erode the right of private citizens and business owners to deny services to any person.

Desegregation of Public Accommodations

Unlike Connally, the new US secretary of defense, Robert McNamara, stepped up the pressure on municipal authorities and business owners to desegregate. On July 26, 1963, Secretary McNamara issued Directive 5120.36 mandating that military base commanders use financial resources against businesses that practiced racial discrimination against soldiers and their families. The secretary threatened to use legal action if discrimination continued in public accommodations servicing military personnel and their dependents.[18]

In Texas, the secretary's directive did not convince most business owners or city municipalities to voluntarily desegregate. Only El Paso, San Antonio, Corpus Christi, and Galveston had already complied or were in the process of doing so. These cities were the homes of military bases, and it was in the best interest of business owners to voluntarily desegregate or at least improve services for people of color. The city councils in Galveston and Corpus Christi encouraged establishments to desegregate, but did not change their segregation ordinances.[19] Galveston's city council also introduced a comprehensive desegregation plan for all public schools. The schools affiliated with the base had already desegregated. This initiative failed, however, after some citizens opposed to the plan asked the governor's office to intervene on their behalf. The governor's staff informed the city council that the plan violated state law because municipalities were required to hold an election before schools could integrate (HB 65; see chapter 5). If the voters approved, the city could move on with their initiative. If the city council defied state law, the governor's office was prepared to withdraw all state funding to the schools. Across Texas, state law made it difficult to desegregate schools, since the majority of voters did not favor integration, and it was useless to hold an election when only a minority of residents wanted change.[20]

During the summer of 1963, African Americans, Mexican Americans, and liberal whites intensified their pressure to desegregate Texas. They were not satisfied with the voluntary desegregation plans that cities had adopted. They demanded direct action and immediate nullification of exclusionary ordinances. On August 28, 1963, thousands of people joined the Freedom Now March that descended on the Texas Capitol to place pressure on Governor Connally to follow President Kennedy's desegregation plan. Among the organizers of the march was Albert Peña Jr., who bused people into Austin, and worked with Booker T. Bonner, the leader of the march and member of the NAACP.[21] Following the march, the NAACP, PASSO, and other multiracial coalitions placed renewed pressure on the City of San Antonio to adopt a desegregation ordinance similar to the one passed in El Paso. Council members refused, but announced that they had obtained the voluntary desegregation of 173 restaurants, 38 hotels and motels, and all lunch-counter establishments downtown.[22] They also announced that they were in the process of establishing several committees to find ways to resolve discrimination practices in the city and that they were addressing the concerns raised by Secretary McNamara.[23] The committee on Military-Civilian Cooperation would address problems experienced by military families, and the complaints raised by local civil rights organizations would be studied by the Committee on Discrimination in Privately-Owned but Publicly-Used Facilities, the Committee on Equal Employment, and the Committee on Education.[24]

Civil rights activists opposed the superficial solution that the city had adopted. County Commissioner Albert Peña Jr. was disappointed with the committees' composition, since the mayor had appointed mainly conservatives who supported voluntary desegregation. Many of the committees' members had publicly voiced opposition to civil rights organizations that used pickets, boycotts, sit-ins, and marches to pressure business establishments. For Peña, the only solution was to run candidates for office who would be willing to change local and statewide laws. Acknowledging that electing Mexican Americans to office would require a massive get-out-the-vote campaign, he favored working with labor leaders such as Hank Brown of the AFL-CIO, along with the NAACP.

During the 1963 PASSO convention, held in San Antonio, Peña pushed the membership to endorse for office a slate of multiracial candidates running under the Democratic Coalition. Many conservatives, who were also members of LULAC, were against the coalition. They saw Peña becoming excessively partisan in support of labor issues and electoral politics that did not concern Mexican Americans. Regardless of the opposition, the majority of the delegates supported Peña, and in the upcoming election, PASSO chapters endorsed the liberal Democratic slate of national, state, and local candidates. At the end of the 1964 election, the results were disappointing. PASSO's multiracial coalition floundered when nearly all of its state and local candidates lost. Joe Bernal won the state House seat representing

Bexar County, and Peña was reelected to the Bexar County Commission but all African American and labor candidates lost.[25]

President Johnson's Civil Rights Legislation and the Great Society

On November 22, 1963, President Kennedy was assassinated in Dallas, and Vice President Johnson became president. Johnson kept his commitment to support Kennedy's civil rights agenda, regardless of the political cost. Nearly half of Americans, including many members of Congress, were not prepared to end segregation. Five days after Kennedy was assassinated, President Johnson went before a joint session of Congress to call for the enactment of civil rights legislation.[26] He had gone against the advice of allies who told him that he had to remove the public accommodations clause of the civil rights bill if he wanted to remain president. Johnson firmly believed that the cause of civil rights required a federal mandate prohibiting discrimination in all public facilities on the basis of race, color, national origin, or religion. Without a federal law, minorities would continue to be discriminated and harassed.[27] To gain national support, Johnson asked Black leaders, labor unions, and church councils to support him, and he invited many groups to the capital to discuss the national impact of his civil rights agenda.

Johnson's closest friends advised him against asking Congress to vote on desegregation legislation during his first year in office. He needed to first secure his party's upcoming presidential nomination and afterward win the presidential election in 1964. This may have been a safe plan politically, but Johnson knew that the nation was ready to make a radical change and that he had to take this opportunity. Congressional representatives from the northern and western sections of the country were prepared to pass civil rights legislation, and following the assassination of President Kennedy, many people in the South were also ready.[28]

On March 26, 1964, House Resolution 7152, which came to be known as the Civil Rights Act of 1964, was passed by the US House of Representatives, despite southern opposition to the legislation. Three months later, after Republicans asked for moderate revisions of the bill, it passed the Senate on June 10. Liberal Democrats had obtained the support of moderate and liberal Republicans, thereby defeating the southern bloc. Forty-four Democrats and twenty-one Republicans joined forces.[29] The bill returned to the House for further debate and passed on July 1. The next day, President Johnson signed the bill into law, and the Civil Rights Act of 1964 empowered the federal government to begin requiring states to nullify their segregation laws.[30]

The act prohibited discrimination on the basis of race, color, religion, or national origin. Title 2 prohibited these types of discrimination in the provisioning of services to the public, whether owned by government agencies or private citizens. As long as services were provided to the public, people could not be discriminated against. For example, hotels, motels, restaurants, cafeterias, theaters, stores, transportation agencies, and other businesses open to the public could not deny or restrict services on the basis of any protected class. Only private clubs not open to the public were exempt from the act.[31] Likewise, titles 3 and 7 of the act were directed toward stopping state and municipal governments from discriminating against people on the same grounds. Title 3 prohibited governmental agencies from denying access or requiring separate facilities for people on account of race, color, religion, or national origin, and title 7 prohibited employment discrimination. Title 6 was designed to enforce the law's mandates by withdrawing federal funds from offending entities that received financial assistance from the federal government, such as universities and colleges. Several provisions of the act were designed to improve federal oversight of the electoral process, such as the federal collection of voter registration data and the establishment of a new federal monitoring system in which people could report voting obstructions (titles 1, 5, 8, 10, 11).

Title 4 addressed segregation in the public schools. This was the second-most sensitive clause of the act, following the public accommodations mandate. Many state governments had vowed never to desegregate their schools. In negotiating this section of the act, congressional representatives agreed to not mandate the immediate end of school segregation. Such a move would have been unrealistic and unenforceable at the local level. Instead, the act looked toward the future and prohibited the assignment of students to particular schools based on race, color, religion, or national origin. School districts were not required to overcome the racial imbalances resulting from a history of school segregation—unless communities filed class-action suits. The desegregation of schools was generally left to the courts, but title 4 authorized the US attorney general to file suits against school districts that purposely continued to assign students to schools based on race, color, religion, or national origin. In sum, the federal government encouraged desegregation and would support communities to desegregate when hostile municipalities obstructed change.

After passage of the Civil Rights Act of 1964, President Johnson moved on to make further civil rights reforms. He could push through his agenda, having won an overwhelming victory in the November election. Johnson won in a landslide, with 486 of the 538 electoral votes, and 61.4 percent of the popular vote. This stunning victory demonstrated to Congress that most Americans supported the president's political agenda. After the president lobbied Congress, the Senate and the House passed the Voting Rights Act, and President Johnson signed the act into law on August 6, 1965.[32] The act was designed to address problems that had not been resolved under the Civil Rights Act of 1964 or the Civil Rights Act of 1960.[33] The Voting Rights Act of 1965 prohibited discrimination in voting procedures and nullified state laws that used literacy tests to deny or abridge a person's right to vote. The act contained enforcement provisions to prevent voter intimidation, establishing a federal monitoring system to ensure that qualified voters were allowed to register and placing federal observers in polling locations where it was public knowledge that Blacks were not allowed to vote.

From 1964 to 1965, President Johnson pushed his Great Society programs. They grew out of a philosophy based on the humanist concepts that the rich should help the poor, and the articulate should represent the illiterate. In 1965, Congress passed the Higher Education Act, which increased financial assistance to students in postsecondary education and gave working-class students in particular financial assistance to further their education and move toward a path of social mobility. The Elementary and Secondary Education Act doubled the educational budget for kindergarten through the twelfth grade. Johnson pushed health care reforms that culminated in establishing Medicare for the aged and Medicaid for the poor. All these programs helped the poor. Great Society programs gave racial minorities the means to help themselves, and his civil rights legislation removed many obstacles to their taking full advantage of the ballot box. Culturally, the public accommodations reforms of the Civil Rights Act of 1964 struck a blow against the belief that for generations had reified as truth the myth that only whites deserved equal treatment.

The Desegregation of Public Colleges with Deliberate Speed

Neither the Texas governor's office nor the Texas Legislature endorsed most of President Johnson's civil rights agenda. The legislature refused to begin revising the Texas Constitution to nullify the state's public accommodation laws. Debating the end of de jure segregation would have to wait. Governor Connally personally supported the desegregation of the schools, but left the issue to the courts, local communities, and college boards. Unlike the state government's slow response to the desegregation mandates of the Civil Rights Act of 1964, public universities immediately began to desegregate all aspects of university life. Most public universities in Texas had offered admissions to Blacks following the *Brown* decision but had refused to desegregate athletics and student life, under the rationale that the ruling applied only to admissions. This was a common position taken by universities across the country.[34] By November 1963, only six public colleges in Texas had refused to desegregate, along with six junior colleges, including one Black junior college.[35] Most private colleges had desegregated, with the exception of Baylor University, the University of Mary Hardin-Baylor, Rice University, and the University of Houston. Three smaller Black private colleges had also refused.[36]

After the passage of the Civil Rights Act, Texas college boards once again waited to see how the University of Texas System regents would respond. If the regents resisted, other college systems would likely follow a similar policy.[37] The regents had made substantial progress in desegregating campus dining halls and developing plans to desegregate athletics, but they resisted desegregating dormitories or requiring students to integrate their clubs. The regents knew that under the Civil Rights Act, it was necessary to require the full-scale desegregation of university life.[38] If the regents failed to comply, financial penalties amounting to 14.9 percent of the system's budget would be imposed.[39] They had already been warned by the US Commission on Civil Rights that title 3 and title 6, mandating the desegregation of all domains of student life, would be enforced. The governor had notified the commission that Texas public colleges had desegregated or were in the process of doing so.[40] The Office of the Commission on Civil Rights required proof of the system's desegregation compliance.[41] The regents responded that the board had voted 6–1 on May 17, 1964, to comply with federal law.[42]

Letters were sent to all university presidents, deans, student organizations, and administrators, telling them that all institutions affiliated with the University of Texas System had to comply with title 6 of the Civil Rights Act. The regents also reported that all varsity athletics had been desegregated.[43] Likewise, student clubs and organizations across the system were notified that they had to adopt a nondiscrimination policy or they would not be allowed to operate on campus. After the regents submitted their report to the civil rights commissioners, only the sororities and fraternities on some campuses refused to desegregate. The regents did not suspend the groups' affiliation, but informed their governing councils that they had to hold rush membership drives off campus.[44] At UT-Austin, fraternities sus-

Kappa Sigma fraternity celebrating Texas Independence Day at the University of Texas at Austin, 1966

pended their discriminatory membership rules in 1968, and the sororities did so in the 1980s.[45] Managers and owners of off-campus housing affiliated with UT System colleges were likewise required to end discriminatory renting practices.[46]

The changes made by the regents certainly made attending UT System colleges more welcoming for minorities. At UT-Austin, however, fraternities and sororities on occasion made life unwelcoming by purposely ridiculing African Americans and Mexican Americans.[47] On Texas Independence Day, some fraternity members taunted Mexican American students by dressing up as drunken Mexican bandidos and staging dehumanizing skits.[48] African Americans were depicted in similar ways. Several clubs on campus sponsored the Cowboy Minstrel Day to make fun of Black people. White students dressed in blackface acted foolishly while pretending to be African Americans.[49] These practices were very offensive to students and became more problematic as the number of Mexican American and African American students rose. In 1968, 468 Mexican American students were enrolled at the Austin campus, and by 1971 their numbers had increased to 1,000.[50] African American student enrollment had also increased, but remained low in comparison with that of Mexican American students.[51] By

1971, African American student enrollment had increased to 300, from 200 in 1962.[52]

The State of Texas Resists Redistricting Reforms

Although the desegregation of Texas progressed slowly, state legislators moved forward with districting reforms in 1965 that benefited Mexican Americans and African Americans. Several new federal mandates required the redrawing of voting-district boundaries and ending voting fees. The governor's office and the Texas Legislature fought against having to enact these mandates, but in the end were pressured to reform the state's election laws.

The Texas Legislature's political headache began in 1962 when the US Supreme Court ruled in *Baker v. Carr* that many states were not following the "one person, one vote" principle. Under this rule, states were required to form congressional districts containing, as closely as possible, an equal number of residents, and to assign only one representative per district. This rule ensured that densely populated cities, often containing many minority residents, were not underrepresented in Congress and that low-density rural areas, often containing mostly whites, were not overrepresented, as had been the case for decades. For example, the dispute in *Baker v. Carr* arose in Tennessee, which had not adjusted the boundaries of its congressional districts for sixty years, despite the state having become increasingly urban during that time. Over the years, neither Congress nor the courts had maintained oversight over districting boundaries, and many state legislatures purposely drew districts that were malapportioned, either to give certain, often rural and conservative, regions more representation or to dilute the representation of Black and Mexican American voters.[53] Thus, in *Baker v. Carr* the US Supreme Court chose to intervene and ruled that the Constitution required judicial intervention to meet constitutional requirements.

Governor Connally considered the US Supreme Court's ruling unwarranted, since the justices had traditionally chosen not to intervene in what were called "political questions." To stop federal courts from intervening in Texas electoral policies, Connally asked the Fifty-Eighth Texas Legislature to pass House Concurrent Resolution 22, which proposed an amendment to the US Constitution prohibiting any type of federal intervention in lawsuits or controversies relating to the election of state representatives.[54]

Once the legislation was passed, the amendment resolution was submitted to Congress. Needless to say, it did not receive congressional support, and two years later Texas had to comply with the "one person, one vote" rule after the US Supreme Court ruled on reapportionment in a series of cases, thereby empowering lower federal courts to intervene.[55]

In 1964, a federal court in Houston ruled, in *Bush v. Martin*, that Texas had several malapportioned congressional districts and ordered the legislature to redraw all district boundaries by August 1, 1965.[56] The legislature had not redistricted the state since 1950. As a result, areas containing large numbers of Blacks and Mexican Americans were underrepresented in the Texas congressional delegation. Based on the US Census of 1960, Harris, Tarrant, Dallas, and Bexar Counties had grown immensely, but had not been apportioned more representatives.

In January 1965, under federal oversight, the Texas Legislature completed the redrawing of districts for congressional and state legislative seats. At the congressional level, Dallas and Harris Counties each gained an additional representative. At the state level, Harris County received seven new seats in the House of Representatives, Dallas County gained five seats, Bexar County three, and Tarrant one additional seat. McLennan, Travis, Nueces, and Lubbock Counties each lost one seat, and Bell and Taylor Counties lost two seats.[57] In the Texas Senate, Bexar County gained one senatorial seat, Dallas two, and Harris three.

These changes were a welcome relief for Mexican American civil rights organizations. The number of elected officials representing Mexican Americans was expected to increase as a result of them, but also because of ratification of the Twenty-Fourth Amendment in 1964. It prohibited the charging of poll taxes or other kinds of fees to vote in federal elections. This was expected to give poor people a better chance to vote. Within a few months of ratification of the amendment, the Texas Legislature tried to go around federal law by redesigning its voting fee system to instead charge people to register to vote. A Texas Democratic multiracial coalition, which included liberal democrats, PASSO, the NAACP, and the Texas AFL-CIO, opposed the state fee and supported two repeal bills. Coalition members believed that any type of fee prevented poor people from voting for candidates of their choice. Both repeal motions failed.[58]

Regardless of the setback, African Americans and Mexican Americans continued to register voters. To their relief, two years later the US Supreme Court intervened. In *Harper v. Virginia Board of Elections*, the justices ruled that the states could not charge any type of voting fee.[59] This empowered African Americans and Mexican Americans to get out the vote.

PASSO, LULAC, and the GI Forum coordinated voter registration campaigns to increase the number of Mexican American elected officials, while PASSO worked with the Democratic coalition. In 1967, in the aftermath of redistricting and the voting fee reforms, Mexican Americans and African Americans did well in electing representatives of their choice. That year, ten members of the Texas Legislature were Mexican Americans, with one serving in the Senate. This was the first time that such a large number of Mexican American representatives had been elected to the state legislature. African Americans also made significant advances. Two African Americans were elected to the Texas House of Representatives, and Barbara Jordan was sent to the Texas Senate. African Americans had not served in the Texas Legislature since the end of Reconstruction. Over the next decade, the number of Mexican American and African Americans state representative would continue to increase.[60]

The Farmworker Movement in Texas and California

In the mid-1960s, a social movement to end the exploitation of farmworkers in Texas began, replicating the political organization that had taken place in California. Unfortunately, changing the working conditions for farmworkers was very difficult because Governor Connally and the state legislature opposed any state intervention. Despite those obstacles, some changes did take place after the Bracero Program ended.

Into the 1960s, Texas farmers had the reputation across the United States of paying the lowest wages, allowing children to work in the fields, and mistreating guest workers. In general, only when there was a labor scarcity had the governor's office intervened in the affairs of the agricultural industry. During the Bracero Program, which began in 1942, the Mexican government banned Texas from receiving guest workers in 1944 and 1947 because of complaints that workers were mistreated and cheated out of their wages.[61] After the governor's office negotiated agreements with the Mexican consulate, it was common for the bracero bans to be lifted, but they were sometimes reinstituted against some Texas counties.

During most years when the Bracero Program was active, it adversely affected domestic farmworkers across the United States by creating an oversupply of labor. This led to lowering local wages and justifying the exclusion of farmworkers from the federal minimum wage of $1.25. During the early 1960s, braceros were paid on average 88 cents an hour, while domestic farmworkers' wages ranged from 59 cents to a little under a dollar.[62]

In Texas, it was common for farmers to pay farmworkers 40–50 cents an hour.[63]

Since the program's inception, the AFL-CIO (American Federation of Labor–Congress of Industrial Organizations) and civil rights activists in California and Texas had demanded that the US government terminate the Bracero Program because of its adverse effects on the domestic farm labor force. In Texas, the GI Forum and LULAC repeatedly asked the federal government to terminate the program.[64] Congress had long refused to do so because the program significantly cut the agricultural industry's labor costs. In 1962, however, a California Mexican American civil rights organization called the CSO (Community Service Organization) took a proactive stance and initiated the dismantling of the program. The CSO departed from its traditional civil rights agenda—desegregation, voter registration, police violence, and racial discrimination affecting the aged within the Social Security Administration—and turned to helping farmworkers.[65] To launch its farmworker initiative, the CSO hired César Chávez, a well-trained labor activist affiliated with the AFL-CIO. Three years later, Chávez organized Central California farmworkers and formed a strong coalition composed of Mexican and Filipino farmworkers. They then formed a union called the National Farm Workers Association (NFWA). Chávez and Dolores Huerta, who also worked for the CSO, became the cofounders of the NFWA. Chávez was elected president, and Huerta became the head organizer. The union was later renamed the United Farm Workers and became affiliated with the AFL-CIO.

Chávez and Huerta launched a strategic media campaign designed to reach the American public and expose what they perceived to be the inhumane treatment of the most vulnerable people in the United States. They publicized the fact that the average farmworker family lived on an annual income of $500, whereas the median US family household income was $5,600 in 1960.[66] It became common for reporters to follow Chávez and film the problems he spoke about. For example, he reported that many employers knowingly allowed children to work in the fields and that municipalities refused to regulate farm laborers' housing. It was customary for labor camps to be overcrowded and unsanitary, and in violation of basic housing codes. Television reporters captured images of houses with broken floorboards, roofs in disrepair, and stoves, if available, without proper gas hookups. Worst of all, labor camps did not have yards or parks where children could play safely. These violations made living in labor camps dangerous. Chávez argued that these conditions were the outcome of three main problems: the exclusion of farmworkers from the Fair Labor Standards Act, which allowed employers to pay wages as low as possible for farm labor; the failure of state governments to regulate farm laborers' wages and housing; and the Bracero Program. When addressing the American people, Chávez identified the Bracero Program as the first problem to be dealt with; otherwise, Congress would not improve wages or housing conditions. In essence, Chávez argued that for wages to increase, it was necessary for the Bracero Program to end. Without braceros, employers would have to compete for the local farm labor force, and wages would rise immediately.

When Chávez and Huerta took their cause to the American public, they received strong support from news media corporations, college students, the Catholic Church, the AFL-CIO, and many religious organizations. To bring attention to the plight of the farmworkers, Chávez and Huerta organized labor strikes against employers that refused to enter contracts guaranteeing workers higher wages. To lobby county governments to pass codes for farm labor housing, the NFWA organized marches and rallies in front of governmental buildings. The news media televised Chávez's speeches and events, which led to pressure on the US government to make changes. As support for the NFWA grew and abundant research proved that the Bracero Program harmed American farmworkers, President Johnson urged Congress to end the program.

Congress ended the Bracero Program on December 31, 1964, one month after President Johnson won the presidential election.[67] The intent of terminating the program was to put pressure on the agricultural industry to voluntarily restructure itself and improve working conditions. It was expected that farmers would raise wages, offer health benefits, and improve labor camp housing in order to compete for a local dependable labor force.[68]

In California, the competition for farm labor rose immediately, and growers began paying higher wages. Throughout California, large-scale growers offered domestic farmworkers as much as $2.45 an hour, and within the legislature, representatives began talks to establish a commission to oversee collective bargaining between employers and unionized workers.[69] In Texas, things did not go as smoothly. The legislature was not willing to make any reforms. Its only change was to end child labor and abolish state laws that exempted child farmworkers from attending school. In 1963, representative Eligio "Kika" de la Garza introduced House Bill 165, which placed children employed in agriculture under the same child labor laws applied to other Texas children.[70] The bill passed, and children younger than fourteen were now required to attend school and could not be employed in agriculture.[71] Unfortunately, employers did not follow the reforms. The following year, the US Department of Labor found Texas farmers to be illegally employing 1,763 minors, of which 363 were under nine years of age, 941 under thirteen, and 454 between the ages of fourteen and fifteen.[72] Only Georgia had close to the same number of child labor violations, with 1,113 children illegally employed in agriculture.

After Congress terminated the Bracero Program, César Chávez unionized many workers in California. His ultimate goal was to make the NFWA a national organization and to change federal law to include farm laborers in the nation's minimum-wage policies. That would force state legislatures to raise farmworkers' wages. Public support for the NFWA was galvanized by the March to Sacramento. On March 17, 1966, Chávez led a twenty-five-day march for three hundred miles from Delano, California, to the Capitol in Sacramento. Catholic pastors, interfaith coalitions, students, and civil rights activists hosted the marchers and prepared food and lodging for them.[73] The main NFWA planned to use the march to recruit farmworkers to join the union and to bring public attention to the abuses that farmworkers were subjected to by the agricultural industry. In addition, Chávez and Huerta hoped that the march would inspire other farmworker communities across the nation to replicate this form of social protest.

Less than two months after the march, Eugene Nelson, a NFWA labor organizer, asked Chávez to be reassigned to Texas, his home state. In May 1966, Nelson and two Starr County merchants, Margil Sánchez and Lucio Galván, organized a rally in Rio Grande City to recruit workers to form a union. Sánchez was the chair of the local PASSO chapter, and Galván was a community activist trying to organize the workers to go on strike.[74] Within a week, they had recruited seven hundred members and formed the Independent Workers Association (IWA). Starr County farmers paid among the lowest wages in the nation. The county was located along the border, and employers could easily hire undocumented workers for very little pay.[75] On June 1, 1966, 1,400 melon workers employed by La Casita Farms and five other corporations went on strike. Their main demand was for their hourly wage to be raised from 50 cents to $1.25.[76] The strikers voted to become affiliated with the NFWA in expectation of receiving financial assistance from the union. Chávez supported the affiliation but was not prepared to heavily invest in Texas, since the political atmosphere did not support improved working conditions or wage hikes. Unlike California farmworkers, those in Texas did not have enough allies in the legislature to institute reforms. Furthermore, it was common knowledge that local officials had the Texas Rangers and the local police arrest farmworkers if they threatened to strike.[77]

During the first days of the strike, hundreds of outsiders came to observe and help the strikers. As the strike drew media attention, A. Y. Allee, captain of the Texas Rangers, traveled to South Texas and told the Rangers to keep the strikers under control.[78] Particularly troublesome for the captain were the activities of Eugene Nelson, the strike leader, who was organizing blockades of roads. Strikers would sit in front of the roads outside farm entrances to prevent trucks carrying the daily harvest from leaving the farms. The same technique was used along the international bridge to Mexico. To dissuade Mexicans across the border from coming into Starr County, Nelson and other strikers met workers on the bridge and asked them to return home. This was a way of preventing scab labor from replacing the *huelgistas* (strikers). Because this was an effective strategy, Allee ordered Nelson and the other organizers to be arrested for disturbing the peace.[79] Judges tried to keep the organizers and union leaders in jail by imposing fines of up to $2,000.[80] Other workers were fined $50–$500. During the strike, many people were beaten and arrested, and the lead organizers were repeatedly jailed. Among the harassed was state senator Joe Bernal, who was temporarily detained and personally roughed up by Captain Allee for allegedly misbehaving in the picket line. Bernal was released after the captain learned that the senator was an observer there to monitor the strike.

To bring public attention to the problems experienced by Texas farmworkers, the strikers decided to replicate the Sacramento march. Father Antonio Gonzáles from Houston, the Baptist minister James Novarro, Father Sherrill Smith from San Antonio, and Father Robert Peña from Rio Grande City would lead the march, and Eugene Nelson was to coordinate the march activities on the way to the Capitol.[81] The strikers voted to organize a five-hundred-mile march from the Rio Grande Valley to Austin. They expected to meet Governor Connally in Austin and ask him to introduce a bill to set the state's minimum hourly wage for farm labor at $1.25.

La marcha, as it was called, began July 4, 1966, and ended on Labor Day, September 5. The marchers received monetary aid from PASSO chapters, Catholic parishes, the United Auto Workers, the NAACP, the Texas AFL-CIO, and the Southern Christian Leadership Conference.[82] They also received monetary, spiritual and public support from the dioceses of Brownsville, Corpus Christi, and San Antonio. The farmworkers moved southeast from the Valley to Harlingen and then turned to Corpus Christi before heading northwest to Austin. At night, they rested in places arranged by churches and student organizations. When the marchers got close to Austin, they were joined by ten thousand supporters.

Governor Connally had publicly denounced the strike and attempted to stop the farmworkers from reaching Austin. On August 31, in a last attempt to convince the marchers to turn back, the governor decided to meet the march organizers on the highway in New Braunfels. The governor met with Father Gonzáles, Father Novarro, Eugene Nelson, and Henry Muñoz Jr., an AFL-CIO organizer.[83] The governor insisted that the legislature and the governor's office were doing as much as they could for the farmworkers. The government had funded many poverty programs to help migrant youth, and he was prepared to sponsor other programs if they turned back. The governor insisted that the farmworkers' problems could not be resolved by the legislature, since their plight was the outcome of being poor and uneducated. Novarro responded that what the Texas farmworkers needed was a fair living wage and employment protection from the state. Charity did nothing to improve their social conditions. When the organizers continued to echo Father Novarro's sentiments, the discussion turned into a heated argument, and Connally informed them that he would not support a minimum-wage law nor take responsibility for having caused their problems.[84] Everyone parted ways, and the march continued.

César Chávez and Andrew Young, the executive director of Martin Luther King's Southern Christian Leadership Conference, greeted the marchers at St. Edward's University in Austin. Chávez and Young were there to provide advice and help negotiate. During the march to the Capitol, they were joined by US senator Ralph Yarborough, US congressman Henry B. González, Barbara Jordan, Joe Bernal, Dr. George Sánchez, and four other state senators, and fourteen state representatives. The strikers and members of the NAACP, the Texas AFL-CIO, and the IAW, along with Yarborough and Chávez, gave electrifying speeches supporting the minimum-wage demand. At the end of the rally, Connally issued a public statement opposing the strikers.[85] It truly must have been an embarrassment for the governor when news reporters announced that the rally was the largest in Texas history.

After the rally, the marchers returned to the Rio Grande Valley and resumed the strike for another year. By this time, the NFWA had been incorporated into the AFL-CIO, making more money available for the union and its affiliated chapters. This allowed the melon strikers to receive long-term support. Chávez sent Antonio Orendain, the secretary of the NFWA, to assist Nelson, since farm labor strikes had broken out in nearby Cameron and Hidalgo Counties.[86] Orendain was an experienced organizer in setting up road blockades to prevent trucks from bypassing the strike line. In Starr County, violence against the strikers worsened: two strikers were severely beaten, and Nelson and Orendain were repeatedly arrested and jailed. The local police, with the assistance of the Texas Rangers, easily dismantled the strikes and intimidated supporters giving assistance to the farmworkers. It became common for bystanders taking photographs to be roughed up and arrested, even if they were women or priests.[87] On one occasion on January 27, 1967, the Texas Rangers followed a group of bystanders to the home of Kathy Baker, and the Rangers roughed up her guests. Captain Allee participated in the raid and brutally beat two men.[88] The attack was so heinous that Francisco "Pancho" Medrano, a United Auto Workers officer who routinely brought food to the strikers, organized the group to file legal charges against Allee and the Rangers. Medrano had been previously arrested for taking photographs of strike activities.

Because of the ongoing violence and the hundreds of arrests, Senator Yarborough called for an investigation of the melon strike. During June 1967, the US Senate Subcommittee on Migratory Labor investigated strikers' complaints of police brutality.[89] Yarborough chaired the committee, which held hearings in Starr and Hidalgo Counties. This gave strikers the opportunity to document their grievances and allowed PASSO and the AFL-CIO to inform the committee about other types of farm labor abuses taking place in other parts of Texas. The committee submitted its report to Congress as part of a national investigation into farm labor conditions in the United States. Although no local issues were resolved in Texas after the committee submitted its report, the findings propelled the California Legislature to institute reforms. The Johnson administration lobbied Congress to set a minimum federal wage for farmworkers. In 1967, Congress mandated that farmworkers' wages could not be below $1 an hour, which was 40 cents lower than the national minimum wage.[90]

The strike ended when Hurricane Beulah made a direct hit on South Texas in late September. During and after the strike, Governor Connally continued to oppose legislation to improve the working and housing conditions for farmworkers. In January 1967, the Sixtieth Texas Legislature passed House Bill 208, which was meant to improve housing conditions in the labor camps. The governor vetoed the bill. If the legislation had been adopted, labor camps would have been required to meet minimum health standards such as providing toilets and meeting sanitary conditions, and would have been supervised by health inspectors.[91] The governor likewise continued to oppose any bill that placed restrictions on the use of pesticides and herbicides in the fields.[92]

Despite Connally's obstructive practices, a few years later the US Senate subcommittee's investigation brought additional changes to Texas. The investigation had obtained critical information proving that the Texas Rangers had used excessive force against the melon strikers. This evidence was used in charges filed in federal court in Brownsville by Francisco Medrano and the other plaintiffs against the Texas Rangers.[93] After losing at trial, the Rangers appealed; the US Supreme Court upheld the lower court's decision.[94] In *Allee v. Medrano* (1974), the justices ruled that local police and the Texas Rangers had selectively arrested labor organizers as a means of ending the strike. The Court also ruled that some of Texas's antipicketing laws were unconstitutional, and it prohibited the Rangers from intervening in farm labor strikes from then on.

Even though new labor laws were instituted in Texas, Chávez retreated from giving Texas farmworkers the union's full financial support because "conditions were not favorable to winning labor strikes."[95] Instead, Chávez focused on reforming national policies affecting farm labor. In 1975, in response to the union scaling back its financial contributions, Antonio Orendain formed a new union called the Texas Farm Workers Union (TFWU).[96] He was moderately successful in organizing wildcat strikes and winning local victories but was unable to garner statewide support or receive financial assistance from the Catholic Church. Most chapters of the TFWU collapsed in the early 1980s from a lack of funds. On the other hand, the Texas UFW continued to represent farmworkers, but primarily focused on helping workers recover unpaid wages, offering referrals to civil rights or immigration attorneys and funding community activities.[97]

In the end, although the melon strike did not change the legislative agenda in Texas, it was a monumental success in energizing social activism and inspiring a new generation of youth to demand immediate change. Soon, Texas youth joined a national movement organized by college students to end segregation and remove social barriers impeding the social mobility of Mexican Americans.

The Chicano Movement in Texas

Across the nation, in the aftermath of the Higher Education Act of 1965, the entrance of racial minorities and working-class whites into universities and colleges increased substantially.[98] Grants and financial aid intended for middle- and low-income students became available, thus providing the monetary basis for racial minorities to fund their college education. In Texas as in other states, officials anticipated that student enrollments would increase, so the legislature worked with the boards of public colleges to develop plans to expand the state's university systems.[99] In 1969, the legislature authorized the establishment of several affiliate universities under the University of Texas, Texas A&M, and Texas Tech Systems.[100]

Throughout the United States, when racial minorities entered universities and colleges in large numbers, they formed civil rights organizations on campus. Their main concerns were desegregation, voting rights, increasing the college enrollment of racial minorities, and advocating for the poor. By the late 1960s, many Mexican American students had begun to call themselves Chicano, an ethnic identifier associated with Aztec culture.[101] It signified their pride in being people of color. The term "Chicano" was introduced by college students, but its use soon spread to high school students, and was adopted by thousands of Mexican Americans across the country.[102] The Mexican American civil rights movement eventually came to be known as the Chicano Movement, and it formed an important sector of the civil rights movement. In Texas, many people adopted the term "Chicano," but most preferred to continue calling themselves Mexican American, in recognition of their Mexican ancestral roots.

Central to the growth of the Chicano Movement in Texas was the founding of the youth student organization MAYO (Mexican American Youth Organization). On July 4, 1967, MAYO was established in San Antonio by college students from St. Mary's University.[103] José Ángel Gutiérrez, a student from Crystal City, became the chairperson of MAYO, and within a year, chapters had been established in colleges and high schools throughout Texas. The students were inspired by the direct action taken by the farmworkers in Starr County. The laborers had taken a political position demanding immediate change and then made their plight known to the people. MAYO students did not limit their membership to college students—on the contrary, they were determined to mobilize Mexican American youth in order to empower them to establish economic improvement projects in their communities. At first, MAYO received some assistance from established Mexican American civic leaders. In San Antonio, Albert Peña Jr. gave the students advice on how to recruit community activists, and a LULAC merchant gave them office space.[104]

MAYO students were inspired by other political movements taking place across the United States and in Texas.[105] The Southern Christian Leadership Conference, led by Martin Luther King, promoted a national agenda to desegregate America, end police brutality, and demand equal rights. Across Texas, African Americans were organizing sit-ins, boycotts, and pickets to challenge local forms of discrimination.[106] The most inspirational social issues for MAYO, however, were the struggles that Chicano leaders advocated. They did not want handouts or charity from private sources and governmental agencies. Instead, they demanded that US laws be reformed so that their communities could have an equal chance at social mobility. In

California, César Chávez had exposed the reluctance of federal and state officials to extend the national minimum wage to 3.6 million farmworkers.[107] In Colorado, Rodolfo Gonzáles, the founder of the Crusade for Justice, was mobilizing communities and leaders to run for political office and take control of their city governments. His campaign against social injustice also emphasized ending police brutality. In New Mexico, Reies López Tijerina, the founder of the Alianza Federal de Pueblos Libres (Federal Alliance of Free City-States), was the leader most widely admired by youth.[108] He publicly defied the status quo and used militant tactics to advance his cause. Tijerina had launched a campaign to reclaim land grants that the US government had illegally stolen from Mexican Americans in New Mexico following the Mexican-American War. He charged that when the federal government pushed most Mexican farmers off their land and gave the water rights of Mexican American communities to large-scale farmers, families lost their source of income, became impoverished, and had to turn to farm labor for their livelihood.

When MAYO was founded, Tijerina was in the midst of many lawsuits. Some litigation involved land grants, but the most serious lawsuits involved federal charges against Tijerina for committing crimes against the government. Tijerina was charged with inciting riots, assaulting forest rangers and police officers, and holding illegal meetings. The political attacks against Tijerina incensed many youth, and when he called for a national meeting to be held in Albuquerque, New Mexico, on October 21, 1967, José Ángel Gutiérrez and other MAYO members attended.[109] The top priority of the meeting was to discuss the main problems that Mexican Americans were experiencing and to organize coalitions that would formulate action plans.

First, however, an urgent matter had to be addressed by the conference participants. The Johnson administration, like the previous one, was ignoring Mexican American issues. The President's Committee on Equal Employment Opportunity (PCEEO) was funding many antipoverty programs in Mexican American communities as part of Johnson's Great Society, yet most other civil rights issues affecting Mexican Americans were being ignored. Bilingual education, farm labor problems, police brutality, school segregation, the land grant controversy, and employment discrimination were given secondary importance by the PCEEO. Johnson had also failed to place a Mexican American on the commission. In 1966, when the commission held a conference in New Mexico to set its agenda for the coming years, no panel addressed Mexican American issues. Mexican American participants were so angered at the lack of inclusion that they staged a walkout. In response, President Johnson appointed Vicente Ximenes to the PCEEO. He was expected to diversify the goals of the PCEEO and initiate plans to address Mexican American affairs. The president also established the Inter-Agency Committee on Mexican American Affairs and asked Ximenes to organize a meeting in Texas in late October 1967.[110]

At the conference organized by Tijerina, the attendees learned that the Inter-Agency Committee meeting was restricted to elected officials, government personnel, the leading members of LULAC and the GI Forum, and AFL-CIO labor activists such as Ernesto Galarza and Bert Corona. This was insulting. The administration had failed to invite César Chávez and other activists recognized by Mexican Americans to be the main leaders of the Chicano Movement, including Rodolfo González and Reies López Tijerina. Worse, Johnson had convened the meeting on the day when he was to meet Mexico's president, Gustavo Díaz Ordaz, at the border between Ciudad Juárez and El Paso. A large-scale ceremony, including a motorcade parade, was planned to begin in downtown El Paso and end at the border, with a ribbon-cutting ceremony signifying the end of the Chamizal border dispute, which dated back to disagreements that began in 1852 regarding the location of the border between Ciudad Juarez and El Paso when heavy rains shifted the flow of the Rio Grande. Johnson's actions indicated that he was unwilling to give Mexican Americans his full attention. Both events were scheduled to take place in El Paso on October 28, and the Chamizal ceremony was expected to take most of the president's time.[111]

To protest the selective inclusion of participants and to find a way to pressure the government to address Mexican American issues, attendees at the Albuquerque meeting decided to quickly organize a conference to be held the same day as the Inter-Agency Committee meeting. They planned to boycott the meeting by asking Mexican Americans not to attend. During the discussions, the MAYO activists José Ángel Gutiérrez and Mario Compean surfaced as outspoken leaders and strategists. They presented many ideas on how to create a national unity movement. Gutiérrez proposed that Mexican Americans needed to forge a national identity based on the concept of "la raza." His idea became part of the leading ideological philosophies surfacing at the time and being debated as unifying symbols of peoplehood. Gutiérrez and Compean volunteered to take the lead in organizing the conference in El Paso and within a few days to prepare for the arrival of thousands of Mexican Americans.[112]

A few hours later, Ximenes learned of the counterprotest planned by the Chicano activists and alerted the president, advising him to cancel the Inter-Agency Committee meeting. Johnson disagreed, not believing that

Mexican Americans would organize any kind of protest. On the contrary, he expected to be greeted warmly. His record on Mexican American civil rights far exceeded President Kennedy's, and he considered the Chamizal agreement to be of great value to Mexican Americans. The president did not realize that Mexican Americans and Mexicans did not necessarily share the same identity or interests. Mexican Americans, who were an American minority group, were concerned with the problems that Mexican immigrants experienced, yet their concerns went beyond immigration and the well-being of Mexico. Without a doubt, bringing closure to the long-standing Chamizal border dispute and agreeing on the location of the US-Mexico border in Texas was an important issue, but not as critical as listening to their complaints about school segregation and employment discrimination.[113]

From October 27–28, 1967, Mexican American civil rights activists held their national meeting in El Paso, calling it "La Raza Unida Conference." It was held in El Segundo Barrio at the Sacred Heart Church community center, located one block away from the US-Mexico border.[114] Participants both attended the conference and picketed the Inter-Agency Committee meeting. When President Johnson arrived at the Inter-Agency Committee meeting in downtown El Paso following the Chamizal ceremony, protesters surrounded the building's perimeter. As the president entered the building and walked the halls, protesters hissed, booed, and shouted taunts at Governor Connally, who accompanied the president. This allowed Johnson to learn how much the governor was disliked by Mexican Americans. Johnson was also informed that many invitees were boycotting the Inter-Agency Committee meeting or were also attending the conference organized by Mexican Americans activists.

After picketing the president's meeting, attendees met at La Raza Unida Conference to discuss short- and long-term goals. During the conference, activists attended classes to learn how to coordinate regional and national networks and to organize national meetings. They also agreed that boycotts, rallies, and pickets were needed to pressure the Anglo-American establishment for immediate change. This national agenda was put into practice. On March 23, 1969, the National Chicano Youth Liberation Conference was held in Denver, Colorado, and within a month was followed by a meeting in Santa Barbara, California. Around a year later, the Chicano Moratorium was organized to protest the Vietnam War.[115]

Following the El Paso meeting, MAYO activists established many organizations in their communities, applied for government funding, and began addressing municipal issues affecting Mexican Americans.[116] Within a year,

President Lyndon Johnson and President Gustavo Díaz Ordaz meeting in Ciudad Juárez–El Paso, October 28, 1967

Mexican American attorneys had established a national organization called the Mexican American Legal Defense and Educational Fund (MALDEF). This marked a major milestone. The organization began to coordinate campaign drives to finance lawsuits against employment discrimination, school segregation, and inequitable funding for minority schools. The main office was established in San Antonio but was moved a year later to San Francisco, since the political differences in Texas among MAYO youth, Mexican American politicians, and the Anglo-American establishment limited MALDEF's activities. Within three years, branch offices were established in San Antonio, Chicago, Atlanta, Washington, DC, and Los Angeles.[117]

By 1969, MAYO activists and many long-standing Mexican American civil rights activists had clashed over which political tactics to use to confront local governmental officials. Many Mexican American civic leaders felt that MAYO threatened the gains they had made and the relationships they had established with Anglo-American allies. The most contentious confrontation involved a dispute between Representative Henry B. González and MAYO activists who sponsored a march and rally in Del Rio. González was not against challenging racist traditions.[118] He be-

Sacred Heart Church,
El Segundo Barrio,
El Paso

lieved, however, that immediate change caused only trouble and violence. It was best to negotiate with governmental officials and enact change by supporting President Johnson's Great Society programs and working with Democratic allies. González had been instrumental in convincing President Johnson to combat poverty in Texas by directly giving federal funds to local organizations with a long history of advocating for the poor, rather than turning the funds over to the state government. Because of his lobbying efforts, grants were directly awarded to churches and community organizations. The GI Forum, LULAC, and PASSO, which received many grants, were in the process of establishing programs for the poor, including job training, housing assistance, rural health clinics, and legal aid. MAYO chapters across Texas received grants and used the funding to establish VISTA (Volunteers in Service to America) programs and voter registration projects. Regrettably, the unconventional political tactics used by some MAYO activists when dealing with local officials antagonized González, and he responded by withdrawing his support for their funding.

Sacred Heart Church, community center, location of La Raza Unida Conference,
October 27–28, 1967

MAYO chapters obtained financial support from the Ford Foundation and the federal government. They received funding to pay volunteers and rent office space. Their main source of income came from VISTA, a federal program established by President Johnson to help fight poverty in poor communities. VISTA funds were to be used to develop economic-opportunity projects. Officially, VISTA volunteers and staff were independent from MAYO, but since the proposals were written by MAYO students, VISTA offices often housed MAYO chapters, and the groups cosponsored activities. MAYO and VISTA volunteers organized rallies and local marches, and attended city council or county commissioner meetings to demand social services for Mexican American communities.

The dispute between MAYO and Representative González climaxed in the spring of 1969. The problems began after the Val Verde county commissioners in Del Rio complained to the governor that VISTA staffers were breaking federal law by working with MAYO activists to finance projects against the government. The commissioners wanted to get rid of VISTA because Mexican American youth had picketed outside the county courthouse to protest police brutality. The commissioners asked the governor to end the VISTA program in Val Verde County. Preston Smith, who had recently become governor, was opposed to direct action and was investigating MAYO chapters across Texas. The governor supported the commissioners and immediately closed down the VISTA offices. In response, Mexican American, organized a protest march in Del Rio on March 14. Students notified MALDEF of the upcoming events and asked for assistance. In anticipation of many people being arrested, MALDEF attorneys waited for the protesters at the police station where the march was to end. To mock the police, the march took the form of a funeral procession to emphasize the outcome of police brutality. When the protesters arrived at the station, thirty-four participants were arrested, and MALDEF attorneys intervened to post their bail.

On March 30, 1969, MAYO led another march and held a rally in Del Rio to protest the governor's actions and police brutality. More than three thousand people attended the rally. During one of the speeches, locals introduced the Plan de Del Rio, which chronicled the history of segregation and the mistreatment of Mexican Americans in Del Rio and in other parts of Texas. The speaker used the governor's recent closure of the VISTA offices as another example of the abuse that Mexican Americans experienced in Texas. Among the other speakers were state senator Joe Bernal, Héctor García, and Albert Peña Jr. George Sánchez and other members of LULAC and PASSO also attended the conference but did not speak. José Ángel Gutiérrez gave an inspirational speech decrying racial oppression, but used inflammatory metaphorical language that enraged the governor and Representative González. He referred to the government as "gringo oppressors" and called for an end to "taco politics," an insult directed at González for not stopping the governor from ending VISTA.

After the rally, MAYO and VISTA chapters in South Texas organized demonstrations criticizing the governor and raising local issues. By mid-1969, MAYO was encountering severe criticism from local governments and Representative González. They complained to the Ford Foundation and asked it to stop funding MAYO. VISTA offices were closed down throughout South Texas. González then pressured MALDEF to fire Gutiérrez, who at that time was one of the law firm's researchers. He threatened to ask the Ford Foundation to defund MALDEF if it continued to associate with MAYO. A few months later, MALDEF relocated to California to avoid the contentious Mexican American politics in Texas.

Despite the problems that MAYO chapters encountered, they continued to organize demonstrations and rallies. In late November 1969, MAYO worked with PASSO and the UFW to support workers who were on strike against the Economy Furniture Company in Austin. The company was one of the largest furniture factories in the Southwest, and when the workers formed a union, the company refused to negotiate with its elected officers.[119] Over 90 percent of the workers were women, the majority of them Mexican Americans, and many had not received a wage increase in fifteen years. To gain support from state representatives, seven hundred people participated in a march to the Capitol. When the company and the strikers could not come to an agreement, the strike lingered for over a year. Besides boycotting and organizing larger demonstrations, the strikers took their case to court. In January 1971, the Third Court of Appeals in Austin ruled in support of the workers to unionize.

Other times, MAYO members joined multiracial coalitions to help protest against the Vietnam War, which had escalated during the Johnson administration. For Mexican Americans, the fact that soldiers of color were being disproportionately placed on the front lines was a major concern.[120] By the time the war ended in 1975, Latinos numbered 11 percent of the US population but accounted for 19.4 percent of combat deaths; African Americans accounted for 12 percent.[121]

MAYO chapters also helped high school students organize marches to protest school inequities. In California and Texas, Mexican Americans had won numerous lawsuits to end school segregation, yet students in many counties remained segregated in Mexican schools or in separate classrooms. When Mexican American students organized a boycott of the schools in East Los Angeles, Mexican-descent students in Texas were inspired to do the same. From March 1 to March 8, 1968, five thousand students attending East Los Angeles high schools participated in a series of walkouts in support of equal educational opportunities.[122] This event came to be known as the "East Lost Angeles Walkouts," and is often referred to as the "Chicano Blowouts." The walkouts brought national and international attention to problems associated with segregated schools. Students challenged the idea that Mexican Americans should be satisfied with the unequal educational opportunities they were offered. The students' main grievance was that they were being pushed out of high school and not provided the academic skills to enter college.

In Texas, one year after the Chicano Blowouts, students in Crystal City High School organized a similar walkout and raised nearly identical demands.[123] They were given technical advice by MAYO activists, including Gutiérrez. The Crystal City walkout was not the first in Texas; MAYO had recently worked with two other high school organizations in South Texas to replicate the East Los Angeles walkouts. The Crystal City walkout, however, became the best known because it triggered further social activism in South Texas.

The problems in Crystal City coincided with José Ángel Gutiérrez's decision to move back there, his hometown. Gutiérrez and his wife, Luz, planned to set in motion a plan to organize local activists to take over the city councils and school boards in Hidalgo County and in Zavala, Dimmit, Frio, and La Salle Counties, known as the Winter Garden Region.[124] Gutiérrez had recently completed his master's thesis on the Winter Garden Project, which proposed that the social mobility of Mexican Americans could be best achieved by focusing on the local level. He believed that Crystal City was the place to begin his project, since six years earlier, a coalition of PASSO and labor activists had organized locals to take over the city council. In 1963, five Mexican Americans were elected to the council, giving them a majority and, hence, control.[125] Anglo-American residents displeased with the election outcome decided to overturn the election results. They removed one council member by accusing him of writing a bad check, and another for being delinquent in his utility payments. Both claims were legitimate reasons to disqualify a person from holding office. During the next election, Anglo-American candidates won most seats in the city council.

During the winter of 1969, Mexican Americans students at Crystal City High School prepared to make their own demands. They were tired of tolerating the ethnic-racial hierarchy that administrators and teachers imposed upon them and that made them feel ashamed and unwanted. Mexican American students were seldom given the opportunity to become student leaders, since the teachers appointed student committees. This created racial tensions between Mexican American and Anglo-American students. School policy also prohibited students from speaking Spanish at school, and teachers were told to punish students if they disobeyed. Students were finally driven to organize a walkout after two incidents involving the cheerleading squad and the selection of the homecoming queen. Although 60 percent of Crystal City High School students were Mexican Americans, the school allowed only one of the six cheerleaders to be of Mexican descent. The teachers selected the cheerleaders and did not allow students to vote. Likewise, the football coach, not the students, nominated the homecoming queen, called the Tournament Sweetheart. During the fall semester of 1969, when two cheerleader vacancies became available, Mexican American students petitioned the administration to allow the student body to elect the cheerleading squad and the Tournament Sweetheart.[126] They pointed out that it was unfair that Mexican American girls were never chosen to be the Tournament Sweetheart. The faculty committee denied their request.

The faculty's response angered Mexican American students, and they assembled a committee to meet with the district superintendent. He supported the students' petition and ordered the high school's administrators to organize an election. The superintendent's actions outraged the all-white school board, and they vetoed his decision. In the meantime, parents and students met to discuss the students' complaints. Luz and José Ángel Gutiérrez attended those meetings, and during the discussions, they introduced the idea of the Winter Garden Project. By this time, Gutiérrez and Luz had made significant connections with local civic leaders, who agreed to help the students. Plans were also being formed to mobilize a larger political movement in the Winter Garden Region.

On December 9, 1969, around two thousand students walked out of their classrooms, and their parents picketed the schools.[127] Severita Lara, a student leader, organized the walkout, and to the astonishment of the school board, students from middle and elementary schools joined them. When news of the walkout reached other cities in Texas, PASSO and more MAYO activists came to support the students. MALDEF attorneys arrived when Severita was arrested for picketing outside a grocery store.

Nearly two weeks after the walkout, the Texas Education Agency tried to intervene because Mexican American parents refused to allow their children to return to school. At the same time, the school board refused to agree to any of the students' demands. The students had asked the board to end the punitive penalties for speaking Spanish during school hours; to offer courses on Mexican American history, culture, and literature; and to hire Mexican American teachers and administrators. After Christmas break, the school boycott continued, and Texas senator Ralph Yarborough intervened. He invited Severita and two other student leaders to visit him in Washington, DC. After speaking to the students, the senator alerted the Civil Rights Division of the Department of Justice and the Department of Health, Education, and Welfare, requesting that agents investigate the students' complaints. On January 9, 1970, after federal officials negotiated a settlement, the school board reluctantly approved the students' demands.[128] By then, the walkout had sparked a social movement in Crystal City, and Mexican Americans working with MAYO and PASSO activists organized a campaign to run candidates for office in the Winter Garden Region.

After a series of meetings, Mexican Americans led by José Ángel Gutiérrez voted to form La Raza Unida Party (RUP) and run candidates for office. On January 23, 1970, Gutiérrez signed an application to officially register the party in Zavala County.[129] The same thing was done in the Hidalgo, Dimmit, and La Salle Counties. In Crystal City, news spread about RUP, and Anglo-Americans who opposed the party activated their political coalition called CASAA (Citizens Association Serving All Americans), which included some conservative Mexican Americans who opposed MAYO and PASSO. A similar countermobilization effort occurred in the other counties. In the elections in March and April, RUP candidates were overwhelmingly elected to office. In Crystal City, they won three of the vacant seats on the city council and elected three candidates to the school board. Similar results took place in Cotulla and Carrizo Springs. Given these unprecedented results, other Mexican Americans in South Texas established RUP chapters and won many elections. By January 1971, Mexican Americans had taken control of the Crystal City city council. In many South Texas communities, MAYO members ran for office, and once they were elected to office, MAYO chapters were transformed into RUP chapters. MAYO was absorbed into RUP, which became an official third party.[130]

Chicano Studies Departments and the Student Movement

Following the East Los Angeles Walkouts, Mexican American college students across the country began to pressure university administrators to establish ethnic studies departments. Their goal was to diversify the curriculum. Ethnic studies courses exploring race, ethnicity, gender, institutional racism, segregation, and inequality were expected to sensitize students and lead to the dismantling of the stereotype that minorities were poor because they were lazy and intellectually dull. In April 1969, Mexican American students held a conference in Santa Barbara, California, where they wrote "El Plan de Santa Barbara."[131] The Texas MAYO delegation pushed forward the idea that students should also demand Chicano studies centers with work-study programs.[132] This would provide an avenue for Chicano research and would show university administrators that it was critical to educate students to become college professors.

Many administrative boards responded favorably and in 1969 began funding research centers, cultural centers, and academic departments.[133] The California State University System and University of California System led the way. In Texas, the University of Texas System regents were the first to establish ethnic studies centers, which housed research and academic units. In 1970, UT–El Paso became the first campus to launch a Mexican American studies program, and the following year UT-Austin inaugurated its Mexican American and African American studies programs.[134] Among Catholic universities of Texas, Our Lady of the Lake in San Antonio established the first Mexican American studies program in 1971.[135] By 1975, many universities across the United States had founded Mexican American studies departments or were offering courses on Mexican Americans; six hundred Spanish-surnamed faculty members were employed as college professors.[136]

De Jure Segregation Officially Dismantled in Texas

In 1967, the Texas Legislature reluctantly began to comply with the Civil Rights Act of 1964, but only regarding governmental agencies. The legislature was not prepared to nullify state laws pertaining to privately owned businesses or to desegregate Texas public primary and secondary schools. The legislature would not terminate all of its discriminatory laws until 1972.

On April 18, 1967, Governor Connally signed into law Senate Bill 185, which ended segregation in government-owned buildings and those leased by the government to private citizens. No longer could municipalities order people on the basis of race, color, national origin, or religion to use separate facilities such as bathrooms, waiting areas, and drinking fountains.[137] Governmental employees were prohibited from denying a license, permit, or certificate to persons for the same reasons. The governor also signed into law House Bill 74, which repealed all intercity segregation policies separating white and Black passengers in carrier accommodations, including railway seating.[138]

In 1969, under the administration of Governor Preston Smith, the Sixty-First Texas Legislature finally began debate to nullify the state's segregation statutes beyond those affecting governmental institutions.[139] Many representatives were appalled at the job that lay before them and refused to pass any bill intended to repeal all discriminatory laws in Texas at once (e.g., SJR 4, HJR 5, SJR 16). Instead, they chose to debate each policy separately and delay the process.

In 1969, state senator Joe Bernal introduced a bill that attempted to immediately repeal all segregation and employment-discrimination laws in Texas. Although his bill did not pass, Bernal documented the needed types of reforms and left a historical blueprint of the type of discrimination that racial minorities were still subjected to five years after the Civil Rights Act had passed. When Bernal introduced Senate Bill 368, he claimed that social discrimination in Texas emanated from the power that the legislature had given police and governmental officials to deprive "certain people" of their equal protection rights.[140] To resolve this problem, he proposed ending all Texas laws designed to discriminate against groups on the basis of race, color, religion, or national origin. He also proposed that the same forms of discrimination be prohibited in the hiring, tenure, and promotion of employees. He put forward in the bill that all employers in Texas should be prohibited from advertising job listings that limited employment to whites. Bernal also identified a series of discriminatory policies that unions used to give white workers advantages.

Concerning public accommodations, Bernal's bill proposed to immediately nullify all exclusion and segregation laws. As part of this reform, he asked that real estate agents and house builders be fined if they continued to use blockbusting strategies to intimidate home owners from selling their homes to minorities and women. Not surprisingly, Bernal's comprehensive plan to rapidly desegregate Texas received little support. Instead, Governor Smith approached desegregation piecemeal, allowing desegregation debates to proceed, but giving representatives who opposed change the chance to set limits. The main problem was schools. If the desegregation of most areas of social life was to be agreed upon, it was necessary that those who favored desegregating the schools accept a long-term plan.

Ending restrictive housing covenants and deed restrictions became an area of the law that was easily agreed on. The legislators did not have much choice, in fact, since federal law and the US Supreme Court had ruled that racial and ethnic discrimination in housing was unlawful.[141] On June 10, 1969, Governor Smith signed House Bill 808 into law, which prohibited corporations and private citizens from placing racial, ethnic, religious, or national-origin restrictions on the sale, rental, or conveyance of property. Any deed containing such a restriction became unenforceable.[142] The significance of this legislation was that city governments would no longer be allowed to ignore federal law, since the state was prepared to enforce nondiscriminatory housing policies.

Associated with the housing reforms, the legislature terminated the authority it had given municipalities to determine who was white or Black for the purpose of segregating residents. This authority had given city officials the power to zone neighborhoods and restrict who lived there. On May 6, 1969, Governor Smith signed House Bill 253, ending a de jure policy that had allowed city governments to manipulate racial definitions and segregate racial minorities in districts that were also zoned for industrial use.[143]

A cemetery bill nullifying Texas segregation policies in the interment of the deceased was approved by Governor Smith on May 22, 1969.[144] Senate Bill 516 revised cemetery policies that had allowed associations to restrict or limit who was offered services in profit and nonprofit cemeteries for any reason deemed necessary by the associations. Additional laws passed in 1969 exclusively called for an end to the segregation of African Americans in libraries (HB 251), prisons (HB 259), student censuses (HB 254), parks (HB 256), teacher meetings (HB 258), and sleeping compartments for train porters (HB 252, HB 255).

One of the most contentious debates surrounded banning the state's antimiscegenation laws. Two bills were submitted in 1969. Bernal introduced Senate Bill 364, and an identical bill was introduced in the House by Representatives David Evans, Curtis Grave, Jake Johnson, and Carlos Truan (HB 261). Both bills died. This was an area that legislators were not willing to compromise on, even though two years earlier the US Supreme Court, in *Loving v. Virginia* (1967), had declared antimiscegenation laws to be unconstitutional. The legislature finally nullified Texas antimiscegenation laws and issued new forms and instructions to county clerks in 1970 after the House Judiciary Committee advised representatives that the State of Texas had to comply with federal law.[145]

Indeed, 1969 was a transformative year, and major civil rights reforms took place during the administration of Governor Preston Smith. The Texas Legislature, however, was not prepared to revise its state constitution by passing an equality amendment that would prohibit the passage of future bills attempting to return to the old apartheid system. The mood of the legislature changed two years later, and in the Sixty-Second Texas Legislature, an equality amendment to the Texas Constitution passed in the House and Senate. On May 5, 1971, Governor Smith signed Senate Joint Resolution 16, calling for an election to revise the Texas Constitution, and on November 7, 1972, voters approved the legislation, with 2,156,536 voting in favor and 548,422 against.[146] Article 1, section 3a of the Texas Constitution was amended to stipulate: "Equality under the law shall not be denied or abridged because of sex, race, color, creed or national origin." This was a historic moment, yet problems in the schools persisted. For many years afterward, schools remained segregated despite the passage of equality reforms.

CHAPTER 7

Mexican American Social Mobility and Immigration

This chapter explores the social mobility and political changes that Mexican American communities experienced in the aftermath of the Civil Rights Act of 1964. Economic opportunities gradually opened for Mexican Americans, but not until 1980 were these changes significant. This chapter also explores the political gains made by Mexican Americans within the Democratic Party and examines why the idea of a third party collapsed. The demise of La Raza Unida Party marked the evolution of the Chicano Movement in Texas and the integration of Mexican Americans within the Democratic Party.

While this chapter focuses on the social and political advances of Mexican Americans, it also examines two major political challenges that they encountered: school segregation and anti-immigration social movements. After the Texas Legislature initiated the desegregation of most areas of Texas life, the desegregation of the schools still moved slowly. The legislature was prepared to desegregate the schools only if parents and school boards did it voluntarily. Representatives preferred to improve the educational opportunities of minorities in Texas by increasing school finances rather than mixing students of different races and ethnicities in the same school. Complicating school politics was a surge in Mexican immigration in the early 1980s and mid-1990s. This demographic change paralleled a national pattern that was not welcomed by many US citizens. Mexican American social and political mobility may have taken place, yet anti-Mexican nativist attitudes persisted.

The Chicano Movement Evolves

In the early 1970s, many Mexican Americans wanted to shift the goals of the Chicano Movement into third-party politics and to expand the political influence of La Raza Unida Party in their states. For many activists, forming a national third party was an effective approach to obtaining representation in state governments. In 1972, Rodolfo "Corky" Gonzáles called for a national convention to be held in June in El Paso to elect a RUP chair and nominate candidates for national positions. Gonzáles had been working with Mexican Americans in California and Colorado to expand RUP outside Texas. José Ángel Gutiérrez, still the chairman of RUP, was not prepared to launch campaigns beyond city and county elections, believing that state and federal elections could not be won.[1] In South Texas, RUP had won majority control of many city councils, and some members were anxious to expand to the state level. They disagreed with Gutiérrez's hesitancy and instead endorsed Gonzáles's enthusiasm. Mexican Americans involved in the Democratic Party shared Gutiérrez's skepticism. They opposed RUP's expansion into state and national politics because RUP candidates would take votes away from Mexican American Democratic candidates and result in defeats for both parties.

During the RUP convention in June, Gutiérrez and Gonzáles ran for national party chair. When Gutiérrez was elected, he tried to keep the party focused on local elections, but when most of the delegates voted to expand, it became necessary to organize statewide campaigns. The party did not nominate candidates for president and Congress, because people were unwilling to put energy into campaigns that could not be won. After the convention, RUP candidates ran for office in Texas, California, Arizona, and Colorado. The results were mixed. In Texas, local candidates did well in South Texas, but in the rest of the states the results were disastrous. Making matters worse, not only were RUP candidates not elected to office, in some areas Democrats lost their elections because the Mexican American vote was split between RUP candidates and liberal Democrats. Among those who lost their seats was Richard Alatorre, a California state assemblyman. He lost to a Republican by a few hundred votes, which the RUP candidate took away. In Texas, state senator Joe Bernal lost to a Republican for the same reason, and county commissioner Albert Peña Jr. lost the primary election by 117 votes; he blamed the RUP candidate, who had gotten 3,500 votes.[2]

After the disastrous experiment, RUP lost nearly all support outside Texas, and the idea of a third party was abandoned. In South Texas, local

RUP candidates did well. This was attributed to Ramsey Muñiz's campaign for governor. Although he received only 6 percent of the vote, his candidacy energized local campaigns and served to get out the Mexican American vote. Two years later, Muñiz ran for governor again, with the same result. His candidacy once again was considered to have energized South Texas voters.

For the Democratic Party, losing voters to RUP was an unwelcome sign. In 1972, the chair of the Texas Democratic Party asked the leadership of the Texas RUP to dissolve the party and return to the Democratic Party. RUP was assured that their candidates would be supported for local and statewide offices. When RUP did not disband, two years later the Texas Democratic Committee changed some of its rules to maintain and attract Mexican American voters. The Democratic leadership required that minorities and women be appointed to committees developing party policy. The Democratic Committee agreed to open most meetings to all delegates and promised to aggressively recruit minorities to run for office.[3]

In 1976, Mexican Americans who ran for office in South Texas continued to do well, whether they ran as Democrats or RUP candidates. Approximately, 31.7 percent of city council positions were filled by Mexican Americans. In the rest of Texas, less than 5 percent of council members were Mexican American.[4] The success of RUP candidates began to dwindle two years later, and the party's potential demise was marked by Mario Compean's devastating defeat. In 1978, Compean, the cofounder of MAYO, ran for governor, but garnered less than 1 percent of the vote.[5] This loss indicated that Mexican American voters had returned to the Democratic Party and did not consider RUP a viable, sustainable third party. La Raza Unida Party was no longer capturing a large percentage of the electoral vote in high-density Mexican American communities; it remained a stronghold primarily in Crystal City and Cotulla. When Mexican Americans won elections, they did so by running as Democratic candidates. In Texas, as in the rest of the Southwest, RUP's influence collapsed.

Indeed, Democrats opened their party to Mexican Americans, and this became evident in various domains of government service. In 1978, the number of Mexican American Democratic delegates was more than double the figure from ten years earlier, going from 4.2 percent to 10 percent of the total delegates.[6] Likewise, Democrats began appointing Mexican Americans and African Americans to important positions in state government. The number of racial minorities appointed to state boards and commissions rose, and both minority groups came to constitute 5 percent of those positions.[7] Judicial appointment rose, too. In 1977, Governor Dolph

Briscoe, a Democrat, appointed Carlos Cadena to be the chief justice of the Fourth Court of Civil Appeals, and he increased the number of Mexican American district judges from 2 to 16, out of a total of 303.[8] He also appointed the first two African American district judges in Texas's history. Although these numbers seem inconsequential, and none of the minority appointments were women, they symbolically signified a step forward as the gates of power began to open for people of Mexican and African descent.

By 1978, Mexican American politics in Texas was proceeding in the traditional parties. PASSO chapters had failed to attract new members, and RUP had lost its popular appeal. Chicano student and community activism dwindled or became integrated in conventional party politics, labor unions, community social service centers; in some cases, it led to the resurgence of LULAC and GI Forum chapters. On college campuses, the goals of the Chicano Movement became institutionalized in ethnic studies departments, whose curricula were designed to teach students how the US ethnic and racial structure has been shaped by racism, capitalism, and gender bias. College research centers also incorporated the goals of the movement, but became focused on investigating and finding solutions to social problems affecting Mexican American communities. Nationally, MALDEF became the leading Mexican American civil rights organization focused on litigating civil rights abuses in education and immigration.[9]

Employment Mobility, 1970–1980

During the 1970s, Mexican Americans made significant gains in the Democratic Party. In other institutions, however, progress was much slower. In 1970, the Texas State Advisory Committee of the US Commission on Civil Rights submitted its findings to Congress regarding all civil rights matters affecting Mexican Americans and African Americans in Texas in the areas of employment, education, and police-community relations.[10] The committee was composed of people of diverse ethnic backgrounds. One of the committee's main charges was to determine to what extent the state government had complied with title 7 of the Civil Rights Act, which mandated nondiscrimination in employment practices. At the time, Blacks and Mexican Americans constituted more than 30 percent of the state's population (2 million Mexican Americans and 1.4 million African Americans).[11] For nearly two years, the committee held community meetings across Texas and interviewed governmental officers and business owners.

The committee reported that no significant advances were made in education, police-community relations, or employment in the first years after the passage of the Civil Rights Act.[12] Most Mexican American and African American students continued to attend segregated schools. Members of both minority groups were still disproportionately harassed by law enforcement agencies, and in some localities they were excluded from jury duty and from employment in courthouses and law enforcement agencies. Farmworkers were paid very low wages. Worst of all, both minorities encountered racist attitudes when they applied for private-sector jobs.

The area most urgently in need of reform was education. The committee's main recommendation was for the ethnic composition of the Texas Board of Education to be diversified. At the time, all twenty-one board members were Anglo-Americans. The committee expected that a more diverse group would generate new ideas and practices to improve the educational system. The committee also recommended that the US Commission on Civil Rights investigate the military school-busing program in Del Rio. The commander of Laughlin Air Force Base had recently ordered military-dependent students attending the San Felipe schools to be transferred to Del Rio schools, where most of the students were Anglo-American. He alleged that this move was necessary because the San Felipe schools were overcrowded. The committee doubted the commander's truthfulness; to its members, this was an obvious attempt to use busing to resegregate the schools. The committee concluded that this was a direct violation of the Department of Defense's educational policies and a step backward in the desegregation of Texas schools. They also found that the integrated schools in San Antonio, El Paso, Houston, and Corpus Christi suffered from severe financial disparities. To resolve this problem, they advised the commission to investigate why new buildings and facilities were being constructed only in schools attended mainly by Anglo-American students, and why no building improvements were planned for the integrated schools.

In employment, the committee recommended that the Office of Federal Contract Compliance begin proceedings against Texas companies that were not following federal civil rights laws. Utility companies, banks, and oil companies receiving federal funds were obliged not to discriminate, yet these kinds of companies seldom hired racial minorities, even if most of the local workforce was Mexican American or African American. Similar problems were found in state and local government. The Committee recommended that Congress enact legislation authorizing the withholding of federal funds from any state or local agency that discriminated against racial minorities. It also recommended that federal agents ask the Texas Employment Commission to discontinue its practice of referring Black and Mexican American applicants only to menial jobs.

In law enforcement, the committee recommended that the US Commission on Civil Rights work with the governor's office to immediately abolish the Texas Rangers and integrate the officers into the State Highway Patrol. Of outmost urgency, the committee asked that the US Department of Justice investigate the employment practices of every law enforcement agency in Texas and demand compliance with title 6 of the Civil Rights Act. At that time, few minorities were employed as law enforcement officers, and it was urgent that these agencies immediately recruit more Mexican American and African American candidates.

Ten years later, the US Commission on Civil Rights established a second advisory committee to revisit many of same issues and determine the changes that had been instituted. School segregation, private employment, and farm labor were not included in the study because of a lack of available data. By 1980, the Spanish-surnamed population in Texas had grown to nearly 3 million, and 92.2 percent were of Mexican descent.[13] They constituted 21 percent of Texas residents.[14]

The worst finding identified by the second committee involved the jury system. Absolutely no improvements had taken place in the intervening ten years, and in some counties, conditions had worsened. The committee wrote: "The jury commissioner system had consistently produced grand juries that underrepresent both women and minorities. Only Travis County did not severely underrepresent its predominant minority-group populations."[15]

The only advancement identified by the committee was in government employment, but even in this area serious problems persisted. By 1977, employment at all levels of government had become accessible to minorities, and in most counties, proportional ethnic and racial representation had been achieved. But discrimination persisted, since agencies hired most minorities for clerical and service occupations.[16] The only groups that had made substantial gains were professional men. Twenty-six percent of Mexican American men and 13.9 percent of African American men employed in state and local government were hired for managerial or professional occupations.

The committee concluded that Anglo-American men continued to dominate all domains of law enforcement. Within state law enforcement agencies, very few minorities were employed as officers, and the Texas Rangers continued to exclude both groups. Only the Department of Public Safety

(DPS) and the sheriff's division had made some improvements. Mexican Americans accounted for 2.4 percent of DPS officers and 3.5 percent of sheriffs, and African Americans 0.6 percent of DPS officers and 0.4 percent of sheriffs.[17] At the local level, no improvements were found. Most police departments did not employ people of Mexican or African descent as officers. This hiring pattern was attributed to the fact that less than 5 percent of the city councils in Texas were composed of minority-group members, and it was the responsibility of city governments to hire police forces. Outside South Texas, most city governments complied with federal nondiscrimination policies by hiring minority women for clerical positions, and men as janitors or service workers. Moreover, although South Texas police departments were identified as the only agencies employing Spanish-surnamed police officers in significant numbers, the committee found that few departments had reached proportional ethnic representation.

Federal employment had reached proportional representation in most divisions. In particular, minorities were found to be well represented in the Bureau of Prisons, the Immigration and Naturalization Service, and the Drug Enforcement Agency. When the data were examined by gender, however, the committee found that the representation of minority women was extremely low. Over 80 percent of Mexican Americans employed by the federal government were men, and 70 percent of African Americans were men.[18] The committee found that at all pay grades, the wages of minorities were lower than those for Anglo-Americans. In sum, some advancements in employment had been made by the late 1970s, yet minorities faced a glass ceiling in most government jobs. They were hired in proportion to their numerical population size, yet they were limited to low-paid clerical and service occupations. In private employment, the committee was unable to evaluate what gains, if any, had been made, because data were unavailable.

In 1980, the US Census offered a somewhat more positive outlook on the social mobility of Mexican Americans. Census data corroborated the committee's main finding, namely, that Mexican Americans continued to be concentrated in service and labor occupations, with a small percentage of Mexican Americans being employed in professional and managerial positions in public- and private-sector jobs. In total, around 99,013 Mexican Americans worked in professional or managerial occupations. In addition, family income had risen significantly by 1980. White households' incomes continued to be much higher, but the disparity was substantially less than it had been twenty years earlier. In 1980, the median family income of Mexican American families had increased to $13,293; for whites it was $20,955, and for African Americans, $13,042.[19] There was also significant social-class diversity. The household income of many Mexican American families was over the state's median income, $19,618; for example, 10,227 families earned over $50,000, and 174,339 families earned $20,000 to $49,999.[20] Furthermore, the lowest-paid people in Texas made some gains when Congress extended the federal minimum wage to farmworkers in 1981, which allowed many families to move out of poverty.[21]

Improved School Finances

When the Civil Rights Act of 1964 was enacted, Congress approached school desegregation cautiously and left the pace of integration to the courts. White parents across the country opposed integration. Because of public opposition, most state legislatures supported improving the financing of minority schools rather than integrating them. By the mid-1970s, most members of Congress had abandoned their commitment to desegregate the nation's schools. In Texas, the same pattern followed. To most governmental officials, instituting equitable school finance policies seemed to be the logical solution, but in reality, they knew that it was a politically unreachable goal. African Americans and Mexican Americans favored school integration and were not convinced that schools would be equitably financed if white students remained separated. When the State of Texas did not show any inclination to integrate the schools, parents of color became determined to at least receive equitable school finances. In some cases, members of both minority groups launched lawsuits, while in other cases Mexican Americans focused on issues only affecting them.

Mexican Americans returned to the courts in 1968 in pursuit of equal education. Parents were demanding integration, and African Americans and Mexican American parents in Corpus Christi joined forces when they found that the school-desegregation gains made after *Brown* had been lost. The Corpus Christi desegregation battle marked an important turning point in Texas civil rights history. In Dallas, Houston, and Corpus Christi, cities where a large percentage of the students were Mexican American and African American, school districts began to desegregate African Americans and Mexican Americans by mixing them in the same schools. In an effort to appear to comply with *Brown*, school districts treated Mexican Americans as white, and left white schools alone.[22] The state did not intervene to stop this practice. On the contrary, the legislative educational reforms instituted in 1957 supported this policy, since school boards were given the authority to mix students of common backgrounds together (see chapter 5).

To end this unique resegregation process, Mexican American and African American parents from Corpus Christi filed a class-action lawsuit in 1968 against the school district for falsely reporting that the schools were unitary when in reality school segregation had intensified. The students were represented by seasoned lawyer James DeAnda, who had worked with Gus García in the *Hernandez* case.

Two years later, the US District Court for the Southern District of Texas, in *Cisneros v. Corpus Christi Independent School District* (1970), ruled in favor of the parents. The district was found to be unlawfully and purposely segregating students by gerrymandering school zones and allowing white students who lived in minority neighborhoods to transfer to white schools. Mexican American students were found to have been improperly used to desegregate African American schools after being classified as "other white students." The result of this process was that 85 percent of the schools had become segregated.[23] To stop this practice, the court declared that Mexican Americans were an identifiable minority group and could not be classified as white for the purpose of desegregating African American schools.

Regrettably, *Cisneros* failed to desegregate most Texas schools outside Corpus Christi, because the ruling was ignored by other courts.[24] Most judges preferred to leave the schools segregated and were opposed to busing because of the transportation costs. After *Cisneros*, the Houston school district continued to desegregate African American schools with Mexican Americans under the rationale that Mexican American students were white. It was one of the many school districts in Texas under federal orders to desegregate. The Houston ISD was the sixth largest in the United States, overseeing 238,460 students in 230 schools. Of the students, 66.9 percent were white, 33.1 percent African American, and 15 percent of the white students were estimated to be Mexican American.[25] In 1970, after the district submitted a plan to mix 14,942 African American students with 6,233 Mexican Americans and 2,368 Anglo-Americans, the court accepted the plan despite the opposition voiced by parents of color. African American parents, with support from the NAACP, launched a lawsuit, *Ross v. Eckels* (1970), against the Houston ISD, but lost. The parents appealed to the Fifth Circuit Court, but it accepted the district's plan and ignored the ethnicity of the white students. The court allowed African American schools to be desegregated with Mexican Americans and left nearly all the white schools alone. Part of the court's justification was fiscal responsibility. Allegedly, state funds could be better spent in hiring more teachers and improving school facilities rather than spending money on busing to mix the students.[26]

Federal courts across the United States issued conflicting opinions and echoed the *Cisneros* opinion. In *Keyes v. School District No. 1, Denver Colorado* (1973), the US Supreme Court ruled that desegregating African American students with another class of students who were equally segregated and attended similarly underfunded schools did not fulfill the equal-education mandate imposed by *Brown*. These divided opinions empowered school districts to follow local norms.

Two years after *Keyes*, desegregating schools was no longer a priority of the federal government, including Congress, because whites throughout the nation protested against forced integration. The main complaint was against the use of busing to integrate the schools. Allegedly, busing students outside their neighborhoods destroyed the students' community ties and prevented them from becoming involved in after-school extracurricular activities. Congressional representatives listened attentively to the complaints and agreed that busing was an unfair burden. Oddly, such decisions did not give consideration to the fact that in the past, busing African American students outside their counties because they were not allowed to attend the local white schools was never considered wrong or abusive. In 1974, after sustained pressure from white citizens to end busing for desegregation purposes, Congress redefined compliance with *Brown* in the Equal Educational Opportunities Act of 1974 (EEOA) and decreed that mixing students of different races in the classroom was not the only method of complying with the court ruling.[27] Under the act, Congress rejected racial balance as the goal of desegregation and ruled that lack of such balance did not constitute denial of equal educational opportunity or equal protection as required by *Brown*. Desegregation was redefined as the assignment of students without regard to race, color, sex, or national origin, and not assignment to overcome racial imbalances.

Three years later, Congress amended the EEOA and passed legislation prohibiting the use of busing to desegregate schools. Only school districts under mandatory desegregation orders could use busing to desegregate their schools, or when busing was to be used by magnet schools. Congress supported magnet schools as the principal voluntary desegregation method to be used by school districts.[28] Magnet schools were neighborhood schools that received special funding from the federal government for voluntarily busing in students from different districts. The goal of the government was to encourage school boards in white neighborhoods to reserve some seats for students of color from outside their district.

The US Supreme Court soon followed in the direction of Congress and no longer supported using busing to desegregate the schools. In *Milliken v. Bradley* (1974), a case dealing with students in Detroit, the justices ruled that suburbs did not have to be included in desegregation orders if the suburbs had not been part of past segregation policies.[29] That is, if a suburb did not exist during the period when de jure segregation separated students of different races and ethnicities, the schools in a suburb could not be included in a desegregation plan. The aim of the ruling was to remove from a court-ordered desegregation plan families who had fled to the suburbs to avoid sending their children to desegregated schools. This ruling, coupled with the ban on busing proposed by Congress, made it virtually impossible to desegregate communities.[30]

Three years later, the *Milliken* decision was appealed by the Detroit School Board and the State of Michigan. The plans delineated by the court to improve the standards in segregated schools (enriched curriculum, remedial programs, voluntary student transfer programs, etc.) were challenged. In *Milliken v. Bradley* (1977), often referred to as *Milliken II*, the US Supreme Court upheld the earlier decision. The justices ruled that programs besides those implementing student reassignment plans could be used to comply with *Brown*, reaffirming the principles enunciated in the earlier ruling. In the aftermath of the EEOA and the *Milliken* rulings, desegregation across the nation proceeded voluntarily except in cases where school boards were found to purposely continue assigning students to schools on the basis of race, color, or national origin. Across the nation, the provision of equal educational opportunity moved from mixing students in the classrooms to equalizing funding.

In Texas, national policies allowed school districts that planned to desegregate to do so, and at the same time they sheltered communities that were opposed. Following the federal government's commitment to no longer forcibly desegregate schools, the main problem for the Texas Legislature was how to equalize school funding. The EEOA required that students be given equal educational opportunities to learn, which meant that the financing of schools could not be intentionally or radically unbalanced. This was a serious problem in Texas. Over the years, the legislature had allowed wealthy districts to assess taxes beyond what was required by state law. This system created wealthy and low-wealth school districts, leading to an unequal educational finance system across the state.[31] To comply with the EEOA, the unbalanced school finance system had to be restructured by the legislature.

Complicating the legislature's job, Mexican immigration began to increase during the late 1970s, and this made the equalizing of school finances more complex. Many schools attended mainly by Mexican American students became overcrowded. A public debate soon emerged over the racial and ethnic composition of Texas schools: was school segregation increasing in Texas because of Mexican immigration or because school boards controlled by white parents wanted schools to resegregate? The case of El Paso schools illustrated this political controversy.

In El Paso, school desegregation proceeded voluntarily after *Brown*. Mexican American parents, however, complained that although the schools were integrated, schools with a higher percentage of white students were better funded. In 1979, in *Alvarado v. El Paso Independent School District*, the Fifth Circuit Court of Appeals ruled that the El Paso School Board had purposely underfunded schools attended primarily by Mexican American students, in contrast with the schools attended by white students.[32] MALDEF represented David Alvarado and the other Mexican American students who sued the school district. Vilma Martinez, the president of MALDEF, was lead counsel.

This was a complicated ethnic-discrimination case because Mexican American students were distributed across all of El Paso's schools, and many benefited from the better-funded white schools. El Paso's student population was 59 percent Mexican American, 3.2 percent African American, and 37.2 percent Anglo-American.[33] In court, attorneys for the school district argued that Mexican American students were not being discriminated against, since many of them attended the better-funded schools. The financial problem facing schools, according to the school district attorneys, was due to heavy immigration from Mexico, which had created both a fiscal problem and overcrowding in some schools. The appellate court disagreed, ruling that the El Paso School Board purposely gerrymandered school boundaries to ensure that six out of seven Anglo-American students were clustered in schools where the majority of students were white. And the schools attended by most of the white students were better financed. For example, white students attended schools that had been renovated and air-conditioned, while most Mexican American and African American students attended schools without air-conditioning. The court ordered the district to diversify its management staff, too, since nearly all mid- and high-level administrative positions were held by Anglo-Americans.

In 1989, the Texas Supreme Court heard an appeal involving students from San Antonio, and in *Edgewood ISD v. Kirby*, it ruled unanimously that the Texas school finance system was unconstitutional.[34] The court ordered the legislature to overhaul the school finance system by May 1, 1990, and offer an equity plan.[35] The legislature complied, raising state taxes to increase the funding of low-wealth school districts, which benefited minority students. Taxes were then redistributed across the state to address funding imbalances. This plan did not end Texas school finance problems, and litigation continued for more than sixteen years.[36]

Mexican Immigration Surges in the 1980s and 1990s

During the early 1980s and again in the mid-1990s, waves of immigrants from Mexico entered the United States, leading to a large increase in the foreign-born population. Many of these immigrants settled in Texas, and by the turn of the twenty-first century they had significantly changed the nativity of the Mexican American population. In 1970, a decade before the migration waves began, 88 percent of Mexican Americans in Texas were born in the United States; thirty years later, this rate had fallen to 63 percent.[37] This pattern was replicated across the United States (appendix 7.1). The migrations of the early 1980s were caused by international politics and Mexico's allegiance to the United States. In 1981 when the price of oil fell, Mexico experienced its worst economic disaster since the Mexican Revolution. Mexico blamed US officials for its predicament because it had aligned itself with the US government against the interests of OPEC, the oil cartel. At that time Mexico, was the world's fifth-largest exporter of oil.[38] Mexico's economic crisis began after its government supported the United States during the US-Iran conflict of 1979. In support of Iran's accusations that the US government had meddled in its national affairs, several Middle Eastern countries organized an oil embargo against the United States. OPEC expected Mexico to remain neutral and not interfere. Instead, Mexico demonstrated its solidarity with the United States by escalating its production of oil, providing the United States with 40 percent of its imported oil.[39]

After the embargo ended, OPEC nations planned to maintain the price of oil at high levels and needed Mexico to cooperate. To keep prices high, Mexico was asked to reduce its oil production and follow OPEC's pricing. Mexico did neither, and President José López Portillo ordered Pemex, the agency that managed the Mexican oil industry, to continue producing as much oil as the United States needed. For OPEC, Mexico had become a threat, and with its massive oil reserves, Mexico was developing into an antagonistic competitor. In 1981, OPEC nations retaliated by releasing their reserves and flooding the market. At that point, the price of oil fell by 50 percent and the Mexican economy was temporarily ruined. Within a year, Mexico's inflation rate rose to over 100 percent, the poverty rate increased to 53 percent, and the peso's value fell 100 percent.[40] At first the US government was reluctant to help Mexico, but when the International Monetary Fund (IMF) informed officials that not aiding its neighbor would hurt the US economy and cause Mexican immigration to surge, President Ronald Reagan agreed to issue Mexico long-term high-interest loans amounting to $12 billion.[41]

After the loans were dispensed, the Mexican economy continued spiraling downward because of a series of disastrous events. In 1985, the price of oil continued to fall. Mexico experienced a succession of earthquakes, ranging in magnitude from 7.5 to 8.1, that devastated Mexico City. Mexican elites lost their investments on "Black Monday," October 19, 1987, when the US stock market crashed; Mexican investors lost 75 percent of the worth of their US stocks.[42] With the economy in shambles, many firms defaulted on their foreign loans, and the Mexican federal government chose to bail out the private sector. The government assumed private-sector debt and converted it into public debt. To finance the bailout, the Mexican government had to borrow more money from the United States and institute austerity policies to raise the revenue to repay the loans. The government reduced public spending by an additional 65 percent, increased the price of electricity 57 percent, and laid off 25,000 government employees.[43]

In the meantime, thousands of people fled to the United States as the price of consumer goods skyrocketed and unemployment increased. As plans to stabilize the economy failed, out-migration became the solution that many Mexicans adopted to improve their austere living conditions. The exodus began in the rural areas and then spread to the urban areas when employment became increasingly scarce.

During the 1980s crises, Mexicans entered the United States as permanent legal residents, but also as unauthorized migrants. From 1980 to 1989, over one million Mexicans obtained visas and entered legally. The US government, however, estimates that at least two million additional people entered without permission.[44] In Texas, the foreign-born Mexican population doubled during Mexico's economic crises, going from 498,181 in 1980 to 907,432 in 1990 (see appendix 7.1). The number of undocumented people is uncertain.

The entry of a mass number of undocumented migrants was a new phenomenon that resulted from revisions in immigration law. In 1965, Congress made legal entry virtually impossible for working-class Mexicans, who in past decades would have qualified for permanent resident visas. Under the Immigration and Nationality Act of 1965, Congress implemented new income and occupational restrictions, which disqualified most Mexicans from legal entry unless they had relatives in the United

States who would sponsor them.[45] Applicants without US relatives, therefore, qualified only if they were physicians, surgeons, lawyers, architects, teachers, college professors, engineers, or artists, or were independently wealthy.[46] Unskilled and semiskilled occupations were no longer needed in the United States, and people reporting those occupations became ineligible to immigrate.

In 1976, qualifying for legal immigration became more difficult after Congress placed an annual limit of twenty thousand immigrants for countries in the Western Hemisphere, including Mexico.[47] Previously, only countries from the Eastern Hemisphere were held to that limit. Congress also changed its adjustment policies for undocumented residents. Parents who had US-born children were required to return to Mexico and process their adjustment applications when their children turned eighteen. As a consequence of these immigration reforms, many Mexicans who entered the United States during Mexico's economic crises came without authorization and became undocumented immigrants.

In 1986, after Mexico's devastating earthquakes, Congress offered Mexico economic relief by adjusting the political status of the unauthorized population. The decision was motivated largely by the interests of the agricultural industry. Representatives of agricultural associations testified in Congress that throughout the nation, farmers were experiencing an agricultural labor shortage and that most of their workers were undocumented aliens. After prolonged negotiations, Congress passed the Immigration Reform and Control Act (IRCA) to address the concerns of the agricultural industry and to assist Mexico.[48] In 1986, 2 million undocumented Mexicans adjusted their status to permanent legal residents (out of 2.7 million amnesty recipients). In addition, the government instituted an agricultural guest-worker program to increase the farm labor force and allowed the imported workers to adjust their status to permanent legal residents. The immigration policies significantly contributed to Mexico's financial recovery, since the undocumented population and the guest workers were not under the threat of deportation, which gave them stability and the capability to send remittances to their families back home.

The Mexican economy stabilized in 1989, and Mexico resolved its conflicts with OPEC. But the recovery was short-lived: Mexico experienced a banking crisis in 1994 related to President Carlos Salinas de Gortari's mishandling of the financial system and the North American Free Trade Agreement (NAFTA). NAFTA did not work as projected and caused a banking crisis. The banks' instability was set in motion after Salinas initiated a treasury-securities partnership with the private sector after the recovery. Banks were authorized to sell high-interest treasury bonds and notes carrying interest rates of 14–37 percent. The investments were guaranteed by the federal government and upon maturity were to be paid back in US dollars.[49]

As the banks attracted thousands of national and international investors, Mexican economists warned Salinas that foreign products entering Mexico under NAFTA needed to enter in phases and that the quantity of shipments needed to be limited. They added that agricultural tariffs in the corn industry should be gradually removed. The president did not listen to this advice. When NAFTA took effect on January 1, 1994, Mexican industrialists and farmers were not prepared to compete with the less expensive products flowing in from the United States and Canada. After most tariffs had been removed, US and Canadian products flooded the markets and Mexicans stopped purchasing the more expensive Mexican commodities.[50] Four months later, the banking industry showed severe signs of distress after thousands of farmers and midsize industrialists, unable to sell their products, defaulted on their loans. As the economy unraveled, foreign corporations stopped investing in Mexico, and by December they had pulled out $67 billion.[51] Foreign investors also cashed in high-interest treasury bonds purchased from the banks. Matters worsened. In the state of Chiapas, subsistence farmers whose livelihood had been devastated by President Salinas's economic policies established the Ejército Zapatista de Liberación Nacional (EZLN) and declared war against the Mexican state. Because the economy was in shambles, thousands of corporations, restaurants, and retail stores went bankrupt and people lost their jobs. The IMF informed Salinas and the US Treasury that unless the Mexican economy received a massive infusion of cash, Mexico's financial collapse was imminent. The US government was warned that if it did not assist Mexico financially, it should expect a mass entrance of undocumented immigrants.

During the economic crisis, Ernesto Zedillo became the new president of Mexico on December 1, 1994. Upon taking office, he began negotiations with the IMF and the US government for monetary assistance. His administration expected President Bill Clinton to support some type of immigration relief, paralleling President Reagan's backing for IRCA during Mexico's earlier economic crisis. By this time, the banks were near collapse, and most were unable to redeem the treasury bonds that foreigners and Mexican elites had purchased. The banks had a liquidity deficit of over $37 billion and also shared the treasury's bond debt of $30 billion.[52]

In March 1995, President Clinton agreed to issue Mexico a $40 billion loan package but required the government to implement additional austerity policies. This was necessary if Mexico was to accrue sufficient funds to pay back the past and current quarterly loan installments. The Mexican Congress agreed to reduce domestic spending by 40 percent and implement a series of new deregulation policies that included allowing banks to be fully owned by foreign investors.[53] President Zedillo accepted the loan agreement, but was displeased when he learned that Clinton did not support extending amnesty to undocumented immigrants. On the contrary, Clinton wanted to deter undocumented migration and had previously worked with Congress to enact policies to stop, dissuade, and discourage Mexicans from working in the United States. Only temporary agricultural guest workers were welcome.[54]

On September 17, 1994, at the peak of Mexico's economic collapse, Operation Gatekeeper was funded to stop border crossers in California. Based on a Texas plan, it was designed to stop the movement of people across the border. One year earlier, Operation Hold the Line had effectively reduced unauthorized entry through Texas. A few months after Operation Gatekeeper was instituted, Mexicans shifted their route to Arizona, where crossing through the desert was simpler but much more dangerous. Operation Safeguard was then implemented in Arizona.[55] Mexicans were so desperate to enter the United States that as one entry point became difficult to penetrate, they traveled to other regions.

While President Clinton enacted policies to improve security along the US-Mexico border, Congress finalized an immigration plan to discourage legal immigration from Mexico.[56] On September 30, 1996, Congress passed the Illegal Immigration Reform and Immigrant Responsibility Act (IIRIRA).[57] Congress did not want US citizens and permanent legal residents to sponsor relatives, and to dissuade them, it erected financial obstacles. Persons who sponsored a relative would become responsible for paying for all government benefits used by the new immigrant. The only benefits that sponsors were not responsible for were public schooling, emergency services, and soup kitchen relief. To discourage unauthorized immigration, Congress increased the funding of border security along the US-Mexico border. One thousand border patrol agents were added, a border fence was to be constructed along parts of the California-Arizona border, new immigration detention centers were to be built, and the number of immigration inspectors conducting work-site raids was to increase.

By late 1996, Mexico had received several disbursements of the US-IMF loans, and the economy was recovering. The infusion of cash, however, did not benefit all citizens. The Mexican government once again used a substantial part of the loans to bail out the private sector and pay its debts. The Mexican government was also unable to produce the number of jobs needed for the unemployed, and citizens continued to live under austere public-spending measures.[58] Consequently, millions of Mexicans continued to seek refuge in the United States by entering clandestinely or applying for US residency.

After the IIRIRA became law, border enforcement failed to deter Mexicans from trying to make the United States their home. In 2000, the Immigration and Naturalization Service reported that the number of Mexicans thought to be undocumented and living in the United States had grown to nearly 4.7 million.[59] They constituted around 55 percent of the total undocumented population of the United States. Most undocumented Mexicans were assumed to have entered from 1995 to 2000, during the period when Mexico instituted the round of austerity-mandated cutbacks and tax increases following the NAFTA crisis. At the time, Mexico's poverty rate remained over 60 percent.[60] In Texas, the size of the Mexican undocumented population in 2000 was uncertain. The Department of Homeland Security, however, estimated that approximately 1.8 million of the 3 million foreign-born residents of Texas were Mexican.[61]

In 2000, when Vicente Fox became president of Mexico, the economy improved and the distribution of governmental resources reached the common people. Five years later, the economic pressures for people to leave lessened, and migration to the United States temporarily slowed down. Fox instituted policies to improve the life of the common person. He reduced some of the nation's austerity policies by increasing public spending on schools, health care, and infrastructure. He also extended financial assistance to small and midsize businesses in order to stimulate the economy and improve employment.[62] Mexico's poverty rate fell to 43 percent during his tenure in office.[63]

The Mexican American and Latino Demographic Profile in Texas

In the United States, the number of Latin American immigrants from countries other than Mexico increased significantly during the late 1980s, leading to the diversification of the Latino population. Central Americans were the main groups that entered at that time. Migration from Latin America continued, and by 2010, people of Mexican ancestry constituted only 60 percent of the Latino population of the United States.[64] The demographic pattern in Texas was different from that in other states. The growth of the foreign-born population was steady, but the number of non-Mexican immigrants was relatively small. In 2010, the Latino population in Texas numbered 9,464,713, and people of Mexican ancestry accounted for 88.7 percent of the total.[65] Of the Mexican-origin population, nearly 2.4 million were foreign born, and they accounted for the largest percentage of the immigrants from Latin America.[66] After Mexican Americans, Salvadorans composed the second-largest Latino group (246,028), followed by Puerto Ricans (138,136), Hondurans (103,038), and Guatemalans (76,944).[67]

Excluding Puerto Ricans, who are US citizens, more than two-thirds of Central Americans were foreign born. One of the main differences distinguishing Puerto Ricans from other Latino groups is that Congress instituted a separate immigration and citizenship process for people arriving from Puerto Rico. Since 1917, Puerto Ricans who migrate to the United States have obtained automatic citizenship. This privilege is bestowed on them because Puerto Rico is a US territory.

For most of the Latino foreign born, including those in Texas, if they entered with authorization, they were considered economic immigrants and they held permanent resident visas or were US naturalized citizens. Latinos who entered the United States unauthorized were considered undocumented if they did not receive amnesty under IRCA or the Nicaraguan Adjustment and Central American Relief Act (NACARA) of 1997. NACARA was a special program designed to adjust the status of Central Americans who did not qualify for IRCA, since they arrived in the United States after the congressional cutoff date of January 2, 1982, or were made ineligible by IIRIRA.[68]

Economic factors generally led people to migrate, but in Central America, political instability also prompted large-scale migration. Migrations from Central America in the mid-1980s were made by people trying to escape the civil wars in their countries. By the mid-1990s, the wars had ended, but migration continued because countries remained economically and politically unstable during the postrevolutionary period.[69] The Department of Homeland Security estimated that in 2011, the largest number of undocumented people in the United States, after Mexicans, came from El Salvador and Guatemala. The total number of unauthorized immigrants was estimated at 11.5 million, of which 60 percent were Mexican.[70] In Texas, demographers estimated that 16 percent of the US undocumented population lived in Texas.

Latino and African American Ethnic Growth
and Texas Electoral Politics

Currently across Texas, Mexican Americans and African Americans constitute the majority of residents in many cities. This demographic fact has led to their increasing influence in Texas electoral politics. In 2010, Mexican Americans and other Latinos accounted for 37.4 percent of the state's population, and African Americans 12.4 percent.[71] Latinos and African Americans made up 60 percent of Harris and Dallas Counties.[72] A similar pattern was found in Bexar County, where Latinos accounted for 59 percent of the residents, and together with African Americans composed over 67 percent of the county's population. Furthermore, in 115 of Texas's 254 counties, Latinos and African Americans constitute at least 40 percent of the population. Demographers have attributed this population trend to increasing Latino birthrates and immigration, which in turn have enhanced the electoral influence of people of color in Texas. Approximately one-third of the Latino population in Texas is foreign born (3 million).[73]

In many cities, African Americans and Latinos live in adjacent neighborhoods and therefore they have often been placed in the same state and congressional electoral districts.[74] Although less than one-quarter of the Latino foreign born are eligible to vote, when electoral districts are composed and representatives assigned, the foreign born are part of the population represented. This political fact benefits minorities running for office and helps the Democratic Party because most minorities in Texas vote for Democrats. For example, in Texas counties with over 700,000 residents, such as Dallas, Tarrant, Hidalgo, El Paso, Travis, Harris, Bexar, and Collin, the foreign-born population ranges from 10.4 percent in Bexar to 29 percent in Hidalgo. In northern and southeastern Texas counties where African Americans constitute a large percentage of the population, the immigrant population is also large. Dallas has over 500,000 foreign-born residents, Harris around 1 million, and Tarrant and Denton together have nearly 400,000.[75]

Along the US-Mexico border, the population is predominantly of Mexican descent, and this had allowed residents to elect Latino representatives. Of the thirty-two counties designated by the State of Texas as forming the border region—none of them located more than sixty-two miles from the Rio Grande—only four have a majority Anglo-American population. The rest have a Latino population ranging from 96 percent in Starr to 56 percent in Kinney. Most of the Latinos are of Mexican origin, and the size of the foreign-born population parallels that found in the rest of the state, with the average being around 16 percent of the county. In the border region, El Paso County has the largest number of residents, 804,338, of whom 82 percent are Latino. Of the Latino population, 30 percent (199,603) are foreign born.[76]

In the last few years, African Americans and Latinos have made great advances within the Texas Democratic Party, while their influence lags behind in the Republican Party. In fact, the current leadership of the Texas Democratic Party is predominantly composed of minorities. It is uncertain whether Anglo-Americans left the Democratic Party for philosophical reasons, or whether there are structural causes for their diminishing role within its leadership. To address this query and provide background for the Democratic Party's compositional ethnic change, I momentarily examine why many white Americans left the Democratic Party.

In Texas after Reconstruction, most citizens, including Mexican Americans, supported the Democratic Party (see chapter 3). During the administration of President Franklin D. Roosevelt, the political stance of the Democratic National Committee became more liberal and overwhelmingly favored legislation offering employment and housing opportunities to minorities. As a result, Texas Democrats became divided into liberal and southern conservative camps.[77] After the election of President Eisenhower in the 1950s, many white Democrats in Texas became Republicans because they favored the party's fiscal conservatism, particularly its promises to cut taxes and federal spending. When President Lyndon B. Johnson moved to enforce the Civil Rights Act of 1964 and the Voting Rights Act of 1965, his agenda caused more Democrats in Texas to defect to the Republican Party.[78] Not all conservative Democrats left the party, because they continued to support policies to benefit the ordinary people. The liberals and southern conservatives agreed on many issues but diverged on civil rights and school segregation.

By the late 1960s, the Democratic Party in Texas had become more inclusive of Mexican Americans and African Americans and supported policies that benefited them.[79] The party, however, continued to be controlled by the southern wing, and its leadership persisted in excluding both minority groups from shaping the party's political agenda. In the early 1980s, Democrats remained in control of most congressional and state legislative positions. But because of political pressure from minorities, the party's leadership increased its support of Mexican American and African American candidates. For example, the party supported minority candidates running for statewide office in heavily populated minority districts in the counties of Dallas, Harris, Bexar, and El Paso, and in South Texas. As a result of this philosophical political shift, by 1985 twenty-three Mexican Americans and fourteen African Americans had become state representatives.[80]

When Texas Governor George W. Bush became president in 2001, more Democrats defected to the Republican Party, including some minorities. That year, 10 percent of African American voters and 25 percent of Latino voters registered as Republicans.[81] After President Bush's election, white voters did not return to the Democratic Party, and three years later, Republicans won the majority of the seats in the Texas Legislature. The same white electoral voting pattern occurred at the federal level.

By 2017, the Texas Democratic Party's leadership had become primarily composed of Latinos and African Americans. By then, it had become difficult for white Democrats to win elections at the state level. Democrats who ran in districts predominantly populated by white voters lost to Republican candidates. In the Texas House of Representatives in 2017, out of fifty-five Democrats, forty-four were Latino or African American, and in the Senate, nine out of eleven Democratic senators were people of color. The Republican leadership remained nearly all-white.[82] Most of the Democratic representatives continued to come from districts heavily populated by minority voters. This political shift has not translated into political gains for African Americans and Latinos because the Republican Party, which has controlled state government since 1994, does not share the same political goals as the Democrats. By 2019, the number of Democratic state representatives had increased slightly, but the pattern remained the same.[83]

The demographic ethnic shift of legislators in the Democratic Party in the early twenty-first century has been primarily attributed to the changing liberal outlook of its membership across the generations. This attitudinal evolution is closely interwoven with the state's redistricting after the release of each decennial census. The party in control determines the redistricting boundaries, and this has affected who is elected to office and who will likely control the legislative agenda.

By law, Congress requires states to redraw their district voting boundaries every ten years to ensure that congressional and state districts are substantially equal in population (see chapter 6). Over the years, both parties have been accused of manipulating district boundaries to maximize the advantages for their party.[84] For example, from the 1980s to early 1990s, before the Bush Republican shift, liberal Democrats controlled the legislature, and they established voting districts where the majority of voters were minorities.[85] Congress permitted the creation of majority-minority districts as a way to avoid minority vote dilution, which helped ensure that racial- or language-minority groups that shared political interests were not denied an equal opportunity to elect candidates of their choice.[86] This created safe seats for Democrats and allowed minority candidates to be elected to both chambers of the Texas Legislature. The Democratic-controlled legislature created other safe districts to ensure that Democrats were elected to state positions. In districts populated by white voters, neighborhood boundaries were drawn to split Republican voters into separate districts and ensure that the majority of voters in each district were Democrats.

Ten years later, the Republican-controlled Texas Legislature reconfigured state legislative districts. In 2003, it formed ten additional minority districts where Latinos and African Americans constituted the majority of voters.[87] This allowed more minorities to elect representatives of their choice to the Texas Legislature as long as they lived in districts that were overwhelmingly populated by people of color. In districts predominantly inhabited by whites, the strategy previously used by Democrats was replicated, which led to losses for Democrats and gains for Republican candidates. The end result was that minorities who were Democrats were elected to the state legislature, while Democrats who were white and ran in white or predominantly white districts lost elections.[88] Safe seats had been created for minorities to elect Democrats, but in the rest of Texas, it became difficult for Democrats to elect candidates. This scenario did not empower minorities, because the majority of the legislature was Republican.

In response to the 2003 redistricting plan, MALDEF, the GI Forum, LULAC, and the NAACP filed suit in Texas, alleging unconstitutional gerrymandering and other voting-rights violations. The federal district court ruled against them, and they appealed to the US Supreme Court three years later in *League of United Latin American Citizens v. Perry* (2006).[89] The civil rights organizations charged that state district lines in some counties, particularly in South Texas, had been drawn to reduce the number of Democratic state legislators. Although safe majority-minority seats had been created in large urban areas in Texas when the redistricting plan was developed, Mexican American and African American civil rights organizations charged that Republicans had failed to give Democrats adequate representation in other zones. Many districts where minorities resided exceeded the lawful population size of a voting district and had been purposely packed to avoid assigning a second representative to those districts. In other cases where minorities constituted the majority of the residents of a district, the redistricting plan had allegedly gerrymandered their neighborhoods. This was particularly troublesome in South Texas, where counties that had white voting populations of 30 percent or higher were used to dilute majority-Latino districts. Minority districts were divided, separated, and adjoined to districts where the majority of voters were Republican and white. After hearing the charges, the justices upheld the state's redistricting plan, but reversed the lower court's opinion on District 23 in South Texas. It was found to have been intentionally packed and in violation of the Voting Rights Act.

Disputes over redistricting led African American and Mexican American civil rights organizations to bring suit again, after district lines were redrawn in response to the 2010 census. In *Perez v. Abbott* (2017), MALDEF, the NAACP, LULAC, and the GI Forum charged that the state's legislative plan was intentionally designed to dilute minority voting strength.[90] On April 20, 2017, a three-judge panel of the US District Court for the Western District of Texas found that part of the redistricting plan violated the "one person, one vote" rule.[91] The court concurred with part of the charges presented by the civil rights organizations. The voting districts for Nueces, Hidalgo, Bell, and Lampasas Counties were concluded to be shaped to pack Latino voters into minority districts while other nearby districts were underpopulated. In El Paso, Bexar, Nueces, Harris, western Dallas, Tarrant, and Bell Counties, evidence of vote dilution was shown by the formation of malapportioned districts drawn to ensure that they contained a majority of Republican voters. The districts had the same number of voters, but the lines were drawn to ensure Republican victories. The state legislature was ordered to redraw some of the district lines.

The court's ruling was appealed by the governor's office to the US Supreme Court, and on June 25, 2018, by a vote of 5–4, it was reversed.[92] Only state House District 90, which contains part of Tarrant County, was found by the Court to have been intentionally gerrymandered. African American and Latino residents make up 88 percent of the district. In response to the Court's decision, the lower court was asked to retain oversight of the redrawing of District 90. Before accepting the new legislative plan, the district court also asked the legislature to modify some other boundaries where minority-vote dilution was apparent, namely, in Bexar, El Paso, and Nueces Counties and in some North Texas counties.[93] This was a modest victory for minority civil rights organizations.[94]

Although the Supreme Court decision was a disappointing loss for Mexican American and African American civil rights organizations, the political coalition they established continues to pressure the Texas Legislature to draw a more equitable map for the 2020 decennial redistricting plan. Political strategists project that the 2020 census will show that Texas's demographics continue to change and that more representatives will be apportioned to districts containing both minority groups. It is projected that the white population of the state will fall to 39 percent.[95]

The growth of immigrant and minority populations in Texas and other states has prompted some citizens to ask Congress to change the methodology used to determine voting districts.[96] The intent of their proposal is to reduce the apportionment of the number of congressional and state legislative seats representing districts with large immigrant populations. In Texas, if such a law were adopted, the number of seats apportioned to Dallas, Tarrant, Bexar, Harris, and El Paso Counties, and the counties in South Texas, would decrease. A citizen-only map would strip Latino and African American voters of majorities in two or three state Senate seats and six or seven state House seats. The change at the state level might be welcomed by those who believe that immigrants dilute the choices of US voters. Such a change, however, would have long-term effects on the representation of states with large immigrant populations, regardless of which party was in power. APM Research Lab, a politically independent institute, projects that if citizen-only maps were to come into effect, 100 congressional districts would be affected.[97] Since Texas has one of the largest immigrant concentrations in the nation, it would likely lose congressional seats, and that could affect the funds and federal resources the state receives.

Nonetheless, in 2016 members of the Project on Fair Representation, a nonprofit legal defense organization in favor of counting only US citizens when forming election districts, filed a lawsuit against the State of Texas and lost. The US Supreme Court ruled in favor of Governor Abbott in *Evenwel v. Abbott* (2016).[98] The justices stated that the "one person, one vote" rule is based on the equal protection principle and that total population, not just the number of eligible voters, must be counted when designing legislative districts. The Court, however, ruled that the legislatures can use different measurement systems in designing state districts, and that those districts not need be perfectly equal in population. In the aftermath of the ruling, from 2017 to 2019, four bills were introduced in Congress to count only citizens when forming election districts and four bills were introduced to add a citizenship question to the 2020 US Census. Many Democrats, MALDEF, and the American Civil Liberties Union charged that the intent of the bills requiring a citizenship question on the census was to determine where immigrants resided and then use this information to design citizen-only maps, even if Congress did not change its methodology in determining the composition of electoral districts.[99] On June 27, 2019, the Supreme Court blocked the use of a citizenship question on the census, and by then Democrats had introduced legislation prohibiting the use of citizen-only maps.[100]

Republican and Democratic Political Disputes

With the shift in political control in Texas from Democratic to Republican, both parties have fought not only over redistricting but also over voting requirements.[101] Democrats have charged that Republicans are trying to dilute the voting power of minorities because minorities overwhelmingly vote for Democratic candidates. In 2011, Republicans passed Senate Bill 14, known as the "Texas Voter ID Law," which required a person to present a government-issued photo identification before being allowed to vote in Texas. The allowable forms of photo IDs were a Texas driver's license, an ID card issued by the Department of Public Safety and Transportation, a Texas election identification certificate, a US passport, a military identification card, and a handgun license.[102] The law was considered to be the toughest voter ID policy in the nation. Immediately, Democrats, MALDEF, and the NAACP charged that it violated the Voting Rights Act, since the law was intentionally designed to discriminate against minorities, specifically the elderly and poor people in rural areas. They argued that over 600,000 people in Texas, mostly elderly minorities, did not have identification cards that qualified under the new law. Furthermore, Democrats argued that in rural areas, many additional people would be politically disenfranchised, since they would not be able to easily obtain a government-issued ID card; in some cases, the nearest Department of Public Safety and Transportation Office was located 137 miles away. The US Justice Department in the Obama administration concurred, offering the opinion that the law violated the Voting Rights Act, as well as the Fourteenth and Fifteenth Amendments.[103] In response, Greg Abbott, who was then Texas's attorney general, sued the Justice Department. After a series of federal court hearings, the Fifth Circuit Court of Appeals, on July 20, 2016, affirmed previous rulings that Texas's voter ID law violated the Voting Rights Act.[104]

After the Supreme Court refused to hear the appeal, the Texas Legislature rewrote the law.[105] On June 1, 2018, Governor Abbott signed Senate Bill 5 into law.[106] The new ID requirements were softened for people who did not possess a current government-issued photo identification and were unable to attain one. Before they could vote, however, they had to sign an affidavit explaining their problem, and they were subject to a criminal penalty if they lied. To be eligible to vote, people could present government-issued IDs that had expired no more than four years earlier or else show a secondary document such as a government document with their address, a utility bill, a bank statement, a government paycheck, or a birth certificate (if born in the United States).

In 2013, another voter ID law was challenged by civil rights organizations alleging that it violated the Fourteenth Amendment rights of American-born children. The law, it was charged, would have long-term effects on voting if not struck down. The controversy began in 2010 when Texas House representative Leo Berman introduced House Bill 292, "An Act relating to birth records of children born in this state; creating an offense." Berman attempted to make two patently unconstitutional claims with this legislation: children born in Texas whose parents are undocumented are not US citizens, and children whose parents are not US citizens, permanent legal residents, or US nationals cannot be issued a birth certificate.[107]

The legislation failed because the Fourteenth Amendment, which provides for birthright citizenship, can be changed only by another amendment. The bill received little support from Republicans and was opposed by Democrats.[108] But one aspect of the legislation could have been implemented if the attorney general of Texas had succeeded. On January 1, 2013, the Office of the Attorney General ordered the Department of State Health Services' Vital Statistics Unit to not issue birth certificates to the parents of children who were undocumented unless they could provide US-issued identification cards or current voter IDs from their country of origin.[109] To immigrant-rights advocates, the transparently obvious intent of this new mandate was to pressure undocumented people to leave Texas.

In 2014, the South Texas office of the Texas Civil Rights Project filed a lawsuit against the State of Texas on behalf of parents. It claimed the birth certificate ID law violated their children's Fourteenth Amendment rights. One of the lead attorneys, Efrén Olivares, argued that because of the law, many US-born children in Texas would not be able to enroll in school, because to do so, they would need to present a birth certificate as evidence of their identity.[110] They would also not be able to travel because they needed an identification card to leave the state, and without a birth certificate, they could not get a government-issued ID. In sum, the State of Texas was creating a class of people without proof of birth or nationality, which in the future would prevent them from voting or receiving the privileges associated with US citizenship.

A year later, after additional parents from counties across Texas joined the lawsuit, Texas attorney general Ken Paxton filed a lawsuit in the US District Court for the Western District of Texas, asking for a dismissal of the suit. In October 2015, Judge Robert Pitman rendered a decision allowing the state to continue enforcing this policy for a probationary period of nine months but also issued an opinion that the law might not be constitutional. He also allowed the civil rights suit to move forward. By this time, the Mexican government had joined the suit. Following Pitman's ruling, the State of Texas backed down and allowed for international identifications such as marriage licenses, voter ID cards, school transcripts, or passports to be used in Texas to obtain a child's birth certificate.[111] This was the policy used in Texas before Paxton tried to institute the more restrictive policy.

Republican representatives are divided on the issue whether children born to undocumented parents should be given the rights of citizens. Legislation on this topic has not succeeded in Texas, and powerful Republicans have openly been against it. In 2010, during the Texas Republican Convention, the party's platform contained a plank stating that Congress should deny a child born to undocumented parents US citizenship. But many Republicans opposed their party's position, including Governor Rick Perry, who stated that it was a divisive plank and not right for Texas.[112]

The Republican Party's position has not changed since then, and during the Texas Republican Convention in 2020, members once again endorsed rescinding birthright citizenship when parents were undocumented.[113] The Republican platform endorsed other political policies that have been traditionally alienating to Democrats, Latinos, and African Americans, such as repealing the Voting Rights Act of 1965, asking Congress to mandate that the US Census collect data only on US citizens, requiring proof of legal residency before allowing children to attend public schools, and requiring photo IDs and proof of citizenship before voting.[114]

Has Social Mobility Slowed Down for Mexican Americans?

US Census and Texas Educational Agency (TEA) data provide mixed findings on the current social mobility of Mexican Americans. More Mexican Americans with college educations are entering higher-paid positions, and school segregation has declined substantially. But the median household income of Latinos in comparison to non-Latino whites shows only slow improvement. In 1980, Mexican Americans earned around 63 percent of what non-Latino whites earned, and by 2010 it had improved to 72 percent.[115] Mexican Americans in the last thirty years continued to be heavily represented in service and labor occupations, with approximately 40 percent of the total working-age population found in those occupations. The number of people working in sales and administrative support also remains the same, at around 24 percent. The lack of advancement may be related to how the growing foreign-born population, in particular the undocumented sector, obscures the social mobility of native-born Latinos.[116] This supposition, however, fails to explain why African Americans followed an economic pattern similar to that of Mexican Americans and other Latinos. In 2010, African Americans and Latinos earned comparable median household incomes, and whites earned considerably more. The figures are $40,165 for Latinos, $38,541 for African Americans, and $59,221 for whites.[117]

Although according to the US Census, Mexican American households earn less than Anglo-Americans in Texas, there have been great advances in the educational attainment of Mexican Americans, which has translated into occupational mobility. Mexican Americans and Latinos with advanced degrees earned a median income of $53,695, which is substantially more than most Latinos' household earnings.[118] In 2010, 10.2 percent of Mexican Americans in Texas (age twenty-five and older) had advanced degrees (i.e., professional, bachelor, and doctoral degrees), as did 11.2 percent of Latinos in general.[119] The college graduation rate had more than doubled since 1990, and it paralleled a similar growth rate for Mexican Americans in professional and managerial occupations. Of particular significance are the employment gains made by Mexican American women, who in the past were nearly absent from these higher-paid positions. In 2010, they surpassed men in these job activities: 24.2 percent of Mexican American women in Texas were found in managerial and professional occupations, in comparison to 14 percent of Mexican American men.[120]

In regard to educational improvements, the equalization of funding for primary and secondary schools has improved significantly, and the level of school segregation has fallen. The Texas Education Agency reported that in 2005, only 28.9 percent of schools in the state continued to be racially imbalanced.[121] The agency also reported that since the late 1980s, the funding of minority-isolated schools has improved significantly under the recapture funding system instituted by the state legislature. This funding system redistributes part of the local taxes obtained from wealthy districts and distributes them to poor districts. Scholars, however, argue that although segregated schools may be better funded than they were in the late 1980s, when the state's educational budget is cut, programs for low-income students in segregated schools are the first to go.[122] Likewise, school construction or building improvements needed in poor neighborhood schools are often stalled from a lack of funds.[123] For example, in 2011 the legislature cut $5.4 billion from the Texas educational budget, and the first programs terminated in response were programs designed for poor students, who were overwhelmingly found in segregated schools.[124] In 2013, Judge John K. Dietz, of the 250th District Court in Austin, ruled that the distribution of the recaptured funds following the state's financial disbursement led to the inadequate funding of many school districts across Texas, and he ordered $3.4 billion of the funds to be returned to the affected districts. Litigation soon followed as the judge's orders were appealed, which led to a rehearing of the case by the Texas Supreme Court. The Texas Education Agency and the governor's office opposed the funds being returned, whereas MALDEF, the NAACP, and the National Education Law Center represented the low-wealth schools suing for the return of the funds.[125] On May 13, 2016, in *Morath v. Texas Taxpayer & Student Fairness Coalition*, the Court ruled that while the Texas school finance system was imperfect, it was not unconstitutional. The judges concluded that the inequities in funding poor schools is a problem that cannot be completely resolved, and as long as all students receive a basic education, they are being prepared to move forward.

After the court loss, MALDEF and the civil rights coalition it was part of continued to litigate cases in support of low-wealth school districts. The new strategy is to litigate individual cases rather than to file one lawsuit representing numerous schools. Overall, substantial improvements have been made in the schooling experiences and occupational mobility of some Mexican Americans. Problems continue, nevertheless, especially in the area of school finances. Thus, Mexican American civil rights organizations continue their vigilance and struggle to improve the opportunities of poor students, many of whom are the children of immigrants.

Anti-Latino Movements and the Trump Administration

During the 2016 presidential campaign, Donald Trump, then a Republican candidate, promised that if elected, he would put an immediate end to undocumented migration by building a great wall separating Mexico and the United States. He promised that Mexico would pay for the wall. To gain popular support for his candidacy, during several campaign speeches he stereotyped Mexican immigrants as rapists, drug pushers, and criminals. On June 16, 2015, Donald Trump stated: "When Mexico sends its people, they're not sending their best. They're not sending you. They're not sending you. They're sending people that have lots of problems, and they're bringing those problems with us. They're bringing drugs. They're bringing crime. They're rapists. And some, I assume, are good people."[126] In later speeches, Trump portrayed US-born Mexican Americans as untrustworthy people with stronger allegiance to Mexico than the United States. His negative portrayal of Mexican-origin people as untrustworthy, disloyal alien citizens and undesirable immigrants gave energy to a racist public discourse that for years had been critiqued for being stereotypical and untrue. Trump's hateful comments, repeated throughout the campaign and afterward, gave prominence to an unacceptable political undercurrent, moving many Mexican Americans to contest these negative stereotypes.

Anti-immigrant movements and discourses occasionally appear in US history, and Mexican Americans are accustomed to dismissing this racist rhetoric. For generations, Latinos, particularly Mexican Americans, have endured the myth that they are alien citizens.[127] Thus, when Trump used anti-immigrant rhetoric to generate support from voters who believed that Latinos, especially those who were undocumented, were the cause of US economic problems, it was not a shock. But when Trump, in the middle of his campaign, began to state that people of Mexican ancestry might not be able to perform their jobs because of their ancestry, it marked an unprecedented attempt to demonize all people of Mexican descent. Trump was no longer attacking immigrants; he was making it acceptable to question the morals and American patriotism of all Mexican Americans.

On May 28, 2016, Trump publicly criticized US district judge Gonzalo Curiel during a campaign rally in San Diego, California, for failing to dismiss two class-action lawsuits filed against him. During the rally, Trump called on the crowd to castigate the judge for being unfair and partisan. Trump called Judge Curiel a hater and one-sided, claiming that his ethnicity prevented him from rendering a fair decision.[128] The following day, Trump was criticized by many in the news media and by members of Congress for attacking the judge and making false statements about how a person's ethnicity affected their belief system. This time, Trump was not attacking the character of Mexican immigrants; he was insulting the judgment and allegiance of a highly respected US citizen who happened to be of Mexican descent. It had become apparent that Trump distrusted people of Mexican ancestry. A week after the rally, Paul Ryan, the Speaker of the US House, publicly disavowed those statements and issued a stinging criticism. Ryan remarked that saying a judge could not preside over a lawsuit involving Trump's business because of his Mexican heritage was "the textbook definition of a racist comment."[129]

Despite the firestorm surrounding his comments, Trump defended his statements against Judge Curiel and argued that his views were not racist. In a CNN interview on June 3, 2016, Jake Tapper asked Trump why he had called Curiel biased and a Mexican, when in fact he was a US citizen born in Indiana. Tapper also queried Trump on his presupposition that people of Mexican ancestry could not do their jobs because of their heritage. Trump defended himself by arguing that the judge could not be impartial because he, Trump, was promising Americans that during his administration, a wall would be built separating Mexico and the United States. In his own view, Trump argued, Mexicans like Curiel did not like this project, and those types of people were prejudiced against him.[130]

When Trump won the presidential election, neither he nor his cabinet members apologized or retracted any part of the president's hurtful comments. For many Americans, his reluctance was a symbol of the president's attempt to transform racist beliefs into respectable, everyday, commonsense ideas. The president, by his words, had made it acceptable for bigoted people to believe that their negative views of Latinos were indeed "facts," because the nation's leader said so. News reporters also proposed that Trump's use of the "immigrant invasion" discourse was politically motivated, an old strategy of blaming immigrants for US economic problems. In the recent past, this scapegoating technique had been successfully used in California, and in the mid-1990s it initiated a social movement against Latinos.[131]

Trump's campaign discourse mirrored California governor Pete Wilson's 1994 reelection campaign rhetoric. Wilson was supported by Save Our State (SOS) political activists, whose members blamed the high cost of living in California on the immigrant invasion. At the time, Mexico was experiencing its second economic crisis caused by NAFTA. Wilson claimed that undocumented people were a financial drain on California's social service budgets, specifically on schools and county hospitals. SOS then organized a ballot initiative, Proposition 187, to establish a state-run citizenship-screening system to prohibit undocumented immigrants from using health care, public education, and other social services in California. SOS expected that this initiative would be replicated by other states and help Wilson's campaign. Indeed, SOS's projections were correct: Proposition 187 passed, and Wilson received 55 percent of the vote, gaining a second gubernatorial term in office. MALDEF and the American Liberties Union challenged

Proposition 187 in federal court, wining an injunction on most provisions of the law. Three years later, the law was found to be unconstitutional for infringing on the federal government's exclusive jurisdiction over immigration matters.[132] Nonetheless, the damage was done. SOS's other goals gained popular support among people who saw Latinos as a problem. Latinos who were US citizens became the next target of SOS.

SOS planned not only to make California a hostile place for undocumented immigrants to live, but also to purge the US electoral system of unqualified voters. SOS members charged that many Mexican Americans were illegitimate voters because they were not true Americans, since they were the children of undocumented aliens. According to SOS members, those kinds of people should not be allowed to vote. Following the failure of Proposition 187 to be enacted, SOS supported a series of proposals in Congress to end birthright citizenship. The intent was to safeguard future elections by ending automatic citizenship and removing illegitimate voters from the electoral process. Legislation to end birthright citizenship, however, was rejected by most members of Congress. Representatives of both parties charged that undocumented migration was a problem, but taking away the citizenship of US-born people was not the best way to address this problem. Immigration reform had to be addressed in other ways.

Although initiatives to end birthright citizenship failed, many states continued to promote anti-immigrant legislation. The SOS movement sparked regional social movements, and many state legislators studied what actions to take. On January 5, 2011, Republican legislators from forty states met in Washington, DC, to discuss ways to pressure Congress to curtail immigration.[133] At the conference, it was decided that the best way to reduce immigration to the United States was to pass state laws that would be hostile to undocumented people. The main strategy was to require state citizenship for a person to receive state services. The bills would deny state citizenship to the children of residents whose parents were either undocumented, nonpermanent legal residents or temporary workers. These initiatives replicated the intent of Proposition 187. Although representatives acknowledged that the bills were unconstitutional, they believed that the resolutions could easily pass and mobilize their congressional representatives to pass federal laws forcing undocumented people to leave the United States.

After the conference, around twenty-one state legislatures introduced state citizenship bills, but none gained enough votes to become law.[134] The legislatures passed other laws affecting Latinos in general, though, such as requiring law enforcement officers to ask a person's immigration status during a detainment, including traffic stops, as opposed to only when a person was arrested. The legislatures also adopted laws requiring county sheriffs and police departments to cooperate with federal authorities in deporting undocumented residents. In Texas, House representative Leo Berman headed the anti-immigrant movement but was unsuccessful in passing any bills. He submitted a series of bills to make life miserable for Latinos, such as allowing police officers to arrest persons suspected of being undocumented, requiring noncitizens to prove legal entry before being issued driver's licenses, ending birthright citizenship, prohibiting sanctuary laws allowing churches to protect undocumented aliens, and increasing state taxes on money transfers to Mexico. Although Berman's efforts were unsuccessful, some of his proposals were later adopted.

The State of Texas at that time was more concerned with challenging federal policies adopted by the Obama administration. Any federal policy affecting immigrants would have great consequences in Texas because of the state's large foreign-born population. In 2014, when Attorney General Greg Abbott was running for governor, he organized twenty-five other states to support a lawsuit against President Obama's administration. With his executive discretionary authority, the president established two programs to temporarily suspend the deportation of some families and youths. Under the DAPA program (Deferred Action for the Parents of Americans), the president planned to permit undocumented people who were parents of US-citizen children, and who had no felony convictions, to be issued work permits. Their deportation would be temporarily suspended. The president's DACA (Deferred Action for Childhood Arrivals) program, instituted two years earlier, was designed to temporarily suspend the deportation of some people who had been brought unauthorized as children by their parents to the United States. They were permitted to apply for renewable two-year work permits.

By the time the lawsuit was heard by the Fifth Circuit Court of Appeals, Abbott had won the election for Texas governor. In *State of Texas v. United States* (2015), the plaintiffs argued that the president had exceeded his executive authority because only Congress has the power to enact immigration policies. After a series of court hearings that the administration lost, the appeal reached the US Supreme Court, and on June 23, 2016, the justices deadlocked, which allowed the lower court's ruling to remain in place.[135] DAPA was blocked from being instituted, and new DACA permits would not be issued. People already holding DACA permits were allowed to renew their permits.

After Trump became president, Governor Abbott was prepared to support the policies that Leo Berman had fought to institute for years. The political atmosphere had changed. Trump had ushered in a new era in which openly talking about Mexicans and Latinos as a problem was acceptable. Within a month of taking office, Trump supported federal legislation to end sanctuary cities in the United States. Sanctuary cities are municipalities that limit how much local law enforcement can cooperate with federal authorities to apprehend and deport undocumented people. On May 7, 2017, Governor Abbott signed into law Senate Bill 4, which banned sanctuary cities in Texas. The bill was not solely about undocumented people. It also affected Latinos who were US citizens because it permitted racial profiling. Law enforcement officers were ordered to detain any person who appeared to be undocumented and ask for proof of their legal status.[136] This policy overwhelmingly affected more Latinos than any other ethnic group in Texas.

In sum, in this day and era, racism can be camouflaged or subtly expressed. Violent acts and racial and ethnic slurs targeting a person in public because of their ancestry are rarely tolerated, even by people who avoid associating with minorities. Hate speech, however, especially when it comes from leaders, can incite a person to take violent action and externalize racist beliefs normally contained within that person's social circles. During the summer of 2019, two mass shootings targeting immigrants, Mexican Americans, and Latinos were committed by men who endorsed Trump's rhetoric. On July 28, 2019, a young man, Santino William Legan, attended the Gilroy Garlic Festival, located in an agricultural workers' community in California where 58 percent of the residents are Latino. He opened fire on the crowd with a WASR-10 semi-automatic rifle. Fortunately, the police were able to stop him before he finished emptying his 75-round drum magazine. The gunman shot himself after being wounded multiple times by the police. Legan killed three people and wounded fifteen. Before his death, Legan posted a message on his Instagram account: "Why overcrowd towns and pave more open space to make room for hordes of mestizos and Silicon Valley white twats." He instructed his followers to read "Might Is Right," a proto-fascist manifesto that promotes racial violence against allegedly biologically inferior people of color; the screed is popular in white-supremacist circles.[137]

On August 3, 2019, a far more devastating incident took place in El Paso, Texas, when a young man named Patrick Crusius brought an AK-47 assault rifle to kill Mexicans in a Walmart store. Another predominantly Latino community was targeted for carnage. The shooting has been described as the deadliest anti-Latino attack in recent US history. Crusius shot and killed twenty-two people and injured twenty-four others, and all except one person was Latino. After being arrested, Crusius informed police that he had traveled from Allen, a suburb of Dallas, to El Paso, where he was assured of killing many Mexicans. In a manifesto that the FBI confirmed was written by Crusius, the shooter stated that he was acting against a migrant invasion, using language mirroring Trump's campaign rhetoric. In his white-supremacist manifesto, Crusius stated that Democrats would soon be in control of the United States, and he attributed this political shift to the numerical growth of the Latino population. He proposed that immigration and the importation of guest workers from Mexico had led to the uncontrollable growth of the Latino population. This created a Hispanic voting bloc that was unfair to whites. Crusius's intent in selecting El Paso was to "remove the threat" of a Latino invasion by terrorizing Mexican Americans to the point that they would leave the country or become too intimidated to challenge the status quo.[138]

President Trump condemned the shooting as hateful and cowardly. The president's critics, however, stated that it was Trump's hateful speech that had spurred the shooter to act. News reports highlighted the association between the shooting and Trump's recent irresponsible comments. During a Trump reelection campaign rally in May 2019, an audience member suggested shooting illegal migrants crossing the border. The president, rather than condemning the comment, tried to make a joke: "Only in the Panhandle you can get away with that."[139]

I hope this scenario will never be repeated in Texas, and that the anti-Latino atmosphere will soon fade away, as did the SOS movement in California. For now, however, Mexican American civil rights organizations must remain vigilant to protect the political rights of immigrants and ensure that the civil rights of minorities are upheld.

Epilogue

This book chronicles the long presence of Mexican Americans in Texas and their sustained struggles to obtain social and economic equality. Over the years, in spite of the odds of prevailing against institutional racism and a judicial system that reflected the social prejudices of those in power, Mexican Americans defended themselves and accomplished many achievements. During the 1980s, substantial social mobility took place when employment and educational opportunities were opened to them. Since then, many Mexican Americans from Texas have advanced socioeconomically, and as discussed earlier, many have achieved notable and distinguished positions. Among those are the forty Democrats and one Republican Spanish-surnamed representatives currently elected to the Texas House and Senate. Within government service, Alberto R. Gonzales reached one of the highest-ranking positions in the executive branch when he served as President George W. Bush's attorney general. He had served as Texas secretary of state and a Texas Supreme Court justice. Other notable Mexican American trailblazers are the doctors of philosophy Juliet García and Ricardo Romo, who served as university presidents in the University of Texas System for nearly two decades. Dr. Romo was president of the University of Texas at San Antonio from 1999 to 2017, and Dr. García was president of the University of Texas at Brownsville from 1986 to 2014.

In the area of philanthropy, Teresa Lozano Long, who was originally from Premont, Texas and the daughter of a successful dairy farmer, donated millions of dollars to the UT Law School and to the Lozano Long Institute of Latin American Studies. Sadly, Dr. Lozano Long passed away on March 22, 2021. She and her husband, Joseph Long, gave millions of dollars to the arts in Texas, and their most cherished investments were their donations to the University of Texas at San Antonio's Health Science Center, where they funded three scholarships a year for medical students from communities in South and West Texas. The scholarships pay for all the students' medical school expenses. The purpose of the scholarships is to aid students from communities that lack medical facilities; upon graduation, they pledge to return to their hometowns and improve local medical services. The medical school at UTSA is named for the Longs. Dr. Lozano Long was also an important contributor to the development of this manuscript. As a member of the University of Texas Press Advisory Board, she generously provided advice, encouraging me to examine the resiliency of the Mexican American people and to explore the activism of Dr. George I. Sánchez and Gus García.

In the arts, Robert Rodríguez, a filmmaker, began his career with a low-budget film about life in South Texas called *El Mariachi*. The film was purchased by Columbia Pictures in 1992 and distributed nationwide, propelling Rodríguez to national fame. Since then, he has produced many films in the science fiction and thriller genres, giving many Mexican Americans the opportunity to play leading roles. Among the leading actors in Rodríguez's films are the director and filmmaker Salma Hayek and the actor Antonio Banderas. Both actors appeared in Rodríguez's two sequels to *El Mariachi*. In 2011, Rodríguez's *El Mariachi* trilogy was added to Library of Congress's National Film Registry to be preserved as films that are culturally, historically, and aesthetically significant.

In the academic domain, many Mexican Americans have left their mark, writing books that have shaped the hearts and minds of readers. Among the most notable books is Gloria Anzaldúa's *Borderlands/La Frontera: The New Mestiza* (1987), a narrative that explores the border as a metaphor and a social reality. According to Anzaldúa, Mexican Americans are a people who must daily navigate and negotiate social borders that are constructed to exclude them on the basis of their race and culture. For many Mexican Americans, the social borders they experience are intensified because they undergo double forms of oppression related to their gender and their sexual preference. As part of her ontological analysis, Anzaldúa offers a vivid description of the poverty and hardships that farmworkers experience in South Texas, and their endurance through inner spiritual strength. Although Anzaldúa's analysis openly discusses her anger at the prejudices she experienced for being a Chicana lesbian, the book was written to encourage Mexican Americans to be proud of their heritage and culture. An equally compelling book is *"With a Pistol in His Hand": A Border Ballad and Its Hero*, by Américo Paredes (1958). In this study of an oral tradition, Paredes reconstitutes the life of a man from South Texas who was unjustly persecuted by

Texas Rangers during the late 1800s. The book has remained a classic text about racism and bigotry in Texas. Paredes's account of Gregorio Cortez has influenced generations of Mexican American writers to critically write about racism while presenting their prose in a diplomatic style that uses parody, irony, and gentle humor in order not to alienate readers.

Américo Paredes and Teresa Lozano Long were both students of George I. Sánchez. Sánchez, as discussed in earlier chapters, was a leading pioneer of educational issues involving racial minorities. Along with the attorney Gustavo García, Sánchez dedicated his life to eradicating school segregation. While Paredes used a humorous and literary approach in his critique of racism in Texas, Sánchez wrote as a social scientist, supporting his assertions with statistical data and legal arguments. Sánchez's assertive tone and criticism of the state government led him to be censured by the University of Texas System, and for fifteen years of his career, he was not given a raise because of his liberal politics and activism against school segregation.[1] Nonetheless, Sánchez established an academic blueprint for how to muster empirical data to support one's critique.

Many problems remain. The most serious one is the ongoing scapegoating of Mexican immigrants and other Latino immigrant groups, who are accused of causing most US economic problems. This popular political trope is used to camouflage deep prejudices against Mexican-origin people, regardless of whether they are US citizens. Of specific concern is how Senate Bill 4 will unfold in Texas, since it allows the racial profiling of Latinos who appear to be undocumented. Furthermore, many prejudiced people continue to see Mexican Americans as alien citizens. They would prefer for the old segregation system to be reinstituted and for minorities to again not be allowed to compete for social mobility. They see the political and socioeconomic gains that Mexican Americans have made over the years as illegitimate forms of mobility, achieved by usurping or slowing down opportunities for Anglo-Americans. Many advances have also been accomplished in education, yet the problem of school finance remains. Many poor children continue to attend segregated schools that are underfunded.

In the area of party politics, Mexican Americans and African Americans have been integrated into the Democratic Party and have made great advances in the party's leadership. Voter ID bills, SB 4, and the conflict over birth certificates are reasons why both groups lean Democratic and are increasingly being pushed away from the Republican Party. Not all Mexican Americans, however, are alienated from the Republican Party. In the 2016 presidential election, 69 percent of Hispanics nationwide identified as Democrats, 21 percent as Republicans, and 10 percent as independents.[2]

In Texas, 18 percent of Hispanic voters supported Trump in the 2016 presidential election, and 77 percent voted for Hillary Clinton.[3] According to Geraldo Cadava in his book *The Hispanic Republican: The Shaping of an American Political Identity, from Nixon to Trump* (2020), Democratic-Republican Latino issues are complex, and in his perspective, many Republican Latinos do not believe that Trump is a racist, but rather that he is a sloppy speaker. Cadava is uncertain whether this is a minority opinion, and he proposes that studies of the 2020 presidential election are needed to provide a clearer response.

In 2020, Joe Biden decisively won the presidential election against Donald Trump, and according to national exit polls, with the exception of Cuban American voters, the Latino support for Democrats increased considerably. At the national level, 74 percent of Latinos voted for Biden, and 23 percent for Trump.[4] In Texas, the findings were mixed. Although Texas Latinos mostly followed the national pattern, support for Democrats fell in border counties. Statewide, Latinos voted 67 percent for Biden, yet the margin fell around 10 percentage points from the 2016 presidential election.[5] This decline has been attributed to South Texas voting patterns, where even though Biden received the most votes, the percentage favoring Democratic candidates fell. It is uncertain why this took place. Was it the result of lower Latino voter turnout, or the Democratic Party's lack of attention to Mexican American voters? Perhaps both assessments are valid. That is, although the state's voter turnout was the highest in thirty years, reaching 66.2 percent, in South Texas the turnout was much lower, and four counties had the lowest turnout in the state, failing to top 45 percent.[6] Further complicating matters, Hispanics compose 71–79 percent of the registered voters in South Texas counties, and research is needed to determine whether the non-Hispanic vote surged and the Latino vote declined.[7] What is also probable is that Latino turnout was affected by Biden's failure to visit South Texas during the presidential campaign.

Few changes occurred at the state level. Most incumbent Republican and Democratic candidates retained their seats. Only Peter Flores, a Republican state senator from the South Side of San Antonio, lost his seat to the Democratic candidate Roland Gutierrez.[8] The changes in election patterns in South Texas will surely become a heated issue in Texas as redistricting politics take center stage. In the last redistricting challenges posed by MALDEF, LULAC, and the GI Forum, these organizations were disappointed with the federal rulings dismissing their claims that Latinos were packed in districts in order to split the Democratic vote. Given that the 2020 US Census data is projected to report a substantial increase in the Latino population, coupled with the fact that new congressional and state electoral maps will be drawn in 2021, redistricting politics and ID voting policies will continue to be contentious issues in the upcoming decade.

Finally, I bring this book to closure by sharing a memory of a meeting I attended in San Antonio in the winter of 2014. Los Bexareños Genealogical and Historical Society invited me to present a paper on Ricardo Rodríguez, whose ordeal led to the landmark case *In re Rodriguez* (1897). In this case, the federal courts affirmed that Mexican Americans were US citizens and that Mexican immigrants had the right to apply for US citizenship. In looking back at Texas history, it seems that Mexican Americans are periodically forced to defend their right to political representation. Nonetheless, at the end of my presentation, I asked the audience whom they considered the most important historical figure in Texas. The audience responded that without a doubt it was Gus García, the civil rights activist who from the late 1930s to early 1960s encouraged others to fight social injustice, even if the barriers appeared insurmountable. A few people in the audience had met García, and they recalled that he professed that every person had to be treated with dignity and respect, regardless of their social status or humble birth. In retrospect, I concur with the audience's response. After undertaking this long-term, time-consuming project, which led me to read countless books and articles and immerse myself in Texas archives and legal documents, I came to see Gus García as an example of courage and selfless dedication in service to those who cannot defend themselves. García, like many of those whom I have written about, chose a hard road in life when he did not have to. He chose to advocate for the civil rights of Mexican Americans when he could have taken an easier path by accepting the status quo and not challenging the state's hierarchical racial structure, especially during a period when being of African or Mexican ancestry was a sign of inferiority. I am optimistic that a new generation of Mexican American scholars, activists, and politicians will devote their careers to the struggle for social justice that Gus García worked tirelessly and courageously for.

Acknowledgments

I dedicate this book to Dr. Carlos E. Castañeda, Dr. George I. Sánchez, and Gustavo García, who have been inspirational in my academic career and pursuit of social justice. This book would not have been possible without the financial contributions of the University of Texas at Austin. The Teresa Lozano Long Institute of Latin American Studies provided support for this research with funds granted to the institute by the Andrew W. Mellon Foundation. The funds were used to visit the Archivo General de la Nacíon in Mexico City during the summer of 2019. The University of Texas Press provided research funds for the reproduction of archival photographs and for extended travel to visit archival depositories at the El Paso Public Library's Border Heritage Center, the National Archives at Fort Worth, and the Louis J. Blume Library Special Collections and University Archives of St. Mary's University. The writing of this manuscript was also facilitated by a one-semester Faculty Research Grant from the University of Texas at Austin.

Finally, I would like to thank my family for the encouragement to pursue this study.

Appendixes

Appendix 3.1: Population of South Texas Counties and Selected Other Texas Counties, 1870 and 1890

South Texas	1870	1890	South Texas	1870	1890
Atascosa	2,915	6,459	Medina	2,078	5,730
Cameron	10,999	14,424	Nueces	3,975	8,093
Dimmit	109	1,049	San Patricio	602	1,312
Duval	1,083	7,598	Starr	4,154	10,749
Encinal	427	2,744	Uvalde	851	3,804
Frio	309	3,112	Webb	2,615	14,842
Hidalgo	2,387	6,534	Zapata	1,488	3,562
Karnes	1,705	3,637	Zavala	133	1,097
Kinney	1,204	3,781	*Other*		
La Salle	69	2,139	Bexar	16,043	49,266
Live Oak	852	2,055	El Paso	3,671	15,678
Maverick	1,951	3,698	Presidio	1,636	1,698
McMullen	230	1,038	Victoria	4,869	8,739

Source: US Census, *The Twelfth Census of the United States, Taken in the Year 1900, Volume 1, Part I* (1901), 40–42.

Appendix 3.2: Population Growth of Mexican Immigrants in the United States and Texas, 1900–1920

Year	US	Texas	Texas as % of US
1900	103,393	71,062	68.7
1910	221,915	125,016	56.3
1920	486,418	251,827	51.7

Source: US Census, *Thirteenth Census of the United States Taken in the Year 1910. Population, Volume 1* (1913), 804; US Census, *Abstract of the Fourteenth Census of the United States, 1920* (1922), 309.

Appendix 4.1: Nonwhite and White Persons of Mexican Descent in Selected Texas Cities and Counties, 1930

	Nonwhite Mexican-origin families		Mexican-born whites	
	Total[a]	Foreign born[b]	City[c]	County[d]
Austin	902	514	23	Travis: 30
Corpus Christi	2,399	1,151	46	Nueces: 57
El Paso	12,430	11,091	416	El Paso: 467
Fort Worth	756	659	52	Tarrant: 60
Galveston	485	382	83	Galveston: 94
Houston	2,822	2,190	320	Harris: 351
Laredo	5,067	4,252	—	Webb: 268
Port Arthur	351	316	11	Jefferson: 17
San Angelo	548	254	4	Tom Green: 4
San Antonio	16,860	11,226	765	Bexar: 886
Waco	310	232	21	McLennan: 30

Note: In 1930, the total number of Mexican foreign-born nonwhite persons in the United States was 616,998; the number of Mexican foreign-born white persons was 23,743; see US Census, *Abstract of the Fifteenth Census of the United States*, 134–135, Table 62: Foreign-born white by country of birth and foreign-born nonwhite, by divisions and states, 1930.

[a] Figures from US Census, *Fifteenth Census of the United States: 1930, Population, Special Report on Foreign-Born White Families by Country of Birth of Head, with an Appendix Giving Statistics for Mexican, Indian, Chinese and Japanese Families*, vol. 6, *Supplement*, 211–212, Table 39: Mexican, Indian, Chinese, and Japanese families by tenure, for cities of 25,000 or more having in their population 1,000 or more of the specified race, 1930.

[b] The US census designates a family to be foreign born if the head of household is an immigrant. Figures from ibid., 213, Table 40: Mexican families by nativity, for cities of 25,000 or more having in their population 1,000 or more Mexicans, 1930.

[c] Figures from US Census, *Fifteenth Census of the United States: 1930, Population, Volume 3, Part 2*, 1019, Table 18: Foreign-born white by country of birth, for counties and for cities of 10,000 or more, 1930.

[d] Each county is the one where the city in the same row is located. Figures from ibid., 1016–1019.

Appendix 7.1: Foreign-Born Mexicans in Texas and the United States, 1970–2000

	Texas			United States		
	Mexican ancestry	Foreign born	%	Mexican ancestry	Foreign born	%
1970	1,619,064[a]	193,639[b]	12	4,532,435[a]	759,711[b]	17
1980	2,752,487[a]	498,181[c]	18	8,740,439[a]	2,199,221[d]	25
1990	3,890,820[e]	907,432[f]	23	13,393,208[g]	4,459,837[g]	33
2000	5,071,963[h]	1,879,369[i]	37	20,640,711[j]	9,177,487[k]	45

Notes: "Foreign born" indicates those of Mexican ancestry who were not born in the United States.

Percentages are the percentage of those with Mexican ancestry who were foreign born.

In 1980 the Census Bureau recalculated the "Mexican ancestry" category for 1970.

[a] US Census, *Persons of Spanish Origin by State: 1980: Supplementary Report* 12, Table 7: Mexican origin persons in selected states by rank, 1980 and 1970.

[b] US Census, *Distribution of Foreign Stock Population: 1970, Census of Population Supplementary Report*, 17, Table 2: Persons of foreign stock by nativity and country of origin for selected states, standard metropolitan statistical areas, and places: 1970.

[c] US Census, *General Social Economic Characteristics of Texas, 1980*, "Characteristics of Population," PC80-1-C45, 45–107, Table 61: Selected Social and Economic Characteristics by Race, 1980 and 1970.

[d] US Census, *General Social and Economic Characteristics, United States Summary, 1980*, vol. 1, pt. 1, 1–17, Table 79: Country of Birth of Foreign Born Persons, 1980 and 1970.

[e] US Census, *1990 Census of Population: General Population Characteristics, Texas*, 29, Table 3: Race and Hispanic Origin: 1990.

[f] US Census, *1990 Census of Population: Social and Economic Characteristics, Texas*, sec. 1 of 3, 144, Table 19: Place of Birth of Foreign-Born Persons, 1990.

[g] US Census, *1990 Census of Population: Persons of Hispanic Origin in the United States*, 5, Table 1: General Characteristics of Selected Hispanic Origin Groups by Nativity, Citizenship, and Year of Entry: 1990.

[h] US Census, PHC-T-10, Table 1–44: Hispanic or Latino Origin for Texas: 2000, https://www2.census.gov/programs-surveys/decennial/2000/phc/phc-t-10/phc-t-10.pdf.

[i] US Census, "Place of Birth by Year of Entry by Citizenship Status for the Foreign-Born Population [104], Decennial Census, 2000: DEC Summary File 4," Table ID: PCT 048 (Texas, foreign born, Mexico), https://data.census.gov/cedsci/table?q=Texas,%20Mexican%20foreign%20born,%202000&tid=DECENNIALSF42000.PCT048.

[j] US Census, PHC-T-10, Table 1-US: Hispanic or Latino Origin for the United States: 2000, https://www2.census.gov/programs-surveys/decennial/2000/phc/phc-t-10/phc-t-10.pdf.

[k] Nolan Malone, Kaari F. Baluja, Joseph M. Costanzo, and Cynthia J. Davis, "The Foreign-Born Population, 2000" (US Census Bureau, December 2003), 5, Table 2: Top Ten Countries of Birth of the Foreign-Born Population: 2000.

Notes

These chapter notes are offered to readers who want to explore more thoroughly the historical material I used in writing this book and the main authors I consulted in constructing my representation of Mexican Americans in Texas history. The archival data for this study are located in the Texas State Library and Archives Commission, Austin; the Dolph Briscoe Center for American History and the Nettie Lee Benson Latin American Collection, both at the University of Texas at Austin; the Louis J. Blume Library Special Collections and University Archives of St. Mary's University, San Antonio; the El Paso Public Library's Border Heritage Center; the National Archives at Fort Worth; the Legislative Reference Library of Texas, Austin; the Archivo General de la Nación, Mexico City; and US Census data. Documents that were reviewed include Texas legislative debates, governors' records on segregation and minority affairs (e.g., depositions, rulings, transcripts of court proceedings), student directories, college admission data, University of Texas System records (e.g., admission, housing, and segregation/desegregation files), yearbooks from the University of Texas at Austin and St. Mary's University, nineteenth-century Spanish runaway slave records, Mexican population labor statistics, Texas Advisory Committee to the US Commission on Civil Rights reports on desegregation, federal documents on the Salt War Riots, and nineteenth-century photographs.

The literature produced by scholars on Texas history and Mexican Americans is substantial. Because of the topic of this book, the primary literature I incorporated in this text concerns political economy, US-Mexico relations, government, race relations, and schooling. This book differs from other historical accounts in that it is not focused on one region of the state and instead provides an overview of events that occurred throughout Texas and had statewide or national impact.

I wish to acknowledge some of my main sources of information and inspiration. The two best-known works produced on the history of Mexican Americans in Texas history are the books by Carlos E. Castañeda and David Montejano. They both advanced historical chronologies that have become master narratives for Mexican American history. Castañeda's first volume of *Our Catholic Heritage in Texas* appeared in 1936 and was followed by six additional volumes chronicling Texas's Catholic heritage from the Spanish period to 1950. His work is considered the foundation of Mexican American history because six of the volumes are largely based on Spanish and Mexican archives and provide an overview of Mexican American history. David Montejano's classic text *Anglos and Mexicans in the Making of Texas, 1836–1986* unfolds the history of Mexican Americans within a larger narrative about the development of capitalism in Texas. In other writings, Montejano further examines Texas history by exploring electoral politics and the Chicano Movement.

Among the studies I cite in this book for the Spanish period are the foundational texts by Gerald Poyo, Gilberto Hinojosa, Alicia Tjarks, Jesús de la Teja, María Elena Martínez, and Antonio Feros. The texts by Martínez and Feros offer an overview of the expansion of the Spanish Empire in Mexico and provide a social and legal overview of how the *mestizaje* process unfolded within elite and common social circles. The other texts examine Texas history and rely heavily on the conclusions introduced by Castañeda. These works, however, move beyond identifying the exploration and settlement of Spanish Texas, since they critically examine the politics and social hierarchies that developed within the colonial settlements. Of specific significance are the complicated analyses they advance regarding how many mestizos, *afromestizos*, and Indians over the generations came to identify racially and culturally as *Español*.

The best-documented period in Mexican American history runs from Texas Independence to the late 1800s. Américo Paredes, Ana Carolina Castillo Crimm, Andrés Tijerina, Neil Foley, Arnoldo De León, David Weber, Josefina Vázquez, and Félix Almaráz are among the best-known authors who examine the transition of power from Mexican to US rule. Anglo-Mexican race relations, land grants, and the Texas Rangers are the main topics of study.

The best-known studies on segregation during the nineteenth and twentieth centuries have been produced by Ignacio García, Patrick J. Carroll, Carlos Kevin Blanton, Mario García, Gilberto Hinojosa, Monica Perales, Cynthia Orozco, Félix Almaráz, Max Krochmal, Jennifer Najera, and Michael Olivas. Their topics have covered housing covenants, oral histories, biographies, LULAC, civil rights, multiracial coalitions, segregation within Catholic parishes and schools, and community histories of Mexican American neighborhoods. Some members of this academic cohort are educational scholars who specialize in school segregation. Guadalupe San Miguel Jr. and Richard Valencia, among the most prolific scholars on this topic, have produced historical studies on school segregation and integration, school finance, deficit thinking, and bilingual education. Their research reflects the activist-scholar tradition pioneered by George I. Sánchez, who dedicated his life to proving that the segregation of Mexican Americans was not the result of social class and language differences, but rather was due to racism. Sánchez's work focused on bilingual education, school segregation, and educational policy. During the 1940s and 1950s, he collected the educational data that was used by Mexican American attorneys during school segregation litigation.

Studies on Texas politics cited in this book offer an analysis of the Chicano Movement, the history of the GI Forum and LULAC, and the treatment of Mexican Americans in the Democratic and Republican Parties. Armando Navarro, David Montejano, and Rodolfo Rosales advance critical overviews of how racism led to the rise of the Chicano Movement in Texas. Julie Pycior also examines the Chicano Movement, but focuses on President Lyndon B. Johnson's relationship with the Mexican American community, specifically with LULAC, PASSO, and the GI Forum. Benjamin Márquez's work concentrates on traditional party politics. His analysis offers a comprehensive overview of the gradual integration of Mexican Americans within the Democratic

Party. He also examines the ascendance and decline of LULAC, the GI Forum, PASSO, and La Raza Unida Party. Steve Bickerstaff and Henry Flores, like Márquez, study traditional party politics, focusing on the formation of electoral districts. Although Robert Caro and Ricky Dobbs do not focus on Mexican Americans, their historical overviews of Texas politics provide valuable information on Texas race relations and examine why the Texas Legislature opposed *Brown v. Board of Education of Topeka* and the passage of the Civil Rights Act of 1964.

The literature on immigration cited in this book is mainly based on primary documents, including news articles, Department of Homeland Security reports, International Monetary Fund studies, and court records. The historical chronology on Mexican immigration relies on anthropological studies by Patricia Zavella, Leo Chavez, Daniel Rothenberg, David Stoll, and my research on US-Mexico relations.

Abbreviations

The following abbreviations and short forms are used in the notes.

AGI: Archivo General de Indias, Seville, Spain

AGN: Archivo General de la Nación, Mexico City

Bexar Archives: Bexar Archives, Digital and Microfilm Collections, Dolph Briscoe Center for American History, University of Texas at Austin

Briscoe Center: Dolph Briscoe Center for American History, University of Texas, Austin

Chancellor's Records: University of Texas System, Chancellor's Office Records, boxes 34, 53, 69, 85, 102, 123, and 145, Desegregation Folders, Dolph Briscoe Center for American History, University of Texas at Austin

Duren Papers: Almetris Duren Papers, Dolph Briscoe Center for American History, University of Texas at Austin

García Papers: Gustavo García Papers, Benson Latin American Collection, University of Texas at Austin

HB: House Bill

HCR: House Concurrent Resolution

HJR: House Joint Resolution

LRL: Legislative Reference Library of Texas

Morehead Papers: Richard M. Morehead Papers, box 3F279, Dolph Briscoe Center for American History, University of Texas at Austin

Stevenson Records: Records, Governor Coke R. Stevenson, Interracial Discrimination Files

Sánchez Papers: George I. Sánchez Papers, Series 2, Benson Latin American Collection, University of Texas at Austin.

SB: Senate Bill

SJR: Senate Joint Resolution

Stat.: *United States Statutes at Large*

TSLAC: Texas State Library and Archives Commission, Austin

UTCOR: University of Texas Chancellor's Office Records

Note on the Epigraphs

Margaret Mead's comment dates from 1978, when she was named Planetary Citizen of the Year. Dolores Huerta's remark is from a 2012 White House meeting when she encouraged Congress to reauthorize the Violence Against Women Act. The observation by Joseph Heller was attributed to a 1970 film adaptation of his novel *Catch-22*, but because similar sayings appeared earlier, the quotation's origin is debated.

Introduction

1. When applied to individuals, the term "Mexican American" refers only to US citizens. When in reference to Mexican American communities, the ethnic label includes immigrants and American-born people of Mexican descent.

2. Following the Mexican-American War (1846–1848), Mexican Americans became a numerical minority of the population. They also, however, became ethnic minorities because of their distinct national origin and culture, and they were considered racial minorities because most Mexican Americans were of a mixed racial heritage. In this book, the terminology emphasizing their ethnic or racial minority status is fluid and changes depending on the historical period and case study under discussion.

Chapter 1: The *Pobladores* and the *Casta* System

1. Borah, *Justice by Insurance*, 26; Thornton, *American Indian Holocaust*, 24.

2. Dobyns, *Native American Historical Demography*, 1, 11; Feagin and Feagin, *Racial and Ethnic Relations*, 138; Thornton, *American Indian Holocaust*, 25–32; Thornton, "Population History of Native North America," 12.

3. Díaz del Castillo, *Conquest of New Spain*, 326.

4. Gibson, *Tlaxcala*, 159, 181–189; Deeds, Meyer, and Sherman, *Course of Mexican History*, 109, 121.

5. Powell, *Soldiers, Indians, and Silver*, 194.

6. Hammond and Rey, *Don Juan de Oñate*, 17; Wilcox, *Pueblo Indian Revolt*, 131.

7. Forbes, *Apache, Navaho, and Spaniard*, 174; Kessell, *Spain in the Southwest*, 123, 152.

8. Burton and Smith, *Colonial Natchitoches*.

9. Chipman and Joseph, *Spanish Texas*, 69.

10. Ibid., 86.

11. Bannon, *Spanish Borderlands Frontier*, 102.

12. Chipman and Joseph, *Spanish Texas*, 75; Morfi, *Relación geográfica e histórica*, 96–97.

13. Newcomb, *Indians of Texas*, 36.

14. Campbell, *Extinct Coahuiltecan Populations*; Chipman and Joseph, *Spanish Texas*, 103–109.

15. Bannon, *Spanish Borderlands Frontier*, 112; Castañeda, *Catholic Heritage in Texas*, 2:47.

16. Castañeda, *Catholic Heritage in Texas*, 2:45–47; Poyo, "Hispanic Texas Frontier," 394.

17. Castañeda, *Catholic Heritage in Texas*, 2:87.

18. De la Teja, "Forgotten Founders."

19. Castañeda, *Catholic Heritage in Texas*, 2:35.

20. De la Teja, *Faces of Béxar*, 54.

21. Weber, *Spanish Frontier in North America*, 193.

22. R. Ramos, *Beyond the Alamo*, 55.

23. Weber, *Spanish Frontier in North America*, 167.

24. Kessell, *Spain in the Southwest*, 217.

25. Chipman and Joseph, *Spanish Texas*, 121.

26. Burton and Smith, *Colonial Natchitoches*, 9; Chipman and Joseph, *Spanish Texas*, 122.

27. Weber, *Spanish Frontier in North America*, 168; Morfi, *Relación geográfica e histórica*, 125.

28. Bannon, *Spanish Borderlands Frontier*, 121.

29. Castañeda, *Catholic Heritage in Texas*, 4:23, 25.

30. Weber, *Spanish Frontier in North America*, 195.

31. Hamnett, *End of Iberian Rule*; M. E. Martínez, *Genealogical Fictions*; Ortega, *Recopilación de leyes de los reynos de las Indias* (1774; first ed., 1681), vol. 1, book 2, title 16, law 32; Perez de Soto, *Recopilación de leyes de los reynos de las Indias*, vol. 2, book 7, title 3, law 5.

32. Sanchíz, "La limpieza de la sangre."

33. Perez de Soto, *Recopilación de leyes*, vol. 2, book 7, title 5, law 15.

34. M. E. Martínez, *Genealogical Fictions*, 148.

35. Ibid., 148; Perez de Soto, *Recopilación de leyes*, vol. 2, book 6, title 5, laws 6–8.

36. Perez de Soto, *Recopilación de leyes*, vol. 2, book 4, title 5, law 8, and vol. 2, book 7, title 5, laws 1–3.

37. Aguirre Beltrán, *La Población Negra de México*, 256–257; Love, "Legal Restrictions on Afro-Indian Relations," 135.

38. Vinson, *Before Mestizaje*.

39. M. E. Martínez, *Genealogical Fictions*, 148; Cope, *Limits of Racial Domination*, 18.

40. Feros, *Speaking of Spain*, 146; Haring, *Spanish Empire in America*, 201.

41. Haring, *Spanish Empire in America*, 203, 253; M. E. Martínez, *Genealogical Fictions*, 148.

42. Feros, *Speaking of Spain*, 74; Haring, *Spanish Empire in America*, 156.

43. Feros, *Speaking of Spain*, 121.

44. From 1537 onward, Indians were declared by law to be human beings, with the right to be Christianized and own property, and they could not be enslaved; see Hanke, *Spanish Struggle for Justice*, 72–73.

45. Cutter, *Legal Culture of Northern New Spain*; Ortega, *Recopilación de leyes*, vol. 1, book 1, title 1, laws 1, 3 and 9.

46. Cope, *Limits of Racial Domination*; Perez de Soto, *Recopilación de leyes*, vol. 2, book 7, title 4, laws 1, 4.

47. Schwaller, *Géneros de Gente*.

48. M. E. Martínez, *Genealogical Fictions*, 153; Sanchíz, "La limpieza de la sangre," 120–123.

49. M. E. Martínez, *Genealogical Fictions*, 195.

50. Feros, *Speaking of Spain*, 218.

51. Vinson, *Bearing Arms for His Majesty*, 2.

52. Borah, *Justice by Insurance*, 26; Dobyns, *Native American Historical Demography*, 40; Miller, *Mexico*, 141.

53. Aguirre Beltrán, "Slave Trade in Mexico," 431.

54. Deeds, Meyer, and Sherman, *Course of Mexican History*, 167.

55. Feros, *Speaking of Spain*, 157.

56. Ibid., 163.

57. Ibid., 188; Nuñez, "Nation-Building and Regional Integration," 204.

58. M. E. Martínez, *Genealogical Fictions*, 243.

59. Nuñez, "Nation-Building and Regional Integration," 204.

60. Deeds, Meyer, and Sherman, *Course of Mexican History*, 203.

61. DePalo, "Nuevo Vizcaya Militia"; Herrera, "Juan Bautista de Anza."

62. Haring, *Spanish Empire in America*, 295–296, 312.

63. Deeds, Meyer, and Sherman, *Course of Mexican History*, 135; Hamnett, *End of Iberian Rule*, 25.

64. Feros, *Speaking of Spain*, 223–225.

65. Frederick, "Without Impediment," 499; M. E. Martínez, *Genealogical Fictions*, 240–242.

66. Cottrol, *Long, Lingering Shadow*, 41; Feros, *Speaking of Spain*, 224.

67. Frederick, "Without Impediment," 211.

68. Feros, *Speaking of Spain*, 220–225.

69. Saether, "Bourbon Absolutism and Marriage Reform," 477, 491.

70. Feros, *Speaking of Spain*, 224–229.

71. De la Teja, "Forgotten Founders"; Tjarks, "Demographic Analysis of Texas."

72. Schwaller, *Géneros de Gente*.

73. Poyo, "Canary Islands Immigrants," 41.

74. Castañeda, *Catholic Heritage in Texas*, 3:269–273.

75. Each mission community formed its own town council; see Tijerina, *Tejanos and Texas*, 26.

76. AGN, *Provincias Internas*, vol. 163, exp. 7, fs. [page] 173.

77. Ibid., 178–179.

78. Ibid., 181–184.

79. Chipman and Joseph, *Spanish Texas*, 137–138; de la Teja, *Faces of Béxar*, 62.

80. Benavides, "Sacred Space, Profane Reality," 14; de la Teja, *Faces of Béxar*, 60.

81. Gerald Poyo argues that the Isleños controlled the *ayuntamiento* up to the early 1760s, and when the capital was moved to San Antonio, the governor diminished the council's authority ("Canary Islands Immigrants," 53–58).

82. Morfi, *Relación geográfica e histórica*, 272–274.

83. Chipman and Joseph, *Spanish Texas*, 174.

84. Jones, *Los Paisanos*, 113; Chipman and Joseph, *Spanish Texas*, 188.

85. By the time San Antonio became the capital of Texas, four additional missions had been established from 1720 to 1731 (Weber, *Spanish Frontier in North America*, 192), and the West Texas settlements at San Saba and Candelaria had failed (Chipman and Joseph, *Spanish Texas*, 150).

86. Hendricks and Timmons, *San Elizario*; Weber, *Mexican Frontier*.

87. Alonzo, *Tejano Legacy*, 54.

88. Hinojosa and Fox, "Indians and Their Culture," 107–114; Weber, *Mexican Frontier*, 53.

89. Poyo, "Hispanic Texas Frontier."

90. Aguirre Beltrán, *La Población Negra de México*, 222.

91. Ibid., 222–230.

92. Similar patterns were found in El Paso del Norte and Laredo. The number of Spanish residents exceeded the national percentage. In 1789, Laredo reported that 45 percent of its residents were Spaniards, 22 percent mulatto, *lobo*, or *coyote*, 17 percent mestizo, and 16 percent Indian (Hinojosa, *Borderlands Town in Transition*, 124). In El Paso del Norte, 46 percent were Spanish, 0.015 percent *peninsulares*, 29 percent *castas*, and 25 percent Indian (AGN, *Historia*, vol. 522, exp. 32, f. 252).

93. "Cuadros estadísticos de la población de los presidios de la Bahía del Espíritu Santo y San Antonio de Béjar, y de las poblaciones de la provincia de Texas, 1777," Universidad Nacional Autónoma de México (National Autonomous University of Mexico), Mexico City, Archivo Franciscano, AFRA AF 10/152.1.f.1–4v.

94. "Documentación relativa al número de vasallos y misiones en la provincia de Texas" (report accompanying the census of 1777), in ibid., AFRA AF 10/149.1.f.1–4v.

95. Morfi, *Relación geográfica e histórica*, 67.

96. AGI, *Guadalajara*, legajo 283, cited in Tjarks, "Demographic Analysis of Texas," 298.

97. Bexar Archives, Census Report, Bexar, 1782.

98. Ibid., Census Report, Bexar, 1783.

99. Poyo, "Canary Islands Immigrants"; de la Teja, *Faces of Béxar*.

100. Poyo, "Hispanic Texas Frontier."

101. Separate censuses were conducted for mission residents and the civilian population, but in the provincial census of Texas, all inhabitants were included.

102. Jones, *Los Paisanos*, 115–118. In 1779, the village of Nacogdoches was founded near the old settlements of Los Adaes (48).

103. Bexar Archives, letters of Gov. Pacheco: n.d., roll 165, frame 81; March 1, 1790, roll 20, frame 219; June 26, 1790, roll 20, frame 412.

104. Bexar Archives, letter from Gov. Manuel Muñoz, August 4, 1793, roll 23, frame 703.

105. Humboldt, *Tablas geográfico-políticas* (1803).

106. Bexar Archives, Province of Texas, 1804, e_bx_014762_001.

107. In Texas, the Pragmática Sanción marriage law was seldom invoked. The Bexar Archives contain one case of an African-descent family asking the authorities to stop the marriage of their relative María Trinidad to a mission Indian (de la Teja, *Faces of Béxar*, 94; Bexar Archives, Proceeding concerning María de la Trinidad 1781, e_bx_003536_001). Furthermore, royal administrators informed Governor Manuel Muñoz on March 7, 1799, that his company was not under the jurisdiction of the Ley Pragmática (Bexar Archives, Correspondence of Jose Ramón Mateos to Governor of Texas, 1794, e_bx_010940_003).

108. Real Cédula 15 de Octubre 1802, in *Derecho Internacional Mexicano*, 1:135.

109. Vizcaya Canales, *Instrucción reservada de Salcedo y Salcedo*, 16.

110. Ibid., 7.

111. In 1776, the northern provinces were temporarily divided into the eastern and western provinces, with Texas and Coahuila placed under the eastern division, and California and New Mexico in the western division. In 1792 the provinces were

reunited and renamed the Internal Provinces under one general commander (Vizcaya Canales, *Instrucción reservada de Salcedo y Salcedo*, 13). The viceroy retained oversight only of California, Nuevo Santander, and Nuevo León. Laredo at that time was part of Nuevo Santander.

112. Vizcaya Canales, *Instrucción reservada de Salcedo y Salcedo*, 8–10.

113. Nemesio de Salcedo y Salcedo to King Charles IV, April 26, 1804, in AGN, *Provincias Internas*, vol. 200, exp. 3, fs. 379, 382–383.

114. Almaráz, *Tragic Cavalier*, 17; *State Papers and Publick Documents of the United States*, 12:25–42; Weber, *Spanish Frontier in North America*, 292.

115. Kessell, *Spain in the Southwest*, 347.

116. Castañeda, *Catholic Heritage in Texas*, 5:294.

117. Parise, "Slave Law and Labor Activities."

118. Nemesio de Salcedo y Salcedo, report to Charles IV, January 23, 1805, in AGN, *Provincias Internas*, vol. 200, exp. 3, f. 333.

119. Ingersoll, "Slave codes and Judicial Practices."

120. Kessell, *Spain in the Southwest*, 351; *State Papers and Publick Documents of the United States*, 10:493–496.

121. Salcedo y Salcedo report to Charles IV, in AGN, *Provincias Internas*, vol. 200, exp. 3, f. 391–392; Bernardo Villamil, report, January 22, 1805, in ibid., fs. 333–335.

122. Salcedo y Salcedo report to Charles IV, f. 333.

123. *Esclavitud*, April 14, 1789, in *Derecho Internacional Mexicano*, 3:318.

124. Villamil report, in AGN, *Provincias Internas*, vol. 200, exp. 3, fs. 344–345.

125. Marqués de Casa Calvo to José Joaquín Ugarte, December 26, 1804, in ibid., fs. 335–337.

126. José Joaquín Ugarte to Bernardo Villamil, December 1804, in ibid., fs. 338–339.

127. Villamil report.

128. Salcedo y Salcedo report to Charles IV, fs. 391–392.

129. *State Papers and Publick Documents of the United States*, 10:446–448.

130. Vizcaya Canales, *Instrucción reservada de Salcedo y Salcedo*, 32.

131. Aguirre Beltrán, *La población Negra de México*, 248.

132. Weber, *Spanish Frontier in North America*, 295.

133. Costeloe, "Spain and the Spanish American Wars," 226.

134. Haring, *Spanish Empire in America*, 323.

135. Hamnett, *End of Iberian Rule*, 83–84.

136. Feros, *Speaking of Spain*, 199.

137. Deeds, Meyer, and Sherman, *Course of Mexican History*, 216.

138. Hamnett, *End of Iberian Rule*, 31, 77.

139. Feros, *Speaking of Spain*, 238.

140. Hamnett, *End of Iberian Rule*, 112.

141. Ibid., 122.

142. Feros, *Speaking of Spain*, 211–212.

143. In 1793 and 1810, it was estimated that 0.2 percent of the total population of New Spain had been born in Spain, 10 percent were of African heritage, and 11 percent were mestizo (Aguirre Beltrán, *La población Negra de México*, 234).

144. Borah, *Justice by Insurance*, 395.

145. Ibid., 396.

146. Ellis and Walter, "Protecting Indian Decrees," 53.

147. Chance and Taylor, "Estate and Class in a Colonial City."

148. Almaráz, *Tragic Cavalier*, 142.

149. Ibid., 123.

150. Castillo Crimm, *De León*, 58.

151. Vázquez and Meyer, *México frente a Estados Unidos*, 31.

152. Folsom, *Arredondo*, 72, 75.

153. Bradley Folsom states that San Antonio fell to rebel forces on March 29, 1813 (*Arredondo*, 75), whereas Raúl Ramos gives the date as April 1 (*Beyond the Alamo*, 40).

154. Castillo Crimm, *De León*, 64.

155. Folsom, *Arredondo*, 85.

156. Vázquez and Meyer, *México frente a Estados Unidos*, 31.

157. Feros, *Speaking of Spain*, 244.

158. Hutchinson, *Frontier Settlement in Mexican California*, 80; King, "Colored Castes and American Representation," 53.

159. Fradera, *Imperial Nation*, 69–70.

160. Chipman and Joseph, *Spanish Texas*, 236; Hall and Weber, "Mexican Liberals and the Pueblo Indians," 7.

161. Folsom, *Arredondo*, 4, 89; Vizcaya Canales, *Instrucción reservada de Salcedo y Salcedo*, 27.

162. Castillo Crimm, *De León*, 64.

163. Vázquez and Meyer, *México frente a Estados Unidos*, 42.

164. *State Papers and Publick Documents of the United States*, 12:111–115, 124–125.

165. The Transcontinental Treaty of 1819 took effect on February 22, 1821 (*Derecho Internacional Mexicano*, 1:144). Article 6 stipulated that Spanish citizens who remained in US territory would be extended the political rights of US citizens (140).

166. Adams-Onís Treaty of 1819, in *Derecho Internacional Mexicano*, 1:138–149.

167. *Residents of Texas, 1782–1836*.

168. AGN, *Provincias Internas*, vol. 187, exp. 9, fs. 267–274.

169. Ibid., fs. 268–269.

170. Ibid., fs. 271–273.

171. Tivi reported that her value was $1,000. The denomination of the country's currency was not reported.

172. AGN, *Provincias Internas*, vol. 187, exp. 9, fs. 270–271.

173. Deeds, Meyer, and Sherman, *Course of Mexican History*, 230.

174. Folsom, *Arredondo*, 203.

175. Plan de Iguala, Law 12, in *Derecho Internacional Mexicano*, 3:391.

176. Pantoja Morán, *Bases del constitucionalismo mexicano*.

177. Alonzo, *Tejano Legacy*, 41.

178. Tijerina, *Tejano Empire*, xxii.

179. Weber, *Mexican Frontier*, 4–5.

Chapter 2: New Racial Structures

1. Foley, *Mexicans in the Making of America*, 20; Deeds, Meyer, and Sherman, *Course of Mexican History*, 270.

2. Vázquez and Meyer, *United States and Mexico*, 20.

3. Castillo Crimm, *De León*, 17.

4. Weber, *Mexican Frontier*, 164.

5. Vázquez, *México y el expansionismo norteamericano*, 52.

6. Pantoja Morán, *Bases del constitucionalismo mexicano*, 42.

7. Bugbee, "Slavery in Early Texas," 394; Vázquez, *México y el expansionismo norteamericano*, 55.

8. Bugbee, "Slavery in Early Texas," 395; Vázquez, *México y el expansionismo norteamericano*, 53.

9. Vázquez and Meyer, *United States and Mexico*, 34.

10. Hamnett, *End of Iberian Rule*, 291.

11. Pantoja Morán, *Bases del constitucionalismo mexicano*; Rojas, "La evolución histórica de la cuidadanía." States were to determine residency requirements for immigrants eligible to run for office (Pantoja Morán, *Bases del constitucionalismo mexicano*, 361).

12. Vázquez, *México y el expansionismo norteamericano*, 55.

13. Decreto de 13 de Julio de 1824—Prohibición del comercio y tráfico de esclavos, in *Derecho Internacional Mexicano*, 3:321.

14. Pantoja Morán, *Bases del constitucionalismo mexicano*, 418.

15. Colonel Jared E. Groce, the largest slave owner in Austin's colony, petitioned for a one-year grace period against the enforcement of the decree of July 13, 1824, but was denied an extension (Vázquez, *México y el expansionismo norteamericano*, 55).

16. Torget, *Seeds of Empire*, 79.

17. Vázquez and Meyer, *United States and Mexico*, 33.

18. Castillo Crimm, *De León*, 79.

19. Torget, *Seeds of Empire*, 80; Vásquez, *México y el expansionismo norteamericano*, 54.

20. Chávez et al., *La Constitución de 1824*, 26.

21. Vázquez, *México y el expansionismo norteamericano*, 60; Tijerina, *Tejanos and Texas*, 30, 101.

22. Greaser et. al, "Index to Titles, Field Notes, and Plats," 7–9.

23. Torget, *Seeds of Empire*, 100.

24. "Tejano" is an ethnic term referring to Texas residents of Mexican descent.

25. R. Ramos, *Beyond the Alamo*, 95; Tijerina, *Tejanos and Texas*, 101, 110–114.

26. Torget, *Seeds of Empire*, 119.

27. Foley, *White Scourge*, 18; Vázquez and Meyer, *México frente a Estados Unidos*, 46–48.

28. Vázquez and Meyer, *United States and Mexico*, 33.

29. Torget, *Seeds of Empire*, 97, 156.

30. Ibid., 131.

31. *Derecho Internacional Mexicano*, 3:321.

32. Andrew Torget claims that slavery was not banned in Mexico until 1837, citing the Law of April 5, 1837, as evidence: "Queda abolida la escalvitud en la República, sin excepción alguna" (*Seeds of Empire*, 305). This interpretation is questionable, since the aim of the decree was to initiate the indemnification procedures that President Guerrero proclaimed in 1829 would be implemented in the future (*Derecho Internacional Mexicano*, 3:321–322; Vázquez, *México y el expansionismo norteamericano*, 62).

33. Vázquez, *México y el expansionismo norteamericano*, 65.

34. *Derecho Internacional Mexicano*, 3:139.

35. Vázquez and Meyer, *México frente a Estados Unidos*, 45–47.

36. Campbell, Pugsley, and Duncan, *Laws of Slavery in Texas*, 19.

37. Vázquez and Meyer, *México frente a Estados Unidos*, 45–47.

38. Deeds, Meyer, and Sherman, *Course of Mexican History*, 255.

39. Vázquez and Meyer, *United States and Mexico*, 34.

40. Deeds, Meyer, Sherman, *Course of Mexican History*, 254.

41. Richardson et al., *Texas*, 58, 117, 160.

42. Vázquez, *México y el expansionismo norteamericano*, 78.

43. Reséndez, *Changing National Identities*, 29, 151, 165; Vázquez and Meyer, *United States and Mexico*, 34.

44. Foley, *Mexicans in the Making of America*, 27–28.

45. R. Ramos, *Beyond the Alamo*, 142–165.

46. Deeds, Meyer, and Sherman, *Course of Mexican History*, 256.

47. Texas General Land Office, *Spanish and Mexican Land Grants in South Texas*.

48. Vázquez and Meyer, *United States and Mexico*, 38–39; Weber, *Mexican Frontier*, 266. For a discussion of Texas claims over New Mexico, see Reséndez, *Changing National Identities*, ch. 7.

49. Constitution of the Republic of Texas, 1836, General Provisions, sections 6, 9, and 10, in *Laws of Texas*, 1:1079.

50. Ibid., sec. 10, in *Laws of Texas*, 1:1079.

51. General Land Office Act, sec. 21, in *Laws of Texas*, 1:1276.

52. Foley, *White Scourge*, 19–20.

53. An Act Concerning Free Persons of Color, sec. 8, in *Laws of Texas*, 2:326.

54. Ibid., sec. 3, 2:325.

55. Menchaca, *Recovering History*, 231.

56. Act for the Relief of Certain Free Persons of Color, December 12, 1840, in *Laws of Texas, Supplement, 1822–1897*, 549.

57. M. M. Martinez, *Injustice Never Leaves You*, 10.

58. Alonso, *Thread of Blood*; Chalfant, *Without Quarter*; Weber, *Mexican Frontier*. For a discussion of the failed Texas reservations and settler-Indian conflicts, see T. Smith, *From Dominance to Disappearance*.

59. Minter, "Indian Land Claims in Texas," 50.

60. Keyssar, *Right to Vote*.

61. Montejano, *Anglos and Mexicans*, 82–85.

62. *Debates of the Texas Convention*, 235–236.

63. Ibid., 158.

64. Ibid., 157, 158.

65. Ibid., 123.

66. Reséndez, *Changing National Identities*, 170.

67. Constitution of the State of Texas, 1845, art. 3, sec. 1, in *Laws of the Republic of Texas*, vol. 2, pt. 3 (1845), 1280.

68. *Debates of the Texas Convention*, 212–232, 500.

69. Ibid., 555; Constitution of the State of Texas, 1845, art. 3, sec. 2, in *Laws of the Republic of Texas*, 1280.

70. For a discussion of marriage laws passed by the Republic of Texas in 1837 and 1841, see the following court cases: *Nicholas v. Stewart*, 15 Tex. 226 (1855) (which dealt with the Act of 1841, "Marriage by bond, etc.," article 4608 in *Vernon's Texas*

Civil Statutes), and *Smith v. Smith*, 127 Tex. 621 (1846) (which stated that marriages contracted during the Spanish and Mexican periods were valid and that children were capable of inheritance under the Act of June 5, 1837, and the Act of 1841).

71. Act of June 5, 1837, sec. 1, in *Laws of Texas*, 2:640.

72. For a discussion of marriage laws passed by the Republic of Texas in 1837 validating marriages between *afromexicanos* and whites, see the court cases *Guess v. Lubbock*, 5 Tex. 535 (1851), and *Honey v. Clark*, 37 Tex. 686 (1873). These cases give the rationale that the Texas Supreme Court justices used in upholding the validity of such marriages.

73. See *Hallett v. Collins*, 51 U.S. 174 (1850), for a US Supreme Court review of US laws upholding the validity of marriages contracted during Spanish and Mexican rule in territories that now belong to the United States; see also B. Smith, *Marriage by Bond*.

74. Chabot, *Makers of San Antonio*; *Sam Smith, Appellant v. Maria de Jesusa Smith, Appellee*, 1845–1846. Appeal from the District Court of Bexar County, Fall Term 1846, to the Supreme Court of Texas. Court records contain the court transcripts and depositions for the 1845 and 1846 trials.

75. *Smith v. Smith*, 1845–1846.

76. See *Guess v. Lubbock* (1851) for a discussion of Spanish laws (Siete Partidas) validating marriages between Blacks and whites and the precedent that the Texas Supreme Court established in *Smith v. Smith* (1846) regarding inheritance rights; see also Menchaca, "Anti-Miscegenation History," 286.

77. Menchaca, *Recovering History*, 16.

78. Vázquez and Meyer, *México frente a Estados Unidos*, 55–65.

79. *Derecho Internacional Mexicano*, 1:193–258.

80. Menchaca, *Recovering History*, 17.

81. 9 Stat. 452 (1850).

82. 4 Stat. 729–735 (1834).

83. Cook, *Population of the California Indians*, 44–45, 199; Menchaca, *Recovering History*, 218; Wilcox, *Pueblo Indian Revolt*, chap. 8.

84. 9 Stat. 383 (1849); 519 (1850); 587 (1851).

85. US Constitution, art. 4, sec. 2, cited in Hyman and Wiecek, *Equal Justice under Law*, 517–531, and see also 411, 415–416. For a discussion of the ambiguity of US citizenship laws before ratification of the Fourteenth Amendment, see *Boyd v. Nebraska ex Rel. Thayer*, 143 U.S. 135 (1892).

86. California Constitution, 1849, art. 2, sec. 1, p. 4.

87. New Mexico Organic Law (1850), in *Laws of the Territory of New Mexico*, 20.

88. Lamar, *Far Southwest*, 19; Larson, *New Mexico's Quest for Statehood*, 82; 9 Stat. 449 (1850).

89. Menchaca, *Politics of Dependency*, 21; Vásquez, *México y el expansionismo norteamericano*, 78.

90. Greaser et. al, "Index to Titles, Field Notes, and Plats."

91. In 1850, 21 land claims from Laredo were approved by the Texas Legislature; two years later, it approved an additional 213. Other claims took sixty years to settle (Greaser, *Spanish and Mexican Land Grants*, 137).

92. Texas General Land Office, *Spanish and Mexican Land Grants in South Texas*.

93. Johnson Scott, *Royal Land Grants*, 106; Greaser, *Spanish and Mexican Land*

Grants, 135–138. The number of land grants carried by the *Anson* is disputed; for land grant adjudication, see Alonzo, "Mexican-American Land Grant Adjudication"; for recovered grant titles, see Johnson Scott, *Royal Land Grants*.

94. Garza, *Agencia Mexicana*, 13.

95. Minter, "Indian Land Claims in Texas."

96. Ibid., 36.

97. Metz, *El Paso Chronicles*, 41; Cool, *Salt Warriors*.

98. Bowden, *Spanish and Mexican Land Grants*.

99. Metz, *El Paso Chronicles*, 33.

100. Beckham, *Ysleta del Sur Pueblo Archives*; Minter, "Indian Land Claims in Texas."

101. Metz, *El Paso Chronicles*, 14–15; Minter, "Indian Land Claims in Texas," 24–26.

102. *Hardy v. De Leon*, 5 Tex. 211, 213, 219 (1849).

103. Ibid., 221.

104. Ibid., 214.

105. Ibid., 219.

106. In *McKinney v. Saviego and Pilar, Wife*, 59 U.S. 235 (1855), the US Supreme Court ruled that Mexicans who left Texas after the declaration of independence and lived permanently in Mexico became aliens and lost their property.

107. *Hardy*, 5 Tex. at 234.

108. Ibid., 246.

109. Castillo Crimm, *De León*.

110. Ibid.

111. *Cook v. De La Garza*, 9 Tex. 358, 359 (1853).

112. W. Paschal, petition for reconsideration of judgment, in *William M. Cook v. Antonio De La Garza*, 1852–1854, box 201–4021, file M2617, no. 404, 2, TSLAC.

113. William Cook, petition appealing Texas Supreme Court judgment of fine, filed in Victoria district court, August 2, 1853, in ibid., 6.

114. *Cook*, 9 Tex. 358.

115. W. Paschal, petition for reconsideration of judgment, in *William M. Cook v. Antonio De La Garza*, 1852–1854, box 201–4021, file M2617, no. 404, 1, TSLAC.

116. Grounds for error, filed December 11, 1853, in ibid., p. 28.

117. Final judgment, September 9, 1853, in ibid., 19.

118. *Cook*, 9 Tex. 358.

119. Answers filed September 7, 1853, A. A. Cunningham, attorney for Antonio De La Garza, in *William M. Cook v. Antonio De La Garza*, 1852–1854, box 201–4021, file M2617, no. 404, 12, TSLAC.

120. *Cook v. De La Garza*, 13 Tex. 431 (1855).

121. After the De La Garza suit, Cook filed additional lawsuits against other land grant heirs; see, for example, *Burnley and another v. Cook and others*, 13 Tex. 586, p. 294 (1855). Although, the land grant lawsuits placed Cook on the wrong side of history, largely in a villainous role, he must be credited for helping develop the infrastructure of the Victoria–Matagorda Bay and Calhoun region.

122. *Sheirburn v. De Cordova et al.*, 65 U.S. 243 (1860).

123. Richardson et al., *Texas*, 117; US Census, *Preliminary Report on the Eighth U.S. Census, 1860* (1862), 130.

124. US Census, *Population of the United States in 1860* (1864), 33, 483.

125. Ibid., 484–486.

126. US Census, *The Statistics of the Population of the United States, Ninth Census* (1872), 1:64–65, 372–373.

127. Menchaca, *Naturalizing Mexican Immigrants*, 65.

128. Barr, *Reconstruction to Reform*, 6.

129. Appiah and Gates, *Africana*, 457; Ross, *Justice of Shattered Dreams*, 61.

130. Ross, *Justice of Shattered Dreams*.

131. Texas Constitution, 1866, art. 3, in *Laws of Texas*, 5:860.

132. Richardson et al., *Texas*.

133. 14 Stat., 27–30 (1866).

134. Ibid., 358.

135. The Fourteenth Amendment exempted from citizenship those Indians that were not taxed, which intentionally excluded most Native Americans. In *Elk v. Wilkins*, 112 U.S. 94 (1884), the Supreme Court clarified the language of the amendment and ruled that Indians had no claim to citizenship when born as subjects of an Indian nation, and neither paying taxes nor terminating a tribal affiliation changed that status.

136. 15 Stat. 72–74 (1868).

137. Richardson et al., *Texas*, 204.

138. Barr, "Impact of Race."

Chapter 3: Violence and Segregation, 1877–1927

1. Richardson et al., *Texas*, 220.

2. M. M. Martinez, *Injustice Never Leaves You*.

3. Durham, *Taming the Nueces Strip*, 65; Kingston, *Concise History of Texas*, 87.

4. Menchaca, *Naturalizing Mexican Immigrants*, 76. For lawsuits filed against Texas Rangers by Mexican Americans during the early twentieth century, see M. M. Martinez, *Injustice Never Leaves You*.

5. Cool, *Salt Warriors*; White, *Out of the Desert*.

6. For a discussion of the Unionist-Confederate conflicts in El Paso County, see Cool, *Salt Warriors*, pt. 1.

7. Minter, "Indian Land Claims in Texas," 25.

8. Texas Constitution, 1876, art. 13, sec. 1, Spanish and Mexican land titles, in *Laws of Texas*, 8:821. Unless otherwise noted, references to the Texas Constitution from this point on are to the 1876 version.

9. Minter, "Indian Land Claims in Texas," 26–27.

10. White, *Out of the Desert*, 87, 99–101, 186.

11. Cool, *Salt Warriors*, 37.

12. In *Salt Warriors*, Paul Cool offers a detailed analysis of the conflicts involving powerful white men involved in the Salt War riots. His analysis diverges from other scholarship that focuses on the effects of the Salt War riots on the local Mexican American population.

13. Timmons, *El Paso*, 203.

14. Cardis's diary entry, in US House, 45th Cong., 2nd sess., 1877–1878, Exec. Doc. No. 93 ("Letter from the Secretary of War . . . transmitting reports of the com-

mission appointed to investigate the El Paso troubles in Texas," May 28, 1878), appendix E, 62–64 (hereafter cited as Exec. Doc. No. 93).

15. Cool, *Salt Warriors*, 117, 155, 214–216.

16. Ibid., 110.

17. Ward, "Salt War of San Elizario," 33.

18. Canutillo, another large settlement in the county, was not involved in the Salt War affair, being located at a distance, in western El Paso County.

19. Cool, *Salt Warriors*, 115, 160.

20. Exec. Doc. No. 93, 142; *Report of the Adjutant General of the State of Texas for the Fiscal Year Ending August 31, 1878*, 13–15.

21. Exec. Doc. No. 93, 142.

22. Ibid., 15.

23. Cool, *Salt Warriors*, 81–85.

24. W. B. Blanchard, testimony, in Exec. Doc. No. 93, 70. In *Salt Warriors*, Cool supports the claim that Borrajo and Cardis were trying to make their own claim over the salt lakes. The rumor was advanced by Albert Fountain, but according to the congressional inquiry, this conspiracy was not proved.

25. *Report of the Adjutant General*, 15.

26. Ward, "Salt War of San Elizario," 72.

27. Exec. Doc. No. 93, 24–26; 144–145, 148, 150–158.

28. Cool, *Salt Warriors*, 142–147, 214–216.

29. Ibid., 198.

30. *Report of the Adjutant General*, 16.

31. Exec. Doc. No. 93, 4, 90–91, 95, 104, 113.

32. Ibid., 95.

33. Ibid., 91–92.

34. Ibid., 10, 139.

35. Ibid., 3–5.

36. US House, 45th Cong., 2nd sess., 1877–1878, Exec. Doc. No. 84 ("Letter from the Secretary of War, transmitting report from Colonel Hatch on the subject of 'El Paso Troubles,'" May 8, 1878), 5.

37. Cool, *Salt Warriors*, 224; Exec. Doc. No. 93, 4, 90–91, 95, 104, 113.

38. Exec. Doc. No. 93, p. 87.

39. Ibid., 84, 94–95.

40. Ibid., 21–31.

41. *Report of the Adjutant General*, 13–17; Ward, "Salt War of San Elizario," 141–145.

42. Cool, *Salt Warriors*, 279–282.

43. Levario, "Cuando vino la mexicanadad"; M. M. Martinez, *Injustice Never Leaves You*; Paredes, *With a Pistol in His Hand*.

44. De León, *They Called Them Greasers*, 98.

45. Houston Post, *Houston Post Almanac*, 208.

46. Callahan, *American Foreign Policy in Mexican Relations*, 483; Richardson et al., *Texas*, 225.

47. Clements, "British Investment."

48. Ashton, "Mifflin Kenedy," 3:1064; Montejano, *Anglos and Mexicans*, 63–70.

49. Graham, *El Rancho in South Texas*; M. M. Martinez, *Injustice Never Leaves You*.

50. Kingston, *Concise History of Texas*, 92; Vásquez and Meyer, *United States and Mexico*, 77.

51. Alonzo, *Tejano Legacy*, 228.

52. US Census, *Population of the United States, Eleventh Census: 1890* (1895), 782, 516: US Census, *The Statistics of the Population of the United States, Ninth Census* (1872), xvii; appendix 3.1.

53. Callahan, *American Foreign Policy in Mexican Relations*, 483; M. M. Martinez, *Injustice Never Leaves You*, 13.

54. Colloff, "Blood of the Tigua"; Minter, "Indian Land Claims in Texas."

55. Alonzo, *Tejano Legacy*, 234; Richardson et al., *Texas*, 245–250.

56. Callahan, *American Foreign Policy in Mexican Relations*, 483–491; see Menchaca, *Naturalizing Mexican Immigrants*, 88–90.

57. Miller, *Mexico*, 272.

58. US Census, *Compendium of the Eleventh Census: 1890, Part III* (1897), 50, 65.

59. Registers of Elected and Appointed State and County Officials, reel 13, 1889–1894, and reel 14, 1894–1897, TSLAC; Lasater, *Falfurrias*; Menchaca, *Naturalizing Mexican Immigrants*.

60. Hackney, "Contemporary Views of Populism," 1.

61. Abramowitz, "Negro in the Populist Movement"; Martin, *People's Party in Texas*.

62. For an analysis proposing that racism did not propel the People's Party to politically disenfranchise Mexican Americans, see Cantrell, "Very Pronounced Theory of Equal Rights."

63. Menchaca, *Naturalizing Mexican Immigrants*, 11.

64. *San Antonio Daily Express*, May 12, 1896, 5.

65. *In re Rodriguez*, 81 F. 337, 349 (W.D. Tex. 1897); *San Antonio Daily Express*, May 4, 1897, 5.

66. *In re Rodriguez*, 81 F. at 349, 354–355. Depositions in the case are available from the National Archives, SWD, NRF-0210-San-0001, Court Opinion, 6, 13.

67. 16 Stat. 254–256 (1870).

68. Williams, *Supreme Court of the United States*, 395–397. Fourteenth Amendment, sec. 1, clause 2: "No State shall make or enforce any law which shall abridge the privileges or immunities of citizens of the United States."

69. *Slaughter-House Cases*, 83 U.S. 36, 37 (1873).

70. Williams, *Supreme Court of the United States*, 76, 97, 117.

71. Ross, *Justice of Shattered Dreams*, 193, 194.

72. Williams, *Supreme Court of the United States*, 76, 97, 117.

73. *Slaughter-House Cases*, 83 U.S. 36.

74. Stephenson, "Separation of the Races."

75. Rabinowitz, "From Exclusion to Segregation," 106, 110; Woodward, "Strange Career of Jim Crow," 49.

76. Texas Constitution, art. 7, sec. 7, in *Laws of Texas*, 8:811; SB 97, ch. 41, 22nd Leg., reg. sess., 1891, in *Laws of Texas*, 10:46.

77. *Manning v. San Antonio Club*, 63 Tex. 166 (1884).

78. See, for example, *Terrell Wells Swimming Pool v. Rodriguez*, 182 S.W.2d 824 (Tex. Civ. App. 1944), in *Texas Digest, 1840 to 1961*, 8:282.

79. Brkich, "Bexareños Democratas."

80. Matovina, *Tejano Religion and Ethnicity*, 52–59; De León, *They Called Them Greasers*.

81. SB 117, ch. 14, sec. 1, in *General Laws of the State of Texas*, January 8, 1907 to April 12, 1907, 21–23.

82. Texas Constitution, art. 11, sec. 5, "Municipal Corporations," in *General Laws of Texas* (1913), 284.

83. McCorkle, *Texas City*.

84. Carroll, *Felix Longoria's Wake*; Luckingham, *Minorities in Phoenix*; McCorkle, *Texas City*; Tretter, *Austin Restricted*.

85. J. Márquez, *Black-Brown Solidarity*; Menchaca, *Mexican Outsiders*; Vigil, *Rainbow of Gangs*.

86. Montejano, *Quixote's Soldiers*, 10, chap. 1; Najera, *Borderlands of Race*, 17, part 1.

87. D. Smith, *When Did Southern Segregation Begin?*; Vigil, *Rainbow of Gangs*, chap. 3.

88. Matovina, *Tejano Religion and Ethnicity*, 51–52.

89. Ellsworth, *Population of El Paso*, 6.

90. García, *Mexican American Mayor*, 5; Houser, "Tigua Settlement of Ysleta," 32.

91. Perales, *Smeltertown*, 47.

92. J. Márquez, *Black-Brown Solidarity*.

93. De León and Stewart, *Tejanos and the Numbers Game*; Menchaca, *Naturalizing Mexican Immigrants*.

94. González Ramírez, *La revolución social de México*, 21.

95. J. Márquez, *Black-Brown Solidarity*, 77–78, 95.

96. Treviño, *Church in the Barrio*, 26–30.

97. US Census, *Thirteenth Census of the United States Taken in the Year 1910: Population, Volume 1* (1913), 804; US Census, *United States Bureau of the Census Abstract* (1922), 309.

98. Brooks and Rose, *Saving the Neighborhood*, 39.

99. League of Texas Municipalities, "Notes from the Cities" (July 1916), 103; Glasrud, "Jim Crow's Emergence in Texas," 55.

100. Smith 2002: 20–22.

101. League of Texas Municipalities, "Legislation from Texas Cities" (1917), 151–155.

102. US Department of Commerce, *Standard State Zoning Enabling Act*, iii.

103. Ibid., 4n6.

104. SB 275, 40th Leg., reg. sess., 1927; article 1015b, *Vernon's Annotated Revised Civil Statutes of the State of Texas*, vol. 2A (1963), 267.

105. *Buchanan v. Warley*, 245 U.S. 60 (1917).

106. C. Ramos, "Racially Restrictive Covenants."

107. SB 275 was codified under ch. 103, arts. 1293a and 1293b, sec. 204, and in art. 1015b in *General and Special Laws of Texas*, vol. 25 (1927).

108. Repeal of Act of 1927, ch. 103, art. 1293a and 1293b. sec. 204, HB 808, June 10, 1969; repeal of Act of 1927, ch. 103, art. 1015b, HB 253, May 6, 1969.

109. *Corrigan v. Buckley*, 271 U.S. 323 (1926).

110. For a legal history of housing covenants, see *Clifton v. Puente*, 218 S.W.2d 272 (Tex. Civ. App. 1949); Olivas, "Legal Career of Perales," 324.

111. Secs. 1–3, in *General and Special Laws of Texas*, vol. 25 (1927), 424–425.

112. Auyero, *Invisible in Austin*; J. Márquez, *Black-Brown Solidarity*.

113. Tate, "Austin, Texas, in Sociohistorical Context," 28, 30.

114. Koch and Fowler, *City Plan for Austin*, 51.

115. Ibid., 56–57.

116. For cases upholding the policy of "separate but equal," see *Plessy v. Ferguson*, 163 U.S. 537 (1896); *Hall v. DeCuir*, 95 U.S. 485 (1877); *United States v. Dodge*, 25 F. Cas. 882 (W.D. Tex. 1877).

117. Koch and Fowler, *City Plan for Austin*, 51, 56.

118. Ibid., plate 11.

119. US Census, *Fifteenth Census of the United States: 1930, Population, Volume 3, Part 2* (1932), 969, 972, 1015.

120. Busch, "City of Upper-Middle-Class Citizens," 982.

121. Tate, "Austin, Texas, in Sociohistorical Context," 30.

122. Busch, "City of Upper-Middle-Class Citizens," 982.

123. Tretter, *Austin Restricted*.

124. "Austin[,] Texas[,] Street Guide," map, Miller Blue Print Co., 1934, copy in PCL Map Collection (National Archives, Record Group 145, Austin Texas Folder), University of Texas at Austin.

125. *Delgado, et al. v. Bastrop ISD, et al.*, Civil Case No. 388 (W.D. Tex. 1948). As the population of Austin grew, city officials instituted plans to increase the energy capacity of the city, and in 1960 they built the Holly Power Plant in East Austin. The plant was constructed in the center of several Mexican American neighborhoods and next to Metz Elementary School. Although the plant produced much-needed electricity for Austin, it caused the Mexican American neighborhoods to experience environmental problems. The plant's machinery generated noise, polluted the air, and on occasion created hazardous conditions when tanks storing chemicals spilled over. In 1962, Interstate 35 was built just east of downtown, contributing to noise pollution in the East Side. The city council callously voted to site the freeway for the convenience of Austin residents, rather than putting it a few miles east in agricultural-garden lands, where noise pollution in neighborhoods would have been greatly reduced (Busch, "City of Upper-Middle-Class Citizens," 986).

126. The public school system in Texas was established in 1876, but it was not funded immediately, because many legislators stated that educating all children was unnecessary (Braden et al., *Texas Constitution*, 3, 16).

127. Braden et al., *Texas Constitution*, 3, 12; Texas Constitution, amendment of 1884, art. 7, sec. 8, in *Laws of Texas*, 9:572–575, 582.

128. Cubberly, "High School in US," 264.

129. In 1884, the legislature allocated public land to counties to construct schools (Texas Constitution, amendment of 1884, art. 7, sec. 6, in *Laws of Texas*, 9:571).

130. Texas Constitution, amendment of 1884, art. 7, sec. 3, in *Laws of Texas*, 9:570.

131. Ibid., art. 7, sec. 8, 71, and 75, in *Laws of Texas*, 9:584–585.

132. Registers of Elected and Appointed State and County Officials, reel 9, 1882–1884, and reel 13, 1889–1894, TSLAC; Martin, *People's Party in Texas*.

133. Texas Constitution, amendment of 1884, art. 7, sec. 8 and 78, in *Laws of Texas*, 9:586.

134. Braden et al., *Texas Constitution*, 12–13.

135. In 1919, taxes were increased to pay for schoolbooks for students in public schools (HB 183, ch. 23, *General Laws of Texas* [1919], 60).

136. Webb, *Education in Texas*, 15.

137. Cubberly, "High School in US," 265–266.

138. Webb, *Education in Texas*, 4, 23.

139. Ibid., 50–53.

140. Braden et al., *Texas Constitution*, 20; HJR Res. 9, 39th Leg., reg. sess., 1925, TSLAC, HJR Res. folder 9.

141. Braden et al., *Texas Constitution*, 4, 17.

142. The Fortieth Texas Legislature authorized cities to pass residential districting ordinances, and counties were later given this authority for neighborhoods in unincorporated areas (SB 171). Senate Bills 171 and 375 and House Bill 449 affirmed the authority of cities and counties to draw residential and school district boundaries, including assigning students who lived outside the city limits to specific school districts (*General and Special Laws of Texas* [1927], 81, 124, 239).

Chapter 4: Challenging Segregation, 1927–1948

1. Olivas, "Introduction," xii. For biographies of LULAC's founders, see Orozco, *No Mexicans, Women, or Dogs*. Ben Garza was the first president of LULAC.

2. Almaráz, *Knight without Armor*, 115; Overtfelt, "Del Rio, Texas."

3. Gournay, *Texas Boundaries*, 107.

4. US Census, *Population of the United States, Eleventh Census: 1890* (1895), 340, 785.

5. Braudaway, "Desegregation in Del Rio," 241.

6. Braudaway, "Old San Felipe High School," 1; Braudaway, *Del Rio: Queen City*, 129.

7. US Census, *Fifteenth Census of the United States: 1930, Population, Volume 3, Part 2* (1932), 962, 989, 1007, 1018.

8. Almaráz, *Knight without Armor*, 115.

9. Braudaway, "Desegregation in Del Rio," 242.

10. Registers of Elected and Appointed Officials, reel 19, 1918–1925, TSLAC.

11. Braudaway, "Desegregation in Del Rio," 242.

12. *Independent School District v. Salvatierra*, 33 S.W.2d 790 (Tex. Civ. App. 1930).

13. Ibid.

14. Ibid., 790, 794.

15. Ibid., 794–795.

16. Ibid., 796.

17. *Salvatierra et al. v. Independent School District et al.*, 284 U.S. 580 (1931).

18. Valencia, *Chicano Students and the Courts*, 18.

19. Almaráz, *Knight without Armor*, 117.

20. Ibid., 128–132.

21. M. García, *Mexican Americans*, 70.

22. *Delgado, et al. v. Bastrop Independent School District, et al.*, Civil Case No. 388 (W.D. Tex. 1948).

23. Castañeda, *Catholic Heritage in Texas*, 7:37; Hinojosa, prologue, 20.

24. Schmitz, *Society of Mary in Texas*, 26.

25. Castañeda, *Catholic Heritage in Texas*, 7:292.

26. Hinojosa, prologue, 76.

27. Castañeda, *Catholic Heritage in Texas*, 7:285–358.

28. Schmitz, *Society of Mary in Texas*; Talmadge Moore, *Acts of Faith*; Wright, "Mexican-Descent Catholics."

29. Schmitz, *Society of Mary in Texas*, 100–115.

30. Hinojosa, prologue.

31. Ibid., 22.

32. Ibid., 41.

33. Wright, "Mexican-Descent Catholics."

34. Treviño, *Church in the Barrio*.

35. Ayala, "Negotiating Race Relations"; Menchaca, *Naturalizing Mexican Immigrants*; Pycior, "La Raza Organizes." Gabriela González's "Jovita Idar" (2015) is a short biography of the president of the League of Mexican Women in Laredo. Idar's family was involved in many civil rights activities in Texas, including organizing the Primer Congreso Mexicanista in 1911 and publishing articles in their family-owned newspaper, *La Crónica*, exposing vigilante activities of the Texas Rangers.

36. Treviño, *Church in the Barrio*, 132.

37. Talmadge Moore, *Acts of Faith*.

38. Ibid., 187–221. Formerly a vicariate missionary region, Brownsville was elevated to a diocese in 1912 (38).

39. Ibid., 38.

40. Castañeda, *Catholic Heritage in Texas*, 7:295, 340.

41. Nuesse, "Segregation and Desegregation," 66.

42. For the history of segregation in the US Catholic Church, see La Farge, *Catholic Viewpoint on Race Relations*.

43. Schmitz, *Society of Mary in Texas*, 115.

44. Ibid., 137.

45. A composite analysis of the percentage of Mexican American students attending the St. Louis Academy is based on the school's catalogues from 1895 to 1924 (copies held at St. Mary's University, Louis J. Blum Library, Archive Division).

46. Foley, *Mexicans in the Making of America*, 51; Gratton and Merchant, "La Raza," 2.

47. The US Censuses of 1850, 1860, and 1910 discuss how Mexican-origin people were counted (Menchaca, *Naturalizing Mexican Immigrants*).

48. Gratton and Merchant, "La Raza," 4; Hochschild and Powell, "Racial Reorganization," 80.

49. Reisler, *By the Sweat of Their Brow*, 137.

50. US Census, *Fifteenth Census* (1932), 1014; US Census, *Abstract of the Fifteenth Census of the United States* (1933), 81; US Census, *Fifteenth Census of the United States: 1930, Population; Volume 2: General Report Statistics by Subjects* (1933), 32.

51. US Census, *Fifteenth Census of the United States: 1930, Population, Special Report on Foreign-Born White Families by Country of Birth of Head, with an Appendix Giving Statistics for Mexican, Indian, Chinese and Japanese Families; Volume 6, Supplement* (1933), 199.

52. Ibid., 6, 199.

53. Ibid., 212, 213; US Census, *Fifteenth Census* (1932), 1019. The census indicates that in 1930, out of the 616,998 foreign-born Mexicans living in the United States, 23,743 were white (3.8 percent); see US Census, *Abstract of the Fifteenth Census* (1933), 134–135. In Texas, out of 266,364 foreign-born Mexicans, 3,692 were white (1.3 percent).

54. Gratton and Merchant, "La Raza," 8.

55. M. García, "Mexican Americans and the Politics of Citizenship," 188.

56. Gratton and Merchant, "La Raza," 18.

57. Hochschild and Powell, "Racial Reorganization," 81.

58. US Census, *U.S. Census of Population 1950: Volume 4; Special Reports, Part 3, Chapter C: Persons of Spanish Surname* (1953).

59. SB 117, in *General Laws of the State of Texas* (1907), 21–23.

60. Texas Constitution, art. 11, sec. 5, chap. 147, "Municipal Corporations," in *General Laws of Texas* (1913), 284.

61. See letters in Coke R. Stevenson, records, Interracial Discrimination Files, boxes 4–14/156 and 4–14/183 (hereafter cited as Stevenson Records), TSLAC.

62. Ibid., box 4–14/183.

63. Narcisso Ortiz, notarized statement, in ibid.

64. Orozco, *No Mexicans, Women, or Dogs*, 58–63.

65. Federico P. Jiménez to Gov. Coke Stevenson, April 7, 1942, in Stevenson Records, box 4–14/183.

66. Federico P. Jiménez to Gov. Coke Stevenson, April 8, 1942, in ibid.

67. W. F. Hare, mayor of Uvalde, to Tom Wheat, assistant secretary to Gov. Stevenson, January 30, 1942, in ibid.

68. Tom Wheat to W. F. Hare, February 2, 1942, in ibid.

69. C. P. Spangler, House Rep., Dist. 77, to Gov. Coke Stevenson, February 4, 1942, in ibid.

70. Menchaca, *Politics of Dependency*, 73.

71. Walter Krueger, Lt. Gen., US Army, to Gov. Stevenson, October 14, 1942, in Stevenson Records, box 4–14/156.

72. US Department of State, *Treaties and Other International Agreements of the United States of America, 1776 to 1949*, Executive Agreement Series 278, Migratory Workers, 9:1069–1075.

73. Grebler, Moore, and Guzman, *Mexican American People*, 68.

74. Carroll, *Felix Longoria's Wake*, 147.

75. Ezequiel Padilla, public statement, published by *Talleres Gráficos de la Nación*, July 20, 1943, and sent to Gov. Coke Stevenson; copy in *Rodriguez v. Terrell Wells Swimming Pool* (1943), box 201–510, case no. 11368, file A-108, TSLAC.

76. Blanton, *George I. Sánchez*, 77, 119; I. García, *White but Not Equal*, 42–43, 80.

77. Luis L. Duplan, consul general of Mexico, to Gov. Coke Stevenson, September 30, 1943, in Stevenson Records, box 4–14/156.

78. Foley, *Mexicans in the Making of America*, chap. 3; Raymond, "Faithful Dissent," 178.

79. Ernest J. Boyett, executive secretary to the governor, to H. L. Winfield, Sen. Dist. 22, Fort Stockton, August 9, 1943, in Stevenson Records, box 4–14/156.

80. Pecos Water Improvement Ordinance, July 7, 1943, in ibid.

81. Boyett to Winfield, August 12, 1943, in ibid.

82. Winfield to Boyett, August 16, 1943, in ibid.

83. Stevenson Records, box 4–14/169; Kibbe, *Latin Americans in Texas.*

84. Stevenson Records, box 4–14/169:2.

85. Blanton, *George I. Sánchez*, 79.

86. Report dated November 10, 1944, in Stevenson Records, box 4–14/169.

87. In 1916, Dallas became the first city in Texas to pass laws requiring separate accommodations for whites and African Americans in hospitals, doctors' offices, stores, and youth centers (Glasrud, "Jim Crow's Emergence in Texas," 55; D. Smith, *When Did Southern Segregation Begin?*, 20–22).

88. Good Neighbor Commission folder, in Stevenson Records, box 4-14/169.

89. Carroll, *Felix Longoria's Wake*, 159.

90. I. García, *White but Not Equal*, 43.

91. *Rodriguez v. Terrell Wells Swimming Pool* (1943), Case No. 11368/N.F. 13,737, statement of facts, box 201–510, file 1982/101-W190, TSLAC.

92. Application for writ of error to the Texas Supreme Court, March 20, 1944, in ibid.

93. *Terrell Wells Swimming Pool v. Rodriguez*, 182 S.W.2d 824, 826 (Tex. Civ. App. 1944).

94. Craig, *Bracero Program*, 51; Foley, *Mexicans in the Making of America*, 80.

95. *Journal of the Senate of the State of Texas, 49th Leg., Regular Session* (1945), 869–870. Short title of SB 1: "An Act declaring the policy of this State with reference to citizens of the Americas."

96. Menchaca, *Politics of Dependency*, 74–76.

97. Ibid.

98. Fredrickson, *Racism*, 128–32; Menchaca, *Mexican Outsiders*, 96.

99. Pitti, *Devil in Silicon Valley*; Sickels, *Race, Marriage, and the Law.*

100. McGregor, *Integration of the Armed Forces*, 291.

101. Akers, *Héctor P. García*; M. García, *Mexican American Mayor*, 1998.

102. Menchaca, "Anti-Miscegenation History," 306.

103. "Certificate of Marriage Registry, Andrea Dena Perez and Sylvester Scott Davis Jr.," Los Angeles Certification of Vital Statistics, Los Angeles County, 1949; ACLU, *Open Forum*, October 16, 1948, 1.

104. Sickels, *Race, Marriage, and the Law*, 63.

105. Menchaca, "Anti-Miscegenation History," 300. *Flores v. State*, 60 Tex. Crim. 25 (1910), examines the case of two Mexican Americans who were not allowed to marry because F. Flores was classified as white and Ellen Dukes appeared to be of African descent.

106. Weinberg, *Chance to Learn*; Wollenberg, *All Deliberate Speed.*

107. Valencia, "Mexican American Struggle," 401.

108. Valencia, *Students of Color*, 136.

109. Akers, *Héctor P. García*, 36.

110. Letter in George I. Sánchez Papers, series 2, box 16, folder 17 (hereafter cited as Sánchez Papers).

111. Blanton, *George I. Sánchez*, 167–168.

112. Ibid., 168. See Gus García to George Sánchez, August 22, 1947, in Sánchez Papers, box 16, folder 17, and George Sánchez to Héctor P. García, April 1, 1948, in Sánchez Papers, box 4, folder 9.

113. *Cactus* (1947), 232; Gus García to George Sánchez, May 5, 1948, in Sánchez Papers, box 16, folder 18.

114. *Directory of the Main University and Extramural Divisions* (1946). The number of Spanish-surname students with US residency is based on UT-Austin student directories.

115. SB 171, SB 375, HB 449, and HB 87, in *General and Special Laws of Texas* (1927), 81, 124, 239.

116. Complaint, in *Delgado v. Bastrop ISD* (1947), 9. The complaint was amended on January 17, 1948.

117. Ibid., 11 (for the original complaint).

118. Answer of Defendant to Dismiss folder, Grace and Greenhill, *Delgado v. Bastrop ISD* (1948).

119. L. A. Woods, Defendant Response folder, *Delgado v. Bastrop ISD* (1947).

120. Defendant Response folder, *Delgado v. Bastrop ISD* (1948).

121. Ibid., 85.

122. Travis County school districts 33 and 35 were not included in the *Delgado* suit. Both districts were on the border of Travis and Bastrop Counties near the Colorado Common School District. The Garfield School (in district 35) served white and Mexican American students in separate classrooms, and the Dunlop School (in district 33) served Black and Mexican American students (Travis County Public Schools, Texas Teacher's Daily Register for Public Schools, 1936–1949, boxes 11, 12, and 13, Austin History Center, FP.J.5; Deposition folder, *Delgado v. Bastrop ISD*, 6).

123. Deposition folder, *Delgado v. Bastrop ISD* (1948), 14.

124. Defendant Response folder, *Delgado v. Bastrop ISD* (1948), 24, 49, 119.

125. Final Judgment folder, in *Delgado v. Bastrop ISD* (1948), 1–4.

Chapter 5: The Path to Desegregation, 1948–1962

1. Carroll, *Felix Longoria's Wake*, 35–44.

2. US Department of Labor, *Consultation on Migratory Farm Labor*.

3. Olivas, "Legal Career of Alonso S. Perales," 322.

4. C. Ramos, "Racially Restrictive Covenants," 165.

5. *Clifton v. Puente*, 218 S.W.2d 272, 273 (Tex. Civ. App. 1948).

6. Salinas, "Legally White, Socially Brown," 87; Tretter, *Shadows of a Sunbelt City*.

7. Caro, *Master of the Senate*, 740–741.

8. League of Texas Municipalities, "Judicial Decisions," 179.

9. See HB 46, secs. 14, 30, 49th Leg. reg. sess., 1945, in LRL.

10. Carroll, *Felix Longoria's Wake*, 64.

11. Caro, *Master of the Senate*, 747.

12. Carroll, *Felix Longoria's Wake*, 187.

13. I. García, *White but Not Equal*.

14. US Census, *Fifteenth Census* (1932), 959, 1014.

15. US Census, *Census of Population 1950: Volume 2, Characteristics of Population, Part 43, Texas* (1952), 180; US Census, *U.S. Census of Population 1950: Volume 4, Special Reports, Part 3, Chapter C: Persons of Spanish Surname* (1953), 45, 67. In 1930, 1,988

people of Mexican descent lived in Jackson County, as did 1,908 African Americans (US Census, *Fifteenth Census* [1932], 1014).

16. Haney López, "Race and Colorblindness."

17. I. García, *White but Not Equal*, 36–38, 95.

18. Ibid., 117, 201.

19. Krochmal, *Blue Texas*, 43, 48, 154.

20. Blanton, *George I. Sánchez*, 195; I. García, *White but Not Equal*, 122.

21. I. García, *White but Not Equal*, 132.

22. Neil Foley ("Over the Rainbow") and Ian Haney López ("Race and Colorblindness") concur that the Court in *Hernandez* did not explicitly identify Mexican Americans as white. However, they propose that in this and other rulings, courts have implicitly considered Mexican Americans white. Ariela Gross, in her literature review of Mexican American civil rights litigation, argues that the courts traditionally avoided discussing the race of Mexican Americans and instead made rulings based on treaties, language, and national-origin evidence ("Caucasian Cloak"). She argues that legal scholars have advanced two positions about the Mexican Americans' racial heritage. One group proposes that Mexican Americans are "really white," whereas others state that before 1960, Mexican American attorneys used whiteness as a political strategy to remove them from de jure segregation laws.

23. I. García, *White but Not Equal*, 138.

24. Ibid., 178; *Hernández v. Texas*, 347 U.S. 475, 479 (1954).

25. *Hernández*, 347 U.S. 478.

26. Ibid., 482.

27. I. García, *White but Not Equal*; Blanton, *George I. Sánchez*.

28. State Convention of Latin American Leaders Creating a Texas Pro-Human Relations Fund, July 29, 1951, Corpus Christi, Texas, in Gustavo García Papers, box 1, folder 7, Benson Latin American Collection, University of Texas at Austin (hereafter cited as García Papers).

29. *Brown v. Board of Education of Topeka*, 347 U.S. 483, 489, 496 (1954).

30. Ibid., 493.

31. For public actions taken by Governor Shivers in supporting desegregation while he was simultaneously developing policies to keep Mexican American students segregated, see Houston, "African Americans, Mexican Americans," ch. 3.

32. Castillo, "Bastrop Revives Texas' Undertold Story"; George Sánchez to Gus García, May 18, 1950, Sánchez Papers, box 16, folder 20; Gus García to T. M. Trimble, Office of the State Superintendent of Public Instruction, March 4, 1949, and García to Sánchez, July 2, 1949, both in Sánchez Papers, box 16, folder 19.

33. Gus García to George Sánchez, May 1, 1948, Sánchez Papers, box 16, folder 18; Mixerr Reviews, "Small Colorado School Long Forgotten."

34. Gus García to J. W. Edgar, commissioner of education, October 9, 1950; García to Edgar, November 2, 1951; George Sánchez to Gus García, February 23, 1951, all in Sánchez Papers, box 16, folder 20.

35. Lyle Sanders to Gus García, July 21, 1949, Sánchez Papers, box 16, folder 19.

36. GI Forum, "School Inspection Report on Fourteen Schools," in Sánchez Papers, box 4, folder 9. The school inspection report was submitted to Judge Rice after the September 1949 school compliance deadline. The report was accompanied by correspondence from García to Sánchez dated November 16, 1950.

37. Gus García to George Sánchez, July 2, 1949, Sánchez Papers, box 16, folder 19.

38. Dobbs, *Yellow Dogs and Republicans*, 127.

39. Murph, *The Life of Price Daniel*, 135–137. In 1957 Price Daniel became Governor of Texas and revised Shiver's school segregation policies. The Fifty-Fifth Texas Legislature debated the bills during the regular session (Ibid., 181–184; Dobbs, *Yellow Dogs and Republicans*, 134–137).

40. Ogletree, *All Deliberate Speed*, 126.

41. Ibid., 305; Dobbs, *Yellow Dogs and Republicans*, 125.

42. Salomone, *Equal Education under Law*.

43. Houston, "African Americans, Mexican Americans"; Behnken, *Fighting Their Own Battles*.

44. Hinojosa, prologue, 112; Montejano, *Quixote's Soldiers*, 27.

45. *Dallas Morning News*, August 12, 1955, copy in University of Texas, Chancellor's Office Records, box 34, Desegregation Folder I, 1954–1958 (hereafter cited as Chancellor's Records).

46. McGregor, *Integration of the Armed Forces*, 491: Watson, *Lion in the Lobby*, 245.

47. McGregor, *Integration of the Armed Forces*, 493.

48. Valencia, *Chicano Students and the Courts*; San Miguel, *Let All of Them Take Heed*.

49. George Sánchez to Gus García, May 18, 1959; García to Raul A. Cortez, LULAC president, June 6, 1950; and Nixon School District to García, December 3, 1951, all in Sánchez Papers, box 16, folder 20; letters to Gus García from school districts and attorneys, August 25, 1955, to October 29, 1956, in Sánchez Papers, box 16, folder 21.

50. *San Antonio Light*, October 15, 1972, 1E, copy in García Papers, folder 10; Krochmal, *Blue Texas*, 135.

51. Gus García and other attorneys contacted many school districts about their failure to comply with the court's ruling in *Delgado*. They warned school administrators that litigation could follow if they continued to not comply. The districts contacted included those in the following towns and cities: Bastrop, Baytown, Beeville, Carrizo Springs, Corpus Christi, Curo, Del Rio, Gonzales, Kingsville, Kyle, Mathis, Refugio, Robstown, San Antonio, San Marcos, and Three Rivers, along with the counties of Val Verde and Wharton. See the following correspondence, all in the Sánchez Papers: Gus García to Superintendent Morrison of Curo, January 20, 1949, and George Sánchez to García, February 3, 1949, in box 16, folder 19; Gus García to Billy Lee, assistant attorney general, August 25, 1955, in box 16, folder 20; Gus García to Sánchez, February 20, 1952, in box 16, folder 13; Héctor García to George Sánchez, March 6 and 19, 1956, in box 4, folder 10. See also the following newspaper articles, copies in García Papers, box 1, folder 10: "Edgar Hears Appeal on Kingsville School Segregation," *News Bulletin* of the GI Forum, Austin Chapter, January 1955; "Latins Protest Discrimination," *Corpus Christi Caller*, September 9, 1955.

Other schools identified by Sánchez that refused to comply with the *Delgado* desegregation orders were located in the cities of Austin (Zavala School), Bishop, Cotulla, Driscoll, Edcouch, Encinal, George West, Lockhart, Orange Grove, Pecos, Rio Hondo, Santa Maria, Seguin, Sinton, and Taft, and the counties of Guadalupe and Dimmit (GI Forum, "School Inspection Report on Fourteen Schools"; Sánchez to Gus

García, May 18, 1950, in Sánchez Papers, box 16, folder 2; Héctor García to Sánchez, June 12, 1968, in Sánchez Papers, box 4, folder 10).

52. Behnken, *Fighting Their Own Battles*, 87, 96.

53. For African American and Mexican American political coalitions, see Krochmal, *Blue Texas*.

54. *Bell v. Rippy*, 133 F. Supp. 811 (N.D. Tex. 1955).

55. Behnken, *Fighting Their Own Battles*, 52.

56. *Jackson v. Rawdon*, 135 F. Supp. 936 (N.D. Tex. 1955).

57. Dobbs, *Yellow Dogs and Republicans*, 138–140.

58. Houston, "African Americans, Mexican Americans," 127–148.

59. The educational data for *Hernandez v. Driscoll* was prepared by George I. Sánchez and Henry J. Otto.

60. Houston, "African Americans, Mexican Americans," 156; Murph, *Life of Price Daniel*, 183.

61. HB 231, 55th Leg., reg. sess., 1957, 5, in LRL.

62. Ibid.

63. Institute of Public Affairs, *Fifty-fifth Texas Legislature*, 27; HB 65, 55th Leg., reg. sess., 1957, in LRL.

64. Valencia, *Chicano Students and the Courts*, 58–63.

65. Krochmal, *Blue Texas*, 149–159; B. Márquez, *Democratizing Texas Politics*, 53.

66. *Sweatt v. Painter*, 339 U.S. 629 (1950).

67. After the *Sweatt* ruling, UT System colleges complied with the Court's order to admit Blacks into the professional and graduate schools. From 1950 to 1954, 50 African American students were admitted to Texas Western College (now UT–El Paso) and UT-Austin. The UT medical school at Galveston admitted 24 Black medical students and 350 nursing students; see Tom Sealy, UT System regent, to Fred W. Moore, August 16, 1956, in Chancellor's Records, box 34, Desegregation Folder I, 1954–1958; "All Deliberate Speed," a report on the medical branch's admissions policies, July 20, 1961, in Chancellor's Records, box 85, Desegregation Folder 9-1-1960 to 8-13-1962.

68. Morehead–Dallas Morning Star Survey of Texas Colleges, October 10, 1963, in Morehead Papers, file 23.

69. See "Desegregated-Segregated Status of Institutions of Higher Learning in the Southern United States," US Commission on Civil Rights Report, November 15, 1963, in Chancellor's Records, box 102, Desegregation Folder, 9-1-1962 to 8-31-1964.

70. Maxwell, *General Register of Students*.

71. *Directory of the Main University and the Extramural Divisions*, 1923, 1930.

72. Herschel, *Mexican and Spanish-Speaking Children*, 105–106; *Bulletin of St. Mary's University of San Antonio*, n.s., 4, no. 1 (March 1930) (copy in St. Mary's University, Louis J. Blum Library, Archive Division). In 1930, out of 474 students enrolled at St. Mary's University, 32 were Spanish surnamed. A study conducted by Manuel Herschel in 1928 concluded that Texas's total college student enrollment numbered 38,538, of which around 2,500 were African American and 188 were Spanish surnamed. Of the Spanish-surnamed students, 154 were estimated to be Mexican American, since they were permanent US residents (105–106).

73. Almaráz, *Knight without Armor*, 8. Castañeda was the seventh Spanish-

surnamed student to attend UT-Austin (Maxwell, *General Register of Students*; *Cactus*, 1891–1917).

74. *Cactus* (1929), 399; *Alcalde*, "Red-Letter Dates," 23. The numbers of club members are based on *Cactus* photos.

75. *Cactus* (1933), 224.

76. Mendoza, "Beating the Odds."

77. "S. A. Visitor Writes about Ranger's Story," short biography, June 1, 1960, in García Papers, box 1, folder 10.

78. *Cactus*, 1933–1937.

79. Akers, *Héctor P. García*, 17–30.

80. *Cactus* (1937).

81. Blanton, *George I. Sánchez*, 167.

82. *Directory of the Main University and Extramural Division*, 1945, 1946.

83. *Cactus* (1947), 232.

84. Author's personal communication with Lozano Long, October 27, 2014.

85. The dormitory, sorority, and fraternity housing analysis is based on a review of *Cactus* yearbooks and housing records of the university. The 1985 *Cactus* provides a history of the sororities' and fraternities' admission policies. In 1968, sororities that refused to comply with the university's nondiscrimination race, religion, and color admittance policies were required to move off campus (469).

86. Allen, "Philosophy of Student Housing," 57.

87. City of Austin, Fair Housing Ordinance, May 17, 1968; copy in Fair Housing Ordinance folder, 1968, box 1, AR.2012.006, Austin History Center.

88. Berry, *Scottish Rite Dormitory*, 63.

89. Goldstone, *Integrating the 40 Acres*, 93.

90. Harry Ransom, UT-Austin vice president, to C. P. Boner, UT System vice president, memorandum, September 12, 1956, in Chancellor's Records, box 53, Desegregation Folder I, 1954–1958. In 1955, standardized tests were added to admission requirements for UT System schools. Previously, essays and high school grades were the only requirements. At UT-Austin, a quota limited the number of African American students admitted to around 100 or a maximum of 10 percent of the student body. The following documents, which concern these matters, do not provide any information on Mexican American students: W. B. Shipp, chairman of the Special Committee to Implement the General Recommendations dealing with Selective Admissions, to C. P. Boner, UT System vice president, February 19, 1956; "Memorandum on Testing Centers with Special Reference to Arrangements for White and Negro Students," December 16, 1955; Logan Wilson, UT-Austin president, to high school test administrators, December 9, 1955, all in Chancellor's Records, box 34, Desegregation Folder I, 1954–1958.

91. Logan Wilson, UT-Austin president, to C. P. Boner, UT System regent, H. Y. McCown, UT-Austin dean of student services, and Mr. Bible, October 13, 1956, in Chancellor's Records, box 34, Desegregation Folder I, 1954–1958; Goldstone, *Integrating the 40 Acres*.

92. G. W. Landrum, UT-Austin business manager, to C. P. Boner, July 27, 1956, in Chancellor's Records, box 34, Desegregation Folder I, 1954–1958.

93. H. Y. McCown to Harry Ransom, November 16, 1959, in Chancellor's Records, box 69, Desegregation Folder, 9-1-1958 to 8-31-1960.

94. Mr. Cooksey to Logan Wilson, October 21, 1959, in ibid.

95. Duren, *Overcoming*, 6; Goldstone, *Integrating the 40 Acres*, 93.

96. Duren, *Overcoming*, 7.

97. Goldstone, *Integrating the 40 Acres*, 73; Student Association of the University of Texas at Austin, Report of the Human Relations Commission, June 28, 1957, in Chancellor's Records, box 53, Desegregation Folder I, 1954–1958.

98. Sterling Holloway to Logan Wilson, September 17, 1958, in Chancellor's Records, box 69, Desegregation Folder, 9-1-1958 to 8-31-1960.

99. Goldstone, *Integrating the 40 Acres*, 130.

100. Iber, "In-Field Foes," 136. Once colleges began to desegregate their sports programs, Ricardo Romo, a Mexican American track star, became the president of the UT-Austin Athletic Association in 1966, the first non-Anglo-American to hold that position (*Cactus* [1966], 517, 520). That year, he also became the first Longhorn runner to break the four-minute-mile barrier, running a time of 3:58.8. His school record lasted for forty-two years (Mendoza, "Beating the Odds," 194).

101. Caro, *Passage of Power*, 9.

102. Stern, *Calculating Visions*, 133–138.

103. Ibid., 150–152.

104. Caro, *Path to Power*.

105. Caro, *Passage of Power*, 150.

106. Menchaca, *Naturalizing Mexican Immigrants*.

107. Blanton, *George I. Sánchez*, 212.

108. García Papers, folder 10.

109. Krochmal, *Blue Texas*, 157–160, 258.

110. Pycior, *LBJ and Mexican Americans*, 126.

111. B. Márquez, *Democratizing Texas Politics*, 39, 51; Montejano, *Quixote's Soldiers*, 19, 84.

112. B. Márquez, *Democratizing Texas Politics*, 13, 64.

113. Pycior, *LBJ and Mexican Americans*, 134.

Chapter 6: Institutional Desegregation, Social Movement Pressures, and the Chicano Movement

1. For an overview of Albert Peña Jr.'s political activism and participation in the NAACP, see Krochmal, *Blue Texas*, 158.

2. Behnken, *Fighting Their Own Battles*, 77–82.

3. Krochmal, *Blue Texas*, 203.

4. City of San Antonio, Ordinance 22,555, passed March 22, 1956, *San Antonio City Council Book, July 2, 1964 to July 30, 1964*, 541; also in "City Council Ordinance Book CC March 15, 1956–March 29, 1956, Book 2 of 2, 209, and City Council Minutes, March 22, 1956, 164. Archives and Records, City Council Ordinances digital collections, www.sanantonio.gov/Municipal-Archives-Records /Search.

5. The wealthy Alamo Heights area was not affected by San Antonio's desegregation mandate because in 1922 it had formed a separate city government. The district is located less than a mile from the downtown city center (City of Alamo Heights, "History," www.alamoheightstx.gov/about/history).

6. M. García, *Mexican American Mayor*, 1.

7. W. Guzmán, *Civil Rights in Texas Borderlands*, 104.

8. M. García, *Mexican American Mayor*, 108.

9. For the history of school desegregation in El Paso Independent School District, see *Alvarado v. El Paso ISD*, 593 F.2d 577 (5th Cir. 1979).

10. McGregor, *Integration of the Armed Forces*, 473–499.

11. W. Guzmán, *Civil Rights in Texas Borderlands*, 105.

12. Ibid., 107; Stewart, "Albert Armendariz Sr."

13. Pérez, "Community Gets Credit," 3.

14. Stern, *Calculating Visions*, 88.

15. Steigerwald, *Sixties and Modern America*, 45.

16. P. Brown, "Civil Rights Act," 527.

17. Kuhlman, "Civil Rights Movement in Texas," 231.

18. McGregor, *Integration of the Armed Forces*, 538, 548, 591. For an overview of desegregation within the military and the states' resistance to it, see Watson, *Lion in the Lobby*.

19. Morland, "Lunch-Counter Desegregation"; O'Read et al., *African Americans in Corpus Christi*.

20. Morland, "Lunch-Counter Desegregation," 12.

21. Krochmal, *Blue Texas*, 342.

22. *San Antonio Register*, June 28, 1963, 1.

23. Kuhlman "Civil Rights Movement in Texas," 18; *San Antonio Register*, October 26, 1962, 1; *San Antonio Register*, March 22, 1963, 1.

24. City of San Antonio, Ordinance 31762, in *San Antonio City Council Book, July 2, 1964 to July 30, 1964*, 542.

25. Krochmal, *Blue Texas*, 375; B. Márquez, *Democratizing Texas Politics*, 58; Joe J. Bernal, terms of service, LRL.

26. Stern, *Calculating Visions*, 160.

27. Caro, *Master of the Senate*, 494.

28. Caro, *Passage of Power*, 349.

29. Ibid., 568.

30. Stern, *Calculating Visions*, 182.

31. P. Brown, "Civil Rights Act," 535.

32. Caro, *Master of the Senate*, 569.

33. The Civil Rights Act of 1960 allowed voters to receive translation assistance at the polls. The Texas Legislature complied in 1963 (Institute of Public Affairs, *Fifty-eighth Texas Legislature*, 41–42).

34. Thornton Hardie, UT System regent, to UT System Board of Regents and regents' attorneys, October 26, 1962, in Chancellor's Records, box 102, Desegregation Folder, 9-1-1962 to 8-31-1964.

35. These included the Texas Tech University System, Sam Houston State University, East Texas State College, Stephen F. Austin State University, Tyler Junior College, Tarleton State College, and Kilgore College (Shabazz, "Opening of the Southern Mind," 455). In 1964, the last public colleges in Texas desegregated, under the threat of legal action.

36. Howard Rogerson, acting director of the US Commission on Civil Rights, to Joseph Smiley, UT-Austin president, November 25, 1963, in Chancellor's Records, box 102, Desegregation Folder, 9-1-1962 to 8-31-1964.

37. For details on how the governor's office and the UT Board of Regents worked together to prevent the integration of Texas colleges, see Goldstone, *Integrating the 40 Acres*, 12, 49, 55, 71, 109.

38. UT Board of Regents, memorandum, July 22, 1961, in Chancellor's Records, box 85, Desegregation Folder, 9-1-1960 to 8-31-1962; Interim Report of the Committee on Minority Groups, February 21, 1961, in ibid.; Housing Regulations, UT-Austin, "Rules and Regulations," pt. 2, ch. 10, Auxiliary Enterprises, 59, May 1, 1963, in Chancellor's Records, box 102, Desegregation Folder, 9-1962 to 8-31-1964.

39. US Census Bureau, *Government Finances for 1963* (November 1964), in Chancellor's Records, box 123, Desegregation Folder, 9-1-1964 to 8-31-1966.

40. Shabazz, "Opening of the Southern Mind," 455.

41. Joseph C. Kennedy, UT System assistant comptroller, to Harry Ransom, UT System chancellor, July 30, 1964, in Chancellor's Records, box 102, Desegregation Folder, 9-1-1962 to 8-31-1964.

42. "The Board of Regents Have Voted 6–1 to Integrate UT in All Areas of University Life," *San Antonio Express*, May 17, 1964, 12A.

43. James Colvin, Office of the Business Manager, UT-Austin, notes, June 2, 1964, in Chancellor's Records, box 102, Desegregation Folder, 9-1-1962 to 8-31-1964; Norman Hackerman, vice chancellor, to deans, department chairs, and administration officials, June 1, 1964, in Chancellor's Records, box 123, Desegregation Folder, 9-1-1964 to 8-31-1966.

44. Goldstone, *Integrating the 40 Acres*, 89.

45. *Cactus* (1988), 396; Duren, *Overcoming*, 17.

46. Jack Holland, UT-Austin dean of men and advisor to fraternities, to Norman Hackerman, June 4, 1965, in Dean of Student Records, box CDL2/E32, Integration Folder, 1956–1965, Briscoe Center; Harry Ransom to Prof. Goldstein, September 18, 1965, in Chancellor's Records, box 123, Desegregation Folder, 9-1-1964 to 8-31-1966.

47. Duren, *Overcoming*.

48. *Cactus* (1965), 185; *Cactus* (1966), 298; *Cactus* (1970), 115.

49. *Cactus* (1965), 146–147.

50. Margaret Berry Papers, Affirmative Action Folder, box 2.325/K71b, 1958–1978, Briscoe Center; Duren Papers, box 4A 256/AR81–112, folder Mexican Americans 1971–1981, Briscoe Center; Goldstone, *Integrating the 40 Acres*, 137. In 1967, federal law required that university records identify a student's race and ethnicity; see UT System News and Information, press release, "UT to Meet Federal Compliance Must Ask Students to Identify Their Race," September 5, 1967, in Chancellor's Records, box 145, Desegregation Folder, 9-1-1966 to 8-31-1968.

51. In 1974, the UT System had 79,318 students, of which 9.09 percent (7,211) were Spanish surnamed, 2.13 percent (1,691) were African American, 0.6 percent (474) were Asian American, and 0.3 percent (235) were Native American (University of Texas System Board of Regents, "University of Texas System Enrollment by Ethnic Group 1974," box 2006–023/11, folder UT System Enrollment/BOR 110, Briscoe Center). Mexican Americans were distributed throughout the system; 54 percent attended UT–El Paso, 29 percent UT-Austin, and 17 percent across other campuses.

52. Texas Commission on Higher Education, "Head Count Enrollment, 1952–1962," and Harry Ransom, Chancellor's Survey (Ransom's response to Richard M.

Morehead's college survey on university attendance, October 1962), both in Morehead Papers, College Integration (1962) folder; Goldstone, *Integrating the 40 Acres*, 137.

53. Butler and Cain, *Congressional Redistricting*.

54. HCR 22, 58th Leg., reg. sess., 1963, in LRL; Institute of Public Affairs, *Fifty-eighth Texas Legislature*, 52.

55. For US Supreme Court rulings on reapportionment and the "one person, one vote" rule, see *Wesberry v. Sanders*, 376 U.S. 1 (1964), and *Reynolds v. Sims*, 377 U.S. 533 (1964), cited in Institute of Public Affairs, *Fifty-ninth Texas Legislature*, 4.

56. Ibid.

57. Institute of Public Affairs, *Fifty-ninth Texas Legislature*, 6.

58. Krochmal, *Blue Texas*, 368.

59. Institute of Public Affairs, *Sixtieth Texas Legislature*, 33; *Harper v. Virginia Board of Elections*, 383 U.S. 663 (1966).

60. Behnken, *Fighting Their Own Battles*, 120; B. Márquez, *Democratizing Texas Politics*, 1.

61. Craig, *Bracero Program*, 69; US Department of State, *Treaties and Other International Agreements of the United States of America, 1776 to 1949*, Executive Agreement Series 1858, Migratory Workers, 9:1224.

62. US Department of Labor, *Hired Farmworkers*, 23.

63. US Senate, Subcommittee on Migratory Labor, *Migratory Labor Legislation*, 657.

64. Blanton, *George I. Sánchez*, 147.

65. Pitti, *Devil in Silicon Valley*.

66. US Census, *Current Population Reports: Consumer Income*, Series P-60, No. 37 (1962), 1.

67. Menchaca, *Naturalizing Mexican Immigrants*, 268.

68. Galarza, *Merchants of Labor*.

69. Mines and Anzaldúa, *New Migrants vs. Old Migrants*, 33.

70. HB 165, 58th Leg., reg. sess., 1963, in LRL.

71. Before 1963, children employed as farmworkers were not required to attend school. The federal law prohibiting children twelve and under from being employed did not apply to them (*Penal Code of the State of Texas* (1925), article 1577, 1454; Du Pre Lumpkin, "Child Labor Provisions," 393).

72. US Department of Labor, *Fifty-Second Annual Report*, 197.

73. Street, "FBI's Secret File," 357.

74. US Senate, Subcommittee on Migratory Labor, *Migratory Labor Legislation*, 662.

75. K. Hernández, "Melon Strike 50 Years Ago."

76. Benavidez, "50th Anniversary Celebration," 5, 8.

77. Bowman, *Blood Oranges*, 178; Navarro, 1995: 120.

78. Krochmal, *Blue Texas*, 398, 403.

79. *Medrano v. Allee* 1972: 613.

80. US Senate, Subcommittee on Migratory Labor, *Migratory Labor Legislation*, 697.

81. Ibid., 666.

82. Krochmal, *Blue Texas*, 398–402.

83. US Senate, Subcommittee on Migratory Labor, *Migratory Labor Legislation*, 681.

84. The conversation between Governor Connally and the march leaders was taped (ibid.).

85. B. Márquez, *Democratizing Texas Politics*, 73–74, 81.

86. Bowman, *Blood Oranges*, 179.

87. The confrontation between the Texas Rangers and Kathy Baker was reported in *Medrano v. Allee*, 347 F. Supp. 605, 611–614 (S.D. Tex. 1972).

88. Ibid., 617.

89. US Senate, Subcommittee on Migratory Labor, *Migratory Labor Legislation*.

90. US Department of Labor, "Federal Minimum Wage Rates."

91. HB 208, 60th Leg., reg. sess., 1967, in LRL.

92. Institute of Public Affairs, *Fifty-ninth Texas Legislature*, 76; Bowman, *Blood Oranges*.

93. *Medrano*, 347 F. Supp. 605.

94. *Allee v. Medrano*, 416 U.S. 802 (1974).

95. Rosales, *Chicano!*, 150.

96. Bowman, *Blood Oranges*, 180.

97. Villagran, "Revisiting the 'Midwest Stream,'" 75, 80.

98. Alba, *Blurring the Color Line*, chap. 1 & 2; Foley, *Mexicans in the Making of America*, 170–176; Wells, "Brokerage, Economic Opportunity." Alba found that the number of Jewish and Catholic students in elite universities increased substantially during the 1960s.

99. Institute of Public Affairs, *Fifty-ninth Texas Legislature*, 32.

100. Institute of Public Affairs, *Sixty-first Texas Legislature*, 27–29.

101. Ybarra-Frausto, "Chicano Movement"; Navarro, *Mexican American Youth Organization*, 257.

102. Gómez-Quiñones, *Mexican Students por La Raza*.

103. Montejano, *Quixote's Soldiers*, 59.

104. Rosales, *Chicano!*, 217.

105. Navarro, *Mexican American Youth Organization*, 83, 153.

106. Behnken, *Fighting Their Own Battles*.

107. US Department of Labor, *Hired Farmworkers*, 13.

108. Rosales, *Chicano!*, 154–175.

109. Navarro, *Mexican American Youth Organization*, 151.

110. Pycior, *LBJ and Mexican Americans*, 203.

111. Rosales, *Chicano!*, 166–167; Navarro, *Mexican American Youth Organization*, 151.

112. Navarro, *Mexican American Youth Organization*, 152–153.

113. Ibid.; Pycior, *LBJ and Mexican Americans*, 207–211.

114. Pycior, *LBJ and Mexican Americans*, 211.

115. Rosales, *Chicano!*, 181–183, 197.

116. Blanton, *George I. Sánchez*, 240–241; Montejano, *Quixote's Soldiers*, 60–67.

117. Rosales, *Chicano!*, 265.

118. For an overview of the Del Rio VISTA activism and the procession and march, see Navarro, *Mexican American Youth Organization*, ch. 5; Montejano, *Quixote's Soldiers*, ch. 5; and Rosales, *Chicano!*, 215–219.

119. Navarro, *Mexican American Youth Organization*, 176.

120. Morin, *Valor and Discord*; Westheider, *Fighting on Two Fronts*.

121. Barrios, "'Platoon' without Latinos"; R. Guzmán, *Mexican-American Casualties*, 1, 7; Westheider, *Fighting on Two Fronts*, 13.

122. García and Castro, *Blowout!*, 147–176.

123. Navarro, *Mexican American Youth Organization*, 132.

124. The Winter Garden Region lies north of Laredo and southwest of San Antonio. It gets its name from the year-round agricultural production there.

125. Bowman, *Blood Oranges*, 183.

126. Gutiérrez, *We Won't Back Down*, 58–60.

127. Barrios, "Walkout in Crystal City."

128. Rosales, *Chicano!*, 222.

129. Navarro, *Mexican American Youth Organization*, 215.

130. Montejano, *Quixote's Soldiers*, 117.

131. D. Hernández, *Mexican American Challenge*.

132. Gómez-Quiñonez and Vásquez, *Chicana and Chicano Movement*, 161.

133. Rosales, *Chicano!*, 253.

134. Duren, *Overcoming*, 23; Duren Papers, box 4A 256/AR81–112, folder Mexican Americans 1971–1981.

135. Maribel Láraga submitted the proposal for establishing Mexican American studies at Our Lady of the Lake University. Information provided by Aimee Villarreal, the program head.

136. Gómez-Quiñonez and Vásquez, *Chicana and Chicano Movement*, 170.

137. SB 185, in *Senate Journal, 60th Texas Legislature, Regular Session* (Austin: Von Boeckmann-Jones, 1967), 273, 679, 1775–2171.

138. Institute of Public Affairs, *Sixtieth Texas Legislature*, 20.

139. Institute of Public Affairs, *Sixty-first Texas Legislature*, 16.

140. SB 368, 61st Leg., reg. sess., 1969, in LRL.

141. *Shelley v. Kraemer*, 344 U.S. 1 (1948); *Clifton v. Puente*, 218 S.W.2d 272 (Tex. Civ. App. 1948).

142. See HB 808, 61st Leg., reg. sess., 1969, in LRL; *House Journal, 61st Texas Legislature, Regular Session* (Austin: Nelson Type Setting, 1969), 1:499; repealed articles 1293a and 1293b, sec. 204, ch. 527, "Conveyances, Deeds, Racial Restrictions," in *Vernon's Texas Statutes, 1970 Supplement*, 183.

143. HB 253, 61st Leg., reg. sess., 1969, in LRL; *House Journal, 61st Texas Legislature*, 2:3591.

144. SB 516, 61st Leg., reg. sess., 1969, in LRL; *Senate Journal, 61st Texas Legislature, Regular Session* (Austin: Von Boeckmann-Jones, 1969), 417, 801, 1274, 1375.

145. HB 53 and Judiciary Committee Amendments 10 and 11, 61st Leg., reg. sess., 1969, in LRL; *Texas Family Code*, title 1, ch. 2, sec. 2.01 and 2.23, in *Vernon's Texas Statutes, 1970 Supplement*, 1686.

146. Texas Constitution, art. 1, sec. 3a, added November 7, 1972, 62nd Leg., reg. sess.

Chapter 7: Mexican American Social Mobility and Immigration

1. Rosales, *Chicano!*, 237.

2. B. Márquez, *Democratizing Texas Politics*, 121.

3. Ibid., 90.

4. US Commission on Civil Rights, Texas State Advisory Committee, *Texas: The State of Civil Rights*, 47.

5. Rosales, *Chicano!*, 246.

6. US Commission on Civil Rights, Texas State Advisory Committee, *Texas: The State of Civil Rights*, 50.

7. Ibid., 45.

8. Ibid., 27.

9. San Miguel, *Let All of Them Take Heed*.

10. US Commission on Civil Rights, Texas State Advisory Committee, *Civil Rights in Texas*.

11. US Commission on Civil Rights, Texas State Advisory Committee, *Texas: The State of Civil Rights*, 1.

12. US Commission on Civil Rights, Texas State Advisory Committee, *Civil Rights in Texas*, 1. For findings of the advisory report, see education (4–13), the administration of justice (14–21), employment and farm labor (22–35), and recommendations (45–51).

13. US Census, *Persons of Spanish Origin by State: 1980; Supplementary Report* (1982), 6.

14. US Census, *General and Social Economic Characteristics of Texas, 1980* (1983), 31.

15. US Commission on Civil Rights, Texas State Advisory Committee, *Texas: The State of Civil Rights*, 36.

16. Ibid., 4, 9.

17. Ibid., 29, 33.

18. Ibid., 6.

19. US Census, *Detailed Population Characteristics, Texas* (1983), 1222–1224.

20. Ibid., 1220, 1099, 1230.

21. Menchaca, *Politics of Dependency*, 198.

22. *United States v. Texas*, 321 F. Supp. 1043 (E.D. Tex. 1970); Valencia, *Chicano Students and the Courts*, 271, 309–310.

23. *Cisneros v. Corpus Christi Independent School District*, 324 F. Supp. 599 (S.D. Tex. 1970); Valencia, *Chicano Students and the Courts*, 61.

24. In the aftermath of *Cisneros*, Mexican American parents filed thirteen suits to either end school segregation or to equalize school financing (Valencia, *Chicano Students and the Courts*, 8).

25. Ibid., 64.

26. *Ross v. Eckels*, 317 F. Supp. 512 (S.D. Tex. 1970); *Ross v. Eckels*, 434 F.2d 1140 (5th Cir. 1971); San Miguel, *Chicana/o Struggles for Education*, 35.

27. Salomone, *Equal Education under Law*.

28. Valencia, Menchaca, and Donato, "Segregation, Desegregation," 97, 101–102.

29. *Milliken v. Bradley*, 418 U.S. 717 (1974).

30. Varady and Raffel, *Selling Cities*, 208–209.

31. Braden et. al, *Texas Constitution*, 20.

32. *Alvarado v. El Paso Independent School District*, 426 F. Supp. 575 (W.D. Tex. 1976); *Alvarado v. El Paso Independent School District*, 593 F.2d 577 (5th Cir. 1979).

33. Braden et. al, *Texas Constitution*, 23.

34. *Edgewood ISD v. Kirby*, 777 S.W.2d 391 (Tex. 1989). The case is often referred to as *Edgewood I*.

35. Equity Center, "Texas School Finance History."

36. Valencia, *Chicano Students and the Courts*, 108–114.

37. US Census, *Distribution of Foreign Stock Population: 1970*; *Census of Population Supplementary Report* (1974), 17; US Census, *General Social and Economic Characteristics, United States Summary, 1980*, vol. 1, pt. 1 (1983), 17.

38. Pemex, *Statistical Yearbook*, 6–8.

39. Al-Chalabi, *La OPEP y el precio internacionial*; Grayson, *Politics of Mexican Oil*.

40. Martínez Fernández, *Deuda externa vs. desarollo economico*, 18; Stukey, "Economic Interdependence," 563.

41. US General Accounting Office, *Financial Crisis Management*, 2.

42. Ramirez, *IMF Austerity Program*, 12.

43. International Monetary Fund, Executive Board Specials, EBS/90/10 (1990); International Monetary Fund, Executive Board Minutes, EBM/93/11 (1994).

44. Rytina and Caldera, *Naturalizations in the United States*, 2.

45. 79 Stat. 911 (1965).

46. Ibid., 917.

47. 90 Stat. 2703 (1976).

48. 100 Stat. 3359 (1986).

49. International Monetary Fund, Board Document, Staff Memoranda, SM/94/41 (1994), 46; Instituto Nacional de Estadística y Geografía, *Mexican Bulletin of Statistical Information 18*, 163.

50. Guerrero Andrade, *De la gestión estatal*, 166.

51. US General Accounting Office, *Mexico's Financial Crisis*, 14, 54, 74.

52. Ibid., 6, 11; Girón González, "Deuda externa," 278; International Monetary Fund, Board Document, Staff Memoranda, SM 94/41 (1994), 59; Ros and Bouillon, "La liberalización," 727.

53. Manzo Yépez, *¿Que hacer con PEMEX?*

54. 108 Stat. 4305 (1994); Rothenberg, *With These Hands*, 227.

55. Zavella, *I'm Neither Here Nor There*, 6.

56. Nevins, *Operation Gatekeeper*, 75, 104.

57. 110 Stat. 3009-546 (1996).

58. Menchaca, *Politics of Dependency*, 122–127; Moreno-Brid and Ros, *Development and Growth*, 192, 227–230.

59. Baker and Rytina, *Unauthorized Immigrant Population*, 3, 5.

60. World Bank, *Mexico: Income Generation*; World Bank, "Mexico."

61. US Census, "Place of Birth by Year of Entry by Citizenship Status for the Foreign-Born Population 2000 [104]," PCT048, https://data.census.gov/cedsci/table?q=Total%20population%20of%20Texas&t=-09%20-%20All%20available%20Hispanic%20Origin%3A400%20-%20Hispanic%20or%20Latino%20%28of%20any%20race%29%20%28200-299%29%3AEducational%20Attainment%3ANative%20and%20Foreign%20Born&g=0400000US48&y=2010&tid=ACSDP1Y2010.DP05.

62. Instituto Nacional de Estadística y Geografía, *Anuario estadístico*, 144, 243.

63. Consejo Nacional de la Población, "Chapter 1," 25; World Bank, "Mexico."

64. US Census, *The Hispanic Population: 2010, Census Briefs* (2011), 7.

65. US Census, "Selected Population Profile in the United States: 2010," American Community Survey 1-Year Estimates, Table ID: S0201 (Texas), https://data.census.gov/cedsci/table?t=-09%20-%20All%20available%20Hispanic%20Origin%3AAge

%20and%20Sex%3AEducational%20Attainment&g=0400000US48&y=2010&tid =ACSSPP1Y2010.S0201.

66. Ibid.

67. Ibid.

68. Bean and Lowell, "Unauthorized Migration," 698.

69. Menchú Tum, *Crossing Borders*; Stoll, *El Norte or Bust*.

70. Baker and Rytina, *Unauthorized Immigrant Population*, 3, 5, 7.

71. *US Census, Texas: 2010: Summary of Population and Housing Characteristics*, 256; US Census, "ACS Demographic and Housing Estimates," American Community Survey, 1-Year Estimates, Table ID: DP05 (Texas), https://data.census.gov/cedsci /table?q=Texas%20foreign%20born%202000%20&tid=DECENNIALAIAN2000 .PCT048&hidePreview=false.

72. US Census, *Texas: 2010: Summary Population and Housing Characteristics*, 256–262. In Harris County, 41.6 percent of the population (1.7 million people) were Latino, and 18.9 percent were African American. In Dallas County, 38.2 percent of the residents (905,940 people) were Latino, and 22.3 percent were African American.

73. Baker and Rytina, *Unauthorized Immigrant Population*, 3, 5, 7.

74. Achor, *Mexican Americans in Dallas*; Adler, *Yucatecans in Dallas*; Márquez, 2013; San Miguel, *Brown, Not White*.

75. US Census, "Selected Characteristics in the United States, 2010," American Community Survey, ACS-1 Year Estimates, Table ID: DP02 (Texas, county), https:// data.census.gov/cedsci/table?q=Dallas%20county,%20foreign%20born,%20Texas %202010&tid=ACSDP1Y2010.DP02&hidePreview=false.

76. US Census, "ACS Demographic and Housing Estimates, 2010"; US Census, "Selected Characteristics of the Foreign-Born Population by Period of Entry into the United States, 2010," American Community Survey, ACS-1 Year Estimates, Table ID: S0502. https://data.census.gov/cedsci/table?q=S0502&tid=ACSST1Y2019.S0502 (Texas, foreign-born percentage by region); US Census, *Texas: 2010, Summary Population and Housing Characteristics*," 256–262.

77. Dobbs, *Yellow Dogs and Republicans*, 25; Murph, *Life of Price Daniel*, 145.

78. Caro, *Passage of Power*, see in particular xv, 303, 494, 569–570.

79. Krochmal, *Blue Texas*, 391–395.

80. B. Márquez, *Democratizing Texas Politics*, 98; Texas Politics Project, "Race and Ethnicity in the Texas Legislature."

81. Bickerstaff, *Lines in the Sand*, 34–35; Dobbs, *Yellow Dogs and Republicans*, 150.

82. In the Eighty-Fifth Texas Legislature (2017), three Republican state representatives were Latino and one was African American (https://capitol.texas.gov/Members /Members.aspx?Chamber=H). None of the Republican state senators belonged to a racial minority (https://capitol.texas.gov/Members/Members.aspx?Chamber=S).

83. In 2019, out of 150 Texas House of Representatives seats, 82 were held by Republicans and 66 by Democrats (with 2 vacancies). Three of the Republicans were persons of color. Of the Democratic representatives, 33 were Latino, 13 were African American, 2 were Asian American, and 18 were Anglo-American. Of the 31 members in the Texas Senate, 19 were Republican (1 Latino). Of the 23 Democratic senators, 9 were people of color (2 African Americans, 7 Latinos).

At the congressional level, the Texas delegation of 36 representatives consisted of 23 Republicans and 13 Democrats. Of the Republicans, 2 were persons of color (1 Black, 1 Latino); of the Democrats, 11 were persons of color (6 Latino, 5 Black).

84. Institute of Public Affairs, *Fifty-ninth Texas Legislature*, 6.

85. Bickerstaff, *Lines in the Sand*, 43, 62; Flores, *Latinos and the Voting Rights Act*, 219–223; Texas Politics Project, "Race and Ethnicity in the Texas Legislature."

86. Whitaker, *Congressional Redistricting Law*.

87. Bickerstaff, *Lines in the Sand*, 272.

88. Flores, *Latinos and the Voting Rights Act*, 222–231.

89. *LULAC v. Perry*, 548 U.S. 399 (2006).

90. *Perez v. Abbott*, 267 F. Supp. 3d 750 (W.D. Tex. 2017).

91. Li, Wolf, and Farmer, "Redistricting Litigation."

92. *Abbott v. Perez*, 585 U.S. ___ (2018).

93. *Perez v. Abbott*, 390 F. Supp. 3d 803 (W.D. Tex. 2019).

94. Mexican Americans have filed more than two hundred lawsuits for voting rights violations (Flores, *Latinos and the Voting Rights Act*, 30).

95. Texas Demographic Center, "Texas Population Project Program."

96. Li, Wolf, and Farmer, "Redistricting Litigation."

97. N. Brown, "Republicans Want Census Data."

98. *Evenwel v. Abbott*, 578 U.S. ___ (2016).

99. Brown and LaCrapa, "Trump May Face More Court Battles."

100. Wines, "2020 Census Won't Have Citizenship Question."

101. For the history of Texas redistricting politics from 1980 to 2011 and the use of voter ID laws (e.g., SB 14) to dilute the vote of Latinos and African Americans, see Flores, *Latinos and the Voting Rights Act*.

102. SB 14, 82nd Leg., reg. sess., 2011, in LRL.

103. US Department of Justice, "Justice Department to File New Lawsuit."

104. Malewitz, "Texas Voter ID Law"; Reigstad, "Texas House Approves."

105. Malewitz, "House, Senate OK Compromise"; Park and Ellis, "Texas Voter ID Law."

106. SB 5, 85th Leg., reg. sess., 2017, in LRL.

107. HB 292, 82nd Leg., reg. sess., 2011, in LRL.

108. Menchaca, *Naturalizing Mexican Immigrants*, 310.

109. Ura, "Texas Agrees to Resolve."

110. Quigley, "Texas Eases Birth Certificate Rules."

111. Reigstad, "Texas House Approves."

112. Associated Press, "Texas GOP Passes Immigration Plank."

113. Republican Party of Texas, "Platform, 2020."

114. Alberto R. Gonzales and Rafael Edward "Ted" Cruz have been the most influential Hispanic Republicans in Texas. Gonzales, who was US attorney general (2005–2007), was sympathetic to the plight of undocumented people, since his grandparents entered the United States without authorization. Senator Cruz, who is of Cuban descent and has represented Texas in Washington since 2013, holds anti-immigrant positions that are out of step with the views of other Hispanic Republicans (Cadava, *Hispanic Republican*, 330).

115. Murdock, "Population and Household Change," 33; US Census, *Detailed Population Characteristics, Texas* (1983), 1222–1224.

116. Baker and Rytina, *Unauthorized Immigrant Population*, 7.

117. Murdock, "Population and Household Change," 33.

118. Ryan and Siebens, *Educational Attainment in the United States*, 13. The 2010 median income for Latinos with advanced degrees is for the US total.

119. US Census, "Sex by Educational Attainment for the Population 25 years and

over, 2010 (Hispanic or Latino)," American Community Survey, ACS 1-Year Estimates, Table ID: B15002 (Texas), https://data.census.gov/cedsci/table?t=-09%20-%20All%20available%20Hispanic%20Origin%3AAge%20and%20Sex%3AEducational%20Attainment&g=0400000US48&y=2010&tid=ACSDT5YSPT2010.B15002; Ogunwole, Drewery, and Rios-Vargas, "Population with a Bachelor's Degree or Higher," 3.

120. US Census, "Sex by Occupation for the Civilian Employed Population 16 Years and Over, 2010," American Community Survey, ACS 5-Year Estimates, Table ID: C24010 (Texas, Hispanic Latino), https://data.census.gov/cedsci/table?t=-09%20-%20All%20available%20Hispanic%20Origin%3AOccupation&g=0400000US48&y=2010&tid=ACSDT5YSPT2010.C24010.

121. Valencia, *Chicano Students and the Courts*, 74.

122. Education Trust, *Funding Gap Report*; Valencia, *Students of Color*.

123. Baker and Duncombe, "Balancing District Needs."

124. M. Smith, "School Finance Lawsuits."

125. The Mexican American School Board Association, the San Antonio Hispanic Chamber of Commerce, and the Texas Association of Bilingual Education were also part of the coalition supporting the low-wealth school districts.

126. Ye He Lee, "Trump's False Comments."

127. Ngai, *Impossible Subjects*.

128. East, "Trump Attacks 'Mexican' Judge."

129. Walsh and Raju, "Ryan Rips Trump."

130. D'Antonio, "On Race and Ethnicity, Trump."

131. Chavez, *Latino Threat*.

132. Menchaca, *Naturalizing Mexican Immigrants*, 294.

133. Vedantam, "State Lawmakers Taking Aim."

134. National Conference of State Legislatures, "2012 Immigration-Related Laws."

135. *United States v. Texas*, 579 U.S. ___ (2016).

136. Svitek, "Texas Gov. Greg Abbott."

137. Kwong, *"Gilroy Gunman Cited."*

138. Achenbach, *"Two Mass Killings."*

139. Rucker, *"'How Do You Stop These People.'"*

Epilogue

1. Blanton, *George I. Sánchez*, 139–140.

2. Lopéz et al., "Latino Vote."

3. Pedraza and Wilcox-Archuleta, "Trump Did Not Win."

4. Montoya, "What Conclusions Can We Draw."

5. Arnold, "Message behind Texas' Latino Vote."

6. Wallace, "Texas Voter Turnout Best."

7. Noe-Bustamante et al., "Where Latinos Have the Most."

8. Dexheimer, "Gutierrez Ousts Incumbent."

Bibliography

Abramowitz, Jack. "The Negro in the Populist Movement." *Journal of Negro History* 38, no. 3 (July 1953): 257–289.

Achenbach, Joel. "Two Mass Killings a World Apart Share a Common Theme: 'Ecofascism.'" *Washington Post*, August 18, 2019, https://www.washingtonpost.com /science/two-mass-murders-a-world-apart-share-a-common-theme-ecofascism /2019/08/18/0079a676-bec4-11e9-b873–63ace636af08_story.html.

Achor, Shirely. *Mexican Americans in a Dallas Barrio*. Tucson: University of Arizona Press, 1978.

Adler, Rachel. *Yucatecans in Dallas, Texas: Breaching the Border, Bridging the Distance*. New York: Pearson and AB, 2004.

Aguirre Beltrán, Gonzalo. *La Población Negra de México: Estudio Etnohistórico*. 3rd. ed. Mexico City: Universidad Veracruzana, Instituto Nacional Indigenista, Gobierno del Estado de Veracruz, Fondo de Cultura Económica, 1989.

———. "The Slave Trade in Mexico." *Hispanic American Historical Review* 24, no. 3 (1944): 412–431.

Akers, Cecilia García. *The Inspiring Life of Texan Héctor P. García*. Charleston, SC: History Press, 2016.

Alba, Richard. *Blurring the Color Line: The New Chance for a More Integrated America*. Cambridge, MA: Harvard University Press, 2012.

Alcalde. "Red-Letter Dates for Hispanics and Blacks." September/October 1998, 23.

Al-Chalabi, Fadhil. *La OPEP y el precio internacional del petróleo: el cambio estructural*. Mexico: XXI Editores, 1984.

Allen, Kathryn Ramona. "A Study of the Evolution of the Philosophy of Student Housing at the University of Texas at Austin from 1883 to 1973." PhD diss., University of Texas at Austin, 1975.

Almaráz, Félix D., Jr. *Knight without Armor: Carlos Castañeda, 1896–1958*. College Station: Texas A&M University Press, 1999.

———. *Tragic Cavalier: Governor Manuel Salcedo of Texas, 1808–1813*. College Station: Texas A&M University Press, 2000.

Alonso, Ana María. *Thread of Blood: Colonialism, Revolution, and Gender in Mexico's Northern Frontier*. Tucson: University of Arizona Press, 1995.

Alonzo, Armando. "Mexican-American Land Grant Adjudication." In *Handbook of Texas Online*, Texas State Historical Association, 2016, https://tshaonline.org /handbook/online/articles/pqmck.

———. *Tejano Legacy: Rancheros and Settlers in South Texas, 1734–1900*. Albuquerque: University of New Mexico, 1998.

Anzaldúa, Gloria. *Borderlands/La Frontera: The New Mestiza*. San Francisco: Aunt Lute, 1987.

Appiah, Anthony Kwame, and Henry Louis Gates Jr., eds. *Africana: The Encyclopedia of the African and African American Experience*. New York: Basic Civitas, 1999.

Arnold, Robert. "The Message behind Texas' Latino Vote." KPRC News, December 7, 2020, https://www.click2houston.com/news/investigates/2020/12/07 /the-message-behind-texas-latino-vote.

Ashton, John. "Mifflin Kenedy." In *The New Handbook of Texas*, comp. Ronnie Tyler, 3:1064–1065. Austin: Texas State Historical Association, 1996.

Associated Press. "At Convention, Texas GOP Passes Immigration Plank Similar to Arizona Law." June 13, 2010. Available from Fox News, www.foxnews.com/politics /at-convention-texas-gop-passes-immigration-plank-similar-to-arizona-law.

Auyero, Javier, ed. *Invisible in Austin: Life and Labor in an American City*. Austin: University of Texas Press, 2015.

Ayala, Adriana. "Negotiating Race Relations through Activism: Women Activists and Women's Organizations in San Antonio, Texas during the 1920s." PhD diss., University of Texas at Austin, 2005.

Baker, Bruce, and William Duncombe. "Balancing District Needs and Student Needs: The Role of Economies of Scale Adjustments and Pupil Need Weights in School Finance Formulas." *Journal of Education Finance* 29, no. 3 (2004): 195–221.

Baker, Bryan, and Nancy Rytina. 2013. *Estimates of the Unauthorized Immigrant Population Residing in the United States: January 2012*. Washington, DC: Department of Homeland Security, Office of Immigration Statistics, March 2013. https://www.dhs .gov/sites/default/files/publications/Unauthorized%20Immigrant%20Population %20Estimates%20in%20the%20US%20January%202012_0.pdf.

Bannon, John. *The Spanish Borderlands Frontier, 1513–1821*. New York: Holt, Rinehart and Winston, 1970.

Barr, Alwyn. "The Impact of Race in Shaping Judicial Districts, 1876–1907." *Southwestern Historical Quarterly* 108, no. 4 (2005): 423–439.

———. *Reconstruction to Reform: Texas Politics, 1876–1906*. Dallas: Southern Methodist University Press, 2000.

Barrios, Greg. "A 'Platoon' without Latinos: Mexican-Americans Are Being Denied Their Place in History." *Los Angeles Times*, April 19, 1987. http://articles.latimes .com/1987-04-19/entertainment/ca-1681_1_latino-characters.

———. "Walkout in Crystal City." *Teaching Tolerance* 35 (Spring 2009). www.tolerance .org/magazine/number-35-spring-2009/feature/walkout-crystal-city.

Bean, Frank, and Lindsay Lowell. "Unauthorized Migration." In *The New Americans: A Guide to Immigration since 1965*, edited by Mary C. Waters and Reed Ueda, with Hellen Marrow, 70–82. Cambridge, MA: Harvard University Press, 2007.

Beckham, Irene, comp. *Ysleta del Sur Pueblo Archives*. Vol. 2. Ysleta del Sur Pueblo, TX: Tigua Tribe of Texas, 2000.

Behnken, Brian. *Fighting Their Own Battles: Mexican Americans, African Americans, and the Struggle for Civil Rights in Texas*. Chapel Hill: University of North Carolina Press, 2011.

Benavides, Adán. "Sacred Space, Profane Reality: The Politics of Building a Church in Eighteenth-Century Texas." *Southwestern Historical Quarterly* 107, no. 1 (2003): 1–33.

Benavidez, Severo. "50th Anniversary Celebration to Commemorate the 1966 Starr County Farm Worker Strike and March through San Antonio and on to Austin." *Farmworkers*, special commemorative ed., 2016: 5–12.

Berry, Margaret. *Scottish Rite Dormitory at the University of Texas: A History, 1920–2007*. Waco, TX: Nortex, 2007.

Bickerstaff, Steve. *Lines in the Sand: Congressional Redistricting in Texas and the Downfall of Tom DeLay*. Austin: University of Texas Press, 2007.

Blanton, Carlos Kevin. *George I. Sánchez: The Long Fight for Mexican American Integration*. New Haven, CT: Yale University Press, 2014.

Borah, Woodrow. *Justice by Insurance: The General Indian Court of Colonial Mexico and the Legal Aides of the Half-Real*. Berkeley: University of California Press, 1983.

Bowden, Jocelyn J. *Spanish and Mexican Land Grants in the Chihuahua Acquisition*. El Paso: Texas Western Press, 1971.

Bowman, Timothy P. *Blood Oranges: Colonialism and Agriculture in the South Texas Borderlands*. College Station: Texas A&M University Press, 2016.

Braden, George, Seth S. Searcy III, David Anderson, Darrell Blakeway, Ron Patterson, T. C. Sinclair, and Richard Yahr. *The Texas Constitution: An Annotated and Comparative Analysis; Preliminary Edition for the 1974 Texas Constitutional Convention*. Austin: Texas Advisory Commission on Intergovernmental Relations, 1974.

Braudaway, Douglas. *Del Rio: Queen City of the Rio Grande*. San Francisco: Arcadia, 2002.

———. "Desegregation in Del Rio." *Journal of South Texas* 13, no. 2 (Fall 2000): 240–265.

———. "Old San Felipe High School." Val Verde Historical Commission, 2016. Accessed November 27, 2016. http://vvchc.net/marker/san%20felipe%20high%20 school.html (webpage no longer available).

Brkich, William A. "Bexareños Democratas." In *Handbook of Texas Online*, Texas State Historical Association. tshaonline.org/handbook/entries/bexarenos-democratas.

Brooks, Richard, and Carol Rose. *Saving the Neighborhood: Racially Restrictive Covenants, Law, and Social Norms*. Cambridge, MA: Harvard University Press, 2013.

Brown, Nick. "Republicans Want Census Data on Citizenship for Redistricting." *Reuters*, April 8, 2019. www.reuters.com/article/us-usa-census-redistricting -insight/republicans-want-census-data-on-citizenship-for-redistricting-id USKCN1RK18D.

Brown, Nick, and Lauren Tara LaCapra. "Trump May Face More Court Battles over Giving Citizenship Data to States." *Reuters*, July 15, 2019. www.reuters.com /article/us-usa-census-redistricting/trump-may-face-more-court-battles-over -giving-citizenship-data-to-states-idUSKCN1UA0XI.

Brown, Paulette. "The Civil Rights Act of 1964." *Washington University Law Review* 92, no. 2 (2014): 527–552.

Bugbee, Lester G. "Slavery in Early Texas." *Political Science Quarterly* 13, no. 3 (1898): 389–413.

Burton, H. Sophie, and F. Todd Smith. *Colonial Natchitoches: A Creole Community on the Louisiana-Texas Frontier*. College Station: Texas A&M University Press, 2008.

Busch, Andrew. "Building 'A City of Upper-Middle-Class Citizens': Labor Markets, Segregation, and Growth in Austin, Texas, 1950–1973." *Journal of Urban History* 39, no. 5 (2013): 975–996.

Butler, David, and Bruce Cain. *Congressional Redistricting: Comparative and Theoretical Perspectives*. New York: Macmillan, 1992.

Cactus. Yearbook of the University of Texas. Copies from 1891 to 1988 in the Dolph Briscoe Center for American History, University of Texas at Austin.

Cadava, Geraldo. *The Hispanic Republican: The Shaping of an American Political Identity, from Nixon to Trump*. New York: Ecco, 2020.

California Constitution. 1849. Reprint, San Marino, Calif.: Friends of the Huntington Library, 1949.

Callahan, James M. *American Foreign Policy in Mexican Relations*. New York: Macmillan, 1932.

Campbell, Randolph, William S. Pugsley, and Marilyn Duncan, eds. *Laws of Slavery in Texas: Historical Documents and Essays*. Austin: University of Texas Press, 2010.

Campbell, Thomas Nolan. *Ethnic Identities of Extinct Coahuiltecan Populations: Case of the Juanaca Indians*. Pearce Sellers Series 26:1–16. Austin: Texas Memorial Museum, 1977.

Cantrell, Greg. "'Our Very Pronounced Theory of Equal Rights to All': Race, Citizenship, and Populism in the South Texas Borderlands." *Journal of American History* 100 (2013): 663–690.

Caro, Robert A. *Master of the Senate: The Years of Lyndon Johnson*, vol. 3. New York: Vintage, 2003.

———. *The Passage of Power: The Years of Lyndon Johnson*, vol. 4. New York: Vintage, 2013.

———. *The Path to Power: The Years of Lyndon Johnson*, vol. 1. New York: Vintage, 1990.

Carroll, Patrick, Jr. *Felix Longoria's Wake: Bereavement, Racism, and the Rise of Mexican American Activism*. Austin: University of Texas Press, 2003.

Castañeda, Carlos Eduardo. *Our Catholic Heritage in Texas, 1519–1936*. Vol. 2, *The Mission Era: The Winning of Texas, 1693–1731*. Austin: Von Boeckmann-Jones, 1936.

———. *Our Catholic Heritage in Texas, 1519–1936*. Vol. 3, *The Mission Era: The Missions at Work, 1731–1761*. Austin: Von Boeckmann-Jones, 1938.

———. *Our Catholic Heritage in Texas, 1519–1936*. Vol. 4, *The Mission Era: The Passing of the Missions, 1762–1782*. Austin: Von Boeckmann-Jones, 1939.

———. *Our Catholic Heritage in Texas, 1519–1936*. Vol. 5, *The Transition Period: The Fight for Freedom, 1810–1836*. Austin: Von Boeckmann-Jones, 1942.

———. *Our Catholic Heritage in Texas, 1519–1936*. Vol. 7, *Supplement: The Church in Texas since Independence, 1836–1950*. Austin: Von Boeckmann-Jones, 1958.

Castillo, Juan. "Bastrop Revives Texas' Undertold Story of 'Mexican' Schools." *Austin American-Statesman*, September 22, 2017. https://www.statesman.com/news/20170922/castillo-bastrop-revives-texas-undertold-story-of-mexican-schools.

Castillo Crimm, Ana Carolina. *De León: A Tejano Family History*. Austin: University of Texas Press, 2003.

Chabot, Fredrick. *With the Makers of San Antonio: Genealogies of the Latin, Anglo-American, and German Families, with Occasional Biographies*. San Antonio: Graphic Arts, 1937.

Chalfant, William Y. *Without Quarter: The Wichita Expedition and the Fight on Crooked Creek*. Norman: University of Oklahoma Press, 1991.

Chance, John K., and William Taylor. "Estate and Class in a Colonial City: Oaxaca in 1792." *Comparative Studies in Society and History* 19, no. 4 (1977): 454–487.

Chávez, Alicia Hernández, Fausta Gantús, Florencia Gutiérrez, and María Del Carmen León. *La Constitución de 1824: La consolidación de un pacto mínimo*. Mexico City: El Colegio de México, 2008.

Chavez, Leo. *The Latino Threat: Constructing Immigrants, Citizens, and the Nation*. Palo Alto, CA: Stanford University Press, 2013.

Chipman, Donald, and Harriet Joseph. *Spanish Texas, 1519–1821*. Austin: University of Texas Press, 2010.

Clements, Roger. "British Investment and American Legislative Restrictions in the Trans-Mississippi West, 1880–1900." *Mississippi Valley Historical Review* 42, no. 2 (1955): 207–228.

Colloff, Pamela. "The Blood of the Tigua." *Texas Monthly*, August 1999. www.texas monthly.com/politics/the-blood-of-the-tigua.

Consejo Nacional de Población. "Chapter 1: *Vinculación de la población, El crecimiento economico sostenido, la pobreza y el desarollo sustentable*." In *Informe Ejecución del Programa de Acción de la Conferencia Internacional sobre la Población y el Desarollo 1994–2009*, 11–44. Mexico City: CONAPO, Gobierno de Mexico, 2009.

Cook, Sherburne. *The Population of the California Indians, 1769–1970*. Berkeley: University of California Press, 1976.

Cool, Paul. *Salt Warriors: Insurgency on the Rio Grande*. College Station: Texas A&M University Press, 2008.

Cope, R. Douglas. *The Limits of Racial Domination: Plebeian Society in Colonial Mexico City, 1660–1720*. Madison: University of Wisconsin Press, 1994.

Costeloe, Michael P. "Spain and the Spanish American Wars of Independence: The Comisión de Reemplazos, 1811–1820." *Journal of Latin American Studies* 13, no. 2 (1981): 223–37.

Cottrol, Robert J. *The Long, Lingering Shadow: Slavery, Race, and Law in the American Hemisphere*. Athens: University of Georgia Press, 2013.

Craig, Richard. *The Bracero Program: Interest Groups and Foreign Policy*. Austin: University of Texas Press, 1971.

Cubberly, Ellwood Patterson. "High School in US." In *A Cyclopedia of Education*, edited by Paul Monroe, 3:261–275. New York: Macmillan, 1912.

Cutter, Charles. *The Legal Culture of Northern New Spain*. Albuquerque: University of New Mexico Press, 1986.

D'Antonio, Michael. "On Race and Ethnicity, Trump Has Always Been a Divider." June 4, 2016. Includes "Donald Trump's full CNN interview with Jake Tapper" (video). https://www.cnn.com/2016/06/04/opinions/trump-the-divider-opinion -dantonio/index.html.

Debates of the Texas Convention. W. M. F. Weeks, reporter. Houston: J. W. Cruger, 1846.

Deeds, Susan M., Michael C. Meyer, and William L. Sherman. *The Course of Mexican History*. 11th ed. Oxford: Oxford University Press, 2018.

de la Teja, Jesús. *Faces of Béxar: Early San Antonio and Texas*. College Station: Texas A&M University Press, 2019.

———. "Forgotten Founders: The Military Settlers of Eighteenth-Century San Antonio de Béxar." In *Tejano Origins in Eighteenth-Century San Antonio*, edited by Gerald E. Poyo and Gilberto M. Hinojosa, 27–39. Austin: University of Texas Press, 1991.

De León, Arnoldo. *They Called Them Greasers: Anglo Attitudes toward Mexicans in Texas, 1821–1900*. Austin: University of Texas Press, 1983.

De León, Arnoldo, and Kenneth L. Stewart. *Tejanos and the Numbers Game: A Socio-Historical Interpretation from the Federal Censuses, 1850 to 1900*. Albuquerque: University of New Mexico Press, 1997.

DePalo, William, Jr. "The Establishment of the Nueva Vizcaya Militia during the Administration of Teodoro de Croix, 1776–1783." *New Mexico Historical Review* 48, no. 3 (1973): 223–249.

Derecho Internacional Mexicano. Vol. 1, *Tratados y convenciones concluidos y ratificados por la República mexicana*. José Fernández, compiler. Mexico: Imprenta de Gonzalo A. Esteva, 1877.

———. Vol. 3, *Leyes, decretos y ordenes que forman derecho internacional mexicano o que se reclacionan con el mismo*. Mexico: Tipographia Literaria de Filomeno Mata, 1880.

Dexheimer, Eric. "Gutierrez Ousts incumbent Flores for Senate District 19." *San Antonio Express-News*, November 4, 2020. expressnews.com/news/politics/texas_legislature /article/Gutierrez-takes-early-lead-over-Flores-in-Senate-15699458.php.

Díaz del Castillo, Bernal. *The Conquest of New Spain*. 6th ed. Translated by John M. Cohen. New York: Penguin, 1983. Original manuscript, c. 1578.

Directory of the Main University and Extramural Divisions, 1923–1967. Student directory of the University of Texas at Austin. Copies in the Dolph Briscoe Center for American History, University of Texas at Austin.

Dobbs, Ricky F. *Yellow Dogs and Republicans: Allen Shivers and Texas Two-Party Politics*. College Station: Texas A&M University Press, 2005.

Dobyns, Henry. *Native American Historical Demography: A Critical Bibliography*. Bloomington: Indiana University Press, 1976.

Du Pre Lumpkin, Katharine. "The Child Labor Provisions of the Fair Labor Standards Act." *Law and Contemporary Problems* 6, no. 3 (1939): 391–405.

Duren, Almetris. *Overcoming: A History of Black Integration at the University of Texas at Austin*. Austin: University of Texas Press, 1979.

Durham, George. *Taming the Nueces Strip: The Story of McNelly's Rangers*. Austin: University of Texas Press, 1962.

East, Kristen. "Trump Attacks 'Mexican' Judge in Trump University Lawsuit." *Politico*, May 28, 2016. www.politico.com/story/2016/05/donald-trump-university-judge -gonzalo-curiel-223684.

Education Trust. *The Funding Gap Report 2005: Low-Income and Minority Students Shortchanged by Most States*. Washington, D.C.: Education Trust, 2005.

Ellis, Bruce, and Paul A. F. Walter. "Protecting Indian Decrees." *El Palacio* 10–12. Santa Fe: Museum of New Mexico, 1922.

Ellsworth, Emmons. *Special Census of the Population of El Paso, Texas*. Washington, DC: GPO, 1916.

Equity Center. "History of School Finance." 2018. equitycenter.org/sites/default/files /2018-10/Texas_School_Finance_History.pdf.

Executive Documents of the US House of Representatives, 2nd Session, Forty-Fifth Congress, 1877–1878, Vol. 17, Nos. 74–101 inclusive, except Nos. 89 and 90. Executive Document No. 93: "Letter from the Secretary of War in Response to a resolution from the House of Representatives, transmitting reports of the commission appointed to investigate the El Paso troubles in Texas." May 28, 1878, referred to the Committee on Foreign Affairs and ordered to be printed. US Serials Set, Washington: GOP.

Executive Documents of the House of Representatives, 2nd Session, Forty-Fifth Congress, 1877–1878, Vol. 17, Nos. 74–101 inclusive, except Nos. 89 and 90. Executive Document No. 84: "Letter from the Secretary of War, transmitting report from Colonel Hatch on the subject of "El Paso Troubles." May 8, 1878, referred to the Committee on Foreign Affairs and ordered to be printed. US Serials Set, Washington: GOP.

Feagin, Joe, and Clairece Booher Feagin. *Racial and Ethnic Relations*. Boston: Pearson, 2012.

Feros, Antonio. *Speaking of Spain: The Evolution of Race and Nation in the Hispanic World*. Cambridge, MA: Harvard University Press, 2017.

Flores, Henry. *Latinos and the Voting Rights Act: The Search for Racial Purpose*. New York: Lexington, 2015.

Foley, Neil. *Mexicans in the Making of America*. Cambridge, MA: Harvard University Press, 2014.

———. "Over the Rainbow: *Hernandez v. Texas, Brown v. Board of Education*, and *Black v. Brown*." In *"Colored Men" and "Hombres Aquí": "Hernandez v. Texas" and the Emergence of Mexican-American Lawyering*, edited by Michael A. Olivas, 111–121. Houston: Arte Público, 2006.

———. *The White Scourge: Mexicans, Blacks, and Poor Whites in Texas Cotton Culture*. Berkeley: University of California Press, 1997.

Folsom, Bradley. *Arredondo: Last Spanish Ruler of Texas and Northeastern New Spain*. Norman: University of Oklahoma Press, 2017.

Forbes, Jack. *Apache, Navaho, and Spaniard*. Norman: University of Oklahoma Press, 1994.

Fradera, Josep M. *The Imperial Nation: Citizens and Subjects in the British, French, Spanish, and American Empires*. Translated by Ruth MacKay. Princeton, NJ: Princeton University Press, 2018.

Frederick, Jake. "Without Impediment: Crossing Racial Boundaries in Colonial Mexico." *Americas* 67, no. 4 (2011): 495–515.

Fredrickson, George M. *Racism: A Short History*. Princeton, NJ: Princeton University Press, 2002.

Galarza, Ernesto. *Merchants of Labor: The Mexican Bracero Story*. Santa Barbara, CA: McNally and Loftin, 1964.

Gamio, Manuel. *Forjando Patria: Pro-Nacionalismo*. Mexico City: Libreria de Porrúa, 1916.

García, Ignacio. *White but Not Equal: Mexican Americans, Jury Discrimination, and the Supreme Court*. Tucson: University of Arizona Press, 2009.

García, Mario. *The Making of a Mexican American Mayor: Raymond L. Telles of El Paso*. El Paso: Texas Western Press, 1998.

———. *Mexican Americans: Leadership, Ideology, and Identity, 1930–1960*. New Haven, CT: Yale University Press, 1989.

————. "Mexican Americans and the Politics of Citizenship: The Case of El Paso, 1936." *New Mexico Historical Review* 59, no. 2 (April, 1984): 187–204.

García, Mario, and Sal Castro. *Blowout! Sal Castro and the Chicano Struggle for Educational Justice*. Chapel Hill: University of North Carolina Press, 2011.

Garza, Leonel, comp. *Agencia Mexicana ante la Comisión General de Reclamaciones entre México y los Estados Unidos-Reclamaciones Mexicanas*. In *Indece [sic] de propetarios [sic] originales con la página y número de reclamación*, 1–13, 102–157. Asociación de Reclamantes of Texas Land Grant Heirs, 1980. Reprint of the original 1852 manuscript.

Gibson, Charles. *Tlaxcala in the Sixteenth Century*. New Haven, CT: Yale University Press, 1964.

Girón González, Alicia. "Deuda externa." In *Finanzas públicas de México*, edited by Enrique Arriaga Conchas, 241–285. Mexico City: Instituto Politécnico Nacional, 2001.

Glasrud, Bruce A. "Jim Crow's Emergence in Texas." *American Studies* 5, no. 1 (1974): 47–60.

Goldstone, Dwonna. *Integrating the 40 Acres: The Fifty-Year Struggle for Racial Equality at the University of Texas*. Athens: University of Georgia Press, 2006.

Gómez-Quiñonez, Juan. *Mexican Students por La Raza: The Chicano Movement in Southern California, 1967–1977*. Santa Barbara, CA: Editorial La Causa, 1978.

Gómez-Quiñonez, Juan, and Irene Vásquez. *Ideology and Culture of the Chicana and Chicano Movement, 1966–1977*. Albuquerque: University of New Mexico Press, 2014.

González, Gabriela. "Jovita Idar: The Ideological Origins of a Transnational Advocate for La Raza." In *Texas Women: Their Histories, Their Lives*, edited by Elizabeth Hayes Turner, Stephanie Cole, and Rebecca Sharpless, 225–248. Athens: University of Georgia Press, 2015.

González Ramírez, Manuel. *La revolución social de México*. Vol. 1, *Las ideas—la violencia*. Mexico City: Fonda de Cultura Económica, 1986.

Gournay, Luke. *Texas Boundaries: Evolution of the State's Counties*. College Station: Texas A&M University, 1995.

Graham, Joe S. *El Rancho in South Texas: Continuity and Change from 1750*. Austin: University of Texas Press, 1994.

Gratton, Brian, and Emily Merchant. "La Raza: Mexicans in the United States Census." *Journal of Policy History* 28, no. 4 (2016): 1–31.

Grayson, George. *The Politics of Mexican Oil*. Pittsburgh: University of Pittsburgh Press, 1980.

Greaser, Galen. *New Guide to Spanish and Mexican Land Grants in South Texas*. Austin: Texas General Land Office, 2009.

Greaser, Galen D., Michael T. Moore, Stephen Wilson, and Alexander Chiba, comps. "Index to Titles, Field Notes, and Plats: Spanish Collection." 1988. Unpublished finding aid at the Texas General Land Office.

Grebler, Leo, Joan Moore, and Ralph Guzman. *The Mexican American People: The Nation's Second Largest Minority*. New York: Free Press, 1970.

Gross, Ariela. "The 'Caucasian Cloak': Mexican Americans and the Politics of Whiteness in the Twentieth-Century Southwest." In *Critical Race Theory: The Cutting Edge*, 3rd ed., edited by Richard Delgado and Jean Stefancic, 154–166. Pittsburgh: Temple University Press, 2013.

Guerrero Andrade, Manuel. *De la gestión estatal al mercado global: Los sistemas de intervención estatal en la comercialización del maíz en Mexico, 1936 to 2000*. Mexico City: Universidad Nacional Autónoma de México-Xochimilco, 2005.

Gutiérrez, José Ángel. *We Won't Back Down: Severita Lara's Rise from Student Leader to Mayor*. Houston: Arte Publico, 2005.

Guzmán, Ralph. *Mexican-American Casualties in Vietnam*. Santa Cruz, CA: Merrill College, 1969.

Guzmán, Will. *Civil Rights in the Texas Borderlands: Dr. Lawrence A. Nixon and Black Activism*. Champaign: University of Illinois Press, 2015.

Hackney, Sheldon. "Contemporary Views of Populism: The Omaha Platform of the People's Party." In *Populism: The Critical Issues*, edited by Sheldon Hackney, 1–10. Boston: Little, Brown, 1971.

Hall, Thomas and David Weber. "Mexican Liberals and the Pueblo Indians, 1821–1829." *New Mexico Historical Review* 59, no. 1 (1984): 5–31.

Hammond, George, and Agapito Rey, eds. *Don Juan de Oñate: Colonizer of New Mexico, 1595–1628*. Vol. 5. Albuquerque: University of New Mexico Press, 1953.

Hamnett, Brian. 2017. *The End of Iberian Rule on the American Continent, 1770–1830*. Cambridge: Cambridge University Press, 2017.

Haney López, Ian. "Race and Colorblindness after *Hernandez* and *Brown*." In *"Colored Men" and "Hombres Aquí:" "Hernandez v. Texas" and the Emergence of Mexican-American Lawyering*, edited by Michael A. Olivas, 41–52. Houston: Arte Público, 2006.

Hanke, Lewis. *The Spanish Struggle for Justice in the Conquest of America*. Philadelphia: University of Pennsylvania Press, 1949.

Haring, Clarence H. *The Spanish Empire in America*. New York: Harbinger, 1963.

Hendricks, Rick, and W. H. Timmons. *San Elizario: Spanish Presidio to Texas County Seat*. El Paso: Texas Western Press, 1998.

Hernández, Deluvina. *A Mexican American Challenge to the Sacred Cow*. Los Angeles: University of California, Mexican American Cultural Center, 1970.

Hernández, Kristian. "Melon Strike 50 Years Ago in Starr County Sparked Chicano Movement in Texas." *McAllen (TX) Monitor*, May 31, 2016. Available from Somos Primos, http://somosprimos.com/sp2016/spjul16/spjul16.htm.

Herrera, Carlos. "Juan Bautista de Anza and the Socio-Militarization of Bourbon El Paso, 1778–1788." *Journal of the Southwest* 46, no. 3 (2004): 501–528.

Herschel, Manuel. *The Education of Mexican and Spanish-Speaking Children in Texas*. Austin: University of Texas, Fund for Research in the School of Social Sciences, 1930.

Hinojosa, Gilberto. *A Borderlands Town in Transition: Laredo, 1755–1870*. College Station: Texas A&M University Press, 2000.

———. 1994. Prologue to *Mexican Americans and the Catholic Church, 1900–1965*, edited by Jay P. Dolan and Gilberto M. Hinojosa, 11–125. Notre Dame, IN: University of Notre Dame Press, 1994.

Hinojosa, Gilberto, and Anne Fox. "Indians and Their Culture in San Fernando de Béxar." In *Tejano Origins in Eighteenth-Century San Antonio*, edited by Gerald E. Poyo and Gilberto M. Hinojosa, 105–120. Austin: University of Texas Press, 1991.

Hochschild, Jennifer, and Brenna Marea Powell. "Racial Reorganization and the United States Census, 1850–1930: 'Mulattoes, Half-Breeds, Mixed Parentage,

Hindus, and the Mexican Race.'" *Studies in American Political Development* 22, no. 1 (Spring 2008): 59–96.

Houser, Nicholas. "The Tigua Settlement of Ysleta del Sur." *Kiva* 36, no. 2 (1970): 23–39.

Houston Post. *Houston Post Almanac.* Houston: Houston Publishing, 1897.

Houston, Ramona. "African Americans, Mexican Americans, and Anglo Americans and the Desegregation of Texas, 1946–1956." PhD diss., University of Texas at Austin, 2000.

Humboldt, Alexander von. *Tablas geográfico-políticas, del Reino de Nuevo España que manifiestan la superficie, población, agricultura, fábricas, comercio, minas, rentas y fuerza militar,* Diciembre 1803. In AGN, *Historia,* vol. 72, exp. 24, fs. 14–16.

Hutchinson, Cecil Alan. *Frontier Settlement in Mexican California: The Hijar-Padres Colony and Its Origins, 1769–1835.* New Haven, CT: Yale University Press, 1969.

Hyman, Harold, and William Wiecek. *Equal Justice under Law: Constitutional Development, 1835–1875.* New York: Harper and Row, 1982.

Iber, Jorge. "In-field Foes and Racial Misconceptions: The 1961 Donna Redskins and Their Drive to the Texas State Football Championship." In *Mexican Americans and Sports: A Reader on Athletics and Barrio Life,* edited by Jorge Iber and Samuel O. Regalado, 121–144. College Station: Texas A&M University Press, 2007.

Ingersoll, Thomas N. "Slave Codes and Judicial Practice in New Orleans, 1718–1807." *Law and History Review* 13, no. 1 (1995): 23–62.

Institute of Public Affairs. *The Fifty-eighth Texas Legislature: A Review of Its Work.* Austin: University of Texas, Institute of Public Affairs, 1963.

———. *The Fifty-fifth Texas Legislature: A Review of Its Work.* Austin: University of Texas, Institute of Public Affairs, 1957.

———. *The Fifty-ninth Texas Legislature: A Review of Its Work.* Austin: University of Texas, Institute of Public Affairs, 1966.

———. *The Fifty-seventh Texas Legislature: A Review of Its Work.* Austin: University of Texas, Institute of Public Affairs, 1962.

———. *The Sixtieth Texas Legislature: A Review of Its Work.* Austin: University of Texas, Institute of Public Affairs, 1968.

———. *The Sixty-first Texas Legislature: A Review of its Work.* Austin: University of Texas, Institute of Public Affairs, 1970.

Instituto Nacional de Estadística y Geografía. *Anuario estadístico de los Estados Unidos Mexicanos, 2011.* Aguascalientes, Mexico: INEGI, 2012.

———. *Mexican Bulletin of Statistical Information 18.* Aguascalientes, Mexico: INEGI, 1996.

———. *Resumen de los resultados de los censos económicos.* Aguascalientes, Mexico: INEGI, 2009.

Johnson Scott, Florence. *Royal Land Grants North of the Rio Grande 1777–1821.* Rio Grande City, TX: La Retama, 1969.

Jones, Oakah L., Jr. *Los Paisanos: Spanish Settlers on the Northern Frontier.* Norman: University of Oklahoma Press, 1996.

Kessell, John. *Spain in the Southwest: A Narrative History of Colonial New Mexico, Arizona, Texas, and California.* Norman: University of Oklahoma Press, 2002.

Keyssar, Alexander. *The Right to Vote: The Contested History of Democracy in the United States.* New York: Basic Books, 2000.

Kibbe, Pauline. *Latin Americans in Texas*. Albuquerque: University of New Mexico Press, 1946.

King, James F. "The Colored Castes and American Representation in the Cortes of Cadiz." *Hispanic American Historical Review* 33, no. 1 (1953): 33–64.

Kingston, Mike. 1988. *A Concise History of Texas: From the Texas Almanac*. Dallas: Dallas Morning News, 1988.

Koch, Oscar, and James Fowler. *A City Plan for Austin, Texas: Koch and Fowler Consulting Engineers, 1928*. Austin, Texas: Department of Planning.

Krochmal, Max. *Blue Texas: The Making of a Multiracial Democratic Coalition in the Civil Rights Era*. Chapel Hill: University of North Carolina Press, 2016.

Kuhlman, Martin H. "The Civil Rights Movement in Texas: Desegregation of Public Accommodations, 1950–1964." PhD diss., Texas Tech University, 1994.

Kwong, Jessica. "Gilroy Gunman Cited White Supremacist Manifesto on Instagram Just before Shooting." *Newsweek*, July 29, 2019. www.newsweek.com/gilroy-shooter-white-supremacist-manifesto-instagram-1451586.

La Farge, John. *The Catholic Viewpoint on Race Relations*. Garden City, NY: Hanover House, 1956.

Lamar, Howard R. *The Far Southwest, 1846–1912: A Territorial History*. New York: Norton, 1966.

Larson, Robert W. *New Mexico's Quest for Statehood, 1846–1912*. Albuquerque: University of New Mexico Press, 1968.

Lasater, Dale. *Falfurrias: Ed C. Lasater and the Development of South Texas*. College Station: Texas A&M University Press, 1985.

Laws of Texas. Various volumes: 1 (1822–1838), 2 (1838–1846), 3 (1847–1854), 5 (1861–1866), 8 (1874–1879), 9 (1879–1889), 10 (1891–1897), 11 (1897–1902), *Supplement, 1822–1897* (1898).

Laws of the Territory of New Mexico. Santa Fe, NM: James L. Collins, 1851.

League of Texas Municipalities. "Judicial Decisions." *Texas Municipalities* 6 (November 1919): 159–182.

———. "Legislation from Texas Cities." *Texas Municipalities* 4 (September 5, 1917): 149–180.

———. "Notes from the Cities." *Texas Municipalities* 3 (January 1916): 1–32.

———. "Notes from the Cities." *Texas Municipalities* 3 (July 3, 1916): 65–105.

Levario, Miguel Antonio. "Cuando vino la mexicanada: Authority, Race, and Conflict in West Texas, 1895–1924." PhD diss., University of Texas at Austin, 2007.

Li, Michael, Thomas Wolf, and Alexis Farmer. "The State of Redistricting Litigation (April 2017 Edition)." Brennan Center for Justice, May 23, 2017. www.brennancenter.org/blog/state-redistricting-litigation-april-2017-edition.

López, Mark Hugo, Ana Gonzalez-Barrera, Jen Manuel Krogstad, and Gustavo López. "The Latino Vote in the 2016 Presidential Election." Part 2 of "Democrats Maintain Edge as Party 'More Concerned' for Latinos, but Views Similar to 2012," Pew Research Center, October 11, 2016. www.pewresearch.org/hispanic/wp-content/uploads/sites/5/2016/10/PH_2016.10.11_Politics_FINAL4.pdf.

Love, Edgar F. "Legal Restrictions on Afro-Indian Relations in Colonial Mexico." *Journal of Negro History* 55, no. 2 (1970): 131–139.

Luckingham, Bradford. *Minorities in Phoenix: A Profile of Mexican American, Chinese American, and African American Communities, 1860–1992*. Tucson: University of Arizona Press, 1994.

Malewitz, Jim. "House, Senate OK Compromise on Bill to Soften Voter ID Law." *Texas Tribune*, May 28, 2017. www.texastribune.org/2017/05/28/house-senate -compromise-voter-id.

———. "Texas Voter ID Law Violates Voting Rights Act, Court Rules." *Texas Tribune*, July 20, 2016. www.texastribune.org/2016/07/20/appeals-court-rules-texas -voter-id.

Manzo Yépez, José Luis. *¿Qué hacer con PEMEX? Una alternativa a la privatización.* Mexico City: Grijalbo, 1996.

Márquez, Benjamin. *Democratizing Texas Politics: Race, Identity, and Mexican American Empowerment, 1945–2002.* Austin: University of Texas Press, 2014.

Márquez, John. *Black-Brown Solidarity in the New Gulf South.* Austin: University of Texas Press, 2013.

Martin, Roscoe O. *The People's Party in Texas: A Study in Third-Party Politics.* Austin: University of Texas Press, 1970.

Martínez, María Elena. *Genealogical Fictions: Limpieza de Sangre, Religion, and Gender in Colonial Mexico.* Stanford, CA: Stanford University Press, 2008.

Martinez, Monica Muñoz. *The Injustice Never Leaves You: Anti-Mexican Violence in Texas.* Cambridge, MA: Harvard University Press, 2018.

Martínez Fernández, Raymundo, comp. *Deuda externa vs. desarollo económico: Análisis y síntesis de la Reunión Internacional sobre Deuda Externa y Alternativas.* Mexico City: Foro de Apoyo Mutuo, 1996.

Matovina, Timothy. *Tejano Religion and Ethnicity: San Antonio, 1821–1860.* Austin: University of Texas Press, 1995.

Maxwell, W. J., comp. *General Register of the Students and Former Students of the University of Texas.* Austin: Ex-Students' Association, 1917.

McCluskey, Neil Gerard. *Catholic Viewpoint on Education.* Garden City, NY: Hanover House, 1959.

McCorkle, Stuart. *The Texas City: Its Power to Zone.* Austin: University of Texas, Institute of Public Affairs, 1955.

McGregor, Morris J., Jr. *Integration of the Armed Forces, 1940–1965.* Washington, DC: US Army, Center of Military History, 2001.

Menchaca, Martha. "The Anti-Miscegenation History of the American Southwest." *Cultural Dynamics* 20 (2008): 279–311.

———. *Mexican Outsiders: A Community History of Discrimination and Marginalization in California.* Austin: University of Texas Press, 1995.

———. *Naturalizing Mexican Immigrants: A Texas History.* Austin: University of Texas Press, 2011.

———. *The Politics of Dependency: U.S. Reliance on Mexican Oil and Farm Labor.* Austin: University of Texas Press, 2016.

———. *Recovering History, Constructing Race: The Indian, Black, and White Roots of Mexican Americans.* Austin: University of Texas Press, 2001.

Menchú Tum, Rigoberta. *Crossing Borders: An Autobiography.* New York: Verso, 1998.

Mendoza, Alexander. "Beating the Odds: Mexican American Distance Runners in Texas, 1950–1995." In *Mexican Americans and Sports: A Reader on Athletics and Barrio Life*, edited by Jorge Iber and Samuel O. Regalado, 121–144. College Station: Texas A&M University Press, 2007.

Metz, Leon. *El Paso Chronicles: A Record of Historical Events in El Paso, Texas*. El Paso: Managan, 1994.

Miller, Robert. *Mexico: A History*. Norman: University of Oklahoma Press, 1985.

Mines, Richard, and Ricardo Anzaldúa. *New Migrants vs. Old Migrants: Alternative Labor Market Structures in the California Citrus Industry*. Monographs in U.S.-Mexican Studies 9. San Diego: University of California, 1982.

Minter, Alan H. "Indian Land Claims in Texas during the Twentieth Century." Unpublished paper, 1993. Copy at the Texas General Land Office, Austin, Texas.

Mixerr-Reviews. 2017. "History Pertaining to the Small Colorado School Long Forgotten." *Mixerr Reviews* (blog), June 23, 2017. mixerrreviews.blogspot.com/2017/06/history-pertaining-to-small-colorado.html.

Montejano, David. *Anglos and Mexicans in the Making of Texas, 1836–1986*. Austin: University of Texas Press, 1987.

———. *Quixote's Soldiers: A Local History of the Chicano Movement, 1966–1981*. Austin: University of Texas Press, 2010.

Montoya, Celeste. "What Conclusions Can We Draw about the Hispanic Vote in 2020?" *Fortune*, November 10, 2020. https://fortune.com/2020/11/10/hispanic-latino-voters-trump-biden-2020.

Moreno-Brid, Juan Carlos, and Jaime Ros. *Development and Growth in the Mexican Economy: A Historical Perspective*. New York: Oxford University Press, 2009.

Morfi, Juan Agustín. 2010. *Relación geográfica e histórica de la provincia de Texas o Nuevas Filipinas, 1673–1779*. Compiled by Curiel Defossé. Mexico City: Cien de Mexico, 2010. Originally published 1779.

Morin, Eddie. *Valor and Discord: Mexican Americans and the Vietnam War*. Los Angeles: Valiant, 2006.

Morland, Kenneth. "Lunch-Counter Desegregation in Corpus Christi, Galveston, and San Antonio, Texas." Randolph-Macon Woman's College, May 10, 1960. Special report by the Southern Regional Council, Georgia. Box 1, folder 120, American Left Ephemera Collection, 1894–2008, AIS.2007.11, Archives Service Center, University of Pittsburgh. http://digital.library.pitt.edu/u/ulsmanuscripts/pdf/31735066227822.pdf.

Murdock, Steve. "Population and Household Change in the United States and Texas: Implications for Our Socioeconomic Future." Hobby Center for the Study of Texas, Rice University, February 12, 2016. dallasfed.org/~/media/documents/research/events/2016/16sheltermurdock.pdf.

Murph, Dan. *The Life of Price Daniel, Texas Giant*. Austin: Eakin, 2002.

Najera, Jennifer. *The Borderlands of Race: Mexican Segregation in a South Texas Border Town*. Austin: University of Texas Press, 2015.

National Conference of State Legislatures. "2012 Immigration-Related Laws and Resolutions in the States: January 1–June 30, 2012," https://www.ncsl.org/research/immigration/2012-immigration-related-laws-and-resolutions.aspx.

Navarro, Armando. *Mexican American Youth Organization: Avant-Garde of the Chicano Movement*. Austin: University of Texas Press, 1995.

Nevins, Joseph. *Operation Gatekeeper: The Rise of the "Illegal Alien" and the Making of the U.S.-Mexico Boundary*. New York: Routledge, 2002.

Newcomb, W. W., Jr. 1993. *The Indians of Texas: From Prehistoric to Modern Times*. Austin: University of Texas Press, 1993.

Ngai, Mae M. *Impossible Subjects: Illegal Aliens and the Making of Modern America.* Princeton, NJ: Princeton University Press, 2014.

Noe-Bustamante, Luis, Abby Budiman, and Mark Hugo López. 2020. "Where Latinos Have the Most Eligible Voters in the 2020 Election." Pew Research Center: Fact Tank, January 31, 2020. https://www.pewresearch.org/fact-tank/2020/01/31/where-latinos-have-the-most-eligible-voters-in-the-2020-election.

Nuesse, Joseph. "Segregation and Desegregation at the Catholic University of America." *Washington History,* Spring–Summer 1997, 55–70.

Nuñez, Xosé-Manoel. "Nation-Building and Regional Integration: The Case of the Spanish Empire, 1700–1914." In *Nationalizing Empires,* edited by Berger Stefan and Miller Alexei, 195–246. Budapest: Central European University Press, 2015.

Ogletree, Charles J., Jr. *All Deliberate Speed: Reflections on the First Half-Century of "Brown v. Board of Education."* New York: Norton, 2004.

Ogunwole, Stella, Malcome Drewery Jr., and Merarys Rios-Vargas. "The Population with a Bachelor's Degree or Higher by Race and Hispanic Origin: 2006–2010." Washington, DC: US Department of Commerce, Census Bureau, 2012. https://www2.census.gov/library/publications/2012/acs/acsbr10-19.pdf.

Olivas, Michael. "Introduction: Alonso S. Perales, the Rule of Law, and the Development of Mexican-American Public Intellectuals." In *In Defense of My People: Alonso S. Perales and the Development of Mexican-American Public Intellectuals,* ed. Michael Olivas, ix–xxxviii. Houston: Arte Publico, 2012.

———. "The Legal Career of Alonso S. Perales." In Olivas, *In Defense of My People,* edited by Michael Olivas, 315–343.

O'Read, Mary Jo, Gloria Randle Scott, Cecilia Gutierrez Venable, and Henry J. Williams. *African Americans in Corpus Christi.* Charleston, SC: Arcadia, 2012.

Orozco, Cynthia. *No Mexicans, Women, or Dogs Allowed: The Rise of the Mexican American Civil Rights Movement.* Austin: University of Texas Press, 2009.

Ortega, Andres, comp. *Recopilación de leyes de los reynos de las Indias.* 3rd ed. Vol. 1, books 1 and 2. Published under the royal order of Don Carlos II of Spain. Madrid, 1774.

Overtfelt, Robert. "Del Rio, Texas." In *Handbook of Texas Online,* Texas State Historical Association. https://tshaonline.org/handbook/online/articles/hed03.

Pantoja Morán, David. 2017. *Bases del constitucionalismo mexicano: La Constitución de 1824 y la teoría constitucional.* Mexico City: Fondo de Cultura Económica Senado de la República, 2017.

Paredes, Américo. *With a Pistol in His Hand: A Border Ballad and Its Hero.* Austin: University of Texas Press, 1958.

Parise, Agustin. "Slave Law and Labor Activities during the Spanish Colonial Period: A Study of the South American Region of Río de la Plata." *Rutgers Law Records* 32, no. 8 (2008): 1–30.

Park, Madison, and Ralph Ellis. "Texas Voter ID Law Was Designed to Discriminate, Judge Rules." CNN Politics, November 4, 2017. www.cnn.com/2017/04/11/politics/texas-voter-id-law-discriminate/index.html.

Pedraza, Francisco, and Bryan Wilcox-Archuleta. "Donald Trump Did Not Win 34% of Latino Vote in Texas." *Washington Post,* December 2, 2016. https://www.washingtonpost.com/news/monkey-cage/wp/2016/12/02/donald-trump-did-not-win-34-of-latino-vote-in-texas-he-won-much-less.

Pemex. *Statistical Yearbook* (Anuario Estadistico). Mexico, DF: Pemex, 1988. www .pemex.com/informes/descargables/index.html.

Perales, Monica. *Smeltertown: Making and Remembering a Southwest Border Community.* Chapel Hill: University of North Carolina Press, 2010.

Pérez, Daniel. "Community Gets Credit for Smooth Integration." *El Paso Times*, January 19, 2014. www.elpasotimes.com/news/ci_24943968 (webpage no longer available).

Perez de Soto, Antonio, comp. *Recopilación de leyes de los reynos de las Indias.* 3rd ed. Vol. 2, books 3, 4, 6, and 7. Published under the royal order of Don Carlos II of Spain. Madrid, 1774.

Pitti, Stephen. *The Devil in Silicon Valley: Northern California, Race, and Mexican Americans.* Princeton, NJ: Princeton University Press, 2003.

Powell, Philip W. *Soldiers, Indians, and Silver: The Northward Advance of New Spain, 1550–1600.* Berkeley: University of California Press, 1952.

Poyo, Gerald E. "The Canary Islands Immigrants of San Antonio: From Ethnic Exclusivity to Community in Eighteenth-Century Bexar." In *Tejano Origins in Eighteenth-Century San Antonio*, edited by Gerald E. Poyo and Gilberto M. Hinojosa, 41–60. Austin: University of Texas Press, 1991.

———. "Social Identity on the Hispanic Texas Frontier." In *Recovering the U.S. Hispanic Literary Heritage*, vol. 3., edited by María Herrera-Sobek and Virginia Sánchez-Korrol, 384–401. Houston: Arte Publico, 2000.

Pycior, Julie Leininger. *LBJ and Mexican Americans: The Paradox of Power.* Austin: University of Texas Press, 1997.

———. "La Raza Organizes: Mexican American Life in San Antonio, 1915–1930, as Reflected in Mutualista Activities." PhD diss., University of Notre Dame, 1979.

Quigley, Aiden. "Texas Eases Birth Certificate Rules for Children of Undocumented Parents." *Christian Science Monitor*, July 26, 2016. www.csmonitor.com/USA /USA-Update/2016/0726/Texas-eases-birth-certificate-rules-for-children-with -undocumented-parents.

Rabinowitz, Howard N. "From Exclusion to Segregation: Southern Race Relations, 1865–1890." In *When Did Southern Segregation Begin?*, edited by David Smith, 104–131. New York: Palgrave, 2002.

Ramírez, Miguel. *The IMF Austerity Program, 1983–87: Miguel de la Madrid's Legacy.* Occasional Papers in Latin American Studies 7. Storrs: University of Connecticut, Center for Latin American and Caribbean Studies, 1989.

Ramos, Christopher. "The Educational Legacy of Racially Restrictive Covenants: Their Long-Term Impact on Mexican Americans." *Scholar: St. Mary's Law Review on Minority Issues* 4, no. 1 (Fall 2001): 149–184.

Ramos, Raúl A. *Beyond the Alamo: Forging Mexican Ethnicity in San Antonio, 1821–1861.* Chapel Hill: University of North Carolina Press, 2008.

Raymond, Virginia M. "Faithful Dissent: Alonso S. Perales, Discrimination, and the Catholic Church." In Olivas, *In Defense of My People*, 171–217.

Reigstad, Leif. "Texas House Approves Slightly Relaxed Voter ID Law: Your Texas Roundup." *Texas Monthly*, May 24, 2017. www.texasmonthly.com/the-daily-post /texas-house-approves-slightly-relaxed-voter-id-law-texas-roundup.

Reisler, Mark. *By the Sweat of Their Brow: Mexican Immigrant Labor in the United States, 1900–1940.* Westport, CT: Greenwood, 1976.

Republican Party of Texas. "Platform, 2020." https://www.texasgop.org/2020-state -convention.

Report of the Adjunct General of the State of Texas for the Fiscal Year Ending August 31, 1878. Galveston, Texas. Copy at the El Paso Public Library, Salt Wars Folder, EPVF, Border Heritage Center.

Reséndéz, Andrés. *Changing National Identities at the Frontier: Texas and New Mexico, 1800–1850.* Cambridge: Cambridge University Press, 2004.

Residents of Texas, 1782–1836. Reprint of the Spanish and Mexican censuses. San Antonio: University of Texas, Institute of Texan Cultures, 1984.

Richardson, Rupert, Adrian Anderson, Cary Wintz, and Ernest Wallace. *Texas: The Lone Star State.* 10th ed. Englewood Cliffs, NJ: Prentice-Hall, 2010.

Rojas, Xiomara Avendaño. "La evolución histórica de la ciudadanía: Un punto de partida para el estudio del estado y la nación." In *Historia y nación: Política y diplomacia en el siglo XX mexicano,* edited by Luis Jáuregui and Jose Antonio Serrano Ortega, 171–182. Mexico City: El Colegio de Mexico, 1998.

Ros, Jaime, and César Bouillon. "La liberalización de la balanza de pagos en México: Efectos en el crecimiento, la desigualdad y la pobreza." In *Liberálización, desigualdad, y pobreza: América Latina y el Caribe en los 90s,* edited by Enrique Ganuza, Ricardo Paes de Barros, Lance Taylor, and Rob Vos, 714–765. Buenos Aires: EUDEBA, 2001.

Rosales, Arturo F. *Chicano! The History of the Mexican American Civil Rights Movement.* Houston: Arte Público Press, 1996.

Ross, Michael A. *Justice of Shattered Dreams: Samuel Freeman Miller and the Supreme Court during the Civil War Era.* Baton Rouge: Louisiana State University Press, 2003.

Rothenberg, Daniel. *With These Hands: The Hidden World of Migrant Farmworkers Today.* Berkeley: University of California Press, 2000.

Rucker, Philip. 2019. "'How Do You Stop These People?': Trump's Anti-immigrant Rhetoric Looms over El Paso Massacre." *Washington Post,* August 4, 2019, https:// www.washingtonpost.com/politics/how-do-you-stop-these-people-trumps-anti -immigrant-rhetoric-looms-over-el-paso-massacre/2019/08/04/62d0435a-b6ce -11e9-a091-6a96e67d9cce_story.html.

Ryan, Camille, and Julie Siebens. *Educational Attainment in the United States: 2009*; Population Characteristics. Washington, DC: U.S. Department of Commerce, US Census Bureau, 2012. https://www.census.gov/prod/2012pubs/p20-566.pdf.

Rytina, Nancy, and Selena Caldera. *Naturalizations in the United States: 2007.* Washington, DC: Department of Homeland Security, Office of Immigration Statistics, Policy Directorate, 2008. https://www.dhs.gov/xlibrary/assets/statistics /publications/natz_fr_07.pdf.

Saether, Steinar. "Bourbon Absolutism and Marriage Reform in Late Colonial Spanish America." *Americas* 59, no. 4 (2003): 475–509.

Salinas, Lupe. "Legally White, Socially Brown: Alonso S. Perales and His Crusade for Justice for La Raza." In Olivas, *In Defense of My People,* pp. 75–95.

Salomone, Rosemary. 1986. *Equal Education under Law: Legal Rights and Federal Policy in the Post-"Brown" Era.* New York: St. Martin's, 1986.

Sanchíz, Javier. "La limpieza de la sangre, entre la rutina y la facilidad." In *El peso de la sangre: Limpios, mestizos y nobles en el mundo hispánico,* edited by Nikölaus

Böttcher, Bernd Hausberger, and Max Hering Torres, 113–136. Mexico City: El Colegio de México, 2011.

San Miguel, Guadalupe, Jr. *Brown, Not White: School Integration and the Chicano Movement in Houston*. College Station: Texas A&M University Press, 2001.

———. *Chicana/o Struggles for Education: Activism in the Community*. College Station: Texas A&M University Press, 2013.

———. *Let All of Them Take Heed: Mexican Americans and the Campaign for Educational Equality in Texas*. Austin: University of Texas Press, 1987.

Schmitz, Joseph William. *The Society of Mary in Texas*. San Antonio: Naylor, 1951.

Schwaller, Robert. *Géneros de Gente in Early Colonial Mexico*. Norman: University of Oklahoma Press, 2016.

Shabazz, Amilcar. "The Opening of the Southern Mind: The Desegregation of Higher Education in Texas, 1865–1965." PhD diss., University of Houston, 1996.

Sickels, Robert J. *Race, Marriage, and the Law*. Albuquerque: University of New Mexico Press, 1972.

Smith, Bennett. *Marriage by Bond in Colonial Texas*. Fort Worth, TX: Branch-Smith, 1972.

Smith, David. *When Did Southern Segregation Begin?* New York: Palgrave, 2002.

Smith, Morgan. 2012. "An Updated Guide to the School Finance Lawsuits." *Texas Tribune*, July 3, 2012, www.texastribune.org/2012/07/03/an-updated-guide-to -texas-school-finance-lawsuits.

Smith, Todd. *From Dominance to Disappearance: The Indians of Texas and the Near Southwest, 1786–1859*. Lincoln: University of Nebraska Press, 2005.

State Papers and Publick Documents of the United States. Vols. 10 and 12. Boston: Thomas E. Wait, 1819.

Steigerwald, David. *The Sixties and the End of Modern America*. New York: St. Martin's, 1995.

Stephenson, Gilbert. "The Separation of the Races in Public Conveyances." *American Political Science Review* 3 (1909): 180–204.

Stern, Mark. *Calculating Visions: Kennedy, Johnson, and Civil Rights*. New Brunswick, NJ: Rutgers University Press, 1991.

Stewart, Jocelyn. 2007. "Albert Armendariz Sr., 88; Lawyer Helped Change the Legal Landscape for Latinos." *Los Angeles Times*, October 9, 2007. https://www.latimes .com/archives/la-xpm-2007-oct-09-me-armendariz9-story.html.

Stoll, David. *El Norte or Bust: How Migration Fever and Microcredit Produced a Financial Crash in a Latin American Town*. New York: Rowman and Littlefield, 2013.

Street, Richard Steven. 1996. "The FBI's Secret File on César Chávez." *Southern California Quarterly* 78 (4): 347–84.

Stukey, Elizabeth Smith. "Economic Interdependence and the Sovereignty of Debtor Nations: A Comparison of Mexican and Argentine Reactions to International Monetary Fund Stabilization." *Fordham International Law Journal* 8, no. 3 (1984): 543–588.

Svitek, Patrick. "Texas Gov. Greg Abbott Signs 'Sanctuary Cities' Bill into Law." *Texas Tribune*, May 7, 2017. www.texastribune.org/2017/05/07/abbott-signs-sanctuary -cities-bill.

Talmadge Moore, James. *Acts of Faith: The Catholic Church in Texas, 1900–1950*. College Station: Texas A&M University Press, 2002.

Tate, Maggie. "Austin, Texas, in Sociohistorical Context." In *Invisible in Austin: Life and Labor in an American City*, ed. Javier Auyero, 20–41. Austin: University of Texas Press, 2015.

Texas Commission on Higher Education. "Texas Commission on Higher Education, Head Count Enrollment, Nineteen Fully State Supported Academic Institutions in Texas, Fall Semesters, 1952–1962." 1962. Richard M. Morehead Papers, box 3F 279, Dolph Briscoe Center for American History, University of Texas at Austin.

Texas Demographic Center, "Texas Population Projection Program," (Population 2010–2020, Lloyd Potter, State Demographer). Accessed May 2, 2021. https://demographics.texas.gov/data/TPEPP/projections.

Texas General Land Office. 1988. *Guide to Spanish and Mexican Land Grants in South Texas.* Austin: Texas General Land Office.

Texas Politics Project. "Race and Ethnicity in the Texas Legislature, 1937–2016." Chart. University of Texas at Austin, College of Liberal Arts, 2017. https://www.texaspolitics.utexas.edu/archive/html/leg/features/0304_02/race.html.

Thornton, Russell. *American Indian Holocaust and Survival: A Population History since 1492.* Norman: University of Oklahoma Press, 1990.

———. "Population History of Native North America." In *The Population History of North America*, edited by Michael R. Haines and Richard H. Steckel, 9–50. Cambridge: Cambridge University Press, 2000.

Tijerina, Andrés. *Tejano Empire: Life on the South Texas Ranchos.* College Station: Texas A&M University Press, 1998.

———. *Tejanos and Texas under the Mexican Flag, 1821–1836.* College Station: Texas A&M University Press, 1994.

Timmons, W. H. *El Paso: A Borderlands History.* El Paso: University of Texas at El Paso Press, 2004.

Tjarks, Alicia. "Comparative Demographic Analysis of Texas, 1777–1793." *Southwestern Historical Quarterly* 77 (January 1974): 291–338.

Torget, Andrew J. *Seeds of Empire: Cotton, Slavery, and the Transformation of the Texas Borderlands, 1800–1850.* Chapel Hill: University of North Carolina Press, 2015.

Tretter, Eliot. *Austin Restricted: Progressivism, Zoning, Private Racial Covenants, and the Making of a Segregated City.* Report of the Institute for Urban Policy Research and Analysis, University of Texas at Austin, 2012.

———. *Shadows of a Sunbelt City: The Environment, Racism, and the Knowledge Economy in Austin.* Athens: University of Georgia Press, 2016.

Treviño, Robert. *The Church in the Barrio: Mexican American Ethno-Catholicism in Houston.* Chapel Hill: University of North Carolina Press, 2006.

Ura, Alexa. "Texas Agrees to Resolve Birth Certificate Case with Undocumented Families." *Texas Tribune*, July 25, 2016. www.texastribune.org/2016/07/25/texas-agrees-to-resolve-birth-certificate-case.

US Commission on Civil Rights. Texas State Advisory Committee. *Civil Rights in Texas: A Report of the Advisory Committee to the U.S. Commission on Civil Rights.* Washington, D.C.: US Commission on Civil Rights, 1970.

———. Texas State Advisory Committee. *Texas: The State of Civil Rights: Ten Years Later, 1968–1978.* Washington, DC: US Commission on Civil Rights, 1980.

US Department of Commerce. *A Standard State Zoning Enabling Act: Under which Mu-*

nicipalities may Adopt Zoning Regulations. Washington, DC: Government Printing Office, 1926.

US Department of Justice. "Justice Department to File New Lawsuit Against State of Texas Over Voter I.D. Law." Justice News, 2014. https://www.justice.gov/opa /pr/justice-department-file-new-lawsuit-against-state-texas-over-voter-id-law.

US Department of Labor. *Fifty-Second Annual Report*. Washington, DC: Government Printing Office, 1964.

———. *Hired Farmworkers in the United States*. Washington, DC: Department of Labor, Bureau of Employment Security, 1964.

———. "History of Federal Minimum Wage Rates under the Fair Standards Labor Act, 1938–2009" (chart). 2017. https://www.dol.gov/whd/minwage/chart.

———. *Proceedings of Consultation on Migratory Farm Labor*. Washington, DC: US Department of Labor, Bureau of Employment Security, 1957.

US Department of State. *Treaties and Other International Agreements of the United States of America, 1776 to 1949*, 1972.

US General Accounting Office. *Financial Crisis Management: Four Financial Crises in the 1980s*. Washington, DC: US General Accounting Office, 1997.

———. *Mexico's Financial Crisis: Origins, Awareness, Assistance, and Initial Efforts to Recover*. Washington, DC: US General Accounting Office, 1996.

US Senate. Subcommittee on Migratory Labor. *Migratory Labor Legislation: Hearings Before Subcommittee on Migratory Labor*, 90th Congress, 1st sess., pt. 1, May 17–August 2, 1967. Washington, DC: Government Printing Office, 1968.

Valencia, Richard. *Chicano Students and the Courts: The Mexican American Legal Struggle for Educational Equity*. New York: New York University Press, 2008.

———. "The Mexican American Struggle for Equal Educational Opportunity in *Mendez v. Westminster*: Helping to Pave the Way for *Brown v. Board of Education*." *Teachers College Record* 107 (2005): 389–423.

———. *Students of Color and the Achievement Gap: Systemic Challenges, Systemic Transformations*. New York: Routledge, 2015.

Valencia, Richard, Martha Menchaca, and Ruben Donato. "Segregation, Desegregation, and Integration of Chicano Students: Old and New Realities." In *Chicano School Failure and Success: Past, Present, and Future*, edited by Richard Valencia, 70–113. New York: Routledge, 2011.

Varady, David, and Jeffrey Raffel. *Selling Cities: Attracting Homebuyers through Schools and Housing Programs*. New York: State University of New York Press, 1995.

Vázquez, Josefina Zoraida. *México y el expansionismo norteamericano*. Mexico City: El Colegio de México, 2010.

Vázquez, Josefina Zoraida, and Lorenzo Meyer. 2006. *México frente a Estados Unidos: Un ensayo histórico, 1776–2000*. Mexico City: Fondo de Cultura Económica, 2006.

———. *The United States and Mexico*. Chicago: University of Chicago Press, 1985.

Vedantam, Shankar. "State Lawmakers Taking Aim at Amendment Granting Birthright Citizenship." *Washington Post*, January 5, 2011. http://www.washingtonpost .com/wp-dyn/content/article/2011/01/AR2011010503134.html.

Vigil, James Diego. *A Rainbow of Gangs: Street Cultures in a Mega City*. Austin: University of Texas Press, 2002.

Villagrán, José. "Revisiting the 'Midwest Stream': An Ethnographic Account of Farmwork-ers on the Texas-Michigan Circuit." PhD diss., University of Texas at Austin, 2019.

Vinson, Ben. *Bearing Arms for His Majesty: The Free-Colored Militia in Colonial Mexico.* Stanford, CA: Stanford University Press, 2003.

———. *Before Mestizaje: The Frontiers of Race and Caste in Colonial Mexico.* Cambridge: Cambridge University Press, 2017.

Vizcaya Canales, Isidro, comp. *Instrucción reservada de Don Nemesio Salcedo y Salcedo Comandante General de Provincias Internas a su sucesor.* Centro de Información del Estado de Chihuahua. Chihuahua, Mexico: Gobierno del Estado de Chihuahua, 1990.

Wallace, Jeremy. "Texas Voter Turnout Best in Almost 30 Years?" *Houston Chroni-cle*, November 5, 2020. https://www.houstonchronicle.com/news/election2020/article/Texas-voter-turnout-was-best-in-almost-30-years-15705990.php.

Walsh, Deirdre, and Manu Raju. "Paul Ryan Rips Donald Trump Remarks as 'Textbook Definition of a Racist Comment'." *CNN Politics*, June 7, 2016. www.cnn.com/2016/06/07/politics/paul-ryan-donald-trump-racist-comment/index.html.

Ward, Charles F. "Salt War of San Elizario, 1877." Master's thesis, University of Texas at Austin, 1932.

Watson, Denton. *Lion in the Lobby: Clarence Mitchell, Jr.: Struggle for the Passage of Civil Right Laws.* Baltimore: University Press of America, 2002.

Webb, Annie Blanton. *Historical Statistical Data as to Education in Texas, January 1, 1919 to January 1, 1921.* State Department of Education, Bulletin 133. Austin, 1921.

Weber, David. *The Mexican Frontier, 1821–1846: The American Southwest under Mexico.* Albuquerque: University of New Mexico Press, 1982.

———. *The Spanish Frontier in North America.* New Haven, CT: Yale University Press, 1992.

Weinberg, Meyer. *A Chance to Learn: The History of Race and Education in the United States.* Cambridge: Cambridge University Press, 1977.

Wells, Miriam. "Brokerage, Economic Opportunity, and the Growth of Ethnic Move-ments." *Ethnology* 18, no. 4 (1975): 399–414.

Westheider, James. *Fighting on Two Fronts: African Americans and the Vietnam War.* New York: New York University Press, 1997.

Whitaker, L. Paige. *Congressional Redistricting Law: Background and Recent Court Rul-ings.* CRS Report R44798. Washington, DC: Congressional Research Service, 2017. https://crsreports.congress.gov/product/pdf/R/R44798/3.

White, Owen. *Out of the Desert: The Historical Romance of El Paso.* El Paso: McMath, 1923.

Wilcox, Michael. *The Pueblo Indian Revolt and the Mythology of Conquest.* Berkeley: University of California Press, 2009.

Williams, Stephen, comp. *Supreme Court of the United States, Wallace 15 to 18, Book 21, Lawyers Edition.* Rochester, NY: Lawyers' Co-operative Publishing, 1884.

Wines, Michael. "2020 Census Won't Have Citizen Question as Trump Administra-tion Drops Effort." *New York Times*, July 2, 2019. https://www.nytimes.com/2019/07/02/us/trump-census-citizenship-question.html.

Wollenberg, Charles. *All Deliberate Speed: Segregation and Exclusion in California Schools, 1855–1975.* Berkeley: University of California Press, 1976.

Woodward, C. Vann. "The Strange Career of Jim Crow." In *When Did Southern Segregation Begin?*, edited by David Smith, 47–58. New York: Palgrave, 2002.

World Bank. "Mexico." In "Data Bank: World Development Indicators." http://databank.worldbank.org/data//reports.aspx?source=2&country=MEX&series=&period=.

———. *Mexico: Income Generation and Social Protection for the Poor*. Report 36853. Washington, DC: World Bank, 2005. http://documents.worldbank.org/curated/en/2005/01/6954135/mexico-income-generation-social-protection-poor.

Wright, Robert E. "Mexican-Descent Catholics and the U.S. Church, 1880–1910." *U.S. Catholic Historian* 28, no. 4 (Fall 2010): 73–97.

Ybarra-Frausto, Tomás. "The Chicano Movement and the Emergence of a Chicano Poetic Consciousness." In *New Directions in Chicano Scholarship*, edited by Ricardo Romo and Raymundo Paredes, 81–109. La Jolla: University of California, San Diego, 1978.

Ye He Lee, Michelle. "Donald Trump's False Comments Connecting Mexican Immigrants and Crime." *Washington Post*, July 8, 2015. www.washingtonpost.com/news/fact-checker/wp/2015/07/08/donald-trumps-false-comments-connecting-mexican-immigrants-and-crime/?utm_term=.016db135a0f9.

Zavella, Patricia. *I'm Neither Here nor There: Mexicans' Quotidian Struggles with Migration and Poverty*. Durham, NC: Duke University Press, 2011.

Illustration Credits

p. 106   *Travis Heights restrictive housing covenant*: Courtesy of the Austin History Center, M-20.

p. 110   *Judge Roy Bean*: Courtesy of the El Paso Public Library, Border Heritage Center, Aultman Photo Collection, no. 6016.

p. 129   NO DOGS, NEGROES, MEXICANS: Library of Congress, Manuscript Division, Black History Collection, 024.00.00

p. 143   *Alba Club*: George I. Sánchez Papers, box 75, folder 3, Benson Latin American Collection, University of Texas at Austin; originally published in the *Cactus* yearbook.

p. 144   *Mexican school, Bastrop*: George I. Sánchez Papers, Sanbas02, Benson Latin American Collection, University of Texas at Austin.

p. 145   *Drinking fountain*: George I. Sánchez Papers, Sanbas 11, Benson Latin American Collection, University of Texas at Austin.

p. 145   *Regular school, Bastrop*: George I. Sánchez Papers, Sanbas 07, Benson Latin American Collection, University of Texas at Austin.

p. 146   *Regular school, Elgin*: George I. Sánchez Papers, Sanelg 06, Benson Latin American Collection, University of Texas at Austin.

p. 146   *Mexican school, Elgin*: George I. Sánchez Papers, Sanelg 16, Benson Latin American Collection, University of Texas at Austin.

p. 147   *Privy*: George I. Sánchez Papers, Sanelg 13, Benson Latin American Collection, University of Texas at Austin.

p. 161   *Gustavo García*: Library of Congress, no. WA 17-2/5, United Press photo.

p. 194   *Kappa Sigma fraternity*: *Cactus*, 1966, p. 298. Courtesy of the Dolph Briscoe Center, University of Texas at Austin.

p. 209   *President Lyndon Johnson*: Courtesy of the El Paso Public Library, Border Heritage Center, No. PicCham301.

p. 210   *Sacred Heart Church*: Photo by the author, March 22, 2018.

p. 211   *Sacred Heart community center*: Photo by the author, March 22, 2018.

Index